RECONSTRUCTING RESTORATIVE JUSTICE PHILOSOPHY

Reconstructing Restorative Justice Philosophy

Edited by

THEO GAVRIELIDES

and

VASSO ARTINOPOULOU

ASHGATE

Published by
Ashgate Publishing Limited
Wey Court East
Union Road
Farnham
Surrey, GU9 7PT
England

Ashgate Publishing Company
110 Cherry Street
Suite 3-1
Burlington, VT 05401-3818
USA

www.ashgate.com

British Library Cataloguing in Publication Data
A catalogue record for this book is available from the British Library

The Library of Congress has cataloged the printed edition as follows:
Reconstructing restorative justice philosophy / By Theo Gavrielides and Vasso Artinopoulou, editors.
pages cm
Includes bibliographical references and index.
ISBN 978-1-4094-7071-7 (hardback) -- ISBN 978-1-4094-7072-4 (ebook) -- ISBN 978-1-4094-7073-1 (epub) 1. Restorative justice. 2. Transitional justice. 3. Law--Philosophy. 4. Social justice. I. Gavrielides, Theo, editor of compilation. II. Artinopoulou, Vasso, editor of compilation.

K5250.R43 2013
364.6'8--dc23

2013015213

ISBN 9781409470717 (hbk)
ISBN 9781409470724 (ebk – PDF)
ISBN 9781409470731 (ebk – ePUB)

MIX
Paper from responsible sources
FSC
www.fsc.org
FSC® C013985

Printed in the United Kingdom by Henry Ling Limited, at the Dorset Press, Dorchester, DT1 1HD

Contents

List of Contributors

Mersilia Anastasiadou is a PhD candidate and Research Fellow at the Center for Eastern Studies, Panteion University of Social and Political Sciences, Greece. She has previously worked as assistant to the European Parliament Office in Cyprus at the Directorate General for Communication. She has published articles for the Hellenic Centre of European Studies, the Institute for Democracy Konstantinos Karamanlisin and in the *Hellenic Studies Journal*. Ms. Anastasiadou's research interests relate to international political theory and security, diplomacy, media and foreign policy and international law.

Vasso Artinopoulou is Professor of Criminology and former Vice Rector at Panteion University of Social and Political Sciences, Athens, Greece. Her research interests are in the areas of restorative justice, victimology, family violence, youth justice, and gender and the criminal justice system. She has published widely on these subjects in both English and Greek. She has been the head of many public administration and criminal justice authority boards and is currently head of the Criminal Justice Policy Unit at the European Public Law Organisation. She is also a co-Director of Restorative Justice for All (RJ4All).

John Braithwaite is a Distinguished Professor and the founder of the Regulatory Institutions Network at the Australian National University (ANU). During his academic career, he has specialized in the fields of restorative justice, the application of republican theory to criminal law, shame management and reintegration in criminal justice practice and the application of responsive regulation. Braithwaite has dedicated part of his work to the 20-year comparative project 'Peacebulding Compared'. He is well-known for his books *Crime, Shame and Reintegration* (1989) and *Restorative Justice and Responsive Regulation* (2001) and many published articles. Braithwaite has received a number of international awards and prizes for his work.

Theo Gavrielides is an international expert in criminal justice and human rights theory, policy and practice. His current research is at the cutting edge of restorative and juvenile justice. He is an advisor to governments and international bodies, and is a pioneer of user-led methods of research, policy and legislative reform. He is the founder and Director of Independent Academic Research Studies (IARS), a leading, international think tank with a charitable mission to give everyone a chance to forge a safer, fairer and more inclusive society. He is also an Adjunct Professor at Simon Fraser University (Centre for Restorative Justice) a Visiting

Professor at Buckinghamshire New University. He is also a co-Director of Restorative Justice for All (RJ4All).

Maria Hadjipavlou is an Associate Professor at the Department of Social and Political Sciences, University of Cyprus. Dr Hadjipavlou's research interests include international conflict resolution, gender and conflict, peace education, feminist theories, memory and reconciliation, gender and migration, women and peace. She has published widely in the areas of conflict resolution, the Cyprus conflict, women and peace, ethnic stereotypes, the 'crossings', women and migration, feminism and gender. She is a gender trainer for UNFPA and has trained women in Afghanistan, Tunisia and Bratislava on gender and conflict resolution. As a scholar practitioner she has been a consultant to numerous NGOs and international bodies working in the areas of peace, and gender equality. Her latest book *Women and Change in Cyprus: Feminisms, Gender in Conflict*, 2010 (I.B.Tauris) has become a reference book on gender issues in Cyprus and beyond.

Anne Hayden has served as a victim support volunteer and holds a Churchill Fellowship in victimology. She has a long-standing involvement with restorative justice groups in New Zealand and was commissioned to write the Restorative Conferencing Manual of Aotearoa New Zealand by the Department of Courts. Dr Hayden's research interests are in the areas of victimology and restorative justice. She has studied the use of restorative justice for intimate partner violence and is co-editing a book on the use of restorative justice for family violence.

Gerry Johnstone is the founding Director of the UK-based University of Hull's online MA in Restorative Justice and currently has students based in Africa, Canada, Greece, Hong Kong, Ireland and the UK. He is the author of several best-selling textbooks on restorative justice that are used on relevant courses around the world and have been translated into Chinese, Japanese and Russian. Professor Johnstone has given keynote speeches and led summer schools on restorative justice in China, England, Italy, Macao, Poland, Serbia and Spain.

Robert E. Mackay is a mediator, family dispute resolution practitioner, social worker, researcher and qualified higher education teacher. He currently practises as a family dispute resolution practitioner in Newcastle, Australia. He has recently established Edan Resolutions to undertake research, consultancy, restorative practice and conflict resolution services. He is particularly interested in addressing the aftermath of clergy abuse in Christian churches. Mr Mackay has a long involvement with restorative justice in the UK and has served on the boards of numerous government and EU funded bodies. He developed a theory of 'Law as Peacemaking' as an underpinning for restorative justice practice, and has published on the subject of restorative justice theory.

Giuseppe Maglione is a PhD researcher in theory and history of law at the University of Florence, Italy. He has carried out research on theoretical foundations of restorative justice at the Max Planck Institute in Freiburg and at the University of Oslo. He has been an assistant teacher of philosophy and sociology of law at the University of Florence, trainer in conflict management and mediation at the Interregional School of Local Police (S.I.P.L) as well as victim–offender mediator for the non-profit organization L'altro diritto – Onlus.

Brenda Morrison is Director of the Centre for Restorative Justice and an Associate Professor in the School of Criminology, Simon Fraser University, Canada. She is a social psychologist with field experience in outdoor education, government administration and restorative justice. A particular focus of her work relates to the interplay of individuals and communities and the institutions that serve them. Professor Morrison's teaching and research interests include transformative and restorative justice, responsive regulation, school violence and safety, conflict and cooperation, shame management and social identity, the self and self-interest.

Judah Oudshoorn is a Professor in the Community and Criminal Justice degree program at Conestoga College Institute of Technology and Advanced Learning in Kitchener, Canada. He is also a restorative justice mediator in the Canadian federal prison system. Professor Oudshoorn's research interests included male violence, penology and fatherhood.

Mara Schiff is an Associate Professor in the School of Criminology and Criminal Justice at Florida Atlantic University. She has over 30 years of experience in criminal and juvenile justice research, planning, evaluation, training and teaching, and has focused her work in restorative juvenile justice for the last two decades. Dr. Schiff is the co-author/editor of three volumes on restorative justice and her work has appeared in a variety of academic books and journals. She is also the President of PeaceWorks Consulting, Inc., which specializes in restorative justice training, education and consulting in schools and juvenile justice, and speaks regularly on the subject of restorative justice at major conferences, training and other events.

Marelize Schoeman is a Senior Lecturer in the Department of Criminology and Security Science at the University of South Africa. Her research interests range from babies behind bars, juvenile delinquency and child justice to maritime piracy. Her recent research has focused on traditional and restorative justice as methods of social development and transformation. Dr Schoeman has been a speaker at various national and international conferences and has published widely in accredited journals and subject specialist books.

Susan Sharpe is Advisor on Restorative Justice at the University of Notre Dame, USA. She has long been actively involved with restorative justice as a practitioner, author, teacher, and consultant. Professor Sharpe has worked with government and non-profit agencies in Canada, the USA and South Africa on projects related to restorative justice, and has published academic as well as practical work on issues related to best practice in restorative justice.

Christodoulos K. Yiallourides is Professor of International Politics at the Panteion University of Social and Political Sciences, Greece, where he also heads the Centre of Eastern Studies and the Section of Cultural Management of the Department of Communication, Media and Culture. His teaching and research interests include Greece–Turkey relations, international political theory, foreign policy of the power states: USSR/Russian Federation, Turkish foreign policy, cultural diplomacy, media and foreign policy in the new world order. He has authored numerous books and articles in Greek, German and English.

Howard Zehr, a pioneer in the field of restorative justice, is a Professor of Restorative Justice at the Center for Justice and Peacebuilding of the Eastern Mennonite University where he is also co-leading the Zehr Institute for Restorative Justice. Zehr has served 19 years as Director of the Mennonite Central Committee's Office on Crime and Justice, as well as on the Victims Advisory Group for the US Sentencing Commission (2008–2011), and on various other advisory boards. He has written numerous well-known books and articles on restorative justice and peacebuilding and its practice. His best known books are *Changing Lenses: A New Focus for Crime and Justice* (1990; revised 1995; Third Edition 2005), and *The Little Book of Restorative Justice* (2002). Zehr is also the general series editor of The Little Books of Justice and Peacebuilding.

Evelyn Zellerer is a Professor at Kwantlen Polytechnic University, Canada, and founder and Director of Peace of the Circle – an international organization that works with government, businesses, non-profits, schools, justice agencies and communities. Dr. Zellerer is a facilitator, trainer and speaker specializing in restorative justice, peacemaking circles and conscious governance. She is the author of numerous journal articles and book chapters and has her own blog. For further information, visit: www.peaceofthecircle.com

Editors' Note and Acknowledgements

The editing of a book can be a very lonely process. However, this was not the case for this volume, which was put together precisely because we were able to build on new and existing friendships. In fact, our own friendship was cemented while the foundations of Restorative Justice for All, the first international institute on restorative justice were laid.

We originally had no plans to write this book, as it emerged from the discussions that took place at the First International Symposium of Restorative Justice, which was held in the small island of Skopelos, Greece in June 2012. The book's conceptualisation, the discussions that led to its writing through the holding of a Greek style ancient Symposium, its actual writing, editing and publication were the outcomes of many challenges that left all our fellow travellers transformed. Thus we felt that we had to capture our reflections and experiences.

The journey and thus the book would not have been possible without the support and love that we received from Nikos Kritsilis. He kept us focused and organised while he also offered free accommodation for some delegates in his resort 'Melody".

Many thanks also go to the Mayor of Skopelos, George Michelis, for sponsoring the opening ceremony as well as his special advisor Mrs. Rekka. We are grateful to the Greek Ministry of Culture and the Head of the Department of Archaeology in Thessaly, Volos, Mrs. Ingesiloglou, for entrusting us with the ancient ground of Asklepieion, where we held the closing Symposium ceremony. Thanks also go to Ifigeneia Kovani, the lyric singer, who sang the Orphic Hymns in closing the Symposium.

With no funding and only with a dream to put together something fresh and outside of the box and closed conference venues, we held our sessions on the top of the hills, on beaches, monasteries and ancient grounds. This would not have been possible without the generous sponsorship of Skopelos Holidays spa hotel, the Mojito bar and Caryatids restaurant, Kastani beach bar and the Union of hotel owners. Thanks also go to 'Dolphins of Skopelos' for sponsoring the Mamma Mia's excursions, the Restaurants 'Mousses', 'Gialos, 'kymata' and Nastas for the special dinner prices. We are also grateful to the artists Spyros and Vasso Kosmas for giving us their home, the Minoan Villa, where a special meeting took place. Ms. Kosma also painted the cover image of this book titled 'Chrysalis: the awakening of thought'. We are also thankful to Photogramma for the printing of the Symposium material, Spitalia, Katina and Aeolos hotel for offering some free accommodation to the delegates.

Special thanks go to two young and promising researchers, Ero Michael and Andriana Ntziadima. Ero acted as the Secretariat for the Symposium while Andriana helped with the Index of the book and some of its administration. We are also grateful to Jonathan O' Connor for editing some of the chapters and for his patience while this book was being put together. We are grateful to our publisher, Ashgate, Alison Kirk and her team, for their trust and professionalism. We thought that it was important that we work with a publisher who not only has a strong publishing record in our field, but who also shares our values.

Many thanks to the authors and those who attended the Symposium. They believed in our vision and without any financial support travelled long distances to spend over a week with us, their families and friends. We are also grateful to the authors who did not take part in the Symposium and for responding to our call diligently and professionally.

Last but not least, many thanks should go to our families, Sotiris and Georgia Kritsilis, Sophia, Pavlos and Angela Hadjipavlou, and our many friends and colleagues who put up with our stress, moaning and excitement.

Our ambition is that the book opens up a debate on new methods of writing on restorative justice. Creative and philosophical thinking that takes bold steps in moving outside of empirical evidence from the bottom up is still rare. Even less common are authors and researchers leaving questions unanswered. Much has been written on research trying to address questions of effectiveness and implementation. How often do we take the time to just ask and leave the reader to think freely and creatively?

The writing and editing of this book took just less than a year. At the time of writing this Note, we are back in the island of Skopelos. As we watch the shadows of last year, we reflect on what is to follow. The circle is now complete.

Professors Theo Gavrielides and Vasso Artinopoulou
Skopelos, Greece August 2013

Foreword

John Braithwaite

No one will be able to read this book without wishing they were there for the journey that gave it birth. Rich outcomes are enabled by richness of process. This book succeeds in drawing us into the journey of its travellers. The authors gathered at the Greek island of Skopelos to engage with a Greek Symposium method. The Symposium ethos is to discover deep relationships through love for thinking and the beauty of the mind. As Theo Gavrielides explains in Chapter 1, restorative justice is also an ethos, 'a way of living ... a new approach to life'. A unity of method and subject is evocative in this book, as is its contestation (as in the Maglione chapter). How can we but be drawn to a process that takes the participants from one location to another looking out on the Aegean Sea and the unspoilt natural beauty of Skopelos, from monastery to monastery, to the patio of a Minoan villa, complete with serene Orphic Hymns?

There are many dimensions to Howard Zehr's greatness as an inspiration for a restorative ethos. One of them is the way he urges us to understand our own biographies, how the way we think is shaped by our own culture, by the ways the natural beauty of our own country touches our souls and gifts us a love of place and meaning through belongingness. Brenda Morrison's chapter is about Zehr's idea of a journey of belonging. It is also true that we all become jaded by the daily struggles in our own land. And so we can be renewed by openness to be touched by the beauty of another, by the ideas of another culture, by wisdom preserved from their ancients. The journey of these pages may be no substitute for the relational engagement of being at Skopelos. Yet it is an inviting book that embraces those who imaginatively embark on the beautiful journey of the authors. Good writing also teaches us the art of love, the art of beauty. This is by welcoming us to experience wholeness through transformatively different eyes from our own.

The journey of the book traverses a great deal in an intellectually exciting way: Aristotle (with Artinopoulou and Gavrielides, Oudshoorn), Foucault (Maglione), legal pluralism and conflict of laws (Oudshoorn), paradoxes of power (Schiff), the philosophy of rights (Mackay, Sharpe, Morrison), of universal peace (Hadjipavlou), of co-opting the co-opters from below (Schiff), peacemaking circles (Zellerer), relationality and repair (Sharpe, Morrison), moral and spiritual injury (Mackay), social identity and interaction ritual theory (Hadjipavlou, Morrison), conflict resolution theory with Aboriginal peoples and beyond (Oudshoorn, Zellerer, Hadjipavlou, Morrison), teachings on how to live (Johnstone), restorative pain (Gavrielides), wholeness (Zellerer), among other themes. Prepare for a lot of lens shuffling! Experiential engagement can also help us to escape the trap Gerry Johnstone warns of in his chapter, narrowing our vision to conferencing as a dominant technology and losing sight of the teachings of restorative justice. This book is a grand exercise in critical retrieval, revival, renewal of those teachings, ancient and recent.

There is a great, enduring core of restorative justice teachings that has an increasingly global quality about it. Equally, each local and indigenous version of it has rich particularity that we must continue to learn from and respect by describing it with the name its indigenous adherents use rather than calling it restorative justice. There is much in common between the holism of *shalom* in Christianity and Judaism that integrates justice, peace and relational reconciliation and *salam* that does this in Islam. Islam incorporates the deeper sense of the right of a victim family to forgive even murder if it is the family's wish to leave any punishment to Allah (as in ancient Greece). Pluralizing the religious foundations of rights is one reason why there is a lot of appeal in the more general proposal in Susan Sharpe's chapter to revise rights jurisprudence to include a right to relational repair. The right to relational repair would not be a positive right that the state is obliged to provide but (as in Islam) a negative right that no state should be able to preclude.

A rights discourse that embraces Islam and *ubuntu* (Schoeman's chapter) can be part of a remedy to the feelings of exclusion of the Muslim world and of Africa from the power to infuse meaning into global discourses that Muslims and Africans sometimes see as Christian and Western. All authors in this volume emphasize the imperative to deal with power structures, that silence women, Aboriginal peoples, Africa, that hinder the implementation of restorative justice globally and locally. Along this journey, Maria Hadjipavlou's chapter reminds us that we must get better at acknowledging other traditions, that the distinction between *power over* and *power with* has roots in feminist theory, that leading thinkers of conflict resolution theory such as John Burton, Elise Boulding and Johan Galtung were diagnosing thoughtful strategies for countering power imbalance from the 1960s and earlier.

Shalom and *salam* share much with the holism of *ubuntu*, as evocatively explained in the Marelize Schoeman chapter. Yet *ubuntu* may be a richer communitarian vein for teachings about the opportunity crime creates for building social solidarity across a whole society than we find in western restorative justice writing. It embraces diverse spiritualities in a kind of village humanistic republicanism. I like very much Schoeman's citation of the Venda saying, '*Muthu u bebelwa munwe*' translated as a person is born for the other. It will also be an interesting journey for readers to learn of the strands shared between this African philosophy and Aristotle's Politics (328 BC). As the Epilogue sums up, the connections between Aristotle's theory on justice and restorative justice as a form of social justice recur throughout the volume. The sub-Saharan linguistic preference for replacing *ethics* and *morality* with *character* – something learnt through practical engagement with community struggles – also turns out in this book to have more in common with ancient Aristotelian thought than one might have supposed.

Storytelling becomes more fundamental to character formation than laws under the philosophy of *ubuntu*. Most Westerners would say there is no useful translation of this to urban western criminal justice. Yet perhaps my favourite insight of Western criminology is that you cannot change police culture by changing police rulebooks which police do not read (any more than we academics read university rulebooks). Police culture is a storybook, not a rulebook. To change police culture, you must change the stories police share in the lunch room and out in the patrol car. South African criminologist Clifford Shearing is one of the authors of this insight, with Canadian Richard Ericson. There is nothing so practical for a western criminologist as a good African philosophy.

It shocks me that it is so recent that I have learnt that *ubuntu* is, and has become, a formidably pan-African philosophical tradition, rather than just a Zulu and Xhosa tradition, as I had understood it in the past. More dominant in Western high theory is the Durkheimian argument that formal hard treatment creates more social solidarity than division. Yet, as Brenda Morrison's chapter points out, *ubuntu* has had an influence on the healing edge holistic restorative justice of Nova Scotia. This has been mediated for example through the relational theory of justice of Nova Scotian Jennifer Llewellan.

Just as many African societies have in *ubuntu* a richer philosophical foundation for thinking about social solidarity, so many Asian societies have more philosophically nuanced traditions for thinking about the role of shame in holistic criminal justice than we see in Western teachings. The West should be more open than it is to allowing itself to be enriched by those philosophical traditions, even more ancient than the rich ancient Greek thinking on shame (as in Plato).

This fine collection helps us renew and reconstruct the core of restorative justice teachings at their holistic philosophical foundations while also helping us to look at them with wider historical and cultural lenses. As the Epilogue reminds us, restorative justice lives and evolves in the hands of this generation of travellers on our planet. Our obligation, the Epilogue sums up, is not to be the kind of philosophers whose aim is to define restorative justice more carefully, because if we 'define water too narrowly', we prevent people from seeing its other properties. The practical journey for our generation is therefore to explore the character of restorative justice, through understanding its values and practices (and its internal tensions, as in Maglione). We serve the future better, our editors conclude, by being more interested in 'What happened?' than in 'What works?'. Congratulations to all the authors for sharing the journey back to Greece through their eyes. In each case we get an enriching reflection on the interdisciplinary character of restorative justice. Particular praise must go to Theo Gavrielides and Vasso Artinopoulou for their vision and entrepreneurship in assembling these wise travellers and pointing their compass for the journey.

John Braithwaite
Distinguished Professor and the founder of
the Regulatory Institutions Network at the
Australian National University (ANU)

Preface

Howard Zehr

Depending on how one constructs the history of restorative justice – and like any story, various narratives are possible – the field has had more than three decades of development and application. From a few cautious local experiments for responding to crime it has expanded to a worldwide phenomenon with applications in many arenas beyond criminal justice. Whether all efforts being termed restorative justice are authentically that is another question – and one of the reasons a re-look at the underlying philosophy (or philosophies) of restorative justice dating back as far as Classical Athens is so timely.

Early experiments in victim–offender reconciliation in Canada and the United States during the 1970s are often identified as the beginning of the field, although the term restorative justice was not given to this work until the mid–1980s. Indeed, the field can be said to have emerged from practice more than theory. As one of the early articulators of the restorative justice philosophy, I often think of it as emerging from a desire to conceptualize and communicate what we were doing in practice.

Practice preceded theory or philosophy but of course those involved in the early experiments held a variety of ideological and philosophical commitments that shaped their efforts. In addition to a critical awareness of the limits of the criminal justice approach, these included a commitment to engaging the community, a belief in the power of dialogue and mediation, and a relational concept of human reality. Also included was an intuition about the power and importance of empathy, an intuition that is now being substantiated by neuroscience. For some of the early pioneers a Christian theology of peace and justice also provided an essential philosophical framework.

When telling the story of restorative justice, however, it is important to acknowledge that its roots actually extend much further into the past than the early experiments in North America, New Zealand, Australia and Europe. Indeed, many indigenous groups have traditions with restorative elements and these are deeply enmeshed in their worldviews. Their articulation and philosophical framing of these practices is very different to the way those of European ancestry articulate restorative justice. The members of the Navajo Nation in North America, for example, have a tradition that many view as essentially restorative but, given their long history of it, understandably prefer to use their own terminology. The reconstruction of restorative justice in the following pages is largely the reconstruction of the Western take on restorative justice with some influence from these traditions. Part III of the book, Back to Basics for Restorative Justice, then helps to put this reconstruction in the context of Aboriginal peoples, African traditions of justice and Classical Greece.

As a result of how and where restorative justice emerged in the Western world, the prevailing philosophy (or maybe it is more accurate to say philosophies) has several characteristics that must be considered in a re-examination:

- Having been strongly shaped by practice, its theoretical underpinnings may be somewhat underdeveloped or lack coherence.
- Similarly, the field has developed somewhat eclectically, drawing on various traditions and approaches. This diversity is a source of strength but also may mitigate against coherence.
- Many of the most prominent articulators of restorative justice principles and philosophy have been men of European ancestry. As I often reiterate to my students and audiences, we are shaped by our biographies; no matter how aware of this I try to be, my history, my culture, my gender, my race and ethnicity shape how I think and what I do, and that is true for all of us. Consequently, there are inevitable cultural, gender and other biases in the way restorative justice is articulated and practised.
- Restorative justice philosophy developed as a mid-level theory. It was designed to address a variety of individual and group experiences of harm. However, many note that it has not adequately incorporated underlying issues of social justice, including racism and classism.
- Over the past three decades, I would argue, the dominant philosophy of restorative justice has often been tweaked but has not been fundamentally reoriented. This may point to the strength and resonance of the philosophy but it also warrants a fundamental re-examination.

A critical examination of restorative justice principles and philosophy is especially important because, arguably, the philosophy is more fundamental than specific practices for two reasons. A principled or philosophic approach allows restorative justice to be applied in numerous areas of work and life; indeed, many claim that they view it as a way of life. Second, as a philosophy, restorative justice provides an essential framework or yardstick by which to evaluate practices. This is important as the processes of co-optation and diversion that inevitably accompany social innovation increasingly impact restorative practices.

It is appropriate that this reconstruction of restorative justice is linked with the field of human rights. I have often argued that contemporary restorative justice can be seen as the best of many indigenous traditions combined with modern human sensibilities. But how do these human rights issues get articulated and put into practice in a restorative justice environment and philosophy?

And what does restorative justice have to say to human rights advocacy? My graduate students who come with backgrounds in human rights work often experience a sense of dissonance as they learn about restorative justice. They recognize that so much of their human rights work was done in the punitive deterrence framework of the Western legal system, often combined with a commitment to public shaming. How does one incorporate a restorative justice perspective into this work? How would their work change and how do the two approaches mesh?

Fortunately, the authors in this collection address many of the issues identified above. Then, in their Epilogue – which arguably is not so much an epilogue as a philosophical reflection and synthesis pointing a way forward – editors Gavrielides and Artinopoulou propose a reconstructed philosophy of restorative justice that is much more expansive and inclusive, much less either/or, than the usual approach. There is a place for both structured and unstructured restorative justice, for both law and values, for state-sponsored, community-based, inner personal and interpersonal restorative justice. However, for the restorative justice movement to progress, they argue, first we must reconcile the internal tensions identified by the authors in this volume: conceptual, philosophical, political, personal. Their proposed reconstructed philosophy helps point a direction but, in addition, they suggest some rules for moving in this direction, asking those of us working in and advocating for restorative justice to redirect some of our energies.

The methodology the editors adopted for this volume is significant. Instead of limiting contributions to empirical analysis, they encouraged authors to write freely from a variety of sources and perspectives. To support this approach, the editors encouraged the development of relationships between the authors by bringing them together in an Ancient Greek-style Symposium. This value-based method of reflection and philosophizing on restorative justice is worth exploring further in a world where hard data and statistical information has become predominant, overshadowing the huge potential of deep and personal stories shared through dialogue as well as value- and arts-based approaches to research.

As the library recall notice says, this book is long overdue.

Howard Zehr, PhD
Distinguished Professor of Restorative Justice
Center for Justice & Peacebuilding
Eastern Mennonite University
Virginia, USA

PART I
Reconsidering Restorative Justice

Chapter 1
Prolegomena: Restorative Justice Philosophy through a Value-based Methodology

Theo Gavrielides and Vasso Artinopoulou

Σα βγεις στον πηγαιμό για την Ιθάκη,
να εύχεσαι νάναι μακρύς ο δρόμος,
γεμάτος περιπέτειες, γεμάτος γνώσεις.
Τους Λαιστρυγόνας και τους Κύκλωπας,
τον θυμωμένο Ποσειδώνα μη φοβάσαι,
τέτοια στον δρόμο σου ποτέ σου δεν θα βρεις,
αν μέν' η σκέψις σου υψηλή, αν εκλεκτή
συγκίνησις το πνεύμα και το σώμα σου αγγίζει.
...
Κι αν πτωχική την βρεις, η Ιθάκη δεν σε γέλασε.
Έτσι σοφός που έγινες, με τόση πείρα,
ήδη θα το κατάλαβες η Ιθάκες τι σημαίνουν.[1]

Kavafis' Ithaki, 1910

The Journey Begins

In his poem, *Ithaki*, Kavafis uses the story of Odysseus to remind us that the journey is as important as reaching our destination. After the 10 year Trojan War, King Odysseus set off to his homeland, Ithaki, only to encounter hardship and toil that cost him another 10 years. Ithaki stands for the ultimate objective and the final destination that we all seek through our actions and life. It also acts as the justification for what we do and achieve in our various roles. But the journey to Ithaki and the experiences during that journey are as important because it is through the people and challenges that we encounter on our way that we become ready to embrace and indeed appreciate Ithaki. It is also during this journey that we

1 'As you set out for Ithaki hope the voyage is a long one, full of adventure, full of discovery. Laistrygonians and Cyclops, angry Poseidon—don't be afraid of them: you'll never find things like that on your way as long as you keep your thoughts raised high, as long as a rare excitement stirs your spirit and your body … And if you find her poor, Ithaki won't have fooled you. Wise as you will have become, so full of experience, you will have understood by then what these Ithakas mean' (Kavafis, 1910).

face our fears and weaknesses and that we learn how to think freely and creatively, surpassing what we are and transforming into what we should be. But the journey is also important for two more reasons. Firstly, it is not always certain that we will reach Ithaki. However, the journey itself should be enough for our transformation into a better being and thinker. Secondly, Ithaki is not the same for everyone. We all have our own personal destinations, and it is only through our journeys that we get to understand, embrace and support our respective destinations and together reach a joint purpose.

The writing of this book can only be described as our own personal journey to Ithaki. Although it didn't quite take us 10 years, the book's conceptualization, the discussions that led to its writing through the holding of a ancient Greek-style Symposium, its actual writing, editing and publication were the outcomes of many challenges that left all our fellow travellers transformed. Therefore, the purpose of this chapter is threefold.

First, we want to travel this journey with you, the reader, in the hope that some of our learning, successes and failures are shared and understood. Although your physical presence on our journey is not possible, we hope that, like a time machine, this chapter and book can transport you to the monasteries, beaches, myths and legends that the authors encountered during this voyage. For a philosophical book, this transportation is important not only for understanding its methodological underpinnings, but also for being able to grasp some of the key concepts and norms that it aspires to unravel. While hoping to explain our sympotica methodology, we neither aimed to enter the field of sympotic studies nor to reactivate sympotic cultures and activities. However, we used sympotic qualitative characteristics and values, such as egalitarian dialogue, respect, and team-building processes to achieve open-minded and constructive debates.

Second, this chapter aims to lay the founding values and principles on which the book and the journey were based. These values were agreed with all authors from the outset of our journey, and consequently served as a framework for our philosophical and creative thinking and writing. They are also married to the two disciplines that we aim to challenge through our philosophical thinking; the strands of restorative justice and human rights. As value-based systems of social control and power, restorative justice and human rights are contextualized and challenged through the value frameworks that we, the symposiarchs, adopted and challenged.

Third, as we set off to think normatively about restorative justice we expect, and indeed hope for, an intense debate. We know that this will most likely be critical and, on many occasions, negative. Therefore, it is important to acknowledge our limitations and state our positions from the start. It is paramount that we set the parameters of our work and acknowledge the caveats that any time-bound project with limited resources is expected to face.

The overall ambition of the chapter is to open up the debate on new methods of writing on restorative justice. Undoubtedly, over the last 30 years we have enjoyed an impressive literature on the practices and theory of restorative justice. And yet, creative and philosophical thinking that takes bold steps to move outside empirical evidence from the bottom-up is still rare. Even less common are authors and researchers who leave questions unanswered. Much has been written on research trying to address questions of effectiveness and implementation. How often do we take the time to just ask and leave the reader to think freely and creatively?

As it will hopefully become obvious, each chapter was written by a leading expert in their fields. What is not so obvious is that these experts first became friends in the context of Greek Symposia. Symposium should mean neither academic presentations at conferences nor a social feast. Symposium, as analysed in detail later, should be understood as the life changing process of creating relationships through high level debates, unique life experiences of beauty and love for nature, each others' ideas and personalities, our mistakes and differences.

So, let the journey begin!

An Account of our Journey

The idea for the book and the journey that would lead to it were conceptualized in Athens when the two Editors met to present at a joint conference celebrating the 60th anniversary of the signing of the UN Convention on Human Rights. Following the publication of *Rights and Restoration* (Gavrielides, 2012), and the seminal work of Braithwaite and Strang (2000), it became apparent that more philosophical and critical thinking was needed in understanding the values, connections and foundations of restorative justice, especially within disciplines such as human rights.

It was agreed that this thinking should not be owned by two people. Thus, more travellers were needed. But inviting them to present at a conference simply would not work. We wanted to challenge the participants and indeed ourselves. We felt that the ideas that were planted in our heads needed something radical before they could be communicated. With no funding and while committed to our full-time jobs, we set off to organize an international event that would take the form of an ancient Greek Symposium. We had hoped that this would enable the participants to debate freely and without institutional and professional limitations.

The method of a Greek Symposium was selected not only due to the Editors' Greek background, but also because of its unique ability to create deep relationships through a love for thinking and the beauty of the mind. Symposia are also known for triggering self-observation leading to the betterment of oneself. They were originally treated as cultural institutions with their own formal and comprehensive rules, principally aimed at posing philosophical and rhetorical questions. Ancient Greek symposia were well structured in all their aspects. Formal symposium customs included the number of guests, the special room where the guests gathered (*andron*) and the type of food and drink that was served. For instance, the serving of wine (mixed with water) after eating, as well as the quantity of wine cups, were very important organizational aspects. Moreover, hymns and libations to the Gods before, during and at the end of the symposium were key aspects as they reflected respect for the divine inspiration that was utilized as well as a part of the everyday life of ancient Greeks.[2]

The literature on symposia in ancient Greece and Rome is multidisciplinary and diverse, including rhetoric, philosophy, history, archaeology and humanities. However, there are certain problems of validity and hermeneutics, including the use of original sources and interpretation of ancient Greek. Epistemological issues are also obvious while trying to explain the very old concepts, notions and practices using current logical and theoretical schemes and frameworks. Thus, ancient Greek symposia must be placed within the context of their era and social circumstance.

Nevertheless, a recent trend in humanities focuses on the comprehensive study of the ancient symposium, defined as sympotic studies. This debate started with the publication of O. Murray's *Sympotica: A Symposium on the Symposium* (1990). Likewise, we will use the terms *sympotic* or *sympotica* to refer to the actual cultural institution of the symposium, and *symposiac* or *symposiaca* to refer to the literary genre, which is the symposium.

Admittedly, the most famous symposium in history, Plato's Symposium (Birrell and Leslie, 1925), served as our inspiration:

> The Symposium is a great love treatise which lies somewhere between the Song of Solomon and the Sonnets of Michael Angelo in the past and the works of Mr. Havelock Ellis in the present … Right opinion or orthodoxy to Plato was insufficient to lead the soul which demands that true knowledge of truth, for which Pilate asked and asked in vain. Like a moving staircase, Plato's dialogue rises with the initiated and disentangles law from particulars and unity from multiplicity until suddenly eternal beauty is glimpsed and the soul stands in the real presence of beatific experience (Birrell and Leslie, 1925, p. 2–9).

Our symposium was held on the Greek island of Skopelos on 2–7 June 2012. Following closed invitations from the Editors, twenty international names participated.[3] Our symposium was intended to be a closed scientific event, with no audience or external interventions. The participants came from various corners of the world (Canada, USA, Australia, Europe, Africa), with mixed backgrounds and experiences. This was important in order to achieve a multidisciplinary dialogue that would include all three levels of scientific ambition: academia, research and practice.

The symposium was also differentiated from other forms of scientific activities (such as conferences, seminars, congresses), where the participant usually presents their research findings during a short Powerpoint presentation. In our symposium each contributor had one hour to spend as they wished. There was no technology involved at all. The contributor had to explore and use old ways of debating and

2 See http://www.ontology.co/biblio/ancient-symposia.htm (accessed January 2013).

3 For a full list of participants see http://www.iars.org.uk/content/SkopelosRJ_HR.

keep the participants engaged so that they could then put forward questions and help develop dialogue. Motivation of thinking, using pen and paper and semi-structured questioning, turned out to be our key sympotic techniques.

No papers were requested in advance of the symposium. In fact, the dialogue and questioning served as the vehicle for writing the chapters that are published as part of this volume. Therefore, the symposium sessions were not treated as presentations of new research but rather as an interactive and step-by-step, discourse-based, structuring process, aimed at driving the context of analysis.[4]

Węcowski argues that 'we tend to consider the Greek symposium as a microcosm of the Greek life, especially that of the "Agonistic Age" of Greek civilisation, i.e. of the archaic period' (2002, p. 337). Our symposium was a kind of microcosm of the restorative justice experts who attended, reflecting the *agonistic trends* in academia, research and practice.

Lasting for one week, our symposium turned out to be symbiotic and relational. All our days and evenings were spent in each other's company. All participants shared the seven hour daily programme (four hours every morning and three hours every evening), as well as lunch, dinner and evening drinks. Some participants also brought family and friends who were welcomed to all the activities and in this way strengthened the relationships further. It was important that power was relinquished and a bottom-up debate encouraged.

What really made a difference, however, were the chosen locations for our sessions. Skopelos is one of the most beautiful and unspoilt islands of the Aegean, famous for its blue sea, light, and rich flora and fauna. The locations for each session were different, chosen for their symbolism and unique beauty. For example, the beach-based sessions symbolized the open horizon of the Aegean Sea, encouraging an open mind and creativity. The session held at the old Monastery of Panagia Leivadiotissa, owned by the Monastery of Sinai in Egypt (fourteenth century), represented the continuum between the past and the present, not only in history, but in linking the different countries and cultures present. The Minoan Style villa, designed and painted by the artist Mrs Vasso Kosma reflected the technique and colours of the Minoan Palace at Knossos, Crete, symbolizing the continuum of influence of the Greek civilization through time and space.

The Santa Barbara Monastery, founded in Byzantine times, cut off from other parts of the island and adorned with Byzantine icons, represented peace, calm and self-reflection. We saw Byzantium as the link between ancient philosophies, both Greek and Arab, as well as modern Western thinking. Our selected locations symbolized the continuum in philosophy and spirit, from the past to the present and from East to West, including the values of fairness and justice.

Our closing ceremony at the Ancient Asklipeion of Skopelos, which is referenced as the centre of energy, healing and revealing, was symbolic of our plans to take a step forward in restorative justice and human rights thinking. Healing and revealing social bonds from crime violation and restoring communities,

4 For meaning and forms of sympotic dialogue, see Konig, 2008.

Figure 1 Restorative Justice International Symposium delegates, Skopelos – Summer 2012

while remaining faithful to our core aims in academia, research and policies were emphatically symbolized. Similar to a Greek tragedy's *catharsis* the closing ceremony encouraged further self-reflection, exploration and a transformation into something better. The Orphic Hymns to Dionysus, Dias, and Apollo sung by Iphigenia Kovani, a mezzo lyric singer, and ancient style libations by the host organizers closed the event in an inspiring way.

The event was followed by a painful comedown and countless emails and conversations about the aftermath of our experience and the ideas that flowed from it. Then the writing started, resulting in further debates and, of course, editing. The ultimate Ithaki was the creation of this book, which we hope will encourage the reader to take their own journey of exploration and questioning.

Limitations and Ways Forward

In attempting such a journey and book we were mindful not to be seen as romantic or utopian. Our goals were grounded in academia and the furtherance of philosophical thinking. It was also important that we were not seen as detached from reality. Although the questioning of current models of practice and thinking was encouraged, we did not subscribe to any school of abolition.

Arguably, due to 1970s literature, restorative justice has often been confused with abolitionism and the replacement of the current justice system with something radically different. None of the participants had such an intention. Our writings, questioning and postulation aimed to challenge current ways of thinking about

Figure 2 The journey begins at Kastani beach, Skopelos – Summer 2012

Figure 3 Philosophy in a restorative justice circle, Skopelos – Summer 2012

reality, harm and crime control and the reasons justifying our criminal justice sanctions, practices and ethos. The chapters in this volume may be seen as radical but their intentions are reconcilable, as they aim to help us reposition ourselves in the pursuit of justice for others and ourselves.

Being Greek, both Editors were also anxious to avoid being viewed as promoters of an ancient Greek lifestyle. Although the ideas of Classical Greek thinking and ethos were used, the event was placed within a cultural context that represented its international delegates. It was important that everyone felt comfortable and safe in each other's company. Such is also the power of restorative justice and the universality of human rights.

We acknowledge that the small number of participants in our symposium is not representative of all the trends and perspectives in restorative justice theory, research and practice. However, given the different scientific backgrounds of the participants, the various fields of their work and their diverse professional ideology, we achieved an interdisciplinary dialogue. The multidisciplinary background that we all shared (practitioners, criminologists, philosophers, policymakers and so on) allowed a mixed approach to our critical thinking and to the questions that were raised. The figures of Socrates, Agathon, Phaedrus, Pausanias, Aristophanes, Eryximachus and Alcibiades were used as an inspiration, not an imitation.

What we were also clear about was our ambition to push the theoretical boundaries of restorative justice in order to support current and future practice. Thus, we were determined to draw norms out of practice and the real world as interpreted by the Symposium's international participants. We acknowledge the geographical limitations of our endeavour since not all countries where restorative justice is exercised were represented. We also highlighted the significance of building on what has already been achieved in restorative justice philosophy. Therefore, we were honoured when leading restorative justice theorists, John Braithwaite and Howard Zehr, accepted our invitation to open this volume. Although they were unable to attend the symposium, we believe that their contribution was key in ensuring the continuity of our philosophical thinking.

We encouraged all authors not to be afraid to ask questions. In fact, issues that they were previously not able to ask about due to institutional and other limitations were of particular interest. We were determined to challenge power in all its forms and particularly that between researchers and institutions. In her work *Hope, Power and Governance*, Valerie Braithwaite (2004) speaks of 'collective hopes' that are created through our interactions with others. This interaction, she says, creates shared ways of being and seeing the world. This was the foundation of our Symposium, debates and presence at Skopelos.

Our questioning was also mindful of current social reality and the needs of our times. We did not want to be abstract in our thinking and contribution. We all agreed that both restorative justice and human rights are characterized by an evolving nature and are contextualized by the social, political, financial and cultural environment in which they belong. While developing our thinking we were also mindful of each other's expertise and limitations and through this knowledge we attempted to push our own barriers further out by learning from each other.

We hope that our work reflects current social reality and that most of its limitations lie in the fluidity of societal change and needs. The margins of generalization have been set by these social changes in a rapidly changing world. As Heraclitus said: 'Τα πάντα ρει' (everything moves). Of course, this is the case for every scientific activity. The era of encyclopaedists is long gone. We are now living in the era of universality and globalism of theories and ideas. Relativism and analysis in context are the limits of our work.

Obviously, it was important that the international nature of our venture be put in the context of pre-agreed international conventions and standards while remaining ambitious in taking the next step in proposing new milestones for the construction of a values framework for restorative justice.

Key Terms Explained and Agreed

In order to create a common conceptual framework for the symposium, book and journey, some key terms had to be agreed from the outset. Here we explain their meaning.

Philosophy

Attempting to define *philosophy* is a philosophical task in itself! A linguist would look at the etymology of the word, which derives from the Greek words φίλος (friend) and σοφία (wisdom). They would probably say that it is the act of being or becoming a friend of wisdom. A more conservative approach would be to quote the various definitions in the extant literature. For instance, for Hospers, 'Philosophy is the study of justification' (1990, p. 6). The truth is that 'many people who have been studying and teaching the subject for years woudn't agree on a definition. And a definition wouldn't tell you much anyway. It would give you some words which you could memorise and copy down in notes and spew forth on tests.' (Hospers, 1967, p. 6)

Indeed, the only way to experience the thrill of driving is by driving. Therefore, in our minds, philosophy was the act of questioning with which we engaged before, during and after our journey to Ithaki. But what did we mean by philosophy of restorative justice and what is restorative justice?

Restorative Justice

Admittedly, there are more definitions of *restorative justice* than anyone can remember or quote. According to the literature, the term was coined by Eglash (1977) who distinguished three types of criminal justice: retributive, distributive and restorative. According to Eglash, retributive and distributive justice focus on the criminal act, are informed and dependent on the law, deny victim participation in the justice process and require merely passive participation by offenders. On the other hand, restorative justice, he said, focuses on restoring the harmful effects of these actions, is not dependent on the law and actively involves all parties in the restoration process. Restorative justice provides 'a deliberate opportunity for offender and victim to restore their relationship, along with a chance for the offender to come up with a means to repair the harm done to the victim' (Eglash, 1977, p. 2).

Braithwaite (1999; 2002) and Zehr (1990) spoke about the transformative potential of restorative justice and the 'changing lenses' of how we view crime. Barnett spoke about a 'paradigm shift', claiming that we are living a 'crisis of an old paradigm' and that 'this crisis can be restored by the adoption of a new paradigm of criminal justice' (1977, p. 294). Christie (1977) argued that restorative justice returns conflict as property to the parties involved, taking them away from lawyers.

Restorative justice is now seen by many as an integrated approach rather than as an abolitionist concept. The various definitions in the literature are usually divided into two groups. The first places an emphasis on the process of restorative justice, while the second highlights restorative outcomes. There are also the wider, value-based definitions including, 'Restorative justice is an *ethos* with practical goals, among which is *to restore harm* by including affected parties in a (direct or indirect) *encounter* and a process of understanding through voluntary and honest dialogue.' (Gavrielides, 2007, p. 139) Gavrielides argues that restorative justice 'adopts a fresh approach to conflicts and their control, retaining at the same time certain rehabilitative goals' (p. 139).

Gavrielides (2011) argued that by introducing restorative justice as a radical concept, its proponents were hoping to make the then new concept of restorative justice appealing and interesting enough for writers and politicians who knew nothing about it. However, once the excitement was over, and while restorative justice was leaving the phase of innovation to enter one of implementation, its advocates (like Braithwaite, 1999) started to talk about the need to combine its values and practices with existing traditions of criminal practice and philosophy.

Philosophy of Restorative Justice

Putting the two terms of *restorative justice* and *philosophy* together, we understood them as being integral to our journey to Ithaki. This aimed to explore, understand and master the reasons for and against holding a certain view on restorative justice. While doing so we did not expect to reach any definite conclusions. Indeed, in philosophy, the reasons we can adduce for or against a conclusion are as important as the conclusion itself. There is a saying, 'if you gave me the choice between the truth and the search for the truth, I would take the search'.

Of course we appreciate that not everyone shares our sentiments since our modern society and the bulk of the literature prefer definite conclusions and tend to be impatient with complex arguments. Therefore, we have to warn our readers that most of the issues that are discussed in this volume do not involve definite conclusions that everyone would accept (including those who have thought and written about them for years).

Take for instance one of the key questions of philosophy: 'What is the meaning of life?' Such questions can never be answered and yet their posing triggers a much-needed process of reflection for the appreciation of the good and bad that is to be experienced while living. The study of the search for the truth in such matters helps us understand our own questions. Therefore, it is for you, the reader, to absorb, accept or reject our philosophical thinking and arguments. But ensure whilst doing so you reflect on your own questions and thinking on the issues raised. Then you will also join us in our journey to the realm of philosophical thinking for restorative justice.

Theory

The word *theory* and the act of theorizing are often confused with philosophy and the act of philosophizing. They are not the same, otherwise this book would have been titled *Reconstructing Restorative Justice Theory*.

Aristotle understands theory as the opposite of praxis (practice). Theoria (θεωρία) was to look at, view, behold. In a more technical context, it also meant to refer to speculative understandings of natural beings as opposed to practical knowledge.

Nowadays, theory has come to mean a rational type of generalizing, to think or indeed the results of such thinking. Theories are treated as necessary analytical tools that help us understand and explain or even sometimes be able to make predictions about a given subject matter.

There are many theories in a number of fields of study including criminology. There are even theories within restorative justice. One of the most famous restorative justice theories is Braithwaite's reintegrative shaming (Braithwaite, 1989), which has served as the centre for testing and piloting for years through the RISE experiments in Australia. Thus, a formal theory tends to be syntactic in nature and is only meaningful when given a semantic component by applying it to some content.

The authors of this volume were discouraged from trying to prove or disprove a certain theory. Instead, they were pushed to philosophize by stepping outside the world of empirical evidence and piloting. We wanted them to ask open-ended questions. We were ambitious in our goals of breaching the barriers of both theory and praxis.

Human Rights – Values – Standards – Rights – Principles

Finally, it is also important when talking about *human rights* that we are clear what we mean by rights, values and principles. According to the Universal Declaration on Human Rights (UDHR), 'Human rights refer to the basic rights and freedoms to which all humans are entitled,' or as Article 1 UDHR literally states, 'All human beings are born free and equal in dignity and rights. They are endowed with reason and conscience and should act towards one another in a spirit of brotherhood.' Human rights are minimum standards that are available to everyone simply because of their humanity (Gavrielides, 2005b). For instance, concepts such as citizenship and democracy are not prerequisites for someone's right to be human nor does the enjoyment of those standards protect this qualification.

Similar to restorative justice, definitions for human rights are hardly helpful in unravelling the complexities of its living notion and practices that have travelled through centuries to finally play a role in society's law and order today. For instance, Johnstone (2001) has argued that to develop an understanding of restorative justice, it is necessary to 'engage with accounts of its use in historical societies and contemporary indigenous communities' (p. 10). This is also true for human rights, whose history is rarely explored (Klug, 2000). It is not the intention of this chapter to discuss the definitional ambiguity of restorative justice and human rights. This has been done extensively in the literature, which still strives for further clarity and agreement.

Human rights as *legal articles* are 'by definition justiciable parts of a statute that form the main basis for legal claims in a court of law. They also inform jurisprudence and provide a clear framework for enforcement.' (Gavrielides, 2012) In the case of human rights statutes, some articles are procedural while others are substantial (substantive guarantees). Procedural articles (like Article 1 ECHR, European Convention on Human Rights) are those that define the process that the state and the agents of the law have to follow when a substantive article is engaged. Substantive guarantees (like Article 2 ECHR) refer to the rights and entitlements of an individual under human rights.

Rights may or may not be justiciable. For instance, as argued by natural law and liberal theories, human rights are natural rights given to everyone because of their humanity (George, 1994). However, this does not make them automatically enforceable. They become substantive guarantees when protected by the *legal articles* found in human rights treaties (as in right to life under Article 2 ECHR). Put another way, they give context to legal articles within human rights conventions. Similarly, some rights are procedural (like right to a fair hearing under Article 6 ECHR) while others are substantial (right to life under Article 2 ECHR).

Standards may or may not be legally enforceable but they may be found in a justiciable context. Standards generally suggest that an agreement has proceeded on the minimum level that the practice or notion in question has to be respected or protected. They also suggest that a wide margin is left for the discretionary development of a practice that not only respects the standard but also builds on its minimum protection. Human rights, as standards, signify their evolving nature as they progress and adjust to the realities of the given society and time.

Principles may or may not be justiciable but, when used in the context of legal rights, they constitute the underlying values characterizing them. For instance, being treated with dignity and respect is a key principle underlying the European Convention on Human Rights (ECHR). This principle encompasses: a) respect for the person; b) right to be free from inhumane or degrading treatment; c) recognition of a person's dignity because of his/her humanity; and d) respect for a person's home and family (Gavrielides, 2008). The first three are mainly protected by Article 3 of the ECHR, while the last principle is protected by Articles 8 and 12, though a number of other articles may come into play.

Finally, in relation to *values*, as Klug (2000) argued, it is important when talking about them (as opposed to the legal articles and rights) that we accept, 'they can never be more than a set of broad principles. Although they challenge many assumptions, they are not a substitute for a fully-fledged ideology or belief system which speaks to every facet of human life.' (p. 148) Harvey's argument (2012) is particularly pertinent as he stresses Western democracy's obsession with the legal dimension of human rights and the missed opportunity to read them as shared values that can inform not only our exchanges with the executive, but also how we treat each other.

The Symposium: A Value-based Methodology of Philosophy

We now turn to the values and principles on which the Symposium, this book and our journey to Ithaki were founded. The purpose is twofold. First, it will allow the identification of the values framework within which the event and thus the debates were structured. This framework may then be reproduced for similar future events and the production of new knowledge. Second, it will place the chapters and ultimate objective of this volume within a shared values framework. As Valerie Braithwaite (2004) notes, through collective hopes and shared ways of being we create a values-based framework of further exploration and thinking.

Birrell and Leslie (1925) claim that Plato's Symposium bears the most thorough and in-depth proof of the power and contribution of the method of the Greek Symposium in deconstructing complex notions and norms of life. Furthermore, they argue, 'In form it presents the Platonic Dialogue at its brilliant best. In it may be discerned the germ of the after dinner speech, the modern Essay and the Freudian analysis of the mind.' (p. 2) Using Plato's Symposium we unpick the values that originated from this Greek Symposium methodology and which informed the Skopelos Symposium. Birrell and Leslie (1925) note that one of the most interesting features of Plato's Symposium is 'its treatment of the question of sex, a treatment that is at once faithful and frank, far-fetched and far-searching and in places fantastic' (p. 2). This was also the premise of the Skopelos Symposium.

From the outset, and using the Opening Ceremony of our Symposium as the vehicle of communication, the Symposiarchs (the Editors) laid down the principles to which all participants had to subscribe. These principles can be characterized as the expression of Platonic Love which is synonymous with the affections of the unimpassioned and a metonym for the disaffection or distemper of the virile. So what were those principles?

Equality

The participants were asked to remove their institutional hats while being encouraged to see each other not as professionals filling certain positions of hierarchy within their fields but as equal participants in a joint venture of self-exploration and questioning. Given their diverse backgrounds, we acknowledged that this request demanded a shift in their hearts and minds, and thus we focused on developing personal relationships that would allow us to see each other as friends rather than through our roles in society. Through equality and the absence of institutional hierarchy we hoped to encourage bottom-up thinking for restorative justice's community-based ethos.

Respect and Diversity

We also accepted that our debates would lead to disagreements. We agreed that these would be respected and used to push the boundaries of our thinking. Adversarial models of dialogue that aim to win arguments were discouraged. We promoted the value of respect for each other's strengths and limitations and the acknowledgement that it is through these differences that diversity of opinions, answers and explanations can be achieved. Respect for each other's cultures, religions or non-beliefs, background, sexual orientation, race, political direction and economic status was agreed.

Voluntariness, Independence and Interconnectedness

The event was structured in a manner that allowed participants to take part in the structured programme freely and independently. Most of them came to the island with their families and friends who were also welcomed to observe. The social events were open to everyone, but were not obligatory. Each participant was independent to make their own choices and decide the manner of their participation and presentation. Forced and formal outputs and outcomes were avoided. Instead, we all felt interconnected with each other's critical and constructive interpretation of our thinking and work. Our views and presentation did not exist in a vacuum but were developed and contextualized within the framework of each other's critical thinking and questioning. This helped the Editors to lay strong foundations for a cohesive volume of chapters that are interlinked and complementary.

Brotherhood and Solidarity

The success of the symposium and the context within which its principles were going to be implemented relied on relationship building, trust and mutual understanding. Therefore, a sense of brotherhood and solidarity was pursued right from the start. The participants shared accommodation, introduced their families to each other, ate together and shared their own personal stories. Platonic love and friendship were quickly pursued and achieved in an organic and subconscious manner. It was also hoped that these relationships would endure beyond the actual event and during the drafting of this book. However, it was not expected that all relationships would be equally strong or lasting.

Due Process

It was also agreed that despite the relaxed and informal style of our debates that the participants would respect the due process of the symposium proceedings. This referred to practical issues such as being prompt, respecting the timeline and programme, asking questions but being mindful of the time restrictions and adapting to the locality chosen for each presentation. The participants also agreed to be recorded and on certain occasions filmed, while notes were taken by the Symposium Secretariat.[5] It was also agreed that the opening and closing ceremony would adhere to ancient Greek customs including a libation and Orphic Hymns.

Freedom of Speech and Freedom from Fear

Given that most of the participants were attached to an institution, it was important to agree that their presentation, participation and questioning would take place within a safe environment that would not compromise their position and work. Respect for their freedom of speech was agreed. Fears of being judged, criticized or threatened to be referenced as unscientific were addressed from the outset. The only restriction to these agreed freedoms was respect for others. It was important that creative thinking that goes beyond the boundaries of conservative presentations was encouraged.

Confidentiality

Despite the discussions being recorded, all participants signed confidentiality agreements while accepting that the information shared will be used only for the purposes of the Symposium and this book. As real cases were discussed and interim research data was revealed, it was important that this principle was implemented throughout the proceedings while ensuring that once the event was completed the information gathered was secured and controlled.

5 The Editors are grateful to Ero Michael who acted as the Symposium Secretariat keeping us organized and on time.

Symposium Values – Human Rights and the Restorative Justice Ethos

Reading the Symposium values and their underlying principle of platonic love, we now ask about their relationship with the universal principles of human rights and then their relationship with the restorative justice ethos. Looking at human rights as an umbrella concept encompassing the various values that now underlie it, captured by the Enlightenment and the French Revolution as Liberté, Egalité, Fraternité. These watchwords were used by René Cassin and the other drafters of The Universal Declaration of Human Rights (UDHR) to construct its four pillars of human dignity, liberty, equality and brotherhood (Ishay, 2010). According to Gavrielides, human rights are broken down as:

Equality
Dignity and respect
Fairness, justice and the rule of law
Liberty and individual empowerment
Equity and proportionality
Brotherhood and solidarity
Effectiveness, transparency and confidentiality
Community duty and individual responsibility and
Freedom from fear (2012).

Moving on to restorative justice, a number of international and national documents attempted to identify the key principles underlying its ethos. Some examples include the *UN Basic Principles on the Use of Restorative Justice Programmes in Criminal Matters 2002*, the *Canadian Department of Justice Restorative Justice Values 2010*, the *New Zealand Principles and Values for Restorative Justice 2004*.

These international documents were complemented with volumes of writings. For Braithwaite (2002) and McCold (1999) the principles underlying the restorative justice ethos are victim reparation, offender responsibility and communities of care. McCold argued that if attention is not paid to all three concerns then the result will only be partially restorative. Gavrielides understood this ethos in a broad way, 'Restorative justice, in nature, is not just a practice or just a theory. It is both' (Gavrielides, 2005a). 'It is an ethos; it is a way of living. It is a new approach to life, interpersonal relationships and a way of prioritizing what is important in the process of learning how to coexist'. (Gavrielides, 2007, p. 139) In a similar vein, Daly (2000) said that restorative justice places 'an emphasis on the role and experience of victims in the criminal process' (p. 7), and it involves all relevant parties in a discussion about the offence, its impact and what needs to be done to repair it. The decision-making, Daly said, has to be carried out by both lay and legal actors (see also Zehr, 1990).

It is not the intention of this paper to look at each restorative justice and human rights principle in detail nor to engage in a thorough evaluation of definitional projects in the literature. We conclude with a summary of the common principles underlying our value-based symposium methodology, restorative justice and human rights:

Equality
Respect and Diversity
Voluntariness, independence and interconnectedness
Brotherhood and solidarity
Due process
Freedom of speech and freedom from fear
Confidentiality.

The common ground of these values reminds us of the prerequisite environment that needs to be in place in order for them to manifest themselves and achieve their practical outcomes. Human rights, restorative justice and dialogue-based methodologies of research and philosophy must be developed in a climate of democracy and with genuine intentions of dialogue-based reasoning. For instance, where a participant is silent or fearful to share their thoughts, the values of the symposium should guide the Symposiarchs and indeed the other participants to encourage participation. Where a member of society is marginalized in decision-making processes, human rights values, legal articles and civic society should come into play in making their voices heard. Where a victim is silenced in the process of pursuit for justice, restorative justice should provide the vehicle for sharing, questioning and cleansing.

The contribution of these common values as empowering tools for democratic participation and dialogue-based explorations of justice and ourselves reminds us that even if we do not achieve all our outcomes (Ithaki), the mere process of empowerment is enough to help bring balance.

Structuring Value-based Debates and Reasoning

Sen said: 'To understand the world is never a matter of simply recording our immediate perceptions. Understanding inescapably involves reasoning. We have to read what we feel and seem to see, and ask what those perceptions indicate and how we may take them into account without being overwhelmed by them.' (2009, p. viii) Merely recording the author's perceptions of restorative justice and then expecting to achieve the book's title would have been a naïve exercise and an insult to the reader. The value-based methodology described in this chapter and involving a journey which may or may not lead us to Ithaki, was the Editors' way of achieving this book. We acknowledged the limitations of our chosen method. While some were anticipated, others were unexpected and remained unaddressed. If indeed the reader never reaches Ithaki with us, then the Editors take full responsibility. But as noted, reaching Ithaki was never an expectation.

So, how did we structure our philosophical debates and the reasoning that led us to new paths of knowledge? It is important to stress that each author was given complete freedom to think and write in the style they thought appropriate. To ensure consistency and flow throughout the volume, the authors were encouraged to follow four basic steps in the construction of their normative ideas and the writing of their chapter. These steps were loosely defined.

The first step aimed to build from the extant literature and debate on our selected topics. We hoped that this step would help them elaborate on the conceptual framework of restorative justice rather than remain focused on certain theoretical and/or research aspects. Although we encouraged them to look at the extant literature we also hoped for a critical account of their own achievements and writings. We encouraged them to present state of the art restorative justice theory, research and policy levels, without being limited by geography and by putting this description in the context of their own chapter. Authors were also encouraged to reconstruct restorative justice with material that has never been used before, such as their own personal accounts of restorative justice, practitioners' testimonies and writing and generally writing not considered to be in the mainstream literature. The use of non-English sources was also encouraged.

The second step involved raising key and complex questions on restorative justice as these are informed by its philosophical underpinnings, justification and modern reality. We expected that certain global trends (like the economic crisis) and local challenges would be used as direct or indirect influences on these questions. Putting forward new questions was also seen as a dynamic and interactive process for knowledge production. Pre-constructed models of thought and empirical thinking were discouraged. The questions that were raised during the Skopelos Symposium were reiterated to the authors in the hope that they could act as stimuli for their chapters.

The third step was the most creative part of our thinking and involved deconstructing notions relating to restorative justice theory and practice. *Deconstruction* was approached in two ways. Firstly, it was used as a very broad concept, seen as a process of unravelling some of the restorative justice issues in theory, research and practice. We did not want to use it *stricto sensu*. In other words, we saw it as the process of illuminating some of the colours of the restorative justice spectrum, in our complex postmodern societies, which are characterized by deep social transformations. Secondly, it referred to the process of the Editors re-reading the authors' chapters with the aim of unravelling issues raised by authors' questions and answers. Hermeneutic attempts in authors' views were strictly avoided.

The fourth step involved the reconstruction of notions and ideas that had been challenged by the authors. *Reconstruction* referred to the rebuilding of the deconstructed notion, namely the reformulation of questions and/or presenting new questions for discussion. The authors also hoped to use the concept as a means for a new synthesis, based on previous analyses of authors' chapters. We did not see this synthesis as choosing parts of the chapters and putting them together in a mechanical or logical order, but rather as a process of building and/or restoring the foundations of the restorative justice concept. This was attempted in the Epilogue of the book. Reconstructing restorative justice philosophy does not just refer to the title of the book, but also to the interactive and dynamic process that all authors needed to engage with, and had engaged with, during the Symposium.

The book is introduced by Braithwaite and Zehr. It is generally accepted that their work laid the first foundations for a philosophy of restorative justice. As Zehr notes in this volume, 'Indeed, the [restorative justice] field can be said to have emerged from practice more than theory. As one of the early articulators of the philosophy, I often think of the philosophy as emerging from a desire to conceptualize and communicate what we were doing in practice.' Zehr's statement helped us put the book's chapters in context, keeping them focused and grounded in reality. Normative thinking without a purpose and a contribution to practice was not in our interest.

Braithwaite also agrees with this statement as his publication with Strang concludes: 'There is nothing as practical as a good philosophy and the best philosophy is informed by practice'. (Braithwaite and Strang, 2000, p. 203) They also point out: 'The [restorative justice] philosophy now struggles to keep up with the pace of bottom-up innovation'. Braithwaite's introduction to this book is therefore key to unlocking the paths that we then explore through our journey and chapters. The reader will also realize that the publisher for Braithwaite and Strang (2000) is also the publisher for this book.

The book is broken down into three Parts. Part I takes a more general approach by reconsidering restorative justice through philosophy, law and criminology. Following this introductory chapter, the Editors delve into Classical Greek philosophy to identify the places (τόποι) where Aristotle, restorative justice and human rights meet. The notions of equality and fairness help us reconsider current concepts of justice and the application of human rights by modern institutions. Johnstone then proceeds with an account of restorative justice as a set of teachings or doctrines. He asks: To whom are these teachings addressed? What do they concern? How coherent are they? Would it be prudent to follow these teachings? Would it be ethical to follow them? Maglione then attempts to demythologize explanations and justifications of restorative justice, sketching out a contextual framework for 'interrogating ourselves' while sharpening our intellectual understanding as a preliminary step towards the critical development of new possibilities in the theory and praxis of restorative justice.

Part II moves on with case studies of contemporary issues that are questioned and re-examined in the light of restorative justice philosophy. Although these issues are not extensive and do not reflect the depth and breadth of normative challenges that restorative justice faces in modern society, this part of the book should help the reader contextualize how the book's general objective has practical significance. Mackay uses examples such as that of clergy sexual abuse to ask, what is the nexus between rights and restorative justice, especially where justice is denied? Yiallourides takes a step back by putting restorative justice in the context of universal peace and the reality of international politics. How can restorative justice be pursued at the local level when issues of power and domination overshadow our individual actions at international and state levels? Schiff complements this thinking by looking at the broader institutional power structures within which restorative justice is situated. She argues that Western culture's delicate economic, social and political bases of power require the existence of corresponding class and status imbalances. Sharpe then proceeds to argue that the strength and consistency of benefits such as participation and negotiation arising from restorative justice point to an overlooked relational dimension of human rights. She reminds us of the work of Collectivists in an attempt to understand and use relational and value-based approaches to justice and restorative justice. Morrison continues the reasoning and theorizing of human rights as tools for restorative justice as she looks at the example of Canada and the interplay between the rule of law and restorative practices. Hadjipavlou concludes this part of the book by reminding us that restorative justice is not only an ethos applicable to interpersonal conflicts but also state-to-state and inter-community tensions. She draws learning from the sphere of conflict resolution, which she also connects with restorative justice philosophy.

Part III brings restorative justice back to its basics. In our journey, we were fortunate enough to meet non-Western-based experts who reminded us that the values and norms that have now become the backbone of restorative justice are deeply rooted in traditions such as the Aboriginal peoples of Canada (Oudshoorn's chapter) and practices such as peacemaking circles (Zellerer's chapter) as well as the African concept of *ubuntu* (Schoeman's chapter) and Ancient Greek catharsis (Gavrielides' chapter). This part of the book includes some of its most radical proposals as purist approaches to restorative justice are attempted in the hope that new stimuli can be created for further questioning. We ask that these chapters are read with an open mind and we welcome challenges that continue our philosophical thinking. As explained, this book does not subscribe to the abolition of current models of justice.

The book concludes with an attempt by the Editors to reconstruct restorative justice philosophy by critically analysing and synthesizing the key arguments and reasoning that were developed in its chapters. This attempt should not be seen as the ultimate contribution of the volume but as a summary of what was raised by the authors. The Epilogue also aims to act as a link between the work carried out here and what we hope will follow. As more questions are raised and new methods of thinking and writing for restorative justice are introduced, hopes are raised in encouraging further attempts that follow our paradigm.

It is worth pointing out that although for some authors justice was defined in terms of institutions, for others justice was seen as a fairness set within the context of lives and freedoms of the people involved. As it will become obvious, the issue of power and the imbalances that are experienced in the pursuit and application of justice was repeatedly raised by the authors. This did not just involve power imbalances between the state and the individual but also between the various parties in restorative justice, the parties and the facilitators, the parties and society, society and the state, communities and mainstream justice agencies.

Another common feature is the value-based and relational-based connections that all authors made between restorative justice and the reasoning for its existence. In our exploration of the reasons of what justifies restorative justice, it became clear that most of them are found in the bonds that bind us all. Our interconnectedness, our shared values (such as human rights), our shared ways of being, our collective hopes and our resistance to institutionalized hope and power are all common threads running through the chapters. As a community-born and community-led ethos, restorative justice relies on these connections. It is therefore no surprise why relations and values ended up being the dominant features of our philosophical thinking.

References

Barnett, R. 1977. 'Restitution: A New Paradigm of Criminal Justice' *Ethics: An International Journal of Social, Political, and Legal Philosophy*, 87(4), pp. 279–301.

Birrrel, F. and Leslie, S. 1925. *Plato's Symposium*. The Fortune Press.

Braithwaite, J. 1989. *Crime, Shame and Reintegration*. Cambridge: CUP.

Braithwaite, J. 1999. 'A Future where Punishment is Marginalised: Realistic or Utopian?' *UCLA Law Review*, 46, pp. 1727–50.

Braithwaite, J. 2002. *Restorative Justice and Responsive Regulation*. New York: OUP.

Braithwaite, J. and Strang, H. 2000. *Restorative Justice: Philosophy to Practice*. Aldershot: Ashgate.

Braithwaite, V. 2004. *Hope, Power and Governance*. The Annals, Thousand Oaks: Sage.

Christie, N. 1977. 'Conflicts as Property' *British Journal of Criminology*, 17(1), pp. 1–15.

Daly, K. 2000. 'Revisiting the Relationship between Retributive and Restorative Justice' in *Restorative Justice: Philosophy to Practice*, edited by J. Braithwaite and H. Strang. Aldershot: Ashgate, pp. 33–54.

Eglash, A. 1977. 'Beyond Restitution: Creative Restitution' in *Restitution in Criminal Justice*, edited by B. Galaway. Lexington, MA: DC Heath and Company.

Gavrielides, T. 2005a. 'Some Meta-theoretical Questions for Restorative Justice'. *Ratio Juris*, 18(1), pp. 84–106.

Gavrielides, T. 2005b. 'Human Rights vs. Political Reality: The Case of Europe's Harmonising Criminal Justice Systems'. *International Journal of Comparative Criminology*, 5(1), pp. 60–84.

Gavrielides, T. 2007. *Restorative Justice Theory and Practice: Addressing the Discrepancy*. Helsinki: HEUNI.

Gavrielides, T. 2008.. 'Human rights and customer satisfaction with public services: a relationship discovered'. *International Journal of Human Rights*, 12(2), pp. 187–202.

Gavrielides, T. 2011. *Restorative Justice in the Secure Estate*. London: IARS Publications.

Gavrielides, T. 2012. *Rights and Restoration within Youth Justice*. Whitby, ON: de Sitter Publications.

George, R. 1994. *Natural Law Theory*. Oxford: Clarendon Press.

Harvey, C. 2012. 'A Future for Human Rights?' in *Rights and Restoration within Youth Justice,* edited by T. Gavrielides. Whitby, ON: de Sitter Publications.

Hospers, J. 1990. *An Introduction to Philosophical Analysis*. London: Routledge.

Ishay, M. 2010. 'What are human rights? Six Historical controversies'. *Journal of Human Rights* 3(3), pp. 359–71.

Johnstone, G. 2001. *Restorative Justice: Ideas, Values, Debates*. Cullompton: William Publishing.

Kavafis, K. 1910. 'Ithaca', *The Poems*. Athens: Icarus.

Klug, F. 2000. *Values for a Godless Age*. London: Penguin Group.

Konig, J.P. 2008. 'Sympotic dialogue in the first to fifth centuries CE' in *The End of Dialogue in Antiquity*, edited by S. Goldhill. Cambridge: CUP, pp. 85–113.

McCold, P. 1999. 'Toward a Holistic Vision of Restorative Juvenile Justice: A Reply to Walgrave' in *The 4th International Conference on Restorative Justice for Juveniles*. Leuven, Belgium.

Murray, O. 1990. *Sympotica: A Symposium on the Symposium.* Oxford: OUP.

Sen, A. 2009. *The Idea of Justice*. London: Penguin Books.

Węcowski, M. 2002. 'Towards a definition of the symposium', in *Euergesias charin. Studies Presented to Benedetto Bravo and Ewa Wipszycka by Their Disciples* edited by T. Derda, J. Urbanik and M. Węcowski. Warszawa, pp. 337–61.

Zehr, H. 1990. *Changing Lenses: A New Focus for Crime and Justice*. Scottdale: Herald Press.

Chapter 2

Aristotle on Restorative Justice: Where the Restorative Justice and Human Rights Movements Meet (κοινοί τόποι)

Vasso Artinopoulou and Theo Gavrielides

Introduction

Strong evidence suggests that the roots of restorative justice are ancient, reaching back to the customs and religions of traditional societies (Gavrielides and Winterdyk, 2011). In fact, some have claimed that restorative justice values are grounded in traditions of justice as old as the ancient Greek and Roman civilizations (Braithwaite, 2002b; Gavrielides, 2012a). The actual term, restorative justice, did not appear in the literature (at least in its English translated version) until the 1970s.

Admittedly, it was not until recently that restorative justice advocates took a step back to attempt a self-critique and to evaluate their fast-growing literature. One of the first to have written about the philosophy of restorative justice, Zehr, notes in the preface to this book: 'Depending on how one constructs the history of restorative justice – and like any story, various narratives are possible'.

This chapter aims to give one more narrative on the roots of restorative justice. This is not based on historical sources or empirical evidence but rather on normative thinking and philosophy. Zehr continues: 'Indeed, the field can be said to have emerged from practice more than theory. As one of the early articulators of the restorative justice philosophy, I often think of it as emerging from a desire to conceptualize and communicate what we were doing in practice'.

In this context, Gavrielides, too, has advised the restorative justice movement and eager policymakers that 'before we are able to proceed with implementation, clear philosophical frameworks need to be established … Equally essential is that we realize and accept the conceptual limits of restorative justice so that we move our practices within them.' (Gavrielides, 2005, p. 103)

Furthermore, whilst Gavrielides argued that 'restorative justice comprises two elements: the theoretical and the practical. The restorative theory aims to highlight the importance of the role of all parties in the process of restoring the harm done … Crime is not merely a violation of the law. The restorative practice provides the means to implement these normative assertions' (Gavrielides, 2005, p. 103), Braithwaite and Strang (2000) suggested that a distinctive history of philosophy is being shaped 'by [restorative justice] practices that ordinary citizens find remarkably appealing. As a consequence the philosophy now struggles to keep up with the pace of bottom-up innovation' (xv). For example, Elliot (2011) noted:

> Restorative justice must be more than a programme within the current system – it must be a new paradigm for responding to harm and conflict with its own philosophical and theoretical framework. Facilitating this shift requires a rethinking of the assumptions around punishment and justice, placing emphasis instead on values and relationships. (back cover)

This chapter aims to respond to Elliot's call. As we look for models of philosophical justifications of restorative justice, we look to Aristotle and his interpretation of *harm*, its restoration and the values that drive us in the pursuit of justice and fairness. The chapter is divided into two parts. The first aims at a redefinition of the concepts that are critical in the construction of restorative justice philosophy. As identified within the teachings of Aristotle these are: justice, restoration, community *polis*, equity and punishment. The latter is not examined here in detail as it is the focus of Chapter 14 by Gavrielides. Therefore, the justification that is given by Gavrielides for punishment is adopted by this chapter.

The second part moves on to argue that there are *topoi (τόποι)* where the philosophical origins in Aristotelian thought and restorative justice meet. Justification and contextualization of these *topoi* are discovered both in the renewed contemporary significance of human rights and within the foundations and principles of modern institutions, such as the European Court of Human Rights and international humanitarian law. Without involving the universality of human rights, we finally argue that these *topoi* (*τόποι*) remain the primary social demands in postmodern and complex societies, seeking their practical implementation. To this end, we argue that the restorative justice movement is becoming a new social movement. We finally argue that the restorative justice movement and the human rights movement meet precisely in those common places *(τόποι)*.

Key Concepts Reconsidered

Considering Limitations

A neo-Aristotelian wind is blowing in the humanities, largely reflected in the revival of theories and concepts of virtue (Solum, 2003; Duff, 2003), ethics (Walker & Ivanhoe, 2007), and morality (Mackay, Chapter 5 of this volume; Miller, 2003). According to Lambropoulos (1995), a revival of Aristotelian thought found in the philosophy of law mostly in the US and Australia, has affected new and reformulated theories of law, justice and jurisdiction.[1]

Despite the revival of many contemporary philosophers' interest in Aristotle, the links between his work and restorative justice remain largely undeveloped (Acorn, 2004). Consequently, our analysis involved the examination of Aristotle's original work although we hope we did not develop our thinking under the Sirens' sound. Aristotle and ancient Greek language were central in the authors' basic and graduate education level. Restorative justice is their actual field of interest in study, research and practice over the past ten years. Links, correlations and assumptions between restorative justice and Aristotelian theory on justice inevitably arise. Karalis identified the linguistics and hermeneutics limits:

> Reading his (Aristotle's) works in the original today is extremely hard; even the best translations have to make numberless clarifications in order to warn readers about this bad and obscure style ... What we learn from Aristotle's linguistic approach is the specificity of the things he was talking about. His nouns, adjectives and verbs, the grammatical structure of his idiom, established networks of meaningful relations between the thinking subject and the objects around him. Language itself generated meaning and therefore knowledge. (2008, p. 40)

Nevertheless, the authors have consciously tried to avoid either any biased reading of Aristotle from a restorative justice perspective, or the compressing of the restorative justice concepts and values in a rigid Aristotelian perspective. Furthermore, the authors did not attempt any comparative approach between Aristotle and restorative justice, given the overall epistemological and methodological restrictions; theories, issues and concepts belong to a certain era and fall within a very specific context. A historical approach was not included in our aims either.

Therefore, our analysis of the philosophical idea of restorative justice and justice will avoid looking through the tinted glasses of modern popular culture such as the media, crime fiction, caricatures and films. Instead, we will examine the various modes of action and arrangement of human affairs, which are widely accepted as just. This approach will help us go back to basics, breaking free from the 'Macdonaldised' version of justice.[2]

---

1 Indicatively cited: Rawls, 1971; Weinrib, 1995; Posner, 1979; Nussbaum, 2000; Kelly, 1992; MacIntyre, 1981; Schneewind, 1982; Anton and Preuss, 1991; Aubenque, 1995; Barnes et al, 1973; Black, 1979; Cooper, 1999a; Cooper, 1999b; Curzer, 1995; Engberg-Pedersen, 1983, Engberg-Pedersen and Troels, 1995; Grant, 1885; Irwin, 1988; Jackson, 1973; Joachim, 1951; Kenny, 1978; Kenny, 1992; Keyt, 1995; Kraut, 1989; Kraut, 1979; Leyden, 1985; Miller, 1991; Miller, 1995; Gagarin, 2005.

2 http://www.rj4all.info/content/mcdonaldisationrestorative justice.

Justice Reconsidered

Admittedly, the concept of *justice* dates back to the Homeric period (1400 BC). According to historical sources, the concept of justice was first formulated through the legislation of Dracon, Solon and Cleisthenes. However, it was not until both Plato and Aristotle's work that a comprehensive concept of justice was developed. For Plato, justice is a moral and inherent virtue, constructed by wisdom, self-restraint, and courage; while for Aristotle, justice is reflected in our daily behaviour and gains meaning through our relationships with the *polis* (city state), society and political authorities. Aristotle perceives justice as a dual concept; justice is both a moral/internal and a material/external concept. Reducing social inequality and achieving common wealth (ευ ζην) are the key purposes of justice.

In Aristotle's terms, 'justice is often thought to be the greatest of virtues, and neither evening nor morning star is so wonderful; and proverbially in justice is every virtue comprehended'. Aristotle continues, 'Justice in this sense, then, is not part of virtue but virtue entire, nor is the contrary injustice a part of vice but vice entire'. Virtue and justice, Aristotle said 'are the same but their essence is not the same; what, as a relation to one's neighbour, is justice is, as a certain kind of state without qualification, virtue … If, then, the unjust is unequal, just is equal, as all men suppose it to be'. (Aristotle, *Nicomachean Ethics*, Book V, 1)

The starting point for Aristotle's analysis of justice is the individual as opposed to a condition of affairs. In fact, justice is placed at the top of the values pyramid, since, although other ethical standards (such as mercy, compassion, generosity, benevolence) may be valuable, they are supererogatory rather than required.

But justice, for Aristotle, is not merely a value; justice also means obedience to the law. In fact, he maintains that the law should control the whole range of human (including social and civic) life. He goes on to say that if a particular *polis* state only does this partially that is because it is only a rough and ready adumbration of what the law ought to be. In Nicomachean Ethics, he concludes 'The just, then, is the lawful and the fair, the unjust is the unlawful and the unfair' (Aristotle, *Nicomachean Ethics*, Book V, 1). It is interesting to note that the Greek equivalent of the word just (from the Latin word *jus*) is δίκαιος, which meant 'observant of custom or rule' (Liddel and Scott, 1940:429). In Attic law, αδικείν (to do injustice) was the word used to express any breach of law.

In a broad sense, justice is a moral and inherent principle. It has a general meaning and aims at the moral integration of the individual. It is shaped at a utopian level and represents absolute equality. Moreover, justice according to Aristotle is conceptualized by the ideas and goals of equality. However, equality is required between those of equal status within society. With all acts of injustice, the unjust person is thought to gain advantage while the victim is thought to suffer loss. It is the duty of the judiciary to rectify inequality by imposing a penalty that takes away the wrongful gain. Justice is a zero-sum equation where neither party gains nor loses.

In a narrower sense, justice is materialist and behavioural rather than abstractive. In that sense, justice is defined as specific, aiming to reduce social inequalities, but also to achieve citizens' welfare. This is a form of social justice implemented in everyday social and economic life. It allows equality in exchange and fairness in the distribution of good.

From the above analysis, it becomes apparent that there are two types of justice. One that is attached to the concept of the law, and the other that defines what is fair and equal – we will call it fairness. Although both should be value-based, the former is more easily exposed to arbitrariness and human fault. The latter is closer to the ideal, but is abstract.

Aristotle argues that specific justice is divided into distributive justice and restorative justice (επανορθωτικόν δίκαιον). Distributive justice is concerned with the distribution of wealth, goods and honours within the *polis'* citizens. Restorative justice is applied in individual affairs. Aristotle distinguishes between affairs with the consent (εκούσιες) and without the consent (ακούσιες) of the affected parties.

The gradual transmission from private to public law is reflected in this distinction. Aristotle also identified the acts which, without consent, are included in the restorative justice category: homicide, theft, adultery, robbery, verbal abuse, mutilation and insult. These (kinds of) acts are threatening to social justice, because of the lack of consent from one party (i.e. the victim). Restorative justice, according to Aristotle, aims to restore αγαθά (goods) to individuals. On the other hand, offences are restorable through a judge's intervention or mediation. Consequently, restorative justice is seen as sitting between loss and gain.

According to Irwin, corrective (for us restorative) justice 'is restricted and retrospective; it considers only the harm that has been done and the means of restoring the *status quo ante*' (Irwin, 1998, p. 429). Restoring harm and relationships are the aims of restorative justice (see Sharp, Chapter 8 and Gavrielides, Chapter 14 of this volume).

Restorative Reconsidered

We argue in more detail here that the Anglo-Saxon term for restorative justice is a direct translation of the Greek term *epanorthoticon dikaion* (επανορθωτικόν δίκαιον), as explained above, and was developed by Aristotle in his comprehensive theory on justice. We use the term *restorative* instead of *rectificatory*, *correctional* or *corrective* justice, since in Aristotle's theory on justice it is more complicated than a simple idle adherence. This argument is also, slowly, gaining support in the literature (Otfried 2003, p. 157; Raphael 2003, p. 50).

According to some, 1977 was the year when the term restorative justice was first coined (Van Ness and Heetderks 1997, p. 24). Admittedly, Albert Eglash was among the first to speak of a crisis occurring in the criminal justice system, and of an alternative paradigm, which could fundamentally replace the punitive one.[3] In particular, Eglash distinguished three types of criminal justice: *retributive*, *distributive* and *restorative* (Eglash, 1977). He claimed that the first two types focus on the criminal act, deny victim participation in the justice process and require mere passive participation by offenders. The third one, however, focuses on restoring the harmful effects of these actions, and actively involves all parties in the criminal process. Restorative justice, Eglash said, provides: 'a deliberate opportunity for offender and victim to restore their relationship, along with a chance for the offender to come up with a means to repair the harm done to the victim'. (Mirsky, 2003, p. 2)

Eglash focused on restorative justice in order to describe the harmful effects of criminal acts, and the involvement of the victim, the offender and the society in the criminal process (Eglash, 1977). The impact of victimology, abolitionism and community justice is reflected through the development of restorative justice, as a 'new' way of responding to crime and harm.

Regardless of multiple definitions of restorative justice (see Gavrielides 2008), their core includes the wrongdoer, the person harmed and the restoration process, which is seen as either an individual or a social reaction. Aristotle's definition of restorative justice includes all of the aforementioned key elements. Consequently, the Aristotelian term *epanorthotikon dikaion* means restorative justice, *sensu stricto* (Artinopoulou, 2010a).

The restoration of relationships and of society is significant both in Aristotelian thought and in the restorative justice literature. Indicatively, we cited the work of Howard Zehr who perceives crime as a 'wound in human relationships' and an action that 'creates an obligation to restore and repair' (Zehr, 1990, p. 181, as cited in Gavrielides, 2008).

According to Acorn, in Aristotelian thought there is a close relationship between restorative and corrective justice. Paradoxically however, she perceives restorative justice as sharing elements of retributive justice: 'Restorative justice also shares important ground with retributive justice. Both insist that wrongs must be put right. Both see an essential relation between justice and reciprocity' (Acorn, 2005, p. 21). Acorn moves on to a comparative perspective between restorative justice and the Aristotelian notion of corrective justice:

> Corrective justice, like restorative justice, does not place value on the wilful infliction of suffering on the offender but focuses on repair of the victim's loss. Yet the ambitions of restorative justice are both less precise and more expansive than those of corrective justice … Further distinguishing restorative justice from

---

3 All three have been described as penal abolitionists. The central contention of Abolistionism is that: 'events and behaviours that are criminalized only make up a minute part of the events and behaviours that can be so defined' (De Haan, 1987), and that crime is not the object, but the product of crime control, philosophies and institutions (De Haan, 1987).

corrective justice is its effort to widen the net of our concern in understanding who is affected by wrongdoing. Corrective justice tends to narrow the focus to the primary victim and wrongdoer. Restorative justice, by contrast, seeks to involve and restore all members of community potentially affected by the wrongdoing' (Acorn, 2005, p. 22).

In modern literature, despite the plethora of definitions and studies on the meaning of restorative justice, there is still a considerable conceptual ambiguity (Mackay, 2002; Johnstone, 2004; Gavrielides, 2008; 2012a). For the purposes of this chapter, Gavrielides' definition is accepted: 'Restorative justice is an ethos with practical goals, among which to restore harm by including affected parties in a (direct or indirect) encounter and a process of understanding through voluntary and honest dialogue' (Gavrielides 2007, p. 139). According to Gavrielides, 'restorative justice adopts a fresh approach to conflicts and their control, retaining at the same time certain rehabilitative goals' (p. 139).[4]

The central proposition of restorative justice is very simple. A conflict that occurs between individuals is primarily the concern of those directly affected by the harm that was caused. Restorative justice, therefore, moves the focus away from the past (what happened) and puts an emphasis on the future (what can be done). This suggests a collapse of the legal positivistic understanding of harm as 'crime' and the construction of a philosophical framework that understands fairness and justice in a way that is more aligned with the Natural Law Theory (George 1994). In fact, some historians have argued that restorative justice was favoured by ancient societies because their focus was not to make 'offenders' pay, but make reparation to the person – and not the State – they wronged, building stronger futures at interpersonal levels (Michalowski 1985; Drapkin 1989; Diamond 1935).

Arguably, despite the undoubted differences between the political and social theories of the various philosophers, what modern Western societies understand as 'crime' did not occur until the eighteenth century, principally due to the work of Thomas Hobbes (1588–1679), David Hume (1711–1776) and Jeremy Bentham (1748–1832).

For Aristotle, tragedy affects catharsis through pity and fear, or the purification of such emotions (Van Weyenberg, 2008). Hence, the acknowledgement of the concept of forgiveness is an essential precondition of restoration. Nevertheless, catharsis and forgiveness cannot be achieved through conventional criminal or civil law practices: 'Compared with retributive justice, the restorative mode of justice pioneered by transitional societies demands the application of a greater range of emotional responses to injuries and violations and, in some cases, a challenge to the norms of reasonableness in emotions that applies in established

4 In the literature, there is consensus that restorative justice practices consist of: direct and indirect mediation, family group conferences, healing or sentencing circles and community restorative boards (Walgrave and Bazemore 1999; Crawford and Newburn 2003; Gavrielides 2007).

democracies' (Ure 2008, p. 285). In Chapter 14 of this book, Gavrielides writes extensively on the matter of catharsis, pain, punishment and Greek tragedy.

The conflicts and passions represented in Greek tragedies included complex elements and interactions, such as the begging for forgiveness on the part of wrongdoer, the offender's vulnerability and the recognition of the victim's needs to forgive and revert. Similarly, in many recent restorative practices, such as conference cycles, the strong links between narrative and justice are very interesting (Young, 2000). Narrative and storytelling is related to ancient Greece through discourses, deliberations, epideictic and judicial speeches (Cassin, 2002). Finally, in Attic law, there was a certain process related to the acceptance of forgiveness by the victim's relatives in order to stop the penal process for the offender *(αίδεσις)*. In cases of homicide, if the victim forgave the offender before dying, no penal proceedings were initiated.

According to Derrida, forgiveness cannot be a matter of justice. It is a 'hyperbolic ethics', 'ethics beyond ethics'; it is the 'unthinkably superegocategory' (cited by Acorn 2004: 11). Forgiveness for restorative justice affects not only the emotional foundations of political order and community, but also the processes of reconciliation and doing justice: 'The significance of forgiveness to restorative justice lies in its possible contribution to the ultimate restorative goal of right relation – that is, a lived relationship of mutual equality and respect' (Acorn 2004:11–12).

In ancient Greece, strong emphasis is placed on the offender's accountability and individual responsibility. Still, different penal processes are provided, based on the offences committed, either on purpose or not, or consciously or unconsciously. For example, the offence of homicide was judged by different courts depending on the offender's accountability, if done with or without intent. However ambiguous, this distinction affected the offender's treatment; MacDowell's works on Attic law and homicide gave proof of that distinction (2003).

Community and Polis *Reconsidered*

The restoration of individual relationships and the bond that connects community members gains particular interest in the light of a restorative paradigm because of recognition of the role of the primary parties. As Gavrielides argues, both the victim and the offender are treated as free individuals, responsible for their actions and decisions; they are not strangers, but rather individuals related because of the 'social liaison' that connects them. It does not matter whether they have met before or not. What is important is that they live in the same environment; either social or legal (Gavrielides, 2005). As free individuals, both have rights that must be respected and protected. They also have obligations, including the restoration of balance in the community, which the offence distorted. Therefore, what restorative justice calls them to do is to restore the broken liaison that used to bind them. The primary parties (victim and offender) are considered most appropriate for this task, but need to be guided and supervised by an impartial third party, such as a mediator, chosen by the community. In general, they are both considered mentally competent and hence morally culpable actors, who are expected to take responsibility for their actions, not only to the parties directly injured, but perhaps also to a wider community (Daly, 2000, p. 35).

To return to Aristotle, interestingly, the notion of justice was developed alongside the concept of *polis*. The history of Attic law reflects the ongoing passage from private to public law, from defining the wrongdoing as an individual affair to a punishable offence, from vendetta to the right of the *polis* state authority to punish the offender.[5] The rulings of Areios Pagos and Heliaia – the supreme courts of Ancient Athens – also facilitated the development of a notion, as well as an understanding, of the practice of justice.

Polis, as a key concept in Aristotelian thought, has been analysed thoroughly in the fields of sociology, political philosophy and political sciences. We are not entering into the dialogue of comparing the contemporary communities' characteristics with ones of the Aristotelian *polis*, neither are we joining in the renewed interest in the continuing relevance of Aristotle's philosophy to the process of rethinking community (Little, 2002). Rather, we perceive the notion of *polis* as the community itself, as a complex system of human relationships, as the principal (social) place, to which citizens belong and wherein they interact.

Similarly to Plato and Socrates, the *polis* for Aristotle is the *sine qua non* precondition of doing justice. The *polis*, the city state, is the personification of morality and justice: 'justice is exercised by persons playing their proper role in the community. Justice as complete virtue insures the proper regard and concern for the happiness of the other members of the community' (Roberts 2000, p. 352). The *polis* does not exist without citizens and the citizens do not exist without the *polis*: *póli/polítes*. Political philosophy as a discipline found its origins in Plato and Aristotle. Yet, what is important according to Aristotle is that 'a citizen is one who shares in governing and being governed' (Aristotle, *Politica*, III.13, 1283b42–1284a1). Achieving well-being (ευδαιμονία) is the citizens' end goal. *Polis*, justice and citizenship are interacting, interrelated and interdependent concepts and practices that realize and are realized by the city state.

Normally, the current concept of *polis* is aligned with the concept of community; not only with the involvement of community, but also with the restoration of the community's social bonds, which is of central interest in the restorative justice movement.

Community justice also includes many of the core principles and practices associated with restorative justice. Restorative justice is a new way of thinking about crime that emphasizes one fundamental argument: crime is a violation of individuals, communities, and relationships. If crime is about harm, justice must therefore amount to more than punishing or treating those found guilty of law

5 For the details of Attic law we have to depend on *ex parte* statements in the speeches of the Attic orators, and we are sometimes able to check those statements through the trustworthy, but often imperfect, aid of inscriptions

breaking. Because crime 'creates obligations to make things right' (Zehr 1990, p. 181), restorative justice is best described as including 'all responses to crime aimed at doing justice by repairing the harm, or "healing the wounds," crime causes' (Bazemore and Walgrave 1999, p. 26). And because defining 'harm' and determining what should be done to repair it is best accomplished with input from crime victims, citizens and offenders, restorative justice promotes practices such as victim–offender mediation or dialogue, family group conferencing, and a range of other informal decision-making processes aimed at developing a reparative plan.

Restorative justice, therefore, includes the decision-making processes, the sanctions or obligations that make up such reparative agreements with the offender to 'make things right' with victim and the community. Furthermore, a variety of policies and practices designed to meet the needs of victim, offender, and community. Focused on goals such as rebuilding community relationships, repairing harm and strengthening the capacity of citizens to respond to crime, these interventions go beyond the narrow traditional focus of traditional criminal justice agencies and programs on the needs and risks of individual offenders (Bazemore, 2002).

Artinopoulou (2010a) argues that the increase of community-based restorative justice programmes may be due to the ongoing shift of formal social control from central to community level and the corresponding growth of the community model in crime reduction (since the end of the 1970s). Both the inefficiencies of central policies and the questioning of the state's monopoly over criminal justice policy led to the decentralization of criminal justice policies and the handling of crime problems within, and by, communities. In this context, the model of 'participating justice' emerged, implemented through restorative justice practices, such as community conferences. Participating justice aims to encourage the participation of all the parties that are 'offended' by the wrongdoer's action, aiming to restore the harm done to the victim (as well as the social bond between individuals).

Equity Reconsidered

Equity and justice are interrelated concepts. The notion of equity is used here in the Aristotelian sense, meaning the correction of the law according to the principles of universal justice in situations for which the law is either too abstract or generalized. For Aristotle, equity and justice are closely related; whilst not absolutely identical, they belong to the same genus and are both morally good. In one sense, what is equitable is just, but in another, since equity is the principle applied to correct justice when it errs, it is higher than what is just. Aristotle says that equity is:

> The sort of justice which goes beyond the written law. Its existence partly is and partly is not intended by legislators; not intended, where they have noticed no defect in the law; intended, where they find themselves unable to define things

> exactly, and are obliged to legislate universally where matters hold only for the most part; or where it is not easy to be complete owing to the endless possible cases presented, such as the kinds and sizes of weapons that may be used to inflict wounds – a lifetime would be too short to make out a complete list of these. If, then, a precise statement is impossible and yet legislation is necessary, the law must be expressed in wide terms; and so, if a man has no more than a finger-ring on his hand when he lifts it to strike or actually strikes another man, he is guilty of a criminal act according to the written words of the law; but he is innocent really, and it is equity that declares him to be so (Aristotle, *Rhetoric*, 1374a25–b23).

However, it is worth noting that Aristotle uses another word in Greek to describe equity. It is επιείκεια, meaning leniency, implying both fairness and sympathy and being opposite to rigor and stringency.

Aristotle defines επιείκεια in three ways: a) as a noun; equity/lenience (το επιεικές) is the same as fairness, b) as an adjective; the equitable/clement man, (επιεικής) is a trait in a judge's personality which leads to a fair decision, taking into account the wrongdoer's intentions, his behaviour and the circumstances of the act, and c) in a more general perspective; as a kind of virtue that every wise citizen must have, and more often than not, related to the notion of tolerance which contributed to the kind of individuality permitted to, and expected by the citizens of the *polis*. Aristotle urged citizens to use arbitrators instead of judges for conflict resolution because arbitrators are more *epieikeis* than judges. Aristotle expressed his slight preference for arbitration than for ordinary courts.[6]

It is exactly that broad framework of Aristotle's definition of *epieikia* which, after certain modifications, such as the introduction and implementation of a more regulated and bureaucratically defined legal system, facilitated the Roman concept of *aequitas* (equity). As a concept, equity affected the judicial systems and practices within Roman law. Despite the ambiguity of the term, equity is aligned with justice, restorative justice and social justice. Equity theory, first developed as a theory of justice by John Stacey Adams, is getting away from the Aristotelian concept of *epieikes*, attempting to explain the relative satisfaction in

6 Arbitration and mediation as dispute resolution techniques were used widely in ancient Greece. Arbitration was a strict procedure. Aristotle described the arbitrators' swearing to obey the rules of arbitration procedure. Among other principles, such as right judgement, arbitrators must act under the principle of equity. Arbitration according to D. M. MacDowell was of two kinds: private and public. The first was similar to victim offender mediation, as used recently. It was a voluntary procedure, in which the opposing parties agreed to solve their dispute. The mediator was freely chosen by both parties and the final decision was compulsory for the parties. In the second, the cases introduced to public arbitration were described by law; the arbitrator was not selected by the parties, who kept the right to appeal if the result of the arbitration was not satisfactory to one party (MacDowell, 2003, pp. 324–5).

terms of perceptions of fair/unfair distributions of resources within interpersonal relationships (Adams 1965).

Even if it has been defined in a variety of ways, social justice incorporates the principles of equity and equal rights (Braithwaite 2001). Today, equity is widely used to mean social tolerance and fighting any kind of discrimination.

The distinction between common law and equity is, to a large extent, derived from Aristotle's recognition of equity as a kind of justice superior to legal justice; it is 'a correction of law where it is defective owing to its generality' (Aristotle, *Nicomachean* Ethics Book V, 10).

Moreover, according to Bazemore and Walgrave (1999), equity is one of the three principles of the government's role in restorative justice. The satisfaction of the victim, offender and community, and the legal protection of individuals against unwarranted state action are the other two principles. All parties must be treated with equity, meaning that they and others in similar circumstances will feel that they are treated similarly (Johnstone and Van Ness, 2007).

The '*Topoi*' of Restorative Justice and Human Rights

Shared topoi (τόποι) Explained

The word *topos* is found and analysed in Aristotle's Rhetorics and Topics. Hermeneutics and definitional attempts are many and broad, stemming from logic and argument theories as well as from philosophy (Bochenski, 1951; Evans, 1977; Rubinelli, 2006; Slomkowski, 1997; Tulmin, 2003). An Aristotelian *topos* (place, location) is 'an argumentative scheme that enables a dialectician or rhetorician to construe an argument for a given conclusion … one topos can be used to construe several different arguments' (Stanford Encyclopaedia of Philosophy).[7]

In this chapter, we use *topos* as the partial arguments derived from the dialectical process of identifying the origins of restorative justice in Aristotelian thought. To this end, new questions are posed and normative assumptions submitted, related to the restorative justice movement, such as:

- Which are the *topoi* (τόποι) where Aristotle and restorative justice align?
- And how do they affect the restorative justice values and practices?
- Are they also found or reflected in justice institutions?
- Are they related to human rights doctrines and practices, and if so, how?

The first part of the chapter found *topoi* (*τόποι)* in Aristotelian thought and restorative justice. We identify them as restorative justice *τόποι,* restorative justice normative argumentations. These are:

7 http://www.iep.utm.edu/emp-symp/ (retrieved January, 31, 2013).

1. Restorative justice is a kind of (social) justice aiming to restore the harm and the relationship induced by law violations.
2. Restorative justice's primary values are equity and fairness.
3. Restorative justice punishment involves the processes of catharsis.
4. Restorative justice presupposes the accountability and responsibility of the wrongdoer.
5. Restorative justice is realized in the community (polis) with the participation of active citizens. Justice, community and citizens are integrated elements in restoration the harm and relations.
6. Restorative justice aims for the well-being (ευδαιμονία) of citizens.

Obviously, *τόποι* are the places where restorative justice philosophy lies. *Τόποι* are to be found in the core of restorative justice values and construct the normative arguments for the restorative justice movement.

Τόποι and the Restorative Justice Movement

Based on Giddens' (1990) perspective on historical, social and cultural continuities of criminological theory, research and action, we argue that the restorative justice movement reflects the continuum in criminological thought. But, how is the restorative justice movement defined or, in other words, is restorative justice a social movement?

Artinopoulou explored the contribution of new social movements in criminology, focusing on the law making process and criminal justice policy. She defines social movement 'as the dynamic and interactive social construction that is shaped and developed in a certain social and cultural context and can be distinguished by the mass or the crowd or other organizations such as the political parties' (Artinopoulou 2000, p. 16). Contestation and demand for social change, inclusion of new social practices and new policies in the agenda of the decision-making centres, and collective reactions to certain formal policies are the major criteria for a social movement's definition (Artinopoulou, 2010b). Are these criteria fulfilled by the restorative justice movement?

Restorative justice contests, questions and criticizes the punitive and retributive character of traditional justice systems. This is reflected in the inefficiencies of crime reduction. The increase in prison populations and recidivism rates show that contemporary criminal justice systems are in crisis. Restorative justice focuses upon individual accountability and the offender's responsibility for the damage caused to the victim and for apology and remorse, as well as the restoration of damage and healing of social relationships in the community. Community participation reflects the modern 'deliberation democracy' model, and gives meaning to the community which discusses, participates, realizes, undertakes responsibility and is self-regulated. Hence, restorative justice criticizes the traditional criminal justice model and redefines the crime, the victim, the offender and the handling of the crime issue. *Τόποι* (as addressed above) for restorative justice are the fields of social change.

On the criterion of a social movement's impact in law making and public policies, it is noteworthy that restorative justice practices are widely introduced in national and supranational, binding and non-binding regulations. In the last 30 years, restorative justice practices have widely affected global traditional criminal justice systems, including international organizations and European institutions. For instance, on 24 July 2002 the UN Council adopted Resolution E/CN.15/2002/L.2/Rev.1; 'Basic principles on the use of restorative justice programmes in criminal matters', encouraging countries to use it (UN 1999). Moreover, the Eleventh United Nations Congress passed the Declaration on the Prevention of Crime and the Treatment of Offenders encouraging member states to adopt restorative justice programmes (2005). Noteworthy are the Council of Europe Recommendations R(85)11, R(87)21, R(92)16, R(81)1, (99)19, R(2000)22, R(2003)20, R(2006)8, strongly suggesting to member states that they should implement restorative justice programmes. The European Commission For The Efficiency of Justice – Guidelines for a Better Implementation of the Existing Recommendation Concerning Penal Mediation (CEPEJ, December 2007) is also relevant, as well as the EU Council Framework Decision of 15 March 2001 on non-custodial sanctions (November 2008), and the Opinion of the European Economic and Social Committee on the prevention of juvenile delinquency (15 March 2006). Also noteworthy is the current European Directive on establishing the minimum standards on the rights, support and protection of victims of crime (2012).

The criterion of collectivity (collective reactions) and the adoption of a movement's demands by wide groups of interest or social groups are often realized in public motivation, media coverage and volunteer work for the achievement of a movement's aims. Nevertheless, this criterion is too broad and ambiguous and presents many methodological difficulties in measuring and assessing the collective reactions at a macro level.

Restorative justice practices are implemented in the community at a middle and micro level of interpersonal communication. Social, clinical and cognitive psychology have the proper methodologies and tools to assess the collective and individual reactions and the feelings of participants. As such, scientific interest does not coincide with public information and sensitization about restorative justice values, objectives and practices.

Furthermore, the media (re)produce the stereotypical and punitive representations on crime and criminality, which leads to penal populism (Pratt, 2006, Hough & Moxon, 1985; Melossi, 2000).

Restorative justice involves new qualitative methodologies, such as narrative and life histories. The traditional forms of communication (such as printed newspapers, television) are unable to comply with restorative justice philosophy and practices, with respect to victim's and offender's voices, and human rights have to be protected in all restorative justice practices. In this context, new forms of communication like blogs, internet discussion forums, web platforms[8] and internet scientific journals (*The Internet Journal of Restorative Justice*) are used for promoting restorative justice aims and activities. However, there is a general need for an increase in public information and awareness, possibly through special interest groups, professionals and practitioners.

It is rather controversial for zero tolerance and punitive attitudes to coexist with restorative justice values and goals. The role of the media in changing social representations and social change is crucial. Restorative justice needs media in a paradigm shift orbit to achieve the substantial shift from punishment to restoration.

At the same time, restorative justice *τόποι* challenge human rights institutions and philosophy. Today, the human rights doctrine has been the dominant moral doctrine in globally monitoring and evaluating the status of states and citizens. Even if the discourse on the universality of human rights through moral relativism and different epistemologies is still present, we argue that human rights institutions and philosophy 'provide the contemporary, allegedly post-ideological, geo-political order with a common framework for determining the basic economic, political, and social conditions required for all individuals to lead a minimally good life' (Fagan, 2005).

The origins of human rights philosophy are found in Aristotle's theory on virtue, justice, citizenship, equality, respect and lenience, ideas widely examined by Greek philosophy. For instance, whilst for Plato justice was related to the combination of moral and natural virtue to wisdom, courage and continence, Aristotle introduced justice as it is reflected in the individual's everyday behaviour. Filtered through St. Thomas Aquinas' reintroduction of Aristotelean thought to north west Europe and incorporated in many neo-Aristotelean intellectual movements, including the Enlightenment (and even more so the German and Greek Enlightenments), the wider ideological context of religion (and specifically of Christianity), the ideal of justice was related to the conviction that 'all are equal under God', a collective 'fantasy' (another important *topos*) but also a goal to be achieved. Soon, the notion of equality as coterminous to (social and moral) justice dominated the theories of natural law. In the context of the Enlightenment (this time including the French and Scottish Enlightenments) and the ideas of the French Revolution, the values and principles of equality, liberty and justice redefined the essential ingredients, the foundations, behind the values and ideals of democracy, society and the birth and sociopolitical organization of western European nation states. Here, the role of the city state (society, the supreme *topos*) in the formation and protection of the law is definitive, and remains parallel to the EU ideal of justice as it is defined today. To return to Aristotle, however, in a rather wider approach, restorative justice is perceived as a form of social justice that is applied and practised in the everyday life, and aims to decrease social and financial inequalities.

In most cases, the internalization of this value on the part of the individual (the citizen) defines the wider context of the different theories of social control;

8 See for instance www.rj4all.info.

such internalization of the primary principles of socialization facilitates both the effective social and individual control of primordial instincts and the completion of the individual's personality as a member of the community (the *topos* that has, in turn, facilitated this development). Hence, this process and indeed this interaction, is best understood and concretely realized in relation to a specific sociocultural (either ideal or material) spatial context.

No matter how complex, the Greek philosopher never used the phrase 'human rights' in the meaning we use it today; he constructed the virtue theory on the substantial concept of rights, to the end of well-being (ευδαιμονία). Not surprisingly, restorative justice and human rights are very close relatives.

In drawing from Aristotle, we define restorative justice topoi (*τόποι)* as the ground where justice, respect, lenience and human rights are nurtured and grow up together. They share common philosophical origins and values and they promote and interact for the kind of social change that creates the space for social equality. In this light, human rights activism has spread worldwide – and why not? – to empower restorativists in social change. Restorative justice *τόποι* are *also* human rights *τόποι.*

In the recent global crisis environment these values are tested. Peace, well-being, justice, respect and equity are still social demands, still claimed in every corner of the planet. The priority level and hierarchy of these values change in different societies, not their contents. As John Braithwaite said, 'there is a long way to go before we can be evidence-based about which of the colours in the restorative justice rainbow really do enrich justice. There is even further to travel before we discover whether those colours can come together to form a bright white light to lead us from the darkness of the Guantanamo Bays and the school exclusion policies of this world' (Braithwaite, 2006: 407).

Concluding Reflections

By attempting to explore the philosophical origins of restorative justice we came back to Aristotle's Ethica Nicomachea (Book V) and his comprehensive theory on justice. There, we found the definition of restorative justice (επανορθωτικό δίκαιο) and, like Aristotle, we view restorative justice as a form of social justice, aiming to repair and/or restore the damage or harm done to the victim and the community.

Not all violations of the law are restorable. For Aristotle only individual affairs are restorable. These, he said, had a criminal character, even if the offender had no intention of committing them. Such acts were theft, adultery, homicide, robbery, verbal abuse, mutilation and insult. Excluding homicide and robbery, the remaining types of crime could be restorable, as they are currently.

We claim that common places (τόποι) exist where the restorative justice and human rights movements meet and these are: fairness, equity, restoration, responsibility, punishment, forgiveness, *polis* community and active citizenship. These *τόποι* construct the present day values framework of restorative justice.

Restorative justice is not a mere trend in criminology. Restorative justice is perceived in terms of formulating a new social movement. This is yet to take a specific form. It lives in a dynamic process of maturing. The waves are sometimes big, sometimes low, depending on the wind of change. Fortunately, the pioneers and leaders in the restorative justice movement put their personal stamp on the theory, research and practice.

Ironically enough, Aristotle is standing upright there in the world of ideas, challenging the origins of restorative justice; sometimes, he is wandering into *τόποι*. The debate has just started. We hope that it will continue.

References

Acorn, A. 2004. *Compulsory Compassion: A critique of restorative justice.* Vancouver: University of British Columbia Press.

Adams, J.S. 1965. Inequity in social exchange. *Advances in Experimental Social Psychology*, 62, pp. 335–43.

Anton, J. and Preuss, A. 1991. *Essays in Ancient Greek Philosophy IV. Aristotle's Ethics*. Albany: SUNY Press.

Aristotle, *Nicomachean Ethics*, Book V. Translated by W.D. Ross, Published in 2009 by WLC Books.

Aristotle's *Politica* (ed. W. D. Ross, 1957), Oxford: Clarendon Press.

Artinopoulou, V. 2000. *Criminological aspects of new social movements* (in Greek). Athens, Greece: Nomiki Bibiothiki.

Artinopoulou, V. 2010a. *Restorative Justice. A challenge for current justice systems*. Athens, Greece: Nomiki Bibiothiki.

Artinopoulou, V. 2010b. The 'gray zones' of Restorative Justice. In *Criminality, Confrontation and the Science of Criminology,* Volume in honour of J. Farsedakis. Athens, Greece: Nomiki Bibliothiki. pp. 755–75.

Aubenque, P. 1995. The Twofold Natural Foundation of Justice According to Aristotle in R. Heinaman (ed.), *Aristotle and Moral Realism.* Boulder: Westview Press. pp. 35–47.

Barnes, J., Schofield, M., and Sorabji, R. 1972. *Articles on Aristotle, Vol. 2 Ethics and Politics*. New York: St. Martins Press.

Barnes, J., Schofield, M., and Sorabji, R. 1973. *Articles on Aristotle, Vol. 3 Ethics and Politics*. New York: St. Martins Press.

Bazemore, G. 2002. 'Community Justice Programs', *Encyclopedia of Crime and Punishment*. Sage Publications.

Bazemore, S.G. and Walgrave, L. (eds), 1999. *Restorative Juvenile Justice, repairing the harm of youth crime.* Criminal Justice Press.

Black, H.C. 1979. *Black's Law Dictionary.* St. Paul, MN: West Publishing Co.

Bochenski, J. M. 1951. *Ancient Formal Logic.* Amsterdam: North-Holland Publishing Company.

Braithwaite, J (2001) Restorative justice and social justice. *Saskatchewan Law Review*, 63, 185–94.

Braithwaite, J. 2002a. 'Setting Standards for Restorative Justice', *British Journal of Criminology*, 42(3), pp. 563–77.

Braithwaite, J. 2002b. *Restorative Justice and Responsive Regulation.* OUP.

Braithwaite, J. 2006. Doing Justice Intelligently in Civil Society, *Journal of Social Issues,* 62(2), pp. 393–409.

Braithwaite, J. and Strang, H. 2000. *Restorative Justice: Philosophy to Practice.* Aldershot: Ashgate.

Cassin, B. 2002. 'The Politics of Memory: How to Treat Hate'. *Quest: An African Journal of Philosophy*, XVI/1.2, pp. 18–35.

Commission of the European Communities 2004. *Green paper on the approximation, mutual recognition and enforcement of criminal sanctions in the EU – now Framework Decision on non-custodial sanctions (COM(2004)334 final).* Brussels, November 2008.

Cooper, J.M. 1999a. *Reason and Emotion.* Princeton, New Jersey: Princeton University Press.

Cooper, J.M. 1999b. 'Aristotle on the Goods of Fortune.' in Cooper, John M., *Reason and Emotion.* Princeton, New Jersey: Princeton University Press.

Curzer, H.J. 1995. 'Aristotle's Account of the Virtue of Justice'. *Apeiron*. Vol. 28, pp. 207–38.

Daly, K. 2000. 'Revisiting the relationship between Retributive and Restorative Justice', in Braithwaite, J. (ed.), *Restorative Justice: Philosophy to Practice.* Aldershot: Ashgate, pp. 33–54.

Derrida, J. 2001. *On Cosmopolitanism and Forgiveness*. London: Routledge.

Diamond, S. 1935. *Primitive Law*. London: Longmans, Green & Co.

Duff, A. 2003. 'The Limits of Virtue Jurisprudence'. *Metaphilosophy*, 34(1–2), 214–24.

Eglash, A. 1977. 'Beyond Restitution: Creative Restitution' in *Restitution in Criminal Justice*, edited by B. Galaway. Lexington, MA: DC Heath and Company.

Elliott, E. 2011. *Security with Care*. Halifax: Fernwood Publishing.

Engberg-Pedersen, T. 1983. *Aristotle's Theory of Moral Insight.* Oxford: Clarendon Press.

Engberg-Pedersen, T. 1995. 'Justice at a Distance – Less Foundational, More Naturalistic: A Reply to Pierre Aubenque.' in Robert Heinaman (ed.), *Aristotle and Moral Realism.* Boulder: Westview Press.

European Commission for the Efficiency of Justice, Guidelines for a Better Implementation of the Existing Recommendation Concerning Penal Mediation, (CEPEJ) December 2007.

European Economic and Social Committee, Opinion of the European Economic and Social Committee on the Prevention of Juvenile Delinquency, 15 March 2006.

European Union. Council Framework Decision of 15 March 2001 on the standing of victims in criminal proceedings (2001/220/JHA), *Official Journal of the European Communities*, Brussels, 2001.

Evans, J.G. 1977. *Aristotle's Concept of Dialectic*. Cambridge: CUP.

Fagan, A. 2005. *Human Rights*. Internet Encyclopedia of Philosophy (http://www.iep.utm.edu/hum-rts/)

Gagarin, M. 2005. 'The Unity of Greek Law', in M. Gagarin and D. Cohen (eds), *The Cambridge Companion to Ancient Greek Law*, CUP.

Gavrielides, T. 2005. 'Some Meta-theoretical Questions for Restorative Justice', *Ratio Juris*, 18(1), pp. 84–106.

Gavrielides, T. 2007. *Restorative Justice Theory and Practice: Addressing the Discrepancy*. Helsinki: HEUNI.

Gavrielides, T. 2008. 'Restorative Justice – the perplexing concept: Conceptual fault-lines and power battles within the restorative justice movement', *Criminology and Criminal Justice*, 8(2), pp. 165–84.

Gavrielides, T. 2012a. *Rights and Restoration within Youth Justice*. Whitby, ON: de Sitter Publications.

Gavrielides, T. 2012b. 'Clergy Child Sexual Abuse & the Restorative Justice Dialogue', *Journal of Church and State*.

Gavrielides, T. 2012c. 'Contextualising Restorative Justice for Hate Crime'. *Journal of Interpersonal Violence*, 27(18), pp. 3624–43.

Gavrielides, T. and J. Winterdyk 2011. 'The fall and rise of restorative justice: a historical account of its notion, practices and possible lessons learned', *Pakistan Journal of Criminology*, 2–3, pp. 107–25.

George, R. 1994. *Natural Law Theory*. Oxford: OUP.

Grant, Sir A. 1885. *The Ethics of Aristotle, Essays and Notes*. London: Longmans, Green and Co..

Hough, M. and Moxon, D. 1985. 'Dealing with offenders: Popular opinion and the views of victims. Findings from the British Crime Survey', *The Howard Journal,* 24, pp. 160–75.

Irwin, T. 1988. *Aristotle's First Principles*. Oxford: Clarendon Press.

Jackson, H. 1973. *The Fifth Book of the Nicomachean Ethics of Aristotle*. New York: Arno Press.

Joachim, H.H. 1951. *Aristotle, Nicomachean Ehtics*. Oxford: Clarendon Press.

Johnstone, G. (ed) 2004. *A restorative justice reader*. Willan Publishing.

Johnstone, G. and Van Ness, D. 2007. 'The meaning of restorative justice'. In Johnstone, G. and Van Ness, D. (eds), *Handbook of Restorative Justice*, pp. 5–23, Willan Publishing.

Karalis, V. 2008. 'Aristotle and Us: Some Observations on his Philosophical Language', *Thesis Eleven*, 93, pp. 36–51.

Kelly, J.M. 1992. *A Short History of Western Legal Theory*. Oxford: OUP.

Kenny, A. 1978. *The Aristotlean Ethics: A Study of the Relationship Between the Eudemian and Nicomachean Ethics of Aristotle*. Oxford: Clarendon Press.

Kenny, A. 1992. *Aristotle on the Perfect Life*. Oxford: Clarendon Press.

Keyt, D. 1991. 'Aristotle's Theory of Distributive Justice.' in Miller and Keyt, *A Companion to Aristotle's Politics*. Oxford: Basil Blackwell Ltd.

Kraut, R. 1979. 'Two Conceptions of Happiness', *The Philosophical Review*, 88(2), pp. 167–97.

Kraut, R. 1989. *Aristotle on the Human Good*. Princeton: Princeton University Press.

Lambropoulos, V. 1995. 'The Rule of Justice', *Thesis Eleven*, 40(1).

Leyden, W. Von. 1985. *Aristotle on Equality and Justice*. London: Macmillan Press Ltd.

Liddel and Scott (1940) *A Greek-English Lexicon; Machine readable text*. Trustees of Tufts University, Oxford. http://perseus.uchicago.edu/cgi-bin/philologic/getobject.pl?p.17:14.LSJ (accessed January 12, 2013)

Little, A. 2002. *The Politics of Community: Theory and Practice*. Edinburgh University Press.

MacDowell, D.M. 2003. *The Law in Classical Athens* (in Greek), 4th edn. Athens: Papadima Editions.

MacIntyre, A. 1981. *After Virtue: A Study in Moral Theory*. Notre Dame, IN: Notre Dame University Press.

Melossi, D. 2000. 'Changing representations of the criminal', *British Journal of Criminology*, 40, pp. 296–320.

Michalowski, R. 1985. *Order, Law and Crime*. New York: Random House.

Miller, A. 2003. *An Introduction to Metaethics*. Cambridge: Polity Press.

Miller, F.D. 1995. *Nature, Justice, and Rights in Aristotle's Politics*. Oxford: Clarendon Press.

Miller, F.D. and Keyt, D. 1991. *A Companion to Aristotle's Politics*. Oxford: Basil Blackwell Ltd.

Nussbaum, M.C. 2000. 'Aristotle, Politics, and Human Capabilities: A Response to Antony, Amerson, Charlesworth, and Mulgan', *Ethics*, 111, pp. 102–40.

Otfried H. 2003. *Aristotle*. New York: SUNY Press.

Posner, R.A. 1979. 'The Homeric Version of the Minimal State', *Ethics*, 90, pp. 1–27.

Pratt, J. 2006. *Penal Populism*. London: Routledge.

Raphael, D.D. 2003. *Concepts of Justice*. Oxford: OUP.

Rawls, R. 1971. *A Theory of Justice*. Cambridge, MA: Harvard University Press.

Rhetoric, in Aristotle: The Complete Works. Barnes, J. ed. 1984. Princeton, NJ: Princeton University Press.

Roberts, J. 2000. 'Justice and the polis'. In Rowe, C. and Schofield, M. (eds), *Greek and Roman Political Thought*. Cambridge: CUP. pp. 344–65.

Rubinelli, S. 2006. 'The Ancient Argumentative Game: τόποι and loci in Action'. *Argumentation*, 20, pp. 268–9.

Schneewind, J.B. 1982. 'Virtue, Narrative, and Community: MacIntyre and Morality', *Journal of Philosophy*, 79, pp. 653–63.

Slomkowski, P. 1997. *Aristotle's Topics*. Leiden: Brill Academic Publishers.

Solum, L.B., 2003. 'Virtue Jurisprudence: A Virtue-Centred Theory of Judging', *Metaphilosophy*, 34, pp. 178–213.

United Nations 2002. *UN Economic and Social Council Resolution on the Basic Principles on the Use of Restorative Justice Programmes in Criminal Matters.*

United Nations 2005. *Declaration of the Eleventh United Nations Congress on the Prevention of Crime and the Treatment of Offenders encouraging member states to adopt restorative justice programmes.*

Ure, M. 2008. 'Post –Traumatic Societies: On Reconciliation, Justice and the Emotions', *European Journal of Social Theory*, 11(3), pp. 283–97.

Van Weyenberg, A. 2008. 'Rewrite this Ancient End! Staging Transition in Post-Apartheid South Africa', *New Voices in Classical Reception Studies*, 3, pp. 31–46.

Walgrave, L. 1999. 'Community Service as a Cornerstone of a Systemic Restorative Response to Juvenile Crime', in G. Bazemore (ed), *Restorative Juvenile Justice: Repairing the Harm of Youth Crime.* Monsey, NY: Criminal Justice Press. pp. 129–55.

Walgrave, L. 2002. *Restorative Justice and the Law.* Cullompton: Willan.

Walker, R, and Ivanhoe, P., (eds) 2007. *Working Virtue: Virtue Ethics and Contemporary Moral Problems.* Oxford: OUP.

Weinrib, Ernest, J. 1995. *The Idea of Private Law.* Cambridge, MA: Harvard University Press.

Young, I. 2000. *Inclusion and Democracy.* Oxford: OUP.

Zehr, H. 1990. *Changing Lenses: A New Focus for Crime and Justice.* Scottsdale: Herald Press.

Chapter 3
The Teachings of Restorative Justice

Gerry Johnstone

Introduction

In the light of an upsurge of discussion on restorative justice in recent decades, this chapter starts by asking what that discussion tends to be about and suggests that the focus is predominantly on restorative conferencing and related practices. It argues that, while the emergence of conferencing is without doubt an important and interesting innovation in criminal justice, the tendency to focus upon it to the exclusion of other aspects of restorative justice is leading to an increasingly narrow and impoverished discussion of the phenomenon. The chapter seeks to redress these shortcomings by pointing towards a broader descriptive account of the practices of restorative justice. This account encompasses not only practices such as conferencing but also the teachings of restorative justice, those precepts and guidance that those involved in developing and promoting restorative justice offer to the world. Some of these teachings concern the way we view and respond to those who harm us through criminal conduct. However, the teachings of restorative justice extend to other matters including guidance on how we should live our everyday lives. The chapter suggests these teachings should not be conceptualized as the philosophy underlying restorative justice. Rather, the propagation of certain teachings should itself be seen as an important restorative justice practice; part of the object of study – alongside practices such as conferencing – when we study the practices of restorative justice. This argument will be illustrated with a discussion of a few key teachings of restorative justice and the chapter will then raise some questions concerning these teachings that could form the basis of interesting research projects.

In terms of the objective of this book, that is to develop the philosophy of restorative justice, this chapter has important implications. The most basic implication is to expand our notion of what it is that we are seeking to develop a philosophy of. If we adopt a narrow view of restorative justice – in which the term restorative justice is used as if interchangeable with restorative conferencing – two broad philosophical questions would suggest themselves. The first question concerns the normative justification for intervening in people's lives in the form of conferencing. The issues here are parallel to those which arise with any other penal intervention, for instance is it justified in retributive terms (that people who wrongfully harm others have a moral obligation to make amends, and conferencing is the best or most appropriate way of achieving this) or in consequentialist terms (the purpose of any intervention is to make things better in the future, and restorative conferencing is the most effective and efficient way of doing this)? The second question concerns the philosophical soundness of the ideas that underpin the practice of conferencing itself. The idea that conferencing is a valuable way of intervening in the aftermath of crime rests not just upon the evidence emerging from 'scientific evaluations' of outcomes, but also upon a range of psychological and sociological ideas. For instance, as we shall see, it rests upon some quite complex thinking about emotions. It is quite proper and useful to ask whether these ideas stand up to close philosophical scrutiny.

If we expand our conception of the practice of restorative justice to include the teachings of restorative justice, we find that these teachings embody and seek to disseminate a range of ideas. As we shall see, even from the very brief account provide here, the range of these ideas is quite staggering. The teachings cover matters such as what crime is, what the 'wrongness' of crime consists of and what justice is, through to how we should conduct ourselves in our everyday lives. Just as we should subject the ideas underlying conferencing to philosophical scrutiny, so these teachings also need to be philosophically investigated. What we are likely to find, if we embark upon such an inquiry, is that it takes us broadly and deeply into a wide range of philosophical questions. To think philosophically about the teachings of restorative justice, we need to engage with a much broader literature than that on the normative theories of punishment. We need to engage, for instance, with work in moral philosophy, political philosophy, philosophical studies of emotions and communication and much else.

What We Talk About When We Talk About Restorative Justice[1]

Until the mid-1990s the term restorative justice featured only rarely in the public discourse on crime and justice. Since then, it has become a central term in both academic and policy discussions concerning the future of criminal justice and crime control. Today, books are published regularly on the subject. Indeed, the very first title in a new book series titled 'Debating Law' was *Debating Restorative Justice* (Cunneen and Hoyle, 2010); articles concerning restorative justice appear regularly in academic and practitioner journals focused on crime, justice and punishment; textbooks on criminology, criminal justice and punishment almost invariably contain chapters on restorative justice (such as Newburn, 2012; Brooks, 2012); and there are now at least two journals dedicated to the publication of restorative justice research and scholarship.[2] At the level of policy, the term restorative justice

---

1 This heading is inspired by the Raymond Carver short story 'What we talk about when we talk about love'.

2 *Restorative Justice: an International Journal* will be published by Hart Publishing from 2013; *the Internet Journal of Restorative Justice* was launched in 2012 (see http://www.rj4all.info/wiki/internet-journal-restorative-justice).

first appeared in legislation in the UK in the Crime and Disorder Act 1998. It now features regularly in policy discourse, and in 2012 the UK government introduced a restorative justice action plan.[3] This trend is international, with restorative justice featuring in policy discussions on every continent.[4] Moreover, in recent years the term restorative justice has spilled over from the discourse on crime and justice to a range of other discourses. It now features in discourses concerning the handling of problems such as genocide, gruesome violence committed in the context of political conflict, gross violations of human rights, political oppression and historical injustice (Johnstone, 2011: pp. 149–54). Derivative terms, such as restorative approaches and restorative practices, appear in discourses concerning problems such as disruptive behaviour and underperformance in schools and workplaces, sports misconduct and issues of child protection (ibid.: pp. 145–9).

But what do people talk (or write) about when they talk (or write) about restorative justice? The answer to this question is by no means obvious. Indeed, commentators frequently point to the vagueness of the term restorative justice and there are some lively disputes about the meaning of the term (for an overview, see Johnstone and Van Ness, 2007b). For instance, for some restorative justice is essentially a participatory process and is to be distinguished from processes in which professionals and experts dominate proceedings and make all the decisions, even if they do decide on a reparative sanction. For others, restorative justice is essentially a different conception of what it means to achieve justice, in which justice is achieved not when everyone gets what they deserve but when 'right relations' are (re)established. And (as we shall see) for others, restorative justice is essentially a way of life we should lead; for instance, restorative justice is achieved when power-based relations are replaced with relationships structured in such a way that the needs of all are met (on this, see Sullivan and Tifft, 2013). Increasingly, however, in most discussions of restorative justice it is taken for granted that the subject for discussion is restorative conferencing and related practices. This chapter starts therefore with a brief account of conferencing before seeking to broaden our descriptive image of restorative justice by explaining some of its 'teachings'.

Conferencing

Conferencing is a distinctive social practice which has been established and developed to deal with crime and other forms of wrongdoing (for an analysis of conferencing practices around the world see Zinsstag and Vanfraechem, 2012). Basically, it involves a facilitated encounter between the perpetrator(s) and victim(s) of a wrongful act with others taking part – such as 'victim supporters', 'offender supporters' and people considered to have a stake in the outcome (as in representatives of the 'community' in which the wrong occurs and of the agencies

---

3 See http://www.justice.gov.uk/restorativejustice.

4 For a (now somewhat dated) survey see part 6 of Johnstone and Van Ness (2007a).

which have a responsibility to deal with the matter).. The purpose of the encounter is to discuss and reach agreement upon a number of questions, especially 'what happened?', 'what harm has resulted?' and 'what should be done to repair the harm and reduce the likelihood of further misdeeds by the perpetrator?'. It is now widely agreed amongst advocates and practitioners of conferencing that it should take place: only when the perpetrator has admitted wrongdoing; that participation should be voluntary (although for the wrongdoer the alternative will usually be subjection to less constructive punitive or disciplinary processes); that conferences should be facilitated by a trained facilitator; that preparation of the parties is crucial to a successful encounter; that there should be a clear outcome agreement and that performance of what is agreed should be monitored in some way; and that one of the factors that contributes to a successful conference is the provision of space and time for breaks and refreshments, as it is during these breaks that the dynamic often changes for the better.

Conferencing is advocated and used at various stages of the criminal justice process. In the UK, in particular, it is promoted and used mostly in youth justice, in some places – such as Northern Ireland – it is the presumptive response to first offences committed by youths (Zinstagg and Chapman, 2012). However, there is increasing advocacy of the use of conferencing for adult offences, which in the UK dates to a government strategy paper in 2003 (Home Office, 2003) that was revived when it featured in a government green paper on sentencing and rehabilitation (Ministry of Justice, 2010) and in proposed legislation, the Crime and Courts Bill, 2012–13 (http://services.parliament.uk/bills/2012-13/crimeandcourts.html). In policing, conferencing is often used as a way of dealing with cases to avoid the need for a court appearance. Conferencing is also advocated and used at pre- and post-sentence stages of criminal justice. Outside of criminal justice there is also growing interest in and use of conferencing. For instance, its use is growing in schools (Hopkins, 2004; Morrison, 2007; Cowie, 2010; Drewery, 2010) where it is employed as an alternative to traditional disciplinary practices, and there are experiments in using conferencing for dealing with complaints against the police and for dealing with misconduct and grievances in the workplace.

There are many claims made on behalf of conferencing. For some, it provides a safe and appropriate way for those affected by an offence to participate in deciding what should be done about it; hence, it enables conflicts that for so long have been 'stolen' by lawyers and treatment professionals to be returned to their rightful owners.[5] Another claim is that conferencing leads to better decisions than those which emerge from professionally-dominated processes (such as courtroom sentencing) since those who have most expertise (those directly involved in a situation) participate in the decision-making process. A further claim, influenced by the work of Tyler (2006) on why people obey the law, is that the use of

5 The ideas behind this claim come, of course, from Nils Christie (1977), a major influence on the restorative justice movement.

conferencing results in increased compliance with decisions in the criminal justice process.

However, by far the main claim made on behalf of conferencing is that it has a positive transformative effect on those who take part in it (see O'Connell et al., 1999, on which the following is mostly based). A common claim is that wrongdoers frequently enter a conference indifferent to the harm they have caused others and often with a hardened attitude. As a result of the dialogue that takes place during the conference they frequently undergo a transformation whereby they become repentant, promise to make amends for the harm they have caused, and afterwards refrain from further offending or at least offend less frequently and/or less seriously (Shapland et al., 2008: Chapter 2). Victims of wrongdoing, on the other hand, are said to enter conferencing traumatized, distressed and resentful. As a result of taking part in a conference their recovery from the trauma of victimization tends to be promoted. Many victims become more sympathetic towards the offender, which is actually healing for them (the victim) as it means they are being released from the debilitating and harmful emotions of anger and resentment. Advocates of conferencing claim that, surprisingly, victims often go on to support and even befriend the person who has wronged them. If members of the community in which an offence takes place take part in a conference they too tend to be transformed, according to some conferencing proponents. They discover that they have the capacity to help solve problems in their communities and hence become more confident and less reliant on experts and professionals. Therefore, it is claimed, conferencing has the capacity to contribute to the revival of self-reliant and self-assured communities.

There are various theories about how these transformative effects occur. Amongst the most interesting and influential are those which draw upon a mixture of the psychological theories of Donald Nathanson (1992) and the sociological theories of John Braithwaite (1989), which both focus on the emotion of shame. Drawing upon these ideas, those involved in promoting conferencing and in training conferencing facilitators have produced fascinating suggestions about the psychological routes offenders and victim take during a conference. Wrongdoers, it is said, tend to enter the conference with an indifferent attitude and are then 'brought down': they experience shame when the story of what happened and how it has affected people comes out in the conference in the presence of those (offender supporters) whose opinion of the wrongdoer matters to the wrongdoer. However, in a skilfully facilitated conference, the mood then shifts from negative to positive. A split emerges between the wrongdoer as a person and the misdeed committed by that person. This enables the wrongdoer to join in with the condemnation of the wrongful act, as they can now do so without feeling that their whole person is thereby under attack. Moreover, conferencing then empowers wrongdoers to start to repair the harm they have done through apologies and offers of material reparation. This helps them move from shame to pride and offers them a route to redemption.

Victims, on the other hand, are said to enter conferences traumatized, feeling disempowered and with their world view shattered (see Zehr, 1990: pp. 19–32). The dialogue that takes place during the encounter then uplifts them. The revelation of the full story of 'their crime' helps answer many questions that need to be answered if they are to recover. They experience cathartic release; fearsome images in their minds dissolve; their ability to shape the discussion and outcome returns a sense of power to them; and they recover a sense of autonomy and meaning. Chapter 15 by Gavrielides expands on the point of catharsis and how this may be used in the restorative justice process.

Given the nature of these claims, and the fact that evaluative studies suggest that they are far from implausible, it is not surprising that conferencing has aroused enormous interest within criminology and criminal justice studies and amongst professionals charged with the task of dealing with the aftermath of criminal offences and other wrongful acts. Hence, there has been a wealth of discussion about topics such as: the effectiveness of conferencing; the sorts of offences, offenders and victims for which it is appropriate; the implications of using conferencing within criminal justice systems which pursue a broad range of goals, some of them antithetical to those which conferencing is designed to achieve; how conferencing should be organized and conducted; how power imbalances between different parties participating in a conference may affect the dialogue and outcomes; how these power imbalances might be neutralized; the different models of conferencing that exist and their relative merits and limitations; the desirability of developing practice standards for conferencing, what those standards should be, and the responsibility for seeing that they are met; dealing with practices that claim the mantle of conferencing but do not comply with practice standards; the regimes of accountability that should be established for those running conferences; whether the outcomes of conferences be subject to judicial review and, if so, what the scope of that review should be; how conferencing should be evaluated; the extent to which conferencing is actually happening; and how policymakers, professionals and the public might be convinced of the merits of conferencing.[6]

Within these discussions, however, a slippage of language tends to occur. Discussions of conferencing are often presented as discussions of restorative justice. And, concomitantly, those purporting to discuss restorative justice are increasingly tending to focus on conferencing and related practices such as penal mediation and restorative circles. As Lode Walgrave has put it there is a 'blurring of restorative justice and conferencing in restorative justice literature' (Walgrave, 2012: p. 34). One consequence of this is that, although the literature on the phenomenon of restorative justice would seem to be huge, it is in fact quite narrowly focused. Most of what seems to be literature on restorative justice is in fact literature on just one aspect of restorative justice (that of conferencing and

6 A list of references to this literature would be extremely long. Perhaps it might suffice, then, to point to the compilation of some classic and contemporary literature in Johnstone (2013).

related practices), in which restorative justice is used as if it were interchangeable with conferencing and related practices. Other interesting and important aspects of the phenomenon of restorative justice – such as the teachings (which I will discuss), its underlying philosophy, its organization as a social movement, and its critique of conventional criminal justice – have been largely ignored.

Why this exclusive focus on conferencing? One obvious reason is that conferencing is concrete; an actual organized meeting takes place between people in a certain place at a certain time. This meeting can be observed, described and recorded, so there is something tangible to discuss. We can find out what sorts of venues these conferences take place in, how they are conducted, how long they take, how many people take part in them, what sorts of people take part, and how the dialogue unfolds. We can find out how many conferences are taking place in a certain place in a certain period, the types of offence they are used for, and the stage of the criminal justice (or other) process at which they take place. We can evaluate conferences by asking whether and how the meeting altered the course of events (did it result in change of attitude and conduct by the wrongdoer? Did it have a healing effect for the victim?). The exclusive focus on conferencing, in short, is related to a deeper notion that the empirical is the real or at least is what is important. The existence of conferencing means that restorative justice is not a *mere* idea; it is an idea that is being put into *action* and therefore it matters.

A possible critique of the obsession with conferencing, then, is that it focuses exclusively on the *practices* of restorative justice rather than on the *ideas* or *philosophies* of restorative justice. However, crucially, that is not the point to make here, the argument is rather that the nearly exclusive focus on conferencing and related practices reflects a very narrow perception of restorative justice. One of the key practices of restorative justice is the dissemination of certain social teachings. And this dissemination of teachings is just as tangible, just as observable, just as material, as is conferencing. The dissemination of the teachings of restorative justice takes place through the publication of books and articles, the production and dissemination of videos, organized meetings of restorative justice practitioners and scholars (often also called conferences), blogs and posts on social networking sites and through training and educational courses. Hence, this criticism of the exclusive preoccupation with conferencing is not that it focuses on material aspects of restorative justice to the neglect of ideas, but that it focuses on only a small part of the practice of restorative justice.

The remainder of this chapter will begin to redress this, not by surveying all those aspects of restorative justice which are neglected when one focuses narrowly on conferencing and related practices, but by focusing on one important and interesting aspect that has received little attention: the teachings of restorative justice.

The Teachings

There is a scholarly tradition of elucidating, interpreting and discussing the teachings of certain individuals or institutions. For example, one might explain and discuss the teachings of a major thinker such as Karl Marx (concerning, among other things, how we should conceptualize history, understand specific events, go about achieving certain political goals, or which goals should be pursued) (as in Beer, 1921/2011). Or, one might talk about the teachings of an institution such as the Catholic Church (concerning, among other things, the existence and nature of God, the claims of Jesus Christ, the role and authority of the Church, what we need to do when we commit sins, the permissibility of artificial birth restriction, our duties in the event of war, our obligations towards the sick and poor).[7] As these examples indicate, the concept of teachings in such discussions covers a very broad range of matters. Hence, a working definition of the term teachings in this chapter is an attempt to capture the offering of precepts and guidance covering a diverse range of matters. Crucially, teachings can be offered by an individual, an institution, or a looser entity such as a social movement. They can be direct or indirect and in either case, they are open to different interpretations.

To be quite clear about the purpose here, it is *not* to advocate the teachings of restorative justice nor to criticize them. Rather, a focus on the teachings of restorative justice forms part of a broader sociological concern to make sense of the social movement for restorative justice. From a sociological perspective, the emergence in recent decades of a global campaign which advocates and practises restorative justice is something that calls for explanation. Important questions include what explains the appearance of this campaign and what is its social meaning (as in, what can its appearance tell us about the societies in which we live)? In order to address such questions, it is necessary to have an accurate and adequate portrayal of the phenomenon. This certainly requires an understanding of the nature (and effectiveness) of key practices such as conferencing. However, it also requires an understanding of other aspects of the phenomenon. A study of the teachings of restorative justice is a crucial part of this. The first step in such a study is to describe these teachings. What is offered here is a very brief survey of a few teachings, the goal being to illustrate the nature of the teachings of restorative justice through a few examples.

Teachings Concerning Crime and Justice

At their core, the teachings of restorative justice instruct us on how to think about an issue that will inevitably arise amongst any group of people: what should we do when one member of the group is seriously harmed by the wrongful behaviour of another person? Or perhaps better, the first and most fundamental teaching

7 See http://www.proecclesia.com/page_becoming%20a%20catholic.htm and http://www.beliefnet.com/Faiths/Catholic/2003/03/Official-Catholic-Teaching-On-War.aspx.

of restorative justice is that we should see and define the problem of crime in precisely these terms. That is to say, restorative justice starts *not*, as is commonly thought, by proposing a new way of *responding* to crime, but by proposing a new way of *regarding* and *defining* crime. One of the core teachings is that the way we see and define a problematic situation is crucial. Define it one way and our response is structured by certain questions; define it another way and a different range of questions emerges.

The more habitual question is not the one posed in the previous paragraph but rather: what should we do when one member of the group does something seriously wrong? When we pose this question, our focus is drawn towards the wrongdoer and what to do to with or about him or her. There is still, of course, enormous scope for disagreement. Most people will insist that we ought to punish wrongdoers, but amongst these there will be huge disagreement about how harshly they should be punished and the appropriate method of punishment. Overlapping with this debate, some will argue that punishment should be replaced or accompanied by therapeutic interventions, designed not so much to redress past wrongdoing but to enable the wrongdoer to function better in the future. And, of course, many will argue that the best type of intervention is restorative justice, by which they tend to mean that rather than punishing or treating the wrongdoer, we should encourage him or her to meet with their victims and help repair the harm they have brought about.

The debate about what to do with the wrongdoer is regarded as very important in the teachings of restorative justice. However, a more fundamental teaching is often overlooked: that this whole debate, whilst not unimportant, should be secondary. It needs to be preceded by, and indeed take part in the context of, a rather different debate: what should we do when one member of the group is seriously harmed by the wrongful behaviour of another? Restorative justice teaches us that we tend to neglect this question, or at best treat it as an afterthought. Much of the problematic treatment of crime victims by our criminal justice system stems, it suggests, from the way we define this basic problem.

So, a basic teaching of restorative justice is that when a criminal incident is encountered, our primary question and concern should not be, as it is at present, 'what shall we do to or with the offender?'; rather, it should be 'what should we do for the victim?'. Restorative justice advocates are, of course, well aware that modern societies have many schemes in place for supporting crime victims. But, these are usually *adjuncts* to criminal justice. In the teachings of restorative justice, the goal of helping victims towards recovery from a deeply traumatic experience will be one of the core goals of the system itself. Healing victims will be a central component of criminal justice. So, for instance, if we look at the leading American book about restorative justice, Daniel Van Ness and Karen Strong's *Restoring Justice* (2006), it opens with an account of a sentencing in a rape case. The account is unusual in that the offender and his fate barely figure. Instead, the focus is on the victim's reaction and how what happened in the sentencing process impacted on her psychological recovery. This story is used to introduce an entirely new purpose for criminal justice. Its practitioners are to see themselves as healers pursuing the goals of healing the wounds caused by crime. Later in the book, this concern for healing will also be applied to offenders. But, at the outset, the focus is on healing the 'injuries' suffered by victims. The crucial point is that in a restorative criminal justice, it would be absurd to talk of doing justice and then *also* providing victims with support and help. Rather, restorative justice teaches us that promoting the healing of victims is a core part of what it means to do justice in the aftermath of a crime.

A second teaching of restorative justice is that when it comes to dealing with offenders, the objective of ensuring that they receive their just deserts should give way to the goal of reinstating them to a position of being loved and respected members of the community. Again, the crucial point to appreciate is that this goal of 'recovering' the offender is not an adjunct to or a replacement for 'doing justice'. Rather, in the teachings of restorative justice, healing is part of the essence of justice. Criminal justice itself is to be reimagined. Ensuring that criminal wrongdoers suffer for their misdeeds is dismissed as neither sufficient nor necessary in order to achieve justice in the aftermath of a crime. Rather, justice requires the re-establishment of a 'right relationship' between the offender and the rest of the community. Restorative justice teaches us that offenders should be brought to understand and fully acknowledge the harm they have caused and their responsibility for bringing it about. They must be encouraged to feel and express remorse and contrition for the suffering they have brought upon others. But, when they do so, they should be welcomed back into the community. Offenders who have expressed remorse and a desire to atone should be honoured and cherished. Restorative justice teaches that the return of an offender who has acknowledged and made amends for wrongdoing is a matter of celebration.

A third teaching of restorative justice is that in responding to crime we should be guided by, and give expression to, a different set of values than those which guide and are expressed through the present criminal justice system. It is difficult to be brief in describing the nature of this shift, especially as restorative justice advocates are often quite hazy when it comes to explaining what they have in mind. One useful approach might be to examine the teachings of restorative justice concerning the role that emotions should play in our response to crime.

The commission of a crime often arouses strong emotions and, if we turn our mind to what we would like to see done about the crime, our emotions inevitably influence our thinking. We may feel pity for a young offender who did something stupid rather than malicious, such as get caught up in an orgy of rioting and looting; we may be outraged by the behaviour of another offender; our heart may bleed over the plight of the family of a victim of manslaughter. To some extent, our institutions of criminal justice have been shaped by such feelings. Yet, one of the principles of modern criminal justice is to preclude such feelings from exerting a *direct* influence on decision-making in particular cases. Our system of criminal justice embodies the notion that under the influence of such feelings, we will find it difficult to see or do what is just. Pity for an offender may prevent us from sentencing them to the harsh punishment they really deserve. Sympathy for a victim may result in us sentencing an offender to a much harsher punishment than they deserve. Hence, decision-making in criminal justice, especially sentencing, should be a dispassionate affair. Ideally, it should be entrusted either to people who are distanced from what happened and can be more detached, and/or to people who are trained to follow reason and keep their feelings at bay. Hence, the dispensing of modern criminal justice can often be a sombre, cold, routine, dispassionate affair; it is deliberately designed to be like that.

The teachings of restorative justice are radically opposed to these conventional wisdoms. To quote from John Braithwaite and Heather Strang:

> [T]he power of restorative justice may be connected to the fact that it does not subordinate emotion to dispassionate justice, as in the blindfolded icon of justice balancing the scales. Nor does restorative justice subordinate emotion to rational bureaucratic routines. Space is created in civil society for the free expression of emotions, however irrational they may seem (Braithwaite and Strang, 2001: 10).

So, restorative justice teaches that a justice process must allow and encourage emotions to be expressed. Victims should not only be allowed but encouraged to express their hurt and anger, provided they do so in a civil way and without violence. Offenders should be encouraged to express their feelings, which will hopefully be ones of shame and remorse. But, as restorative justice advocate Chris Marshall suggests in a recent book, the key emotion that a restorative criminal justice process will provide space for is that of compassion (Marshall, 2012).

Indeed, according to the teachings of restorative justice, criminal justice should be an institution that exists, not for the purpose of dispensing 'dispassionate justice', but mainly to encourage and express compassion towards victims of crime. At the same time, it should be an institution which draws upon and is guided by a more compassionate and indeed loving attitude towards those who cause harm to crime victims. To be sure, it will be an institution that is vigorous in its condemnation of criminal conduct. Yet, it will avoid the mistake of contemporary criminal justice, which sees only the offence and assumes that the person who committed it is nothing but an offender. Rather, it will enable us to see the person who committed the offence as a complex human being who has done bad or harmful things, but may be, or at least has the capacity to be, a good person in other respects. Provided they are willing to condemn their misdeeds, express remorse for them and make amends, they can be shown love and compassion. One of the purposes of a restorative criminal justice will be to provide space for this to happen.

Teachings on How to Live

The above only skims through some teachings of restorative justice concerning crime and justice. To provide a richer account, much more would need to be said, for example about the idea that repairing the harm of crime is principally about recreating meaning that has been shattered, or about how the way we see and respond to crime is shaped by the distance between us and those directly involved. However, as it has developed, the restorative justice movement has developed a broader range of teachings concerning how we should live.

To look briefly and quickly at this broader range, we can consider the entry on Howard Zehr's restorative justice blog of 27 November 2009, titled *10 ways to live restoratively* (Zehr, 2009). The ten ways are:

1. Take relationships seriously, envisioning yourself in an interconnected web of people, institutions and the environment.
2. Try to be aware of the impact – potential as well as actual – of your actions on others and the environment.
3. When your actions negatively impact others, take responsibility by acknowledging and seeking to repair the harm – even when you could probably get away with avoiding or denying it …
4. Treat everyone respectfully, even those you don't expect to encounter again, even those you feel don't deserve it, even those who have harmed or offended you or others.
5. Involve those affected by a decision, as much as possible, in the decision-making process.
6. View the conflicts and harms in your life as opportunities.
7. Listen, deeply and compassionately, to others, seeking to understand even if you don't agree with them …
8. Engage in dialogue with others, even when what is being said is difficult, remaining open to learning from them and the encounter.
9. Be cautious about imposing your 'truths' and views on other people and situations.
10. Sensitively confront everyday injustices including sexism, racism and classism.

This is by no means an idiosyncratic contribution to the conversation surrounding restorative justice. It is just one of many discussions on how to live restoratively (see, for instance, Boehrer, 2008) and reflects an important aspect of the broad discourse on restorative justice. These teachings are clearly different from, albeit closely related to, the teachings of restorative justice on the handling of crime. The latter teachings are directed at society or, more specifically, at policymakers and professionals with responsibility for making and carrying out crime policy. Their focus is upon how this professional task ought to be conceived and conducted. The teachings on how to live restoratively are directed more at those who, for whatever reason, have joined in with the dialogue about restorative justice. Their focus is on how these people should live their lives, the moral values that should guide their interaction with others, and how they should regard and deal with certain situations, such as conflict with others. In the context of this book, and the symposium which gave rise to it, they could probably be described as a 'morality of aspiration', similar to the moral teachings found in classical Greek philosophy, as defined by Lon Fuller:

> The morality of aspiration is most plainly exemplified in Greek philosophy. It is the morality of the Good Life, of excellence, of the fullest realisation of human powers .... Generally with the Greeks instead of ideas of right and wrong, of moral claim and moral duty, we have rather the conception of proper and fitting conduct, conduct such as beseems a human being functioning at his best (Fuller, 1964: p. 5).

Analysing the Teachings

These are outlines of different descriptive images of restorative justice. The first is a narrow one, in which restorative justice consists mainly of practices such as conferencing. This is the image around which most of the discussion of restorative justice revolves. The second image is a broader one that encompasses not just practices such as conferencing, penal mediation and circles, but also the teachings of restorative justice. If we adopt this broader image, a whole range of further questions are raised, which need to be part of the conversation about restorative justice. The remainder of this chapter provides a very brief survey of the topics of conversation that might be prompted by this revised image of restorative justice.

First, to whom are these teachings addressed? Answering this question requires interpretation, as those propagating these teachings tend to assume rather than specify an audience/readership. Hence, the teachings on how we should respond to crime seem to be addressed mainly towards those in a position to directly influence the social response to crime: professionals working in the criminal justice system and policymakers. The focus of these teachings is on what the goals of the societal response to crime should be and how they should be conducted (focus on repair of harm rather than on punishment of perpetrators; do not subordinate emotions to dispassionate justice but provide space for the expression of emotions however irrational they may seem). Some, especially members of faith groups, have also sought to reach a broader audience by spreading their teachings amongst fellow members of their faith groups (and presumably hoping that from there they will filter out to a more general public). One prominent concern amongst meetings of restorative justice advocates and practitioners in recent years is that of how to get 'the message' across to the general public. Hence, in the UK organizations such as the Restorative Justice Council have been keen to get positive stories about restorative justice into the popular media, such as the red top newspapers and popular TV dramas. When this concern to get the message 'out there' is discussed, the clear tone is that the restorative justice movement has discovered/developed something of great value for our society, but now more needs to be done to ensure that people learn what it is and overcome the ignorance and prejudice that is likely to act as an obstacle to widespread embracement of the teachings of restorative justice.

The teachings on how to live restoratively, on the other hand, appear to be directed at everyone in principle, although in practice they are targeted at people with an interest in restorative justice, mediation, peacemaking and so on (those people likely to read Howard Zehr's blog and similar material). The focus of these teachings is not so much on how to carry out professional tasks, but rather on how people should conduct their lives. The guidance ranges from the ethico-political (confront racism) to matters of personal ethics (always take responsibility).

Another set of questions which might underpin an analysis of the teachings of restorative justice concerns their tone. As indicated above, the teachings regarding crime and justice are conceived, by those who propagate them, as progressive and enlightened. One of the most fundamental features of the entire restorative justice movement is that those who promote and support its aims have a deep conviction that they are in possession of truth, wisdom and progressive ideas. Their mission is to bring this wisdom and enlightenment to those in the cultural mainstream who are yet to grasp it. Hence, as has often been noted, there is an evangelical, proselytising flavour to much discourse on restorative justice. Often, the teachings of restorative justice are presented not so much as perspectives that need to be argued for, but as self-evident truths, with the goal being to overcome the ideological, political, social and psychological barriers that prevent others from grasping these truths (see Sullivan and Tifft, 2008: p. 3).[8] Such assumptions are in tension with some of the teachings on how to live restoratively. For instance step 8 – 'engage in dialogue with others, even when what is being said is difficult, remaining open to learning from them' – is one which most restorative justice supporters would fervently embrace, yet find difficult to extend to those who advocate positions which run contrary to the values of restorative justice (such as somebody who advocates corporal punishment for young offenders). Many restorative justice advocates will make a fair attempt to listen respectfully to those advocating such positions, but the idea that they might have something to learn from them is something they might find much harder. Likewise, many of the discussions that take place about how to get the message of restorative justice 'out there' are in danger of displaying a lack of caution about imposing truths upon others.

These points take us to perhaps the most fundamental questions concerning the teachings of restorative justice; how feasible and desirable would it be to follow these teachings? With regard to the teachings on crime and justice, perhaps the best test of this is to consider the teachings about compassionate justice. Christopher

8 The restorative justice movement is in this sense by no means unique; rather it shares this tendency with many contemporary 'progressivist' social movements. To be clear, by using terms such as 'evangelical' and 'proselytising', I am not seeking to suggest that restorative justice is more like a religion than a social movement. Much of what I have said here about the restorative justice movement would also apply to the highly secular, contemporary human rights movement.

Marshall opens his penetrating discussion of compassion and criminal justice with a discussion of a New Zealand case in which an eighteen-year-old youth, driving a car that had been illegally modified and was not certified for public roads, careered off a busy suburban road onto the pavement, killing a four-year-old child and injuring his mother and brother. The case is particularly interesting in that the youth, Ashley Austin, was clearly not a malicious or even particularly reckless person. He was not intoxicated, nor driving at high speed and he remained at the scene of the accident and tried to resuscitate the boy who died. As the parents acknowledged, he made a foolish decision with devastating consequences (Marshall, 2012: p. 284). The parents of the dead child forgave Ashley Austin and asked the judge not to send him to prison (he was being sentenced for dangerous driving causing death and serious injury). The judge agreed and sentenced him to six months community detention, community work and a three-year disqualification from driving.

This is clearly the sort of compassionate justice taught by advocates of restorative justice (and, at the risk of labouring the point, since it did not involve a restorative conference or similar process this sort of case would not usually be discussed in conversations concerning restorative justice). The parents clearly had an opportunity to contribute to the discussion of what should be done about the harmful act, they expressed their emotions and the 'justice' which the offender received was a justice that was influenced by those emotions. The case demonstrates that it is certainly feasible for some people to follow the teachings of restorative justice concerning crime and justice. But, the case does raise the question of whether we could expect a significant number of people to behave with such compassion towards somebody responsible for the avoidable death of their young child. Would it be realistic to expect many people to let go of the anger and resentment felt towards the wrongdoer? My guess is that the vast majority of people would find it extremely hard to do so, not simply because they are consumed with irrational emotions of hatred and anger, but because they would regard it as an insult to the memory of their dead child to forgive the person who killed them – a point to which we will return in a moment. Another question here concerns the sorts of conditions that must be in place for such compassionate justice to be feasible.

There is a hint above that there are questions not only over the feasibility but also the desirability of following the teachings of restorative justice concerning compassionate justice. As Marshall goes on to recount, one newspaper columnist was very critical of the court's decision. The columnist acknowledged that he could not have been as compassionate in the same circumstances, a stance which many would share. However, he also questions whether it was *right* to be so compassionate. He argued directly against the core teachings of restorative justice. It is unjust, he argued, to allow the emotions of victims to influence the sentence given to an offender. The point is an important one. Imagine a very similar case happening a year later, but this time the parents demand vengeance, call for the driver to be locked up for life, their demands supported by a public campaign calling for severe punishment of the offender. In such circumstances, we would expect the judge *not* to allow the court's sentencing decision to be influenced by emotions, but to restrict itself to imposing a legally proportionate sentence.[9] The columnist's point was that 'compassion got in the way of justice and heightened the danger for everyone else in the community' (ibid.: p. 285). Nearly all restorative justice advocates and supporters would disagree with the columnist. However, what should be acknowledged is that there are important ethical challenges to the teachings of restorative justice (on this and other points). Those who resist those teachings may be doing so because of ideological, social and psychological obstacles. But they may also be doing so because they are committed to values which are by no means obviously irrational or wrong or unethical, but which proponents of restorative justice find difficult to grasp and embrace.

We turn finally to the guidance on how to live restoratively. This guidance is taken very seriously by many people. Indeed, a number of people responded to Zehr's blog (2009), usually reporting that they regard the ten steps as a very challenging but sound guide to how to conduct themselves in everyday life. It is worthwhile looking at a small selection of these responses:

> I found these very challenging (in a good way!) The particular tension for me is working with 1–9 whilst seeking to do 10.
>
> From my perspective, living a restorative lifestyle – not for the fainthearted – is all there is.
>
> I am going to keep a print of them here next to my computer as a reminder, also for my own personal daily life.
>
> It can seem hard to live based on these rules, but it's worth it.
>
> These principles strike me as wonderful and, on their own, intimidating. I think that we can't make this kind of restoration happen simply by the force of our wills. I think that we need to be connected to deep sources of inspiration and guidance to allow these things to happen, through grace.
>
> I really find the '10 ways to live restoratively' to be a foundation that again can be explored and used in any facet of life at any age. This path is one of honour to follow. Many of us are not able to follow it daily but strive to improve on a daily basis. Keep trying is a good way to practice living with others. There have

9 A common move here by restorative justice advocates is to insist that in a restorative process such as a conference, such emotions – of anger, resentment and so on – would eventually be modified. However, even if there were firm evidence of this (and I suggest the evidence is far less conclusive than is sometimes claimed) this misses the point, which is a principled one in defence of the more emotionally detached decision-making to which our modern legal systems aspire.

> been many programs that use 'steps' or 'keys' to follow and they have proven themselves to be valuable in healing and this is another form of a wonderful guide to enhance the experience of daily living. I think the '10 ways to live restoratively' should be laminated in poster form and placed on every wall above every copier in every business. That would create quite a change in our lives as well as the potential of the world.

It is clear from these responses, and indeed from countless discussions had with restorative justice advocates and practitioners over the last decade, that increasing numbers of people are seeking not only to reform 'external' organizations and social practices in line with the ideas of restorative justice, but to practice principles such as these in their own lives and to encourage others to do so. Nor, for many, is this an optional extra. Rather, there is a fairly widespread view amongst campaigners for restorative justice that it would be contradictory and self-defeating to seek to 'restorativise' the societal response to crime whilst behaving non-restoratively in the workplace and in our everyday lives. Trying to transform the pattern of thinking that guides society's response to crime is currently just one concern – albeit still an extremely important one – of a social movement which aims to propagate a new way of seeing the world and living in it.

References

Beer, M. 1921/2011. *The Life and Teaching of Karl Marx*. London: National Labour Press, reprinted in 2011 in 'Routledge Revivals'. London: Routledge.

Boehrer, F. 2008. 'The Good Samaritan or the Person in the Ditch? An Attempt to Live a Restorative Justice Lifestyle' in Sullivan, D. and Tifft, L. (eds) *Handbook of Restorative Justice*. London: Routledge, pp. 546–54.

Braithwaite, J. 1989. *Crime, Shame and Reintegration*. Cambridge: Cambridge University Press.

Braithwaite, J. and Strang, H. 2001. 'Introduction' in Braithwaite, J. and Strang, H. (eds) *Restorative Justice and Civil Society*. Cambridge: Cambridge University Press, pp. 1–13.

Brooks, T. 2012. *Punishment*. London: Routledge.

Christie, N. 1977. 'Conflicts as Property', *British Journal of Criminology*, 17(1), pp. 1–15.

Cowie, H. 2010. 'Restorative Practice in School: A Psychological Perspective', unpublished, available at http://www.nottingham.ac.uk/EducationResearchProjects/ConflictinSchools/RestorativeApproachestoConflictinSchools.aspx.

Cunneen, C. and Hoyle, C. 2010. *Debating Restorative Justice*. Oxford: Hart.

Drewery, W. 2010. Restorative Practices in New Zealand Schools: A developmental Approach', unpublished, available at http://www.educ.cam.ac.uk/research/projects/restorativeapproaches/seminartwo/ Home Office 2003 *Restorative Justice: the Government's Strategy*. Home Office Communication Directorate.

Fuller, L. 1964. *The Morality of Law, revised edition.* New Haven: Yale University Press.
Home Office 2003 *Restorative Justice: The Government's Strategy*. London: Home Office Communication Directorate.
Hopkins, B. 2004. *Just Schools: A Whole School Approach to Restorative Justice*. London: Jessica Kingsley.
Johnstone, G. 2011. *Restorative Justice: Ideas, Values, Debates* (second edition). London: Routledge.
Johnstone, G. (ed.) 2013. *A Restorative Justice Reader* (second edition). London: Routledge.
Johnstone, G. and Van Ness, D. (eds) 2007a. *Handbook of Restorative Justice*. Cullompton: Willan.
Johnstone, G. and Van Ness, D. 2007b. 'The Meaning of Restorative Justice', in Johnstone, G. and Van Ness, D. (eds) *Handbook of Restorative Justice*. Cullompton: Willan. pp. 5–23.
Marshall, C. 2012. *Compassionate Justice*. Eugene, OR: Cascade Books.
Ministry of Justice 2010. *Breaking the Cycle: Effective Punishment, Rehabilitation and Sentencing of Offenders*. London: The Stationery Office Ltd.
Morrison, B. 2007 'Schools and restorative justice', in Johnstone, G. And Van Ness D. (eds) *Handbook of Restorative Justice*. Cullompton: Willan.
Nathanson, D. 1992. *Shame and Pride: Affect, Sex, and the Birth of the Self.* New York: W.W. Norton.
Newburn, T. 2012. *Criminology* (second edition). London: Routledge.
O'Connell, T., Wachtel, B. and Wachtel, T. 1999. *Conferencing Handbook*. Pipersville, PA: Piper's Press.
Shapland, J., Atkinson, A., Atkinson, H., Dignan, J., Edwards, L., Hibbert, J., Howes, M., Johnstone, J., Robinson, G. and Sorsby, A. 2008. *Does Restorative Justice affect Reconviction: The Fourth Report from the Evaluation of Three Schemes*. Ministry of Justice.
Sullivan, D. and Tifft, L. 2008. 'The Healing Dimension of Restorative Justice: a One-world Body", in Sullivan, D. and Tifft, L. (eds) *Handbook of Restorative Justice*. London: Routledge, pp. 1–16.
Sullivan, D. and Tifft, L. 2013. 'Needs-based Justice as Restorative', in Johnstone, G. (ed.) *A Restorative Justice Reader,* second edition. London: Routledge, pp. 208–16.
Tyler, T. 2006. *Why People Obey the Law*. Princeton, NJ: Princeton University Press.
Van Ness, D. and Strong, K. 2006. *Restoring Justice: An Introduction to Restorative Justice* (third edition). Lexisnexis.
Walgrave, L. 2012. 'The Need for Clarity about Restorative Justice Conferences', in Zinsstag, E. and Vanfraechem, I. *Conferencing and Restorative Justice*. Oxford: Oxford University Press, pp. 33–45.
Zehr, H. 1990. *Changing Lenses: A New Focus for Crime and Justice.* Scottsdale, PA: Herald Press.

Zehr, H. 2009. 10 ways to live restoratively. *Restorative Justice blog*, 27 November 2009. Available at http://emu.edu/now/restorative-justice/2009/11/27/10-ways-to-live-restoratively/

Zinstagg, E. and Chapman, T. 2012. 'Conferencing in Northern Ireland: Implementing Restorative Justice at the Core of the Criminal Justice System' in Zinsstag, E. and Vanfraechem, I. *Conferencing and Restorative Justice*. Oxford: Oxford University Press, pp. 173–88.

Zinsstag, E. and Vanfraechem, I. (eds) 2012. *Conferencing and Restorative Justice*. Oxford: Oxford University Press.

Chapter 4
Problematizing Restorative Justice: A Foucauldian Perspective

Giuseppe Maglione

Introduction

Over the past thirty years, restorative justice (RJ) has slowly emerged worldwide as a popular theory, a relentlessly growing field of research able to inspire concrete actions within (or outside) many criminal justice systems (Daly and Imarrigeon, 1998; Miers, 2001). Taking a closer look at the extensive scholarship focusing on RJ, two overall features can be emphasized. First, it is easy to detect the presence of multiple, shifting, conflicting discourses, even contradictory in nature, regarding its historical roots or main theoretical aspects (Zernova, 2007). Second, a careful analysis can equally easily identify several 'authoritative discourses' which act as shared truths on the historical emergence and theoretical justification of RJ (Daly, 2002). This work is a critical and historical contextualization of these main discourses on RJ from a perspective drawn upon the work of Michel Foucault, with a particular interest in the discursive objects which constitute the authoritative accounts on RJ, their social and cultural embeddeness. How are the vocabularies composed that make possible these authoritative discourses? Where are their historical roots? How have they become authoritative from an epistemic point of view (as in able to define the sayable and thinkable on RJ)? The main goal of this chapter is to address these questions, working out a critical and historical reflection. Foucault's methodological reservoir is conceived as a range of insights to be used, re-elaborated and overcome. As far as the specific research tools are concerned, I argue for a specific interpretation of the foucauldian historical analysis. This stance entails the functional integration (and then the overcoming) of archeological and genealogical approaches in order to diagnose the contingencies of 'one' present. According to this perspective there is no space for the search for static origins or causal explanation, or for the use of universals a priori grids of intelligibility. The goal is not to create *a grand récit*, but only to map out the life course of those discourses and their authority, from singular contingencies to authoritative, taken for granted, narratives on the emergence and justification of RJ.

Archaeology and Genealogy

Foucault's historical project can be described as an attempt to use the distant past in order to gain access to our present, the beliefs, practices and institutions which have reached the state of obvious truths. From this perspective the past is a medium for access to the present rather than a mere object of research or end point, while history is the historicization of our truths rather than the recording activity of a progressive and continuous flow of events. The secondary literature on Foucault used to distinguish three phases in his scholarship: archaeology, genealogy and ethics (Davidson, 1986). I will dwell briefly on the first two, by virtue of their direct methodological relevancy to my study.

Foucauldian archaeology, as a 'way of speaking' about history, analyzes the production of discourse in terms of the conditions for its possibility, excluding the primacy of the consciousness of individual subjects as a precondition of the discourse-making process. The general premise of this approach is that systems of thought and knowledge are governed by rules that operate beneath the consciousness of individual subjects and define a system of conceptual possibilities that determines the boundaries of thought in a given domain and period (Howarth, 2002). In the archaeology the first and main goal is the identification of the *discursive objects* working on their *archive*. In Foucault's framework an archive is composed of multiple and varying discourses, it is 'the law of what can be said, the system that governs the appearance of statements as unique events' (Foucault, 1972, p. 129). The archive then, is not just a passive collection of records from the past, it is an active and controlling system of enunciation. Archeological analysis, starting from the identification of the archive, seeks to describe the history of a specific discourse, the set of 'things said' in all its interrelations and transformations. This analysis forsakes preconceptions about historical unity or continuity, describing instead the processes of discourse in all their disruptions, thresholds, differences, and complex varieties. What must then be detected are the dynamics of formation, transformation and correlation of all the individual components of a discourse (objects, enunciative modalities, concepts and theoretical options), which control the fact that some things can be talked about and the prohibitions about speaking of other things (Foucault, 1991, p. 54). Examples of archaeology are *Madness and Civilization* (Foucault, 1965), which examines the cultural, legal, political and medical construction of discourse on madness in Europe, from the Middle Ages to the end of the eighteenth century. *The Birth of the Clinic* (Foucault, 1973) is a study of the emergence of the *medical gaze* related to epistemic shifts at the end of the eighteenth century. Lastly, in *The Order of Things* (1970), Foucault scrutinizes the underlying conditions of truth of specific scientific discourses that constituted what was acceptable, in an historical dimension.

Genealogy, like archeology, is a way of writing the history of certain objects. Its function lies in describing social phenomena detecting patterns between relations of power on the one hand, and norms, facts and systems of belief and knowledge on the other (Saar, 2002, pp. 231–33). The critical dimension of this perspective rests on both its structural self-reflexivity and on its tension toward the understanding of the present, and expresses itself in deciphering those patterns, with a defamiliarizing attitude (Saar, 2002, p. 235). The overall aim of the genealogist is the historicization of truths, to explore how it is that some truths and knowledge have come to be accepted as unproblematic (Bailey, 1993, p. 120). Rather than seeking the *telos* of a particular concept, genealogy records the singularity of events outside of any finality, isolating the different scenes where they engage in different roles. In this framework 'discontinuity' becomes a category of historical analysis as well as the object of it, from 'the obstacle to the work itself' (Foucault, 1972, p. 9). In other words, rather than being reduced or manipulated to form a linear progression, discontinuities in the history of any phenomenon should be focused upon and explored. Foucault, in fact, believes that 'continuous' histories falsely represent the past as ascribing to a logical flow or pattern (Foucault, 1991, p. 2). He thinks that such histories of continuity obscure the material complexity of events, creating neat narratives from inherently chaotic structures. Another fundamental concept in the foucauldian genealogy is the theme of power. For Foucault, power simply 'produces reality; it produces domains of objects and rituals of truth' (Foucault, 1977, p. 194). Power operates in and through discourses (Gubrium and Holstein, 2000, p. 494), producing what is taken as knowledge or considered truth. The relationship of power and knowledge is neither unidirectional nor exterior. Instead they stand in an interior and reciprocal productivity: 'no power relation without the correlative constitution of a field of knowledge, nor any knowledge that does not presuppose and constitute at the same time power relations' (Foucault, 1977, p. 27). The landmark of Foucault's genealogy, therefore, is the analysis of the mutual productivity of power and knowledge, centered on the everyday, mundane exercise of power rather than grand, all-encompassing explanatory models. This perspective is deployed in well-known books such as *Discipline and Punish* (Foucault, 1977) regarding the history of punishment and the disciplinary society or the *History of Sexuality I* (Foucault, 1978), a genealogy of the 'repressive hypothesis' in the explanation of the relationships between sexuality and bourgeois society.

Problematization: Combining Archaeology and Genealogy

In the mainstream literature there has been much debate about the relationship between Foucault's concepts of archaeology and genealogy (Scheurich and McKenzie, 2005). It has traditionally been said that Foucault's archaeological and genealogical periods are radically different from each other. Just as it is commonplace to distinguish 'between Picasso's Blue period and his Pink period' (Baert, 1998, p. 122), so there is Foucault's archaeology and his genealogy (Bevir, 1999, p. 347). On the other hand, this opinion is not the only interpretative option available and subscribed to by scholars. Some authors, in fact, have argued that archaeology, as Foucault's method of analyzing documents, is indissolubly connected to genealogy, intended as a series of methodological prescriptions that guide the writing of history using the results of archaeology (Dean, 1994, p. 33).

In this work archaeology and genealogy are two research devices combined under the common project of the *problematization* of RJ (Bacchi, 2012). Problematization, as a concept elaborated by Foucault, is an overall methodological perspective which focuses on 'the set of discursive or non-discursive practices that makes something enter into the play of the true and false, and constitutes it as an object for thought' (Foucault, 1989, p. 296). Here discourse is a primary medium of human actions embedded in broader social contexts. Discourse is institutionally situated, constructed (by people, institutions, etc.) and constructive (of people's lived experiences, possibilities, ideas, theories and taken for granted truths). In this view, the legacy of the archaeology is represented by the structural technique of focusing on both discourse and speaker as constructed objects as a necessary step to free ourselves from taking the discourses and practices of this society as simply expressing the way things *are* (Dreyfus and Rabinow, 1983, p. XXVII). The identification of discursive objects enables the raising of genealogical questions: how are these discourses used? What role do they play in society? In the problematization, genealogy moves away from archaeology, intended as an attempt to chart the movement of particular discursive objects in order to unearth the conditions of our present realities. In this way it is possible to diagnose and criticize 'strong narratives', providing a counter-memory that helps to recreate the historical and practical conditions of their present existence (Foucault, 1986, p. 53), opening up new possibilities of understanding and action. In order to operationalize this methodological perspective, I will proceed as follows. First, try to identify and unpack the structure of the authoritative discourses which make up RJ (Tamboukou and Ball, 2003). Then draw up their 'surfaces of emergence', showing the relationship between the authoritative discourses and three main sociocultural constructs, identifying and describing them. In this fashion it is possible to chart the discursive and non-discursive dynamics in the production of authoritative accounts of RJ. Third, map out the common aspects, inner tensions and historical transformations within and between the authoritative explanations and rationalizations of RJ. Lastly, sketch out some conclusive implications of this analytic approach and its findings, raising new questions for RJ theory and calling for new models of explanation and justification.

Two methodological caveats are here necessary. First, the intention is to work out, revising (and maybe distorting) specific foucauldian research devices in order to open up different possibilities of thinking and to generate new kinds of questions on RJ. This means simplifying or reconsidering many aspects of the foucauldian legacy, without worrying about being faithful or unfaithful to the textbook version of Foucault's meta-theory. The second caveat concerns the acknowledgement of some intellectual debts. Kevin Minor and J.T. Morrison (1996) for instance, focusing on RJ, have taken into account the theoretical viewpoint expressed by Michel Foucault. George Pavlich's (1996) *Justice Fragmented: Mediating community disputes under postmodern conditions*, is a genealogical analysis of community mediation in Canada, whereas his *Governing Paradoxes of Restorative Justice* (2005) applies Foucault's concept of governmentality to RJ. However, the contributions made by Kelly Richards (2005, 2009, 2011) are, in my opinion, the most interesting example of a foucauldian study of RJ. In my work I share with Richards both the methodological premises and the main goal. On the other hand, my application of the foucauldian perspective is quite different to Richards' The complementarity of archaeology and genealogy from the problematization's perspective, implies a specific kind of discursive analysis (very different from that one carried out by Richards) as a necessary preliminary step with respect to the genealogical enquiry. This main methodological divergence leads to different conclusions from Richards'.

Authoritative Discourses

The authoritative discourses that act as the main historical explanations and theoretical justifications for RJ are the material – *the archive* (Foucault, 1972, p. 145) – upon which I draw the problematization of RJ. By authoritative discourses I mean the scholarly and advocacy writings published since the late 1970s, which have achieved the status of landmark contributions to the worldwide spread of RJ theory and practice (Braithwaite, 1999; Sylvester, 2003). These discourses are usually the product of long-lasting action research related to the reform of criminal justice. They have blossomed in the attempt to rationalize some innovative criminal justice practices (such as victim–offender mediation) characterized by their borderline positions in the context of well-known strategies for dealing with crime and its aftermath. But notice that they are far from being a cohesive and consistent range of opinions; they should be thought of instead as a cultural construct, a living complex of founding myths and theoretical investigations that often conflict in their approach and outcomes. The relevance of analyzing this authoritative dimension of RJ is related to the fact that they have inspired the mindset of scholars, advocates and practitioners, defining the field of what can be said, discussed, evaluated and thought about RJ. They compound the normative backbone of the RJ world. The problem here is understanding its discursive structure and detecting the contextual factors that have contributed in creating the authority of those discourses.

Authoritative Explanations

One of the most rooted explanations of RJ's emergence is that it represents a response to the shortcomings (or even to the overall failure) of criminal justice systems in contemporary Western countries. As the British RJ activist Tony Marshall emphasizes (1995, p. 230) '[RJ] is a practice that contains the seeds for solving a new problem – the inadequacy of the criminal justice system itself, as it lurches from crisis to crisis, based on a primitive philosophy of naked revenge'.

In the same way, one of the forefathers of the RJ movement, Howard Zehr, claims that 'We know that the system we call "criminal justice" does not work. … We have known that for many years, and have tried many reforms, and they have not worked either' (1985, p. 1–2). Zehr is echoed by Robert Cario, well-known advocate of RJ in France, who states: 'The crisis of the Penal State is evident. The state has troubles maintaining its jealous monopoly of the repression' (2005, p. 11). The breakdown of the criminal justice system seems a tragic, objective fact. Among advocates of RJ we see widespread agreement that current systems of criminal justice are unacceptable on a theoretical level and, from an empirical point of view, ineffectual. Common criticisms include the system's inability to prevent crime, rehabilitate offenders and assist victims. Nevertheless, alternative or more moderate views are present in RJ literature. Gerry Johnstone (2003, p. 5.) for instance, claims that RJ advocates 'present us with a one-sided picture of the values that underpin conventional criminal justice'. He also argues that, despite its shortcomings, the contemporary approach to criminal justice does perform some essential functions with reasonable success. In much of the RJ literature, however, it is taken for granted that the emergence of RJ is a natural consequence of the failure of the criminal justice system (Cohen, 2001, p. 209).

Another typical historical explication of the emergence of RJ, shared by a fair number of scholars and advocates, is that RJ has emerged due to the development of a new awareness of the victims of crime translated into a worldwide victims' rights movement (Shapland, Wilmore and Duff, 1985, p. 2). In this context, starting in the 1980s, RJ has been one of the new ways of dealing with the needs of crime victims. This interpretation is usually complementary to the failure of criminal justice and offers a solid ground on which the victims' rights movement has built up strong political claims and arguments for reform. The connection between these two explanations is probably that the crime victims' claims are shaped first of all as a criticism of the criminal justice system. Clarke and Davies (1994, p 169), for example, argue that 'the increasing use of victim offender mediation programs in Australia and throughout the world can be seen as … a shift in focus in the late 1980s and early 1990s to the rights of victims and the study of victimology'. Likewise, Zehr (2002, p. 15) states that 'the theory and practice of restorative justice have emerged from and been profoundly shaped by an effort to take … [the] … needs of victims seriously'. On the same line, as Antony Pemberton et al. claim (Pemberton et al., 2008) there seems to be little doubt that RJ is in the interest of victims of crime. In academic textbooks the two are often paired and legislation concerning RJ pays tribute to the position of crime victims. Assisting crime victims in their recovery is in fact widely considered to be a core element of any RJ intervention. Lode Walgrave (2003, p. 89), echoing this perspective, argues that RJ can be represented as a victim-centered approach to justice. This is because RJ does not marginalize the victim from the justice process while, at the same time, claiming to offer retribution on the victim's behalf. Instead, RJ recognizes the victim as a central stakeholder within the restorative process, and thus seeks to provide them with a prominent role in shaping the justice process and in deciding upon a just resolution to the conflict (Walgrave, 2003, p. 90).

Along with the failure of the formal criminal justice system and the rediscovering of crime victims' centrality in criminal justice, it is possible to detect another *explanans* regarding the historical emergence of RJ theory and practice, deeply rooted in the RJ literature. The shared factors in the following explain the emergence of RJ: the need of the community to be recognized as a fundamental stakeholder in dealing with crime and its aftermath; its key role in ensuring safety and peace for victims and to foster binding social behavior in offenders; the necessity to be part of the criminal justice system and to escape from being a neglected actor. As Albert Dzur and Susan Olson have emphasized (2004, p. 92.), crime, for advocates of RJ, means more than a violation of the laws of the state and more even than harm to victims. To echo Nils Christie (1981, p. 11), crime is widely conceived by RJ advocates and scholars as a dysfunctional way of saying something and punishment is an equally dysfunctional way of answering. In this picture, the idea that the community has a stake in an offence apart from the victim's and that a larger social network might also be a harmed party, becomes a landmark of RJ. Considering the purely abstract, highly formalized ways in which the community is incorporated in mainstream criminal justice practice, many RJ proponents call for more public participation in the criminal justice process so that the harm to community is more clearly brought to the attention of the offender (Dzur and Olson, 2004, p. 92). Rather than the general claim that communal harm needs to be addressed the best reasons for public participation are more precise ones that link community participation to a better-functioning criminal justice system or other benefits to the community (Dzur and Olson, 2004, p. 92). As usual, the RJ literature is not as peaceful as it might appear, even when talking of community, different and deeply conflicting stances can be easily detected (McCold and Wachtel, 2002).

The claims of reforming the criminal justice system, giving centrality to victims and involving the broader community in dealing with crimes, are usually combined in RJ literature. This complex multifaceted account of recent RJ emergence clashes with one last, very common factor called upon in an explanation of RJ's emergence. This is the conceptualization of RJ's rise as the resurgence of a premodern way of dealing with conflict (Sylvester, 2003; Umbreit et al., 2005; Weitekamp, 1999). This claim, often repeated, has reached the status of a 'myth' (Sylvester, 2003) in RJ literature. John Braithwaite (1999, p. 2), for instance, has synthesized that 'restorative justice has been the dominant model of criminal justice throughout most of human history for all of the world's peoples'. On the other hand, we detect the presence in RJ literature of some sharp criticisms regarding the abovementioned perspective (Sylvester, 2003, p. 493). Some scholars, in fact, rather than seeing RJ as the primary form of criminal justice, describe it as a relatively recent approach to crime and its aftermath, begun in 1970s North America (Mulligan, 2009, p. 142). In this narrative, RJ is seen as a novel and innovative system (Sylvester, 2003, p. 494) which has come to influence justice systems globally over the last three decades (Burkemper et al., 2007, p. 130). One thing must be noted. The 'never-ending' explanation of RJ potentially conflicts with previous ones insofar as they conceive of RJ as the answer to late-modern issues, such as the failure of criminal justice or the community's needs and the crime victims' satisfaction. On the other hand, this conflict is avoided when the claim that RJ is not a product of late modernity is used as a normative justification (RJ is acceptable because it revives ancient traditions) and not as a causal/descriptive explanation of RJ's emergence.

Authoritative Conceptualizations

A well-known archetypal conceptualization of RJ is given by the identification of similarities and differences of RJ with respect to criminal justice at large or penal punishment in particular (Roche, 2007, p. 75). Clearly, this complex range of positions intersects the historical explanations of RJ's emergence as an answer to the failure of contemporary Western criminal justice systems. Early proponents defined RJ as an alternative to the retributive principle informing criminal justice (Zehr, 1985, 1990). This dichotomy has become a standard approach defining RJ. Nevertheless, in more recent years criticisms have arisen against this perspective, deemed as a misrepresentation of a more complex relationship (Ashworth, 1993, 2002, 2003). In fact, various writers in recent times have reached a more positive (or at least more nuanced) view on retribution (Roche, 2007, p. 83).

Within this evolving context there emerges one of the main issues regarding the theoretical conceptualization of RJ, the question of the 'trigger event' (Woolford, 2009, p. 28) for restorative interventions, as in what makes the activation of a restorative practice necessary. As Andrew Woolford has emphasized (2009, p. 29), in RJ literature there are basically three possible (alternative) concepts of RJ trigger events: the *conflict* involving victim, offender and community as stakeholders; the *harm* caused by the offender; the *normative violation* (or the wrong) committed by the offender and suffered by the victim. The idea that the *harm*, rather than the crime, is the trigger event for a RJ intervention is quite common across the literature (Mika and Zehr, 2003, p. 135–152; Sherman and Strang, 2003). In other words, restorative practices respond specifically to interpersonal harms, that is, they address harms caused through interaction between two or more individuals (Woolford, 2009, p. 29). Other scholars, in a different vein, argue that crime is a form of legally categorized *conflict* and therefore they place RJ under the broad rubric of conflict resolution (Christie, 1977). In the RJ literature there is space for another interpretation, according to which RJ is concerned with *normative violations* (Ashworth, 1993). Norms are group's established behavioral codes that guide the activities of an individual belonging to the group. Any RJ intervention must, in this view, focus on these violations, aiming at restoring the balance altered by the wrong committed by the offender.

Closely related to the issue of the trigger event is the theoretical topic of restoration, its meaning and relationship with criminal justice, as a distinctive feature of RJ. The practical ways of applying the vague idea of restoration discussed in the literature are numberless. Nevertheless, the concepts of restitution and reparation appear to be the most recurrent and theoretically relevant. Restoration is usually defined by activities regarding material or personal and private or communal harms, loss and wrongs, shaped usually as restitutive and/or reparative actions (Karp, 2001, p. 730). As for the restitution, the works of Albert Eglash (1958), Gilbert Cantor (1976) and Randy Barnett (1977) are considered key contributions. Eglash's *creative restitution* theory in dealing with crimes, is a perspective based on the idea that the offender, even if self-determined, must be guided toward the restitution, and related constructive acts for a victim or community. Cantor argues for the civilization of offender treatment, which entails restitution and compensation through manageable installments with the agreement of the parties. Barnett analyzes the breakdown of criminal justice as a Kuhnian crisis of the old paradigm of punishment. Barnett's proposal is to overcome the crisis by adopting a new paradigm based on restitution. Within RJ theory it is largely agreed that doing justice involves reparation (Van Ness and Heetderks Strong, 2003; Zehr and Mika, 1998). According to Wright (1991), it seems that the roots of reparation in RJ must be searched for in Margery Fry's *Arms of Law* (1951, p. 124–26), an inspirational and seminal book for the RJ movement. Although it is possible to say that the idea of reparation is basically a must in RJ literature, it must be acknowledged that this concept is shaped, worked out and applied in many different ways. Basically, two different concepts of reparation can be found: material and symbolic/emotional (Retzinger and Scheff, 1996, p. 316). As important as material reparation (for instance monetary compensation) can be in enabling a victim to recover from the effects of a crime, symbolic reparation can be even more significant (Sharpe, 2007, p. 28). This particular form of reparation has apology and forgiveness as a core sequence. In fact it is considered a condition for generating the repair and restoration of the bond between victim and offender, severed by the offender's crime.

Lastly, the relevance of concepts such as shame, love, relationships or healing and forgiveness in RJ literature, is something which cannot be overlooked when we talk of its theoretical features. Indeed, this relational dimension (see Susan Sharpe in Chapter 9), or warm side, is one of the most striking aspects of both scholarly and practice-oriented writings on RJ. Jim Consedine (1999, p. 41) stresses how 'Fairness, truth honesty compassion, respect for people are the basic tenets of an acceptable morality that flows from justice and seeks to protect and enhance the common good'. While Judah and Bryant (2004, pp. 1–6,) argue that 'RJ is holistic, inclusive and affirming of the dignity and worth of every human being'. Well-known authors Zehr and Toews (2004 p. IX), emphasize that 'Restorative values can be distilled to two key underlying values – humility and respect. Furthermore, we should approach our work with wonder'. As Annalise Acorn argues (2004, pp. 18–22), RJ theory tries to mediate and harmonize the two presumptively conflicting realms of love and justice, offering a vision of justice as 'tough love'. Acorn contends that RJ also places an extraordinary amount of faith in the idea that compassion itself, when extended toward and effected between victims and wrongdoers, will have an overwhelming and magically transformative power in the direction of justice. It requires we build better, more respectful, more mutual relationships than those that existed prior to the wrong. It reaches toward an idealized state of right relationships, as its model of the just.

Surfaces of Emergence

From the main authoritative discourses, RJ emerges as an answer to different (and often conflicting) needs, such as those expressed by the crisis in criminal justice, the growing awareness of the crime victims' movement and the claim to be involved in dealing with crimes raised by the community. At the same time, the theoretical main issues faced up to by RJ discourses seem to be drawn essentially from an oppositional comparison to criminal justice; the concept of restoration, the trigger event for RJ interventions (or its object), the relational side of RJ. Through a foucauldian lens it is now possible to cast a critical glace over the authoritative accounts of RJ, problematizing the assumptions that are taken for granted and the obvious truths. This means first of all analyzing their discursive structure and their 'surfaces of emergence' (Foucault, 1972, p. 41). In this perspective, the authoritative accounts seem made not of privileged objects, but rather a dispersal of many objects which compound their basic vocabulary. These objects do not exist before their emergence under certain complex, relational, discursive conditions, and are therefore not defined by their internal, conceptual nature, but by their exterior relations, their triangulation or juxtaposition with other objects. The question, at this point, is to trace back the surfaces of emergence of the objects which constitute the authoritative discourses, the pre-existing fields, normative to some degree, which allow RJ authoritative discourses to define what they are talking about (thereby creating apparently definite objects of discourse) and how. These surfaces are not the historical/theoretical roots of RJ as such, but only the conditions of possibility of the authoritative discourses on RJ, the discursive space from which they come into being.

Victimology and Victim Surveys

The first surface is represented by new knowledge of the victims related to the consolidation of victimology as a scientific and academic discipline and the set-up of new criminological research tools (like victim surveys).

Victimology studies data that describe phenomena and causal relationships associated with victimization, including the victim's experience, its aftermath and the actions taken by society in response to victimization. Therefore, victimology comprises the study of precursors, vulnerabilities and events leading to the victimization (Dussich, 2006, p. 130). Victimology originated with the early writings of Benjamin Mendelsohn (1976) and Hans von Hentig (1948) and became a 'normal science' in the early 1970s. In fact, specific educational programmes for university students interested in understanding victimization and training courses for practitioners wanting to facilitate victim recovery were created in this period.

There was also a growth in this period in the use of victim surveys as a new research device in criminology. A victim survey is a periodic data collection and analysis process within the general population usually conducted by a government entity to study information about crime victims, regardless of whether or not they reported their victimization to the police (Dussich, 2006, p. 131).

This scientific and academic framework has worked as a surface of emergence for both historical and theoretical authoritative discourses on RJ in different ways. This means that the new scientific knowledge on the victims of crime, the identification of their needs detected by victim surveys, combined with the claims of grassroots victims' organizations has opened a fundamental discursive space for the emergence of those discourses on RJ. The empirical and victimological evidence on the involvement of crime victims and their expectations and satisfaction of criminal justice have become key categories in the language of RJ. This is not a natural phenomenon but the consequence of the consolidation and popularization of victimological research. A clear example is the crucial and taken for granted concept of victim participation in RJ processes, quite evidently derived from the victimological research. Even more interesting is how the victimology has informed the category of victim and the concept of victim–offender relationships within the authoritative discourses on RJ. A victim is contextualized, characterized by emotions such as fear and loss of control, in need of empowerment, vulnerable, this is the victim's identity in the authoritative discourses, seemingly drawn from victimological research findings. Likewise, to conceive of the relationship between victim and offender as a dynamic one, including strong emotions and needs to be readdressed, primarily the need to speak out, to talk of the crime's consequences, again seems to be a legacy of victimology and victim surveys.

Abolitionism, Communitarianism, Refeudalization of the Public Sphere

The second surface of emergence is given by the articulation of three different but synchronic discourses:[1] penal abolitionism (especially institutional abolitionism); the rebirth of communitarian philosophy in the late 1970s; and discourses on the refeudalization of the public sphere.

Penal abolitionism is not merely a theory of decarceration, but an approach, a perspective, a methodology, and most of all a way of seeing (Ruggiero, 2011, pp. 1–2). There is clearly an abolitionist element in the proposition that the state centralized administration of penal justice should be replaced by decentralized forms of autonomous conflict regulation (Christie, 1977). But in a general formulation it can be suggested that abolitionists advocate new ways of dealing

1 Due to limited space my account of these discourses lacks the analytical depth such a topic deserves

with undesirable behavior, and in doing so they situate themselves in an original position within the debate around RJ.

Communitarianism finds the sources of social cohesion in shared assumptions so deeply engrained in everyday life that they do not have to be articulated: in folkways, customs, prejudices. (Lasch, 1994, 92). In communitarian perspectives individuals are densely enmeshed in interdependencies which have special qualities of mutual help and trust (see Chapter 14). The interdependencies have a symbolic significance in the culture of group loyalties which takes precedence over individual interests (Braithwaite, 1989, p. 100). Communitarianism can be taken to stand for a highly socialized view of people in which their moral position can be understood only in terms of their social relationships.

In discussing the structural transformations of the public sphere, Jürgen Habermas (1989) clarified that while the market helped create the initial space for civic engagement, it also constantly threatened to colonize public spheres through privatization. He referred to this phenomenon as the 'refeudalization of the public sphere', a process in which the newly created public space would succumb to commercial pressures and reorganize along familiar power hierarchies (Habermas, 1964, p. 49–55). What is particularly interesting is the refeudalization of social decision-making since decisions were removed from public scrutiny (parliaments, boards and so on) and placed within the realm of private spaces (private commercial businesses). Secondly, it is a communicative form that is part of what has been called a refeudalization process as public spaces, whose regulation was previously subject to public scrutiny (through parliaments, public boards and so on), are shifted into private ownership. The growing privatization of public space has spread to a number of sectors, ranging from the airwaves and educational sites to shopping malls. These privatized spaces are designed for commercial profit, not the facilitation of public debate, and the new owners have no vested interest in allowing their private spaces to be used for social dialogue. Several categories of the discourses mentioned above enter the authoritative accounts on RJ, lending out specific discursive elements. The concept(s) of community and its role in restorative discourse seems to emerge from the combination of the idea of community as an alternative to the state in dealing with social conflicts (abolitionism), the idea of social interdependency worked out within communitarian perspectives, and the necessity to resist the privatization/refeudalization of public spheres through investment in the revitalization of 'life worlds'. Community here appears as a kind of antagonist to the state but also to the social atomization processes caused by the privatization of public spaces. In the authoritative discourses the binary opposition between the state (and the criminal justice system as its expression), and a radically different, independent and even alternative virtual space is considered evident and unquestionable. Even if in the authoritative discourses different conceptualizations of community are present, in general this basic conceptual configuration is recurrent and taken for granted. In this perspective, different versions of the 'trigger event' also appear related to that complex discursive combination. The concepts of conflict and damage particularly seem rooted in the idea of a problematic situation, an expression which replaces – in the abolitionist view – the identifying expressions such as offence, crime and criminal act. At the same time the traditional means of state intervention in conflict, appear to be an invasion of the community's domain, an attempt at colonization, able to cause damage and social loss (Christie, 1977).

Spiritual Groups and Psychological ethos

A third surface to be taken into account is given by the vocabulary of spiritual groups and reformist criminal agencies engaged in reconciliatory perspectives since the 1970s and the spreading of the 'Psy-ethos' in the last two decades (Richards, 2005). Most scholars credit the Mennonite Church in Canada with the first initiatives regarding RJ implementation. Today, the Mennonite Central Committee's US Office on Crime and Justice provides information and resources on ministry to victims and offenders, victim–offender reconciliation/conferencing, RJ, the death penalty and other related issues. It also coordinates workshops, research material on restorative justice principles and application, provides consultation to people involved in victim–offender reconciliation/conferencing programs (VORPs) and develops educational and training materials on various crime and justice issues. This is just an example of the direct involvement of a religious group in the reform of criminal justice, analogue discourses might be done for other groups such as Quakers and Catholics. As I will argue, especially when we analyze the conceptualization of the warm side of RJ, we can see the presence of discursive objects, concepts and themes drawing upon the speeches of those religious leaders involved in the reform of criminal justice.

Besides the presence (historically rooted) of religious groups in the criminal justice system, we can observe a similar reforming role played by counselling and therapy experts in the last three decades. Indeed, therapeutic language has informed a range of criminal justice policies that have emerged in recent years, particularly those designed to assist victims of crime, in a way working as the secularized version of the action of religious groups involved in criminal justice reform. It has come to be accepted that crime victims must be offered opportunities to tell the story of their victimization, to express their pain, fear and/or anger about the offence, and to be heard. The popularization of concepts such as self-help, empowerment, healing and being heard act as the surface of emergence for many conceptualizations and justifications for RJ. Many of them often give great importance to the stakeholders' direct expression of emotions and feelings. The goal is to create a space and time for the acknowledgement of deep sentiments, stimulating constructive inner dynamics which allow stakeholders to mirror emotional experiences, heal from inside the personal, emotional and spiritual losses produced by the crime. At the same time there is an emphasis on the relevance of being heard as a complementary need to the expressions of internal states. Both the concept of a direct expression of feeling and the claims of being heard are drawn upon the discursive reservoir of religious movements and therapeutic programs. What is here reproduced is a kind of confessional relationship between the stakeholders, organized by those responsible for the restorative process (such as a mediator or facilitator). This is a basic schema in both secularized and religious ways of dealing with conflicts.

Authorities of Delimitation and Grids of Specification

It it not enough just to identify the discursive space within which the main explanations and justifications of RJ arise. As Foucault said, 'This formation [of discourse] is made possible by a group of relations established between authorities of emergence, delimitation, and specification' (Foucault, 1972, p. 44). Accordingly, it is necessary to take into account at least two other elements which give us a more accurate account of the formation of authoritative discourses on RJ. The authorities of delimitation must be considered. Who has the authority to delimit, designate, name, and define RJ's objects? Who has the right to speak in the authoritative accounts on RJ? These authorities are groups able to produce expert knowledge of RJ, organizing the field in which the legitimacy or not of a particular account of RJ appears and is contested. From this perspective, the crime victims' movement appears one of the strongest voices in the construction of authoritative discourses on RJ. Similarly, religious leaders (Quakers, Mennonites) have had a relevant role in the creation of authoritative conceptualizations of RJ. The professional psychological expertise involved in criminal justice reform is another significant authority of delimitation. Lastly, a specific academic category represented by criminologists has played a role in the set-up and development of those narratives. Their institutional base for speaking is characterized by one main aspect, their primary respect for the object of the offender. An authority which is clearly missing among those who have produced expert knowledge on RJ, is that which speaks on behalf of the offenders. There is not an offenders' movement as there is a victims' one. Therefore, who discursively creates the needs of the offender in RJ? The question is easily answered: criminologists, psy-experts and religious leaders. Their accounts of offender's needs and views are not balanced by the presence of a group directly lobbying the offender's claims. The difference is therefore that victims' needs are elaborated by a specific interest organization and then filtered by the scientific knowledge of criminologists, psy-experts and religious leaders whereas the offender's perspective is entirely shaped by these authorities. Probably the only counterbalance in the definition of the offender's identity in the authoritative accounts on RJ is embodied in the human rights movement which has slowly come to deal with RJ initiatives. In this subject it is possible to see a potential authority of delimitation able to create a narrative on the offender quite divergent from the victim's movement perspective (see the part II of this book).

The *grids of specification* are the systems by which RJ is described, separated, and classified. In this regard, the authoritative explanations appear to be built on the opposition between continuistic/non-continuistic histories whereas the conceptualizations are based on the core comparison with criminal justice. In many authoritative explanations, the events, developments, and inventions regarding RJ seem to be linked in a continuous and necessarily progressive evolution. It is a linear history consisting of a series of events, progressing or regressing in a certain direction, usually culminating in the belief that the current period of time is somehow fundamentally unique from and superior to any other period of time (Weitekamp, 1999). Additionally, in the discussion of RJ origins, events are often considered as agents that can bring about other historical events. In this causal perspective, we see RJ as the product of a genetic connection between specific phenomena (the cause, like the breakdown of criminal justice) under certain conditions (like the emergence of a crime victim movement) that gives rise to or causes something else (RJ). On the other side we detect the presence of non-continuistic histories which stress the innovation brought by RJ, its link to the late modernity of Western societies. The authoritative conceptualizations always appear to be built with reference to the criminal justice system, intended as a complex mindset, an ensemble of professionals, institutional structures and expert knowledge. This reference can be critical and oppositional or constructive and positive, in other words RJ is conceptualized as alternative or complementary (to different degrees) to criminal justice. Looking at the explanatory authoritative discourses as integral to a specific grid of specification, can be emphasized as a last aspect. RJ is often considered a functional answer to a specific crisis or lack or needs. Accordingly, it is possible to define these accounts as functionalist. Underlying the authoritative explanations is the idea that social reality is a complex system whose parts work together to promote stability. In this perspective, when a deficiency or a surplus is present in social reality, natural reactions come into being to fill the gap or eliminate the excess. This idea more or less underlines the rise of RJ: a critical situation (breakdown of criminal justice) asks for a solution (the rise of RJ).

Thresholds and Diffractions

The epistemic authority of the main accounts on historical emergence and theoretical justification of RJ expresses itself in defining what can be talked about, who can speak and how, the thinkable and sayable regarding RJ. Its roots are related to other specific discourses, cultural constructs which have gradually made acceptable those authoritative accounts, as a part of our collective imagination in dealing with crimes.

At this point two last remarks must be made. The first regards the dynamic construction of the authoritative discourses. The surfaces of emergence are static factors, the problem is to set them in motion in order to understand how the authoritative accounts have become possible. The second remark regards the relationship within and between the surfaces, which so far appear isolated and inactive entities. Starting from this second point, it has already been mentioned how the new criminological knowledge on victims shapes the identity of the two main actors of RJ theory. Victim and offender seem to find their needs, claims and identities in the victimological research, which hands out its categories and an overall perspective to the authoritative rationalizations of RJ. At the same time a particular tension emerges between the categories of victim and offender as conceptualized in the authoritative accounts. As already mentioned, while the presence of a crime victim movement filters the identity of victim worked out by the victimological research (and the crime victims' movement), the absence of an offenders' movement defines a lack which potentially affects the role of the offender in RJ theory and practice. This gap marks a tension between the categories of victim and offender in the authoritative accounts, which expresses itself in a less nuanced offender identity, usually depicted as just the counterpart of the victim, the other silenced by expert discourses which speak on his/her behalf, asking to be ashamed, restoratively punished or pushed toward reparation. The existence of epistemic tensions is not only integral to the same surface of emergence but can also be detected between them. This is the case in the relationship between abolitionist/communitarian discourses and victimological knowledge. What can easily be distinguished is the presence of a 'point of diffraction' which characterizes this relationship (Foucault, 1972, p. 65). In fact, victimological research takes for granted what abolitionism accounts deeply deconstruct: the concept of crime (overdetermined in victimology and deconstructed in abolitionism). Similarly, the abolitionism/communitarian view clashes with the spiritual/therapeutic perspective. In the first discursive construct, deprofessionalization and communitarian regulation of problematic situations are unquestionable points. On the other hand, the spiritual/therapeutic discourses imply the strong and regulative presence of experts, creating a vertical way of regulating social conflicts, which, as a consequence of this expert intervention, become inner conflicts. This epistemic shift in knowing the conflict is a relevant point of diffraction between those two surfaces of emergence. These kinds of tensions have implications for authoritative discourses on RJ. For instance, the contraposition between the different concepts of trigger event or the various declinations of restoration seem to be related to the tension abovementioned. The distinction between conflict, harm, normative violation or restitution and reparation, the link with the punishment and the criminal justice, are all dependent on different (and divergent) kinds of knowledge which ground the different authoritative discourses.

The second remark is about what Foucault calls the 'thresholds of emergence' and its application to the authoritative accounts on RJ (1972, p. 186). These thresholds are the historical phases faced up to by a discourse in order to achieve its epistemic authority (or scientificity). Foucault identifies four thresholds: positivity, epistemologization, scientificity and formalization. In the case of the authoritative discourses, we can consider the positivities as the borderline innovative practices of dealing with crimes that, in the 1980s became the target of the rationalization carried out by the authoritative discourses on RJ (such as the Kitchener experiment). Slowly, a system of forming statements explaining and justifying those practices can be discerned. This is the hard core of many authoritative discourses, characterized by a low level of abstraction and a strong procedural attention drawn to practices such as victim–offender mediation or family conferencing. The epistemologization, like the development of a refined epistemic authority and of specific discursive objects and themes, is related to the retrieval of particular theoretical writings which originally were not meant to contribute to RJ at all. This is the case of the sacred texts of RJ, the seminal contributions which have represented the hard core of the authoritative discourses. Authors such as Nils Christie, Randy Barnett and Albert Eglash, widely considered as pioneers in RJ theory, wrote independently and way before the birth of the restorative movement, accordingly ignoring its claims. Only since the 1980s did the advocates of RJ start to reframe those writings, taking possession of them as the forefathers' words on RJ. In this way the authoritative discourses on RJ have gained a more structured and refined epistemic authority, as in a theoretical pedigree certified by the scientific reputation of the forefathers. The scientific threshold is then reached by the emergence of new criminological knowledge on the crime victims combined with therapeutic expert knowledge (as a secularized version of the spiritual/religious one) on the needs of victims and offenders. The formalization threshold is lastly attained through the growing legal codification of many authoritative accounts on RJ (Marshall, 1999; Daly and Hayes, 2001; O'Brien, 2008). This is probably the uttermost certification of the authority of those accounts in defining (normatively) the possibility of what can be said and done in the RJ field.

What must be stressed regarding these thresholds is that they are not regular and successive historical stages. Neither are they definitive and necessary phases in the evolution of the authoritative discourses. In fact, antagonistic accounts are often put forward, destabilizing the earlier epistemic authorities. These thresholds are instead the living and magmatic history of authoritative accounts on RJ, a dynamic ensemble of institutions, practices, academic arguments and practical experiences contingently linked together and synchronically interacting which give to the RJ edifice that appearance of a multifaceted, shifting and conflicting reality.

Conclusions

In this work I have tried to describe some heterogeneous articulations of phenomena which have contributed to make possible the authoritative discourses on RJ. Working out an analysis which detects and combines discursive and non-discursive elements, the vocabulary, as a social and historical living reservoir of words and actions, upon which the authoritative discourses are built, has been unveiled and described. The consolidation of the victimology, the combination between abolitionism, communitarian philosophy and Habermasian perspective, the action (and popularization) of the psy-experts as a secularized version of the religious groups involved in criminal justice reform, have played a crucial role as discursive reservoirs from which authoritative explanations and rationalizations of RJ have drawn their own discursive objects, concepts and strategies. A common meta-theoretical structure of those discourses has also emerged based on specific authorities of delimitations and grids of specifications. Lastly, several internal tensions within and between those authoritative discursive constructs have been displayed, as well as the dynamic construction of their epistemic authority.

Of course, this picture of is only a partial one. Many other aspects could have been identified and analyzed (such as the presence of other authoritative discourses and different surfaces of emergence). Many other questions could have been taken into account (like which kind of subject the authoritative discourses depict and contribute to creating? What the possible embeddeness of the authoritative accounts are in power/knowledge relationships?). This is material available for new, desirable research on RJ.

Nevertheless, at least one general and insightful remark can be conclusively drawn. As a consequence of the problematization carried out, the authoritative discourses have lost their appearance of third, detached and impartial attempts to portray the objective features of RJ, its history and main theoretical issues. They are now deeply rooted in other specific discourses, contextual accounts which feed their objects, concepts and strategies. The authoritative discourses now appear an effect of a number of historical contingencies, linked, juxtaposed and sometimes conflicting. The authority of those discourses which has made RJ a possible and acceptable approach to criminal justice in contemporary Western societies is not a natural quality or an essential attribute. This authority 'is a thing of this world: it is produced only by virtue of multiple forms of constraint … is to be understood as a system of ordered procedures for the production, regulation, distribution, circulation and operation of statements' (Foucault, 1980, p. 131). Bearing in mind this grounded idea of epistemic authority, maybe new spaces for critical and alternative accounts on RJ will emerge more easily.

References

Acorn, A. 2004. *Compulsory Compassion: A Critique of Restorative Justice*. Vancouver: University of British Columbia Press.

Ashworth, A. 1993. Some Doubts about Restorative Justice. *Criminal Law Forum*, 4(2), pp. 277–99.

Ashworth, A. 2002. Responsibilities, Rights and Restorative Justice. *British Journal of Criminology*, 42(3), pp. 578–95.

Ashworth, A. 2003. Is Restorative Justice the Way Forward for Criminal Justice? In: E. McLaughlin, R. Fergusson, G. Hughes, L. Westmarland (eds) *Restorative Justice: Critical Issues*. London: Sage Publications, pp. 164–81.

Bacchi, C. 2012. Why Study Problematizations? Making Politics Visible, *Open Journal of Political Science,* 2(1), pp. 1–8.

Baert, P. 1998. Foucault's history of the present as self-referential knowledge acquisition. *Philosophy Social Criticism*, 24(6), pp.111–26.

Bailey, M. 1993. Foucauldian feminism: Contesting bodies, sexuality and identity. In: C. Ramazanoglu (ed.), *Up Against Foucault: Explorations of some tensions between Foucault and feminism*. London: Routledge, pp. 99–122.

Barnett, R.E. 1977. Restitution: A New Paradigm of Criminal Justice. *Ethics*, 87(4), pp. 279–301.

Bevir, M. 1999. Foucault, Power and Institutions. *Political Studies*, 47, pp. 345–59.

Braithwaite, J. 1989. *Crime, Shame and Reintegration*. Cambridge: Cambridge University Press.

Braithwaite, J. 1999. Restorative Justice: Assessing Optimistic and Pessimistic Accounts. *Crime & Justice: A Review of Research*, 25(1), pp. 11–127.

Burkemper, T.B., Balsam, N. and Yeh, M. 2007. Restorative Justice in Missouri's Juvenile System. *Journal of the Missouri Bar*, 63, pp. 128–34.

Cantor, G. 1976. An End to Crime and Punishment. *The Shingle* (Philadelphia Bar Association) 39(4), pp. 99–114.

Cario, R. 2005. *Justice Restaurative, Principes et Promesses.* Paris: L'Harmattan.

Christie, N. 1977. Conflicts as Property. British *Journal of Criminology* (17)1, pp. 1–15.

Christie, N. 1981. *Limits to Pain.* Oslo and Blackwell: Norwegian University Press.

Clarke, G., Davies, I. 1994. Victim Offender Mediation in Queensland. *The Queensland Lawyer*, 14(5), pp. 169–73.

Cohen, R. 2001. Provocations of Restorative Justice. *Social Justice Research,* 14(2), pp. 209–32.

Consedine, J. 1999. *A Harsh Reality – A Merciful Response.* Paper presented at Reconciling and Restoring Relationships – A Responsibility for All Christians. ICCPPC World Congress. Mexico City. 13 September.

Daly, K. 2002. Restorative justice: The real story. *Punishment & Society*, 4(1), pp. 55–79.

Daly, K. and Hayes, H. 2001. *Restorative Justice and Conferencing in Australia.* Australian Institute of Criminology, Trends and Issues in Crime and Criminal Justice. 186, pp. 1–6. Available at www.aic.gov.au/publications/tandi/tandi186.html

Davidson, A. 1986. Archaeology, Genealogy, Ethics. In: D. Couzens Hoy, ed. *Foucault: A Critical Reader*. Oxford: Basil Blackwell, pp. 221–33.

Dean, M. 1994. *Critical and Effective Histories: Foucault's Methods and Historical Sociology*. London: Routledge.

Dreyfus, H.L., Rabinow, P. 1983. *Michel Foucault: Beyond Structuralism and Hermeneutics* (second edition). Chicago: University of Chicago Press.

Dussich, J.P.J. 2006. *Victimology – Past, Present and Future*. [pdf] Available at http://www.unafei.or.jp/english/pdf/RS_No70/No70_12VE_Dussich.pdf.

Dzur, A.W. and Olson, S.M. 2004. The Value of Community Participation in Restorative Justice. *Journal of Social Philosophy*, 35(1), pp. 91–107.

Eglash, A. 1958. Creative Restitution: A Broader Meaning For An Old Term. *The Journal of Criminal Law, Criminology, and Police Science*, 48(6), pp. 619–22.

Foucault, M. 1965. *Madness and Civilization: A History of Insanity in the Age of Reason*. London: Tavistock.

Foucault, M. 1970. *The Order of Things: An Archaeology of the Human Sciences*. New York: Pantheon Books.

Foucault, M. 1972. *The Archaeology of Knowledge*. New York: Pantheon Books.

Foucault, M. 1973. *The Birth of the Clinic: An Archaeology of Medical Perception*. New York: Pantheon Books.

Foucault, M. 1977. *Discipline and Punish: The Birth of the Prison*. London: Allen Lane.

Foucault, M. 1978. *The History of Sexuality* Vol. I, *The Will to Knowledge*. London: Allen Lane

Foucault, M. 1980. Truth and Power. In: C. Gordon (ed.) *Power/Knowledge: Selected Interviews and Other Writings 1972–1977*. New York: Pantheon Books, pp. 109–33.

Foucault, M. 1986. *The History of Sexuality*, Vol. III: *The Care of the Self*. New York: Pantheon.

Foucault, M. 1989. The Concern for Truth. In: S. Lotringer, ed. *Foucault Live. Interviews*, 1966–84. New York: Semiotext(e), pp. 293–308.

Foucault, M. 1991. Politics and the study of discourse. In: G. Burchell, C. Gordon, P. Miller, eds. *The Foucault Effect. Studies in Governmentality*. Chicago: University of Chicago Press, pp. 53–72.

Fry, M. 1951. *Arms of the Law*. London: Victor Gollancz.

Gubrium, J. and Holstein, J. 2000. Analyzing Interpretive Practice. In: N. Denzin and Y. Lincoln (eds). *Handbook Of Qualitative Research* (second edition). Thousand Oaks: Sage Publications, pp. 487–508.

Habermas, J. 1964. The Public Sphere: An Encyclopedia Article. *New German Critique*, 3 (Fall 1974), pp. 49–55.

Habermas, J. 1989. *The Structural Change of the Public Sphere*. Cambridge, MA: MIT Press.

Howarth, D., 2002. An Archaeology of Political Discourse? Evaluating Michel Foucault's Explanation and Critique of Ideology. *Political Studies*, 50, pp. 117–35.

Imarrigeon, R. 1998. The Past, Present, and Future of Restorative Justice: Some Critical Reflections. *Contemporary Justice Review*, 1, pp. 21–45.

Johnstone, G. (ed.) 2003. *A Restorative Justice Reader: Texts, sources, context*. Cullompton: Willan Publishing.

Johnstone, G. and Van Ness, D.W. (eds) 2007. *Handbook of Restorative Justice*. Cullompton: Willan Publishing.

Judah, E.H. and Bryant, M. 2004. Rethinking Criminal Justice: Retribution vs. Restoration. *Journal of Religion & Spirituality in Social Work*, 23(1/2), pp. 1–6.

Karp, D.R. 2001. Harm and repair: Observing restorative justice in Vermont. *Justice Quarterly*, 18(4), pp. 727–57.

Lasch, C. 1994. *The Revolt of the Elites and the Betrayal of Democracy*. New York: Norton.

Marshall, T.F. 1995. Restorative justice on trial in Britain. *Conflict Resolution Quarterly*, 12, pp. 217–31.

Marshall, T.F. 1999. *Restorative Justice: An Overview*. [pdf] London: Home Office – Research Development and Statistics Directorate. Available at http://www.homeoffice.gov.uk/rds/pdfs/occ-resjus.pdf

McCold, P. and Wachtel, B. 2002. Community Is Not a Place: A New Look at Community Justice Initiatives. In: J.G. Perry ed., *Repairing Communities Through Restorative Justice*. Lanham: American Correctional Association, pp. 39–53.

Mendelsohn, B. 1956. Une nouvelle branche de la science bio-psycho-sociale, la victimologie. *Etudes Internationales de Psycho-Sociologie Criminelle*. France. July–September 1956.

Miers, D. 2001. *An International Review of Restorative Justice*. London: Home Office.

Mika, H. and Zehr, H. 2003. A Restorative Framework for Community Justice Practice. In: K. McEvoy and T. Newburn (eds), *Criminology, Conflict Resolution and Restorative Justice*. Basingstoke; New York: Palgrave Macmillan, pp. 135–52.

Minor, K.I. and Morrison, J.T. 1996. A Theoretical Study and Critique of Restorative Justice. In: B. Galaway and J. Hudson (eds). *Restorative Justice: International Perspectives*. Monsey and Amsterdam: Criminal Justice Press and Kugler Publications, pp. 117–33.

Mulligan, S. 2009. From retribution to repair: Juvenile justice and the history of restorative justice. *University of La Verne Law Review*, 31(1), pp. 139–49.

O'Brien, S. 2008. Restorative Juvenile Justice Legislation and Policy: A National Assessment. *International Journal of Restorative Justice*, 4(2), pp. 100–18.

Pavlich, G. 1996. *Justice Fragmented: Mediating community disputes under postmodern conditions*. London: Routledge.

Pavlich, G. 2005. *Governing Paradoxes of Restorative Justice*. London: GlassHouse Press.

Pemberton, A., Groenhuijsen, M.S., Winkel, F.W. 2008. Evaluating victims experiences in restorative justice. *British Journal of Community Justice*, 6, pp. 99–119.

Retzinger, S. and Scheff, T.J. 1996. Strategy for Community Conferences: Emotions and Social Bonds. In: B. Galaway and J. Hudson (eds). *Restorative Justice: International Perspectives*. Monsey and New York: Criminal Justice Press, pp. 315–36.

Richards, K. 2005. Unlikely friends? Oprah Winfrey and restorative justice. *Australian and New Zealand Journal of Criminology*, 38(3), pp. 381–439.

Richards, K. 2009. Rewriting and reclaiming history: An analysis of the emergence of restorative justice in Western criminal justice systems. *International Journal of Restorative Justice*, 5(1), pp. 104–28.

Richards, K. 2011. Restorative justice and 'empowerment': Producing and governing active subjects through 'empowering' restorative practices. *Critical Criminology: An International Journal*, 19(2), pp. 91–105.

Roche, D. 2007. Retribution and restorative justice. In: G. Johnstone, D. W. Van Ness, eds. *Handbook of Restorative Justice.* Cullompton: Willan, pp. 75–90.

Ruggiero, V. 2011. An Abolitionist View of Restorative Justice. *International Journal of Law, Crime and Justice* 39(2), pp. 100–110.

Saar, M. 2002. Genealogy and Subjectivity. *European Journal of Philosophy*, 10(2), pp. 231–45.

Scheurich, J.J. and McKenzie, K.B. 2005. Foucault's methodologies: Archaeology and genealogy, in *The Sage Handbook of Qualitative Research*, (third edition), edited by N. K. Denzin and Y. Lincoln. Thousand Oaks: Sage, pp. 841–68.

Shapland, J., Wilmore, J. and Duff, P. 1985. *Victims in the Criminal Justice System.* Brookfield, VT: Cambridge Studies in Criminology.

Sharpe, S. 2007. The Idea of Reparation. In: G. Johnstone and D.W. Van Ness, (eds) *Handbook of Restorative Justice.* Cullompton: Willan, pp. 24–40.

Sherman, L.W. and Strang, H. 2003. Repairing the Harm: Victims and Restorative Justice. *Utah Law Review*, 1, pp. 15–42.

Sylvester, D.J. 2003. Myth in Restorative Justice History. *Utah Law Review*, 1, pp. 471–522.

Tamboukou, M. and Ball, S.J. (eds) 2003. *Dangerous Encounters: Genealogy and Ethnography*. New York: Peter Lang.

Umbreit, M.S., Vos, B., Coates, R.B. and Lightfoot, E. 2005. Restorative Justice in the Twenty-First Century: A Social Movement Full of Opportunities and Pitfalls. *Marquette Law Review*, 89(2), pp. 251–304.

Van Ness, D.W. and Heetderks Strong, K. 2006. *Restoring Justice. An Introduction to Restorative Justice* (third edition) Cincinnati: Anderson Publishing.

von Hentig, H. 1948. *The Criminal and His Victim: Studies in the Sociology of Crime*. New Haven: Yale University Press.

Walgrave, L. (ed.) 2003. *Repositioning RJ.* Cullompton: Willan.

Weitekamp, E.G.M. 1999. The history of restorative justice. In: G. Bazemore, L. Walgrave (eds), *Restorative Juvenile Justice: Repairing the Harm of Youth Crime*. Monsey: Criminal Justice Press, pp. 75–102.

Woolford, A. 2009. *The Politics of Restorative Justice: A Critical Introduction*. Black Point: Fernwood Publishing.

Wright, M. 1991. *Justice for Victims and Offenders*. Philadelphia: Open University Press.

Zehr, H. 1985. Retributive Justice, Restorative Justice. *New Perspectives on Crime and Justice – Occasional Papers Series.* Kitchener: Mennonite Central Committee, Canada Victim Offender Ministries.

Zehr, H. 1990. *Changing Lenses: A New Focus For Crime And Justice*. Scottsdale: Herald Press.

Zehr, H. and Mika, H. 1998. Fundamental Concepts of Restorative Justice. *Contemporary Justice Review*. 1, pp. 47–55.

Zehr H. and Toews B. (eds) 2004. *Critical Issues in Restorative Justice.* Monsey: Criminal Justice Press.

Zernova, M. 2007. *Restorative Justice: Ideals and Realities*. Aldershot: Ashgate.

Chapter 5
Gatekeeping in Restorative Justice and Related Research

Anne Hayden

Introduction

A useful definition of gatekeeping was provided by Christopher Forrest who discussed the concept in healthcare regarding general practitioners making referrals of patients to consultants. He stated, 'Within modern societies, gatekeepers are positioned between organisations and individuals who wish to use resources within those organisations. Gatekeepers use discretion when determining who will be granted access to these resources' (Forrest, 2003). It is my impression, however, that in the criminal justice system, gatekeeping is more likely to involve individuals who are not fully informed about resources available to them. This will be explained later on. Notwithstanding, Forrest has raised some thought-provoking points about how gatekeeping has evolved and some of the principles behind it. In the medical arena it has been used in countries with scarce medical resources, and aims to ensure equity by judicially matching services to needs. Furthermore, Forrest noted that gatekeeping alters the behaviour of individuals.

This chapter attempts to apply these observations to the criminal justice environment, starting with the scarcity of resources. It could be argued that precedent-setting initiatives, agents of change or revolutionary movements such as the restorative justice (RJ) movement, are resources which must be used judicially. This could be in order to preserve the status quo in legal systems while at the same time appearing to be liberal and accepting of change. On the other hand, it might represent valuing RJ to the extent that nothing must be permitted to prejudice its future practice or recognition as a successful process.[1] The equity argument could be explained by Jülich's (2001) discussion of equality in the criminal justice system as a presupposition of victims and offenders having equal access to justice (ibid., p. 11). She described two legal forms of equality, one being to treat people the same, the second to accommodate the differences between people. Clearly, Forrest's observations relate to the second form; that is, accommodating

1 At the time the New Zealand Court-Referred Restorative Justice Pilot was being planned, I suggested the inclusion of a small qualitative study of IPV. I was advised that this was not a good idea because 'if something went wrong, that would ruin the chances of RJ becoming an accepted process in New Zealand'.

difference. In the debate about the use of RJ for intimate partner violence (IPV), this could mean that RJ is a way of providing justice to those couples who may be experiencing less serious offending, first time offending, or who do not enter the criminal justice system. For this last mentioned group, the gatekeepers could be counsellors, victim advocates and possibly community police. As far as addressing the alteration of individuals' behaviour is concerned, gatekeeping is possibly more inclined to exercise power over, rather than alter, their behaviour. This is especially so when gatekeeping involves the non-provision of information to the individuals. This is discussed below.

Gatekeeping in Restorative Justice

Gatekeeping is an important issue when it comes to victims and perpetrators having opportunities to access services that might help them. It is often mandated, as discussed in Blagg (1997), Braithwaite (1997), Behrens (2005) and Stewart and Smith (2004). In New Zealand, for example, all youth justice matters are required by law to be referred to the youth justice coordinator (Blagg, 1997; Braithwaite, 1997), thus initially avoiding the mainstream criminal justice system. Braithwaite explained how this model has been 'understudied' by what is known as the Wagga model, where the Wagga Wagga Police Community Consultative Committee of sergeants reviewed cases headed for court, sending many back to the informant to reconsider the possibility of the matter being dealt with by holding a RJ conference (Braithwaite, 1997, p. 502). Blagg (1997) observed that youth justice coordinators in New Zealand used their influence as gatekeepers to empower the indigenous community as well as to facilitate the restoration of their systems of social control (ibid., p. 484 f/n). Blagg's observations of the Wagga model, coming from an indigenous perspective, however, were less complimentary. He stated that the increased power of the police meant that they not only made key gatekeeping decisions, but they also prosecuted the majority of cases in court. Furthermore, citing Dodson, 1991: 160, Blagg commented that in rural areas, where the police presence was prominent, their prosecutor role fuelled Aboriginal perceptions that the police were 'boss of the courts', with more power than the courts, and they despaired of receiving justice (Blagg, 1997, p. 494).

A different view was put by Stewart and Smith (2004) who discussed the advantages of police involvement in RJ as being more informed about the process and as a result were 'enthusiastic supporters of RJ' (ibid., p. 347). In their research into Australian police attitudes towards conferencing, they found significant differences between officers who had attended training, referred youth and attended at least one conference, and those officers who had done none of these things. The former group were more likely to endorse conferencing as a positive process, whereas the latter group, with a more legalistic style of policing, considered it an ineffective process (ibid., p. 355). Accordingly, the more negative the perceptions of gatekeepers, the less likely they were to make referrals, despite, or possibly even because of, their gatekeeper roles and lack of understanding of the process.

As intimated above, there are positive and negative aspects to gatekeeping. On the positive side is its role in ensuring that the most appropriate potential participants are invited, accepted or co-opted into programmes or services. Behrens (2005, p. 224), who examined the needs of victims of IPV with family law issues in Australia, explored the 'dangers and possibilities' of RJ as a means of dealing with such matters. She saw RJ as having a number of gatekeeping processes that were designed to ensure that only those cases that went to RJ were suitable. Criteria of appropriateness included only adult offenders who had been charged, pleaded guilty and accepted responsibility for the offence.

Among the concerns discussed in Behren's paper was the fact that the Australian Capital Territory (ACT) had only recently started treating IPV as a crime, with a pro-arrest, pro-charge and pro-prosecution policy under its Family Violence Intervention Programme, and RJ was seen as 'winding this back' (ibid., p. 224). The potential for the perpetrator to continue abusing the victim during an RJ process by minimizing the violence, and/or applying pressure on the victim to accept an apology, or to reconcile, was also raised. Stubbs (2002, pp. 54–55) raised the possibility of support people colluding with the violence and pointed out that perpetrators of IPV were often adept at apologizing or, in other words, manipulating their partner (2002, p. 58).

Behrens, on the other hand, reminds us that for those cases that never get near the criminal justice system, as in not being reported to the police, 'certain' RJ processes have something to offer IPV victims as a way of possibly improving their situation (ibid., p. 225). Other advantages Behrens puts forward are that victims have the opportunity to experience justice, rather than dispute resolution; rehabilitation; storytelling; creative solutions to victims' needs which are unbounded by the legal system and its categories; it was neither public nor private; and finally, it provided a forum in which the voices of children could be heard.

Accordingly, if one takes a pro-RJ for IPV stance, positive gatekeeping would ensure that suitable people would be given the information to allow them another option. However, an anti-RJ for IPV stance would very likely lead to negative gatekeeping where information about RJ and its potential was withheld from potential couples. Or, in other words, those gatekeepers with concerns about the use of RJ for IPV, would be inclined to make the decision for them not to participate in the process. What are the implications of this scenario? The ethics of informed consent applies in both cases, as explained below.

For people to give informed consent to access a service, they need to be given information about its existence and possible benefits. If they have not been given the relevant information they have been denied the opportunity to give informed consent to participate in the process if they wish to. This is gatekeeping. In the context of IPV, withholding information about the existence and potential of RJ, for example, is not only withholding information, but also withholding opportunities for the use of a different means to deal with their situation, which is an ethical issue.

It could be argued, therefore, that failure to provide relevant information is a form of constraint, leaving those who are denied it without sufficient knowledge or comprehension to make an enlightened decision. In the same way a widely accepted conception that male to female violence is a human rights issue on moral grounds (Barnett, Miller-Perrin and Perrin, 2011), the Universal Declaration of Human Rights, Article 19 provides that everyone has the right to receive and impart information (United Nations, 1993), a factor recognized in the literature (Goldney, 1998; Wilson, Lincoln and Mustchin, 2001). Following the reporting of a crime in Australia, Goldney noted that the police advised victims of their rights to approach the Victims of Crimes Service, pursue litigation and, if necessary, seek therapy. In this context, then, RJ could or should be another agency choice conveyed to the victim.

In the same vein, Wilson, Lincoln, and Mustchin (2001) referred to strengthening victims' right to knowledge. Parsons and Bergin (2010) examined the positive and negative impact on meeting victims' needs by criminal justice involvement. They noted that the responses of legal systems to victims who reported could make the difference between a healing experience and one which exacerbated the initial trauma (ibid., p. 182). They emphasized the importance of providing information to dispel victims' misunderstandings and to create realistic expectations about processes, timescales, court procedure and the availability of services that could help them. Frazier and Haney (1996) examined the attrition in sexual assault cases in their research by gathering data from victims, police and prosecutors in Minnesota. They found that a crucial factor in the case outcome was police decision-making about whether a crime had occurred and how to classify it. Frazier and Haney identified the police as having a significant gatekeeping role. They also found that police sometimes discouraged victims from prosecuting for moralistic or evidentiary reasons, whereas prosecutors would influence victims on the basis of evidence and 'winnability' (ibid., p. 624).

Furthermore, Frazier and Haney considered it was important for these personnel to have some understanding of the basis of their decisions. This is, of course, relevant to their decision-making and the information they provide about the suitability of RJ for IPV cases.

The New Zealand's Victims' Rights Act 2002, in section 8, states that the victim or a member of the victim's family, who has welfare, health, counselling, medical, or legal needs arising from the offence, should have access to services responsive to those needs. The Act also requires that they be given information about programmes, remedies or services available to them. However, certain inadequacies in the distribution of information appear to exist in New Zealand, despite the legislation.

In practice this has meant, therefore, that the welcome acceptance of RJ by many jurisdictions in New Zealand has not extended to IPV cases. Those service providers that have taken these cases have tended to be indigenous or have involved less severe cases. Due to minimal practice in this field, few evaluations have been carried out. This means that professionals are limiting the service provider's practice. While professionals say there needs to be empirical evidence service providers are reluctant to take the risk which means there are minimal opportunities for obtaining empirical evidence. Among these service providers have been police and victim advocates who have played a significant gatekeeping role. This, whether or not intentional, has limited couples' access to RJ.

This is not to say that gatekeeping or withholding information is necessarily an individual's responsibility or decision. Part of a crime prevention policy in New Zealand has been to prevent IPV. When this is considered alongside the frequently expressed concerns about revictimization for victims of IPV attending an RJ conference, the gatekeeping of police attending an incident could be understood in a number of ways. One could be Garland's (1997) sociological explanation of crime control as part of the criminogenic situation which he described as a new site of intervention of governmental practices, somewhat like the economy with its own dynamics and processes. Populated by active people whose actions shaped the processes, the criminogenic situation had 'functional ends of its own that were easily disturbed by heavy handed regulation' (Garland, 1997, p. 3). Thus, the situation could be governed but not completely coercively controlled. 'The aim is to align the actors' objectives with those of the authorities; to make them active partners in the business of security and crime control' (Garland, 1997, p. 3). In this way, various agencies have been standardized with mechanisms like gatekeeping guidelines that can be official or unofficial.

A feminist explanation, on the other hand, could be that gatekeeping is an example of patriarchy. Weedon (1999) discussed feminist considerations of Foucault's theory of power and its link to knowledge. She observed that, while Foucault acknowledged repression had been associated with the use of sexuality over the last 300 years, Foucault reduced the role of repression to a part of a broader strategy of power. Repression, through defences, censorships and denials, was a strategy to become part of a discourse which was 'a technology of power, and a will to knowledge' (Foucault, 1981, p. 12). Foucault noted that the 'will to knowledge' had not come to a halt in the face of a taboo, instead it has persisted to create a 'science of sexuality' (ibid., p. 13) involving many discourses about sex and the exercise of power.

Grosz (1990) has explained Foucault's theory of power as a form of repression in which power exists in its frustrated form rather than its typical functioning which is productive and creative. Thus, for victims of IPV, most often considered to be women, access to RJ has been frustrated or prevented by the paternalistic approach, albeit motivated by the perceived need or wish to protect them. In other words, without gatekeeping or withholding information about a process, victims might be endangered.[2]

---

2 For more on Foucault see Chapter 4 in this book, 'Demythologising Restorative Justice: a Foucaultian perspective', by Giuseppe Maglione.

Power is an integral part of any relationship and may be equal or unequal, particularly in intimate relationships. Power can be positive or negative and in any context. The literature about IPV usually refers to power as abuse against victims, thus taking away the victims' power leaving them relatively helpless. However, my research (Hayden, 2010) revealed that power in intimate relationships is much more complex[3] and involves the use of societal (institutional) power.

Foucault (1982) described societal power as being 'rooted deep in the social nexus' (ibid., p. 781) and as having the following characteristics: power required a certain number of systems of differentiation (such as laws or status and privilege); objectives (such as bringing into action a statutory authority); the means of bringing power into being (such as systems of surveillance); forms of institutionalization (such as legal structures); and degrees of rationalization (for example, greater or lesser technological refinements used in the exercising of power). Power relations, therefore, were rooted in a system of networks. Accordingly, people using formal remedies, such as reporting crimes to the police, are using institutional power and its networks, or one could argue, the tools of gatekeeping.

Research on RJ practice in youth justice in Australia has been the subject of serious concerns regarding police gatekeeping. Stewart and Smith (2004), discussed Wundersitz's (2000) finding that only 18% of apprehensions in South Australia were diverted to a conference, whereas 45% went to court. Despite the pivotal gatekeeping role of police officers, Stewart and Smith observed the limited research on police officers' understandings of, and attitudes towards, conferencing. The research did, however, discuss the views of police officers involved *in* the conference, obtaining enthusiastic responses. Because accessing RJ depended largely on police gatekeeping, there was a need for police to have a greater understanding of the philosophy and practice of RJ. Thus, gatekeepers need to have similar values conducive to restoring balance and reintegration (Winfree Jr., 2004). Indeed, as Stewart and Smith (2004) pointed out, there was a gap in the research which needed to be remedied about our understanding of police decision-making and police discretion.

However, researchers can also be subject to negative gatekeeping.

Gatekeeping in Research

In the process of conducting research into the extent to which using RJ would increase reporting, I experienced gatekeeping while attempting to gain access to participants (Hayden, 2010). Homan (2001) stated that gatekeepers are those who give access to a research field. My experience was the opposite, that using formal channels to access victims was seriously challenging. According to Homan (2001),

3 See Hayden, A. (forthcoming) 'Staying power', in (Hayden, A., Gelsthorpe, L., Kingi, V. and Morris, A. (Eds). *A Restorative Approach to Family Violence: Changing Tack*. Ashgate, UK.

informed consent is a standard feature of ethical procedure in social research. Using a school situation as an example, Homan pointed out that the entitlement to give or withhold consent has often been assumed by gatekeepers, such as teachers who decide whether their pupils could participate in a certain activity. He further explained that the principle of informed consent was standard in a variety of professional practices, as well as social research. It is the professional practice relating to victims and perpetrators that is most relevant to this article. Homan stated that the principle came from the Nuremberg Code of 1946, where internees of concentration camps were used as research subjects (ibid.) without giving their consent. The code specified that voluntary consent meant the person involved should have the legal capacity to give consent without the intervention of any element of force or any other form of constraint or coercion, and that they should have sufficient knowledge or comprehension of the subject matter involved to enable him or her to make an enlightened decision (Homan, 2001).

An early indication of the significance of gatekeeping in my research (Hayden, 2010) occurred when I started making contact with key people in relevant agencies with a view to getting participants for focus groups. The following extract from my critical reflective journal explains:

> I am in the early stages of trying to get my focus groups together and have noticed a marked difference in responses from [a victims' advocacy agency, VAA] and [a men's group, MG]. My meeting with VAA was with the … Manager, who wasn't expecting me, when I expected to meet with [another senior person] …. So it was very ad hoc. VAA refused to be taped and generally I just took a few notes. … I have given my assurance twice that if I get a minimum of four per group I would do separate groups, or interview them informally individually. I have also been required to send details of my supervision [for my selfcare] and post focus group care for the participants. This info is being put to a Leaders' meeting. They have copies of my documentation. I still don't know if they will help with potential participants. I had to wait 2 months for my first meeting which was on ...
>
> In contrast … of the MG has [after receiving my docs and screening criteria] initially left me a telephone message … He felt the screening criteria was too difficult to understand and the words victim and perpetrator were 'meaningless'.
>
> I was able to contact him again and we agreed to have a meeting. It was 3 hours long and he was very enthusiastic about the potential of RJ for these types of cases. I assured him that the terms perpetrator and victim (or similar) were used in much of the literature. I also told him I knew it was not only men who were violent. I said that at any focus group meeting I would acknowledge this to potential participants. He was happy with this. He has [made the offer] for me to go to one of their meetings to talk to the men about my research and RJ to see who would like to participate.
>
> So what we have [are] two very different types of groups, the survivor-driven women's group, and the perpetrator or men's group, both with initial

> reservations about the research, and very different responses to it. On the one hand the women's group has used its protective role as gatekeepers to a marked degree, calling on its infrastructure and procedures to keep the research at bay. On the other hand the men's group is accommodating language (in the words perpetrator and victims) and opening itself to the extent of inviting me to a meeting to talk about my research and RJ.
>
> 27 November 2008 (Hayden, 2010).

The irony of this experience was that the representative from one men's group, whom I expected would be less trusting of me, a researcher with more experience with victims, showed greater interest in my research than those of the victim advocate agency. In some ways, this should not have been unexpected given my knowledge of RJ practice, which was that perpetrators were more likely to be advised to use, and willing to explore the possibility of, RJ than victims or their representatives. There is a distinct benefit for perpetrators to be involved in RJ, as they often are sentenced at the lower end of the sentencing scale.

For victims, however, benefits can be less tangible. When I worked as a RJ practitioner, I found police were significant gatekeepers as far as access to victims was concerned, whereas referrals for perpetrators came most frequently from their legal counsel. The victim agencies' protection of their clients was understandable and justified. They owed their clients a duty of care to protect their privacy, to ensure that any research inviting their participation is not going to endanger their physical, emotional, psychological or emotional well-being. They had codes of practice and protocols to follow to ensure they complied with their own high standards. However, these appeared to deny their clients an opportunity to be fully informed (by me attending a meeting and explaining my research to them) before a decision was made for them that, in effect, my research should be kept at arm's length. Thus, while I complied with the recruitment protocol[4] approved by the University's Ethics Committee, it did not give me access to victims for focus groups. There were other reasons and possible processes I could have employed to improve this. For example, Lofland and Lofland (1995) described a number of factors associated with threats to access including factions, where some kind of distrust and dissent is 'almost universal in human groupings'. It is possible that this was an issue in the current research, between victims and perpetrators and/or between victim advocates and a former practitioner of RJ. Lofland and Lofland made a number of suggestions for dealing with this problem. They included:

- Join one faction, remain aloof from intra-group disputes and be on your group's side in any conflicts within the setting;

---

4 The recruitment protocol for victims and perpetrators required me to contact relevant agencies by telephone, followed by, with their agreement, me sending them the information sheet. I would then telephone them in two weeks to find out whether they would see me, with a view to meeting and introducing the research to potential participants.

- Move among conflicting parties as observers, an outsider to the dispute;
- Initiate trade-offs such as helping in some way in exchange; or
- Use insider understandings. (ibid., p. 58)

So, to apply those suggestions to my research, firstly, it was possible I was seen as a member of one faction, the RJ one, but in my career I had also been a member of the victim faction, although I believe this was disregarded in the research context. Perhaps I was regarded as a defector, having moved to a perspective that related to the opposition or to perpetrators. This took me back to the 1990s when RJ was in its infancy and victim groups saw RJ as 'just another initiative for perpetrators', (see Gavrielides, 2007). Secondly, I was not seen as an independent observer, probably because of my previous roles in victim advocacy, but more recently as a practical and political actor in RJ. Thirdly, I could not offer a trade-off, apart from a cup of coffee if we were in a café. Although I was hearing some very sad stories, it was not possible for me to offer more, such as counselling.[5] The one interviewee who was tearful intermittently during the interview said he had 'plenty of support' including counsellors and medical practitioners. My contribution could only be an ear, empathy and some tissues, along with offers to discontinue the interview if he had wanted. Fourthly, as far as the use of insider understandings was concerned, I used this process with the result that I had 16 key informants. One, a professional stopping violence educator and former perpetrator, volunteered himself as a participant in the perpetrator category.

While, on the one hand, this process of gatekeeping was understood, it was not always beneficial to the people it was aiming to protect. This was obviously not an unknown phenomenon, as acknowledged by Homan (2001) who discussed the need to consider potential contraindications of gatekeeping. Furthermore, there have been other researchers who have experienced similar non-cooperation including Hollander (2009) who researched women's self-defence and their resistance to violence. Because of the funding committee's beliefs that women's resistance to violence was impossible, too dangerous and with implications of victim blaming, Hollander reported that she received 'an array of negative, even hostile' reactions to her research proposal. She identified this as yet another form of resistance which was, in fact, resistance to women's empowerment. In this situation the funding committee were gatekeepers, with the decision-making power to limit opportunities for a sector they most probably wanted to protect. One could even go so far as to say they were being patriarchal or abusing their power. Homan's view that gatekeepers should not act without giving careful consideration to the reasons why that entitlement is being denied the proposed research participants, was most relevant to this research. Equally, it could be argued that well-meaning victim advocates carried out their protective role of their clients so diligently that they denied their clients the opportunity to gain information about, or contribute

5 This was apart from the counselling cited in the information sheet provided to them before they agreed to participate in the research.

their ideas towards, a different way of dealing with IPV. As a result, most victim interviewees were sought privately through people I knew, or their acquaintances, who fitted into the definition of IPV used in this research. Most perpetrators were accessed through my attendance at men's group meetings.

Conclusion

The community is central to human living and, as part of its evolution, has created positive initiatives in many forms. As stated by Frederick and Lizdas (2010) communities can refer to family, friends, neighbours or representatives from other parts of the community such as churches, social services, businesses or criminal justice institutions. Thus, according to Frederick and Lizdas, criminal justice systems are contained within the community. Restorative justice, like other initiatives or self-help programmes, is a part of the community which could, and some would say should, play a more prominent role, given its potential. Zehr (1990) explained what RJ could offer, illustrating an important ability of a community to define justice for itself. He stated '[c]rime is a violation of people and relationships. It creates obligations to make things right. Justice involves the victim, the perpetrator, and the community in search for solutions which promote repair, reconciliation, and reassurance' (ibid., p. 181). Frederick and Lizdas took this further when they described RJ as focusing on mending the harm caused by crime utilizing the resources available within the communities of the parties involved. However the community needs to be able to access resources, including RJ. This is where gatekeeping plays a significant role.

Gatekeeping of victims from RJ processes can deprive them of many benefits. In contrast to a criminal court, a community conference has the ability to offer much to victims. It could facilitate the victim confronting the offender; enable the victim to veto the action plan; and assist the victim towards reintegration by the use of sub-ceremonies (Braithwaite and Daly, 1994). Informants in Herman's (2005) research reported that the focus was on the need for *their* reintegration with their communities, rather than their perpetrators' need.

Gatekeeping, however, depends upon integrity and ethical principles, such as the provision of information and informed consent. This is particularly so when it has the potential to benefit both victims and perpetrators. The implication of withholding helpful information is that a misuse of power has occurred, even if this has been motivated by claims to protect victims. Few people would deny that IPV, although also arising from ancient traditions throughout the world, has continued to be a major problem in New Zealand. Thus, gatekeeping as a means of accommodating difference, referred to by Forrest (2003), could be a useful tool of change for the better for couples experiencing IPV, provided they are given the opportunity to make an informed choice to participate.

Using existing community resources, which may include the criminal justice system, the ethos of restorative justice is to enable a more equitable distribution of power. In other words, according to the RJ movement's rhetoric, it could 'restore the balance'. This is central to its philosophy and is crucial to RJ practice. However, it is necessary for stakeholders to adhere to this value themselves. This is where Gavrielides' (2008) description of 'conceptual fault-lines' in the RJ movement shows particularly well how stakeholders do not necessarily follow their own guidelines. The same follows for research.

Research for the public good needs to be considered along similar lines, where proposals that appear to come out of left field are treated with respect. Sound ethical practice needs to be applied to the consideration of research proposals and access to participants. By this I mean that possible adult research participants should be given the opportunity to choose for themselves whether they want to be involved. They deserve respect as adults rather than being ruled by patriarchy or power, however well-intentioned. Again, relevant to those researching in the field of RJ and IPV is Gavrielides' (2008) comment that 'conceptual tensions encourage the carrying out of different professional battles within the [RJ] movement, while at the same time these battles are feeding the conceptual tensions. A vicious circle is thus created' (ibid., p. 178).

Those of us involved in the RJ movement understand that an important by-product of RJ is breaking vicious cycles or cycles of violence. We need to be mindful that the RJ movement should not be a key participant in such cycles. This can only be remedied if power battles between researchers and practitioners, practitioners and practitioners, practitioners and victims, victims and offenders, top-down and bottom-up, become vehicles for learning and practicing cooperation and peace with the utmost integrity.

References

Barnett, O.W., Miller-Perrin, C.L. and Perrin, R.D. 2011. *Family violence across the lifespan: An introduction.* California: Sage Publications.

Behrens, J. 2005. Meeting the needs of victims of domestic violence with family law issues: the dangers and possibilities in restorative justice. *International Journal of Law in Context*, 1(3), pp. 215–35

Blagg, H. 1997. A just measure of shame? Aboriginal youth and conferencing in Australia. *British Journal of Criminology*, 37(4), pp. 481–501.

Braithwaite, J. 1997. Conferencing and Plurality. *British Journal of Criminology,* 37(4), pp. 502–6.

Braithwaite, J. and Daly, K. 1994. Masculinities, violence and communitarian control. In T. Newburn and E.A. Stanko (eds), *Just boys doing business?* London: Routledge, pp. 189–213.

Forrest, C.B. 2003. Primary care gatekeeping and referrals: effective filter or failed experiment. *British Medical Journal*, 326, pp. 692–5.

Foucault, M. 1981. *The History of Sexuality.* (R. Hurley, Trans. Vol. 1). Harmondsworth: Penguin.

Foucault, M. 1982. The subject and power. *Critical Inquiry*, 8(4), pp. 777–95.
Frazier, P.A. and Haney, B. 1996. Sexual assault cases in the legal system: police, prosecutor, and victim perspectives. *Law and Human Behaviour*, 20(6), pp. 607–28.
Frederick, L. and Lizdas, K. 2010. The role of restorative justice in the battered women's movement. In J. Ptacek (Ed.), *Restorative Justice and Violence Against Women*. New York: Oxford University Press, pp. 39–59.
Garland, D. 1997. Governmentality and the problem of crime, Foucault, criminology, sociology. *Criminological Perspectives: Essential Readings, 2003*, pp. 1–5.
Gavrielides, T. 2007. *Restorative Justice Theory and Practice: Addressing the Discrepancy*. HEUNI: Helsinki.
Gavrielides, T. 2008. Restorative justice – the perplexing concept: Conceptual fault-lines and power battles within the restorative justice movement. *Criminology & Criminal Justice*, 8(2), pp. 165–83.
Goldney, R.D. 1998. Victims of crime: A psychiatric perspective. *Psychiatry, Psychology and Law*, 5(1), pp. 153–7.
Grosz, E. 1990. Contemporary theories of power and subjectivity. In S. Gunew (ed.), *Feminist Knowledge*. New York: Routledge, pp. 59–120.
Hayden, A. 2010. *Why Rock the Boat? Non-Reporting of Intimate Partner Violence* (PhD). Auckland University of Technology, Auckland.
Hollander, J.A. 2009. The roots of resistance to women's self defence. *Violence Against Women*, 15(5), pp. 574–94.
Homan, R. 2001. The principle of assumed consent: The ethics of gatekeeping. *Journal of Philosophy of Education*, 35(3), pp. 329–43.
Jülich, S. 2001. *Breaking the silence: Restorative justice and child sexual abuse* (PhD). Massey University, Albany, New Zealand.
Lofland, J. and Lofland, L.H. 1995. *Analysing social settings: A guide to qualitative observation and analysis* (third edition). California: Wadsworth Publishing Company.
Parsons, J. and Bergin, T. 2010. The impact of criminal justice involvement on victims' mental health. *Journal of Traumatic Stress*, 23(2), pp. 182–8.
Stewart, A.L. and Smith, F. 2004. Youth justice conferencing and police referrals: The gatekeeping role of police in Queensland, Australia. *Journal of Criminal Justice*, 32(4), pp. 345–57.
Stubbs, J. 2002. Domestic violence and women's safety: Feminist challenges to restorative justice. In H. Strang and J. Braithwaite (eds), *Restorative Justice and Family Violence*. Cambridge: Cambridge University Press, pp. 42–61.
United Nations. 1993, June. *Universal Declaration of Human Rights*. Paper presented at the meeting of the United Nations World Conference on Human Rights, Vienna.
Weedon, C. 1999. *Feminism, Theory, and the Politics of Difference*. Oxford: Blackwell.

Wilson, P., Lincoln, R. and Mustchin, M. 2001. *Strategies to integrate and coordinate victims of crime services*. Queensland, Australia: Centre for Applied Psychology and Crminology, Bond University, Gold Coast.

Winfree Jr., L.T. 2004. New Zealand police and restorative justice philosophy. *Crime Delinquency*, 50, pp. 189–213.

Zehr, H. 1990. *Changing Lenses: A New Focus for Crime and Justice*. Ontario: Herald Press.

PART II
Case Studies in Contemporary Society

Chapter 6

The Nexus Between Rights and Restorative Justice: Using a Case Example of an Organization 'C' – the Right – or Moral and Spiritual Claim – to Recognition

Robert E. Mackay

Introduction

This paper addresses two questions, and poses a further six (see Appendix).

The first is theoretical: what is the relationship between rights and restorative justice? This question has both empirical and normative components.

Examination of this question leads to the second question, which is pragmatic: can we pursue restorative aims when access to redress has been limited or denied? This question is addressed by exploring a case example in which a multinational organization is the locus for consideration. The particularities of this case reveal further levels of complexity for restorative practitioners.

Addressing these questions means engaging in an exercise of applied ethics (Singer, 1986). This approach uses moral theory to examine practical questions. In particular, I use an adapted version of Honneth's framework of moral injury as a benchmark to undertake an ethical evaluation of candidate restorative practices for responses to the issues raised in the case example. As I have argued earlier, 'it is not enough simply to justify restorative justice and then select any practice that seems good or related to the idea. One has to be clear that the ethical argument supports the particular practice' (Aertsen et al., 2004, p. 32).

The Theoretical Question

What is the relationship between rights and restorative justice? Before considering the empirical and normative components of this question, we need some working definitions.

Primary Definitions

First we need definitions of rights and restorative justice. Only then can we begin to explore whether or not restorative justice depends on some foundation of rights and, if so, in what way and to what extent.

A right

So what is a right? This I take to be a property of an individual (used as a legitimate having, or holding of, by an individual), either conceived as being inherent in the status of the individual as an individual member of the human community, or granted to an individual by an external authority, which might be a private individual, the individuals' community, or the State.[1] This property is one that is recognized in the sight of others and, in principle, the holder of the property has an expectation, based in law or morality, that it will be respected by others.

What does the property of a right, or the holding of a right entail? A right entails either a permission to act in a certain way, or a protection against others acting in a certain way towards one. Thus the holding of a right in land may involve the right to the exclusive use of the land and the right that others do not use the land.

Restorative justice

What is restorative justice? The approach I take is conceptual, and is based on what others say of it. Restorative justice is a sociolegal ethical principle, which asserts that in cases wherein one party has harmed another, the primary focus for legal intervention should be repair of the harm for the victim and the community, and the reintegration of the offender and the victim. It draws on conventional legal theory (distributive justice) and on ethical theory (such as the need for recognition).

I conceive restorative justice and its related practices as a branch of the wider movement of alternative dispute resolution (ADR) within and alongside the legal system. restorative justice is primarily devoted to the application of ADR within or alongside the criminal justice-penal system, but its practice has come to overlap with ADR in the fields of education and work and, to a lesser extent in family law, where domestic violence has been committed.

What distinguishes what is called restorative justice from other forms of ADR, whether in criminal or civil cases, is that in restorative justice cases there is an adjudicator who is in a position to impose a penalty upon the perpetrator (criminal court, professional panel, employer, education authority, ombudsman, and so on).

1 In this paper, the State means the sovereign body of a country. It may mean the federal government, or a State within a federation. These will be distinguished as necessary.

Analytic and Normative Aspects of the Question

Analytic aspects

RIGHTS

The term rights covers a range of matters. There are rights taken to be natural; those taken to be universal or human, and recognized by such bodies as the UN; rights seen to be absolute or contingent; rights taken to be civil, relating to a person's ability to participate in political processes; legal or procedural rights, the capacity to seek redress, equality before the law and so on; and finally, particular individual rights, such as ownership of particular things recognized by law.

We need to be aware that there are different types of right. There are those which it is claimed inhere in the condition of being human, variously described as universal or natural rights. It is the duty of public authorities to protect these rights. Then there are rights which are said to be civil rights, which may reflect universal or natural rights, but which are contingent upon the values and norms of particular societies. They relate to the rights of citizens, or members of communities. Some rights are seen to be positive, such as the right to education, or the right to vote; others are seen to be negative, in the sense that they represent freedom from aggression from others. Rights may either be substantive, such as the right to life; others are procedural, such as the right to vote. Some rights are deemed to be absolute and can never be abridged; others are contingent, dependent upon the will of the community.

In practice, even if a State recognizes rights as natural and superordinate, such as those of the UN Declaration of Human Rights or the UN Convention on the Rights of the Child, it may not establish the mechanisms to enshrine them in domestic law, or to provide redress.

It is a matter of perennial debate as to whether there are moral claims not enshrined in law which nevertheless have, or should have, the status of rights (Fuller, 1969). In the course of this paper we will need to deal with the overlapping territories of rights and moral claims.

RESTORATIVE JUSTICE

In practice, restorative justice is often taken to be the settling of harms, including relational harms, arising from incidents under the jurisdiction of the criminal law, even when the criminal law has no concern for some aspects of the harm arising from the offence. Furthermore, some restorativists maintain that the settling of criminal events between the parties concerned (especially victims and offenders) should take priority over the requirements of the criminal law. In other words, rights discourse and, more widely, the discourses of distributive and procedural justice, may come to be irrelevant or even detrimental to some relational restorativists (cf. the dispute in restorative circles about the Clotworthy case in New Zealand Court of Appeal, 1998).

Normative aspects

Rights

Where do rights come from? Do they inhere in our human condition or are rights created by law? If one takes the view that rights derive from Natural Law, and that Natural Law is, or reflects, the will of God (an absolute theory of Natural Law), one's approach to rights is going to be different to that of one who argues that our sense of rights, whether universal or particular, reflect our understanding of the needs of human beings living together in community (a sociological view of Natural Law) (Lloyd, 1964).

Hart recognized that a teleological assumption 'is latent in our identification of certain things as human *needs* which it is *good* to satisfy and of certain things done or suffered *by* human beings as *harm* or *injury*' (Hart, 1994, p. 190). That statement may provide a premise for an argument for rights, but only if there is no other way of satisfying needs and protecting people from harm. Finnis (1980) argued that certain human goods (including spirituality) are self-evidently needful for human flourishing and therefore have to be protected. They give rise to natural rights. Law does not create these rights, but must recognize them.[2]

By contrast, Simone Weil argued against recourse to rights theories (Weil, 2003). She maintained that rights was a mediocre notion (ibid., p. 84). It arose within Roman Law from the right to use and abuse property (ibid., p. 82), mostly as she said, people as property. In the French Revolution, rights acquired a materialistic bargaining quality (ibid., p. 80–1).

> The notion of rights is linked with the notion of sharing out, of exchange, of measured quantity. It has a commercial flavour, essentially evocative of legal claims and arguments. Rights are always asserted in a tone of contention; and when this tone is adopted, it must rely upon force in the background, or else it will be laughed at. (ibid., p. 81).

She argues (ibid., p. 83) that rights were not known to the Greek or original Christian mind (the Greeks 'were content with the name of justice' [ibid., p. 82]).

> If you say to someone who has ears to hear: 'What you are doing to me is not just', you may touch and awaken at its source the spirit of attention and love. But it is not the same with words like 'I have the right …' or 'you have no right to …'. They evoke a latent war and awaken the spirit of contention.

She distinguishes a case of a farmer appealing to the right not to sell his eggs with that of a girl being forced into a brothel appealing to rights. Of the latter scenario she states: 'In such a situation the word would sound ludicrously inadequate.' (ibid.). She goes on to remark: 'Thus it is that the social drama, which corresponds

---

2 For a fuller account of rights in the context of restorative justice see Mackay (1994).

to the latter situation, is falsely assimilated, by the use of the word "rights", to the former one' (ibid).

Weil saw rights rhetoric being misused by Germany, claiming it:

> 'had invoked it *ad nauseam* in her role of deprived proletarian nation. It is true, of course, that she allows only one right to her victims: obedience. Ancient Rome did the same' (ibid., p. 82).

Weil wrote before the end of the Second World War, before the motivation to outlaw genocide took root in international legal thinking (Lloyd, 1964). So there is a paradox, that Weil may be wrong about the need for rights discourse, but correct in her intuition that rights discourse is not enough to address the social context and moral milieu of social conduct, and specifically misconduct and social evil. In short, she is arguing for the categorical imperative and priority of moral claims.

This is helpful because she is prefiguring the distinction between the legal *system* and the social *lifeworld* that restorative practitioners and all mediators confront in their work that we find in the work of Habermas (Orts, 1993).

RESTORATIVE JUSTICE

Restorative Justice, as a movement, covers a multitude of practices and theoretical perspectives. I have argued elsewhere that restorative justice is not sufficiently robust a concept to carry these disparate and sometimes mutually contradictory practices and perspectives. However, these different orientations do all have one common denominator, the pursuit of peace. I argue that the greatest contribution of the Restorative Justice movement has been to point to the insight that peacemaking is the fundamental business and purpose (*praxis* and *telos*) of law, as indeed of all state institutions and social practices (Mackay, 2007a, 2007b).

Does a Peacemaking Theory of Law Need a Theory of Rights?

In order to decide this question, we must ask ourselves what we mean by peace? Following a neo-Aristotelian path, peace is a quality that is to be enjoyed by the community as a whole. The quality of peace applies to each and every member of the community. Wherefore do we seek peace? It is to enable optimum human flourishing for the sake of both the individual and the community.

However, with the great variety of human aspirations and diverse types and levels of skill and other attributes within the human community, can it be said that there is sufficient uniformity of human characteristics for us to say that people's participation in the life of the community is best supported by the recognition and implementation of universal human rights? That is, the same rights for everyone, everywhere. Take one example. The most basic of the proclaimed universal human rights is the right to life. In many communities, the ideal of human flourishing for the community is not dependent upon preserving the individual lives of its members. Most communities take seriously the issue of killing a community member, or causing them to be killed (in war for instance), but most permit it, albeit for different reasons. So we have in the example of the right to life an instance of a universal but contingent right. Life may be taken, or caused to be lost, for different reasons at the instance of the particular community to which the individual belongs. We need to explore the reasons for the abridgement of the right to life in order to understand what any community espouses as its means of achieving peace. In other words, in the diversity and particularity of arguments supporting derogations from the universal human right, do there lie more important criteria for a community judging whether it can achieve human flourishing? So it is a serious question whether even such a basic human right as that to life can be an indispensable component of a peacemaking theory of law.

Nevertheless, there is another way of looking at the issue. If we ask, 'How shall we know whether a community is peaceful or not?' we will have to establish criteria of recognition (Hart, 1994). A community may think it is promoting human flourishing, but does not recognize – or, if it does, chooses to downplay or ignore – the fact that certain classes of individuals, sometimes not recognized as being fully or in any way a member of the community in question, or even fully human at all, either by law or by capacity, do not flourish within its boundaries.

MacIntyre (1989) argues that no human community can function, let alone flourish, if it does not honour some basic precepts: namely truth telling, promise keeping and elementary fairness. Habermas's three validity claims perform at a theoretical level a similar function of creating a baseline for normative conduct in a community. For Habermas communicative action involves people rationally motivating each other by testable appeals to truth, objective rightness and integrity in self-presentation (Habermas, 1990, p. 58). These are deontological foundations for morality in society, both connected to a vision of human happiness and *eudaimonia*, or at least stability. A most striking example of belief in this principle is found in a letter from the Japanese neo-Confucian Fujiwara Seika in reply to Lord Huang, Chief of Annam, in the late sixteenth or early seventeenth century, in which he writes:

> Your letter says that the only thing important is the word 'good faith': it is the essence of the morality in the nation and the home. We too hold to the belief that good faith is inherent in our nature, that it moves heaven and earth … its influence is not just limited to contact and communication between neighbouring countries …
>
> It will be seen therefore that men are different in only secondary details, such as clothing and speech. Countries may be a thousand or even ten thousand miles apart, but there is always one thing which is not far apart, not a bit different: that is good faith (Eds. Tsunoda, de Bary and Keene, 1964, p. 338).

One can see that this statement is the foundation for moral claims (and, importantly for this paper, it suggests that good faith is recognizable despite differences of law and culture), but does this approach provide the basis for universal human rights?

One could imagine that a community that did not honour truth telling would fail to be able to decide questions of ownership. One can see how, in the context of particular societies, keeping promises will give rise to rights under contract. One can see that elementary fairness could develop into formal systems for adjudicating reciprocities and settling disputes on the basis of reparation. Established expectations would be crystallized as rights. One could thus incrementally create architectures of rights within particular communities. However, that is a long way from establishing universal human rights. It might be that within international communities which share common philosophies certain types of right could be reciprocally acknowledged and established, for instance in trade, following the example of Fujiwara Seike quoted above, or where different States shared similar value systems (Confucian, Islamic, Christian, Socialist or Enlightenment/Liberal). Indeed, one of the limitations in the universal acceptance of contemporary universal human rights, even when adopted by the United Nations, is that they are couched in a discourse that is Western Liberal. It does not emerge either from within Eastern legal philosophical traditions or from traditional indigenous systems of law.

One means of generalizing rights across communities has been through the imposition of alien systems of law, such as Roman Law throughout Europe and beyond, or English Law throughout the different colonies of the British Empire. However, in view of what Weil has written about rights in Roman Law and her comments that, 'Spaniards and Englishmen who, from the sixteenth century onwards, massacred or enslaved coloured peoples, were adventurers almost without any contact with the fundamental life of their respective countries' (Weil, 2006a, p. 48), we should perhaps be cautious about the value of imperialism as a means of generalizing human rights. Incidentally, it is interesting to note that de Las Casas argued in 1542 that indigenous inhabitants of Latin America had the right under Divine, Natural and Roman Laws to expel the Spanish conquistadores. He also notes that all the conquistadores were 'fortune-hunters' (de Las Casas, 1992).

These considerations aside, are there pressing reasons for us to support the recognition of universal human rights? There are two linked questions to consider in answering this, but they arise from sociopolitical concerns, not from law itself:

1. Do we need universal human rights to sustain claims of right by the vulnerable?
2. And more generally, do we need universal human rights in the global village to help regulate international activities such as trade or to suppress practices such as slavery?

The case of child labour provides a neat example of the relevance of both these questions. In a free unregulated international market, where we buy our commodities and how they are produced is a matter of no consequence. The only issue is the competitiveness of processes at different stages of production.

However, is the international community unconcerned about the consequences of unfettered practices in production? If it is unconcerned, child labour is not an issue. However, if it is concerned, morality raises the question of regulation and enforcement. Strictly, from a freemarket perspective, it would give some producers an unfair advantage in the market if they were able to exploit child labour and others were not. How could this be countered? If, for instance, the European Union was more stringent about the matter than some other States, it might ban the import of commodities produced by child labour. That would induce mutual recrimination in the international trading community. So, rather than engage in trade wars suppose we negotiate. Can we negotiate using any other discourse than that of rights? If not, negotiation could lead, and indeed has led, to the recognition of internationally recognized rights for children not to be exploited (but can they be enforced?).

What can be taken from this is that, following Finnis in a very broad way, rights are a convenient way to handle issues about what constitutes the Good Life (*eudaemonia).* However, Weil's putative rebuttal can almost be heard ringing in our ears. You cannot and must not reduce the evil of child labour to the level of bargaining about rights. Access to a level playing field in the marketplace is seen as taking priority over direct confrontation of a moral evil. You have resolved the question without reference to the needs of the exploited children.

We have therefore, in truth, as well as a conflict about rights, a conflict of rights: a right to trade fairly as between competitors and the rights of children. Can they be resolved equitably? Is there a priority in the ordering of rights? How good are we at managing these issues?

However, even if we could resolve these problems, this only deals with one formal aspect of the recognition of a right. To take it further, how do we enforce rights? How do we provide redress to those who are exploited and victimized; redress, as in access to justice and reparations? Even at this point, we have not dealt with the restorative requirement of engagement of the parties.

The Problem

On the face of it, there appears to be no problem in construing a relationship between rights and restorative justice if one confines the concept of restorative justice to a reparative principle of justice. Implicit in the notion of *harm*,[3] in this definition of restorative justice, is the infraction of someone's rights to material property and, more importantly, to physical and psychological integrity. However, legal realism tells us that things are not so simple.

First, the laws do not recognize all the claims of right that are asserted by members of the community. That is because the translation of universal rights into legally enforceable rights faces two hurdles: (1) Is the universal right recognized

3 There is a debate about terminology here. Should we use *harm*, *injury*, or as my colleague Lyn Beames has suggested, *wound*?

in the State's laws; and (2) even if it is, is there an effective mechanism for redress? Thus the (procedural) right to redress (a property that gives us permission to obtain reparation for harm) may be either restricted or denied, even if a substantive legal right has been infringed. Furthermore, law does not generally provide the opportunity for the healing aspect of the restorative justice agenda. It deals with the past, and to some extent with the future, but it does not deal with the immediate present requirement of both victim and offender, namely the need for moral recognition.[4] What is different about peacemaking is that it supplements the restorative principle of justice (primarily fixing the past), with an approach that also looks to the future (institutive justice), bringing both into the focus of the present (constitutive justice). Perhaps it also brings about the opportunity to test Weil's proposition: 'If you say to someone who has ears to hear: "What you are doing to me is not just", you may touch and awaken at its source the spirit of attention and love' (Weil, 2003, p. 83).

The Pragmatic Question

So, can we pursue ~~restorative~~ constitutive aims when access to redress has been limited and rights have been denied? In addressing this question we must identify that it is an ethical question framed as an attempt to identify whether there is an issue of consistency of moral action in undertaking constitutive practice where rights are impeded. It may be that rights are impeded, including those that constitutive justice would seek to have upheld, but that, notwithstanding, it is ethical to proceed to engage in constitutive practices or one kind or another.

To explore this question, let us turn to the case of the Roman Catholic Church and the clergy sex abuse scandal (the case of C).

The Case of C

C is an international corporate body, which has a spiritual and moral mission in the community. It is an unusual organization, being one of only two sovereign states which have no, or almost no, territory (the other is the Sovereign Military Hospitaller Order of St. John of Jerusalem of Rhodes and of Malta). Its constitutional arrangements both as a State and as a corporate body are autocratic. It has a body of laws that govern its internal operations as an international organization (Canon Law, CL) which, although binding on its officials and members, can be changed by the edict of the Head of C (H). There are no constitutional checks and balances.[5] There are and have been debates about whether a General Council of the Church

---

4 See Susan Sharpe's construction of relational rights (Chapter 9), which provides substance to the chronological categorization of practice orientation.

5 See the website on RC Canon Law, http://www.vatican.va/archive/ENG1104/_INDEX.HTM.

consisting of all bishops had superior authority than H. In the 1340s the great English Franciscan philosopher, William of Ockham, argued that, 'inquiry about what power the pope has "by divine law and immediately from Christ's ordinance" pertains to theologians' (McGrade, 1992, xx, citing William of Ockham). H should defer to the universities on judgement about theological norms. The Sorbonne in Paris enjoyed this role for centuries, until it was replaced by the Roman Inquisition at the Council of Trent (1541–59) (MacCulloch, 2010).

C operates in many countries in the world, providing both spiritual and practical services, including education, welfare and health. The relationship between C and the nation states in which it operates varies. In some cases, where there has been a deep association between the national culture and the values of C, it has enjoyed considerable privileges (such as legal immunities and opportunities), often in the form of concordats. At the other end of the spectrum the State is inimical to C.

C has become involved internationally in a series of major scandals involving clerical sexual abuse of minors. A significant number of its officials became involved in the sexual abuse of thousands of children in C's care in at least three continents over a period of several decades in the latter part of last century. It has been widely argued that C handled this situation very poorly. It is accused of trying to protect its officials from being made accountable to the local State's criminal sanctions,[6] minimizing the harm done to victims, blaming victims for the offences committed against them, exposing victims to further risk of harm by its containment policies and attempting to protect its material assets from legal claims by victims. Cases were vigorously defended, with C denying vicarious liability for the crimes of its officials.[7]

The scandal has led to much suffering for victims and subsequently to a major public outcry. It has also led to a sense of betrayal on the part of non-offending officials and members of C who have not been victimized. Members of the families of victims have been traumatized. It has led to a crisis of confidence in C's authority structures (MacCulloch, 2010, p. 999).

In normal restorative (constitutive) justice practice we are usually dealing with the interface between criminal and civil jurisdictions. In the case of C, we are dealing with the interaction of three legal jurisdictions (with the addition of the

6 The ancient scriptures of C give no warrant for thwarting the authority of the civil power to prosecute crime (Mackay, 2010). A number of senior clerics have been subject to prosecution in the USA and Australia.

7 In one particular sub-federal State it appears that legislation has created a legal loophole whereby C cannot be sued for vicarious liability of its officials because it has transferred its assets to a trust and C does not exist as a legal entity. Although the trustees act according to the instructions of C's officials, and at least one of the trustees is an official of C, the local civil courts have declared that the trust is not responsible for the actions of C and therefore cannot be sued (http://parliament.nsw.gov.au etc.) This has led to demands that the legal immunity of C's trust be removed. In fact, two regional groups of C have waived immunity.

organization's own system of law, CL). Usually, restorative practitioners deal with the combination of practical (physical and material) and psychosocial harms and remedies. In this case, we are dealing with two additional levels of moral and spiritual injury (see the section 'Honneth's theory of recognition and moral injury' below).[8] As extreme as this may appear, the first of these ramifications is common when one takes into account occupational rules and cultures of organizations that are semi-autonomous, such as professions, universities and defence forces.

So, to return to the pragmatic question in a slightly different form: can we, in all conscience, propose to engage in constitutive practices when C has invoked immunity from civil action or has vigorously contested claims of vicarious liability? In other words, where the rights of redress and the right to protection from harm have not been acknowledged voluntarily? This is an analogous position to that in which a criminal defendant does not accept culpability in a restorative justice referral.

The Pragmatic Question Explored

If restorativists[9] take a position that restorative justice is concerned with rectifying quantifiable harms, then they are quickly going to hit a brick wall with the case of C. If redress and damages cannot be achieved, then nothing can be done.[10]

If restorativists say that restorative justice is about healing relationships as well as repairing the harm, the restorative practitioner who engages in such work, faces the critique that they are discounting the material harm of victims and the consequent right to material damages, in order to pursue reconciliation. It might prove to be a futile activity in any event. The victim, knowing that material amends are not forthcoming through the courts or finding their claim heavily defended, is scarcely likely to want to engage in some form of healing of the relationship. Indeed, that could be seen as devaluing the spiritual dimension of healing, rendering it superficial and for show. If the offender is genuinely unable to make material amends, the case is different: non-material amends may be all can be achieved and may be valuable to victims.

8 To distinguish two uses of moral injury. In the sense used before to introduce Honneth's framework, it refers to one of four levels of injury: physical, psychological, moral and spiritual. Honneth (see below) takes moral injury to include injury to self-confidence, self-respect and self-esteem.

9 Having trailed the wish for greater conceptual clarity by calling for a replacement of restorative justice by constitutive justice as a term of art for a principle of a peacemaking theory of law, I revert (pragmatically) to the semantics of current usage for the convenience of the reader.

10 That being said, C has dealt with a number of claims effectively on an *ex gratia* basis. However, the payments are not damages as such, but contributions towards specific measures for victim rehabilitation. In some countries, C has been forced to meet civil claims by the civil courts. In one sub-federal State where C has immunity, some regional Heads of C have waived it and settled claims.

If restorativists argue that the primary aim is to heal relationships, rather than to seek material amends, victims may well retort that this is insufficient. We do not live by bread alone but, and this is the business of terrestrial laws, we do not live without it.

Other Ways Forward?

So are there other ways around this for restorativists?

With practical amends unavailable, restricted or heavily defended in the civil court, and non-material aims apparently lacking credibility, what can be done?

First, we can attempt to engage with C in its own terms.

The restorative justice model sits very well alongside Christian (and other religious traditions) concerning repairing harm. What Ian Elliott,[11] a contributor at the Marquette University conference on restorative justice and the Clerical Abuse Scandal (Milwaukie, Wisconsin, 2011), describes as the 'scriptural cycle' (or sequence) of Confession ➔ Repentance ➔ Forgiveness, is compatible with the principles and processes of restorative practice.

We can also acknowledge that H has recognized that it is necessary for C's pastoral workers to 'have the task of studying and recommending restorative justice as a means and a process for promoting reconciliation, justice and peace, and the return of victims and offenders to the community' (Vatican City, *Africae Munus*). This injunction could be argued to apply reflexively.

Second, we need to recognize the wider context of the restorative movement. No legal system in the world embraces restorative values in their entirety. They apply restorative measures selectively by type of case and level of seriousness within the criminal justice system. Does that prevent restorativists from seeking incremental changes to policy and practice? Most restorativists see legal reform as work in progress, something they seek to encourage and support. The same might be argued in the case of C, but with certain safeguards. One caveat here is that insofar as restorativists are neutral parties, there is a danger that pursuit of legal and community change could be seen as partial to the victim. There is a whole debate about neutrality here, which is outwith the scope of this paper.

Third, we need to invoke the wider peacemaking agenda of the restorative movement. Restorativists now recognize that their field encompasses not only harm created by crime between individuals and groups, but also non-criminal harms committed within communities. They also acknowledge intercommunal conflicts as falling within their purview.

Fourth, we should engage with public bodies that are concerned with addressing the scandal, such as the Parliamentary Inquiry of the Australian State of Victoria into the Handling of Child Abuse by Religious and Other Organisations and the

---

11 Chief Executive Officer, National Board for Safeguarding Children in the Catholic Church in Ireland in 2011.

Australian Royal Commission into Institutional Responses to Child Sexual Abuse (Mackay, 2013).

Fifth, since restorativists are concerned with dealing with harm, it is useful to look at the way we make sense of harm.

As we have noticed before, in the case of C we have people who have been harmed in several ways:

- At a *physical* level they have been sexually assaulted;
- *Psychologically* they have experienced damage to their capacity to develop a normal pathway to sexual expression and relationship;
- At *moral* and *spiritual* levels they have often been blamed, disbelieved and ignored.

This has led to a number of outcomes, most notable of which is that they experience a deep incapacity to trust others. Some have killed themselves. At almost every level of their hierarchy of needs (Maslow) their capacity to move towards self-realization has been hindered. We need to look at differentiating the different types of harm in such a way that can provide indications about the types of remedies that are required.

We also need to see this harm as a whole. Weil writes of this as 'affliction' in an explicitly religious and spiritual context, which may be appropriate for us to consider, granted the nature of the injury:

> There is not real affliction unless the event which has seized and uprooted a life attacks it, directly or indirectly, in all its parts social, psychological and physical. The social factor is essential. There is not really affliction where there is not social degradation or the fear of it in some form or another … [The afflicted] have no words to describe what is happening to them … compassion for the afflicted is an impossibility. When it is really found we have a more astounding miracle than walking on water, healing the sick or even raising the dead … [Worse,] Except for those whose whole soul is inhabited by Christ, everybody despises the afflicted to some extent, although practically no one is conscious of it' (Weil 1959, pp. 78–9, 81).[12]

Honneth's Theory of Recognition and Moral Injury

Taking Hart's direction about harm and injury above, if we turn to Honneth's theory of recognition and moral obligation (Honneth, 1997), we find that 'moral injury consists in the withdrawal or refusal of recognition' (ibid., p. 24).[13] Honneth's theory of recognition is based on the idea that we develop self-consciousness

12 There are also theoretical connections here with the literatures of loss and stigma.

13 I am grateful to Vicky Cowling OAM for having introduced me to the work of Honneth.

through social recognition. This can only be achieved through mutual recognition.[14] Recognition has different levels, broadly relating to the Maslovian hierarchy of needs. In fact, we can helpfully lay the levels of physical, psychological and moral injury over this framework.

On Honneth's model, we develop *self-confidence* through recognizing and having recognized by others the individuality of our basic needs and desires. We develop *self-respect* when we acknowledge our obligations to others, and experience others fulfilling their obligations towards us. Third, we develop a sense of *self-worth* when we recognize our capacities and have these recognized by others. Honneth cites Hegel's differentiation of law (rights), love (mutual obligations in private relationships) and social esteem. The first and the third are fostered by the State (ibid., p. 21; citing Hegel, 1967, p. 133 s207).

Honneth contructs a model of recognition and moral injury by aligning the differentiated modes of self-relation with different levels of moral injury (ibid., pp. 25–7).

(In the third column, Honneth's examples are listed with black bullet points; examples relevant to the case of C are listed underneath in italics with white bullet points.)

Level	Mode of Self-Relation	Level of Moral Injury	Examples of moral injury
1	Self-confidence	Damage to capacity to enjoy physical well-being. Destruction of confidence in the value we hold in each other's eyes	• physical abuse • torture • rape ○ *sexual abuse* ○ *psychological and developmental harm*
2	Self-respect	Disregard for the moral accountability of others. Damage to our self-respect acquired in seeing the value of our judgement recognized by others	• deceit • fraud • systematic discrimination against groups in legal system ○ *breach of trust* ○ *denial of accountability by C*
3	Self-esteem	Humiliation and disregard of our capabilities. Harming the feeling of being socially significant within a concrete community	• not greeting • stigmatization ○ *victims complaints not believed* ○ *blame for the offending* ○ *isolation/stigmatization/ scapegoating within community of C* ○ *not being heard*

14 It would be valuable to explore Honneth's implicit relational theory of development with the theoretical tradition of interpersonal recognition of Buber and other relational theorists in the field of restorative justice.

Honneth's construction of self-relational need with moral injury provides a framework for legal and social harms that allows us to see harmful acts in both their legal and moral dimensions. It is suggested that Honneth's approach is consistent with peacemaking in the sense of providing a theoretical underpinning for peacemaking practice. However, there is a question about how this framework can address spiritual injury as we have recognized from the writing of Weil.

In order to address this question, here is a proposed fourth level for Honneth's theoretical framework. In articulating this, it is necessary to broaden the category of level of moral injury to include spiritual injury. This is entirely consistent with Finnis's approach to the self-evident goods of human life that give rise to rights (Finnis, 1980).

Level	**Mode of Self-Relation**	**Level of Moral and Spiritual Injury**	**Examples of moral injury**
4	Self-realization	Damage to capacity to regard oneself as a spiritual being with potential for development or realization in the way a person's spirituality is expressed (enlightenment, redemption, salvation etc.) Damage to cultural identity	◦ *spiritual condemnation* ◦ *undermining of conscience* ◦ *destruction of a person's spiritual frame of reference* ◦ *denial of right to free religious/spiritual life* ◦ *abuse of spiritual authority* ◦ *betrayal of spiritual trust*

We have already stated that legal systems do not recognize all claims of right, and even if they do they do not always provide means of redress. Moral and spiritual injury often remain unrecognized. This is clearly true with C.

So, can restorativists circumvent the barriers in civil law and still pursue a peacemaking agenda? Such a project will need to address Honneth's extended conceptual framework. It will need to show that it recognizes both the level of self-consciousness and the type of moral injury that Honneth describes. An exercise of this nature constitutes a type of ethical auditing (Aertsen et al., 2004).

A Practical Agenda

There is a range of practical measures that may build towards peacemaking within the community of C and between C and the wider community. We shall examine these measures to discern whether the options meet the requirements of Honneth's framework.

It is proposed that there are five areas in which a restorative approach may be relevant:

1. Support to victims and promote healing
2. Reintegration of offenders within the community

3. Exploring the viability of *bringing the parties together* (victims and those who have caused harm) to facilitate healing (including spiritual healing when possible).
4. Material reparation for appropriate non-litigious means for victims to obtain material reparation
5. Community building, reconciliation and peacemaking within the community of C and between C and the wider community.

One model of restorative justice suggests that there are three types of practice in the criminal justice–penal system. First, there are those that are *non-restorative*. These include pure punishment. Second, there are those that address harm, but focus mostly on one or other party in the triangle of victim–offender–wider community. These might be crime prevention programs, victim support schemes, offender rehabilitation programs or state sponsored compensation schemes. These are viewed as *pro-restorative*. Third, there are those *restorative* programs that directly promote and offer the involvement of victims, offenders and the community in dialogue and resolution (McCold, 2010).

The options we can explore include elements of pro-restorative and restorative practice. If we look at the five areas identified above, it will be seen that the first two address pro-restorative agendas, and the last three address purer, restorative concerns. The five elements constitute a comprehensive restorative and indeed a peacemaking approach.

Developing the Work

Developing the work to support victims and promote healing is *pro-restorative.*

It is important to remember that victimization may take a number of forms. Some forms of abuse are criminal, such as sexual assaults on minors. Criminal suppression of information about abuse is also a form of victimization. Other forms constitute breaches of trust, such as sexual exploitation in pastoral relationships. Victims may need support for referral to specialist agencies that can support them in meeting a variety of needs, whether for independent legal advice or psychological support and counselling.

Initiating Work

Initiating work to support the reintegration of offenders within the community is also *pro-restorative.*

Circles of support and accountability

Integrating offenders presents real challenges to C and the wider community. Some members of C may feel so betrayed that they are unable to contemplate the continuing presence of an abuser among them. However, an abuser who is without support may be more likely to offend. A model of support has been developed in Canada, and has been subsequently adopted in England and Wales. *Circles of support and accountability* were developed to address the need to support released sex offenders and hold them to account. Circles comprise the offender and volunteer members of the community. They meet regularly with the offender. The Circle is supported by an external professional group who provide specialist advice and guidance. Circles have had significant success in reducing reoffending and providing early warning of recidivism (Kirkwood and Richley, 2008).

The additional dimension of C providing such a method of support would be an interesting and possibly unique development internationally. It would enable C to own the offender and to be seen to take responsibility for responding to the offender and to the concerns of C's community and the wider community.

Bringing the Parties Together

Here are three examples of *restorative* practice when exploring the viability of approaches to bring victims and offenders together to facilitate healing (including spiritual healing when possible).

Healing circles[15]

Healing Circles, developed at Marquette University (Wisconsin, USA. See http://law.marquette.edu etc.), provide an excellent model of practice. In this model a number of parties, not necessarily directly known to each other, come together and share their experience of being involved with the issue of the abuse of power by people with power and authority in C. Their experience may be that of a victim; an official or worker who has been touched by the issue in their work; or an offender. Each is encouraged to share their experiences and to receive the experience of being heard and listened to. The Circle provides the participants with the further experience of being validated. This means that they can have the feeling that their statements of need, concern or remorse have been taken seriously by others within the community of C. It is not necessary for an offender to be present at a Healing Circle.

Conferencing

Conferencing covers a number of approaches that bring together victims, perpetrators, their supporters and relevant community members, to address what happened (the incident or episode); how people have been affected, and what can be done to put things right in a way that is both fair and will reduce offending in the future. These approaches are mostly confined to the criminal justice system, workplaces or the education system. Most usually the participants include the victim and perpetrator involved in the same incident or episode. Sometimes more than one victim may be involved. Sometimes there is no victim present.

15 See Evelyn Zellerer (Chapter 13) for an authoritative account of Peacemaking Circles.

In that case, the victim perspective is represented by someone with expertise in victimology.

It should be noted that an offender can also be one who has criminally suppressed information about abuse so could themselves be asked to participate in a conference. Such a person may be more willing to accept responsibility for their offence than primary abusers and therefore be eligible for participation in a conference.

Some conferencing models operate with a closely determined script. This means that the contribution of the facilitator is tightly controlled. There are some difficulties with this method, and it would be advisable to have a more flexible approach to the management of the conference process..

Facilitated meetings between victims and senior clergy

It is proposed that once legal proceedings are completed, or where practical settlements have been achieved, it may be valuable for victims to meet with the senior member of the clergy (bishop or superior) to deal with the outstanding issues and questions that the victim may have. These meetings would be facilitated by a mediator in order to promote democratic participation and a relationship between the participants.

Material Reparation

Exploring mechanisms for appropriate non-litigious means for victims to obtain material reparation.

Mediation can be carried out in a variety of ways. It may be possible for mediation to deal both with the direct abuser and with the question of C's vicarious liability. One could deal with these matters separately, using a conference as an overarching structure. Thus it may not be appropriate for the offender to be part of a discussion about settling the claim of the victim against C.

If mediation of civil claims is considered an option, this can include the presence of lawyers acting in a collaborative way, following some practice developments in the field of Family Dispute Resolution. The lawyers in the room provide a resource to the parties to promote constructive negotiation.

Mediation can also include a specialist supporter for the victim and the offender.

Community Building

By engaging in restorative practices which involve members of C and members of the wider community in expert roles, C is rebuilding its own community and is restoring its relationships with the general public. By demonstrating leadership in addressing the issues squarely, C is making a powerful 'validity claim' about its values and intentions, and thereby encourages its members and others to have confidence in its practices and its integrity.

Truth and Reconciliation Commissions (TRCs) present a further option for community rebuilding. However, this is a wide topic. The application of TRCs raises many questions for legal theory and ethics, which it is not possible to explore within the limits of this chapter. However, the same ethical criteria would apply to a TRC as to other forms of restorative practice. This example nevertheless alerts us to the need to ensure that ethical objectives and the objectives of law are effectively aligned.

Does This Agenda Address Honneth's Criteria?

Level	Mode of Self-Relation	Level of Moral Injury	Examples of moral injury
1	Self-confidence	Damage to capacity to enjoy physical well-being. Destruction of confidence in the value we hold in each other's eyes	• physical abuse • torture • rape ◦ *sexual abuse* ◦ *psychological and developmental harm*

There is a sense in which all damage is irreparable. There are opportunities that are taken away that cannot be replaced. However, victim-centred therapeutic (pro-restorative) work can reduce the impact of harm. The experience of being supported to speak about one's experiences in *Healing Circles* and *Conferences* may also improve self-confidence.

Circles of support and accountability will not help victims, except insofar as they prevent further victimization, but they will help offenders address the question of their own capacity to enjoy well-being without abusing others.

Level	Mode of Self-Relation	Level of Moral Injury	Examples of moral injury
2	Self-respect	Disregard for the moral accountability of others. Damage to our self-respect acquired in seeing the value of our judgement recognized by others	• deceit • fraud • systematic discrimination against groups in legal system ◦ *breach of trust* ◦ *denial of accountability by C*

Healing Circles and *Conferences* may go a long way to restore self-respect. In particular, they can provide an opportunity for C's officials and offenders to take responsibility for what has happened and to own the harm done, both primary and

Level	Mode of Self-Relation	Level of Moral Injury	Examples of moral injury
3	Self-esteem	Humiliation and disregard of our capabilities. Harming the feeling of being socially significant within a concrete community	• not greeting • stigmatization ◦ *victims complaints not believed* ◦ *blame for the offending* ◦ *isolation/stigmatization/ scapegoating within community of C* ◦ *not being heard*

secondary victimization. There is the possibility for an official of C to acknowledge that a particular victim had a right to a childhood unburdened by sexual abuse (UN Convention on the Rights of the Child), and that it did not happen because officials were not providing sufficient protection, or had suppressed information about crimes against children.

There is a particularly damaging way in which victims of sexual abuse can become almost tainted by association with 'impurity' in a community that has particularly restrictive views about the expression of human sexuality. But it is also argued that this tradition of restrictiveness has played a part in the negative formation of some clergy and others in the development of their own sexuality. Have perpetrators themselves been either direct victims of sexual abuse, or subjected to a system of training that failed them in their maturation as adolescents and young adults? There is a need for ownership of these issues by C. (This point has implications at Level 2 above.)

Healing Circles and *Conferences* may help to repair the sense of humiliation that victims have experienced. They may also restore victims to a proper place of esteem within the community of C. They have the capacity to provide moral recognition and, further, spiritual recognition for the *no longer victim, but person once upon a time harmed.* Having been unburdened of their humiliation, such a person can be recognized as an individual, who has capacity, knowledge and understanding that are of special value to the community.

However, it is also important that persons once harmed should be allowed to leave the community of C without a sense of being judged morally or spiritually. Sometimes a *Healing Circle* will be a place where a victim and the community of C recognize a separation in a respectful way, as when a separated couple acknowledge that their personal relationship is over when they settle their future arrangements as parents in a family mediation session. They can go in peace.

Level	Mode of Self-Relation	Level of Moral and Spiritual Injury	Examples of moral injury
4	Self-realization	Damage to capacity to regard oneself as a spiritual being with potential for development or realization in the way a person's spirituality is expressed (enlightenment, redemption, salvation etc.) Damage to cultural identity	◦ *spiritual condemnation* ◦ *undermining of conscience* ◦ *destruction of a person's spiritual frame of reference* ◦ *denial of right to free religious/spiritual life* ◦ *abuse of spiritual authority* ◦ *betrayal of spiritual trust*

Some of the measures identified above may have spiritual benefits for victims. *Facilitated meetings* between victims and senior clergy may help to reduce or reverse spiritual injury if these are addressed directly, and the senior clergy expressly withdraw any imputation of guilt or shame.

Two Conclusions

Integration and Peacemaking

Although, following Hart, rights derive from the need to respond to harm and injury, we still face the problem of which wrongs give rise to legal remedy. The way in which restorative justice transcends the world of law and engages with social life, to return to Hegel's typology, reminds us of Habermas's distinction between *lifeworld* and *system* (Orts, 1993), showing us that peacemaking transcends both domains. We need to be able to integrate the practices of rights within law and formal dispute settlement (system) and achieve moral and spiritual security and healing within our community (lifeworld) if we are to provide the structures (institutions) and spirit (*eudaimonia*) in which our human life can be realized (*telos*).

Mediation in Hell

Nils Christie, one of the great restorative protagonists, stated that he would 'mediate in hell ... Mediation is the basic principle of restorative justice' (Christie, 2002, p. 26). There is no dark corner of human life in which he would not attempt to seek negotiation. Thus he writes of seeking negotiation with terrorists: 'We ought to meet those we think have done something terribly wrong, we must try to understand why they have done it, attempt to convey alternative ways of perceiving the acts, and also look for some common ground' (ibid.).

The metaphor 'Mediation in Hell' perhaps provides an apt counterpoint to St. Paul's observation that 'we are dealing with the spirit of evil in things heavenly' (*Ephesians* 6:12). This level of discourse takes us well beyond the domain of law and the discourse of rights whilst it retains links with the language of reconciliation in which restorative justice is embedded. It also echoes the values of Weil, seeking Grace, the one movement of the soul that defies Gravity (Weil, 2006b, p. 1). Weil's account of spiritual affliction, with its explicit Christian references, goes even further, beyond the professional frames of reference of mediators and restorative practitioners into the realms of theology (Weil, 1959). However, what she addresses is the stuff that some people who have suffered sexual abuse at the hands of the religious may be experiencing.[16] We will need, alongside the formation of an intention to mediate in hell, to develop special insights and skills to enable us to undertake this practice 'in good faith'.

References

Aertsen, I., Mackay, R., Pelikan, C., Willemsens, J., and Wright, M. 2004. *Rebuilding Community Connections – Mediation and Restorative Justice in Europe*. Strasburg: Council of Europe.

Christie, N. 2002. On Mediation in Hell, in *Herstel en Detentie – Hommaage aan Prof. Dr. Tony Peters*, edited by J. Vanacker. Brussels: Uitgeverij Politeia, pp. 23–8.

de Las Casas, B. 1992 (written 1542). *A Short History of the Destruction of the Indies*. Edited and translated by N. Griffin. Harmondsworth: Penguin.

Finnis, J. 1980. *Natural Law and Natural Rights*. Oxford: Clarendon.

Fuller, L.L. 1969. *The Morality of Law* (second edition). New Haven and London: Yale University Press.

Habermas, J. 1990. *Moral Consciousness and Communicative Action*, translated by C. Lenhardt and S.W. Nicholsen. Cambridge UK: Polity.

Hart, H.L.A. 1994. *The Concept of Law* (second edition). Oxford: Clarendon Press.

Hegel, G.W.F. 1967. *Hegel's Philosophy of Right*, translated by T.M. Knox. Oxford: Oxford University Press.

Honneth, A. 1997. 'Recognition and Moral Theory'. *Social Research*. 64(1), pp. 16–35.

Kirkwood, S. and Richley, T. 2008. Circles of Support and Accountability: the case for their use in Scotland to assist in the community reintegration and risk management of Sexual Offenders. *SCOLAG Journal*. October 2008, pp. 236–9.

Lloyd, D. 1964. *The Idea of Law*. London: Penguin.

MacCulloch, D. 2010. *A History of Christianity*. London: Penguin.

Mackay, R.E. 1994. Victimology and Rights Theories. *International Review of Victimology*, 6, pp. 183–94.

MacIntyre, A. 1989. *A Short History of Ethics*. London: Routledge.

16 I use the present continuous tense deliberately.

Mackay, R.E. 2007a. Law as Peacemaking – beyond the concept of restorative justice, in *Images of Restorative Justice Theory*, edited by R. Mackay, M. Bosnjak, J. Deklerck, C. Pelikan, B. van Stokkom and M. Wright. Frankfurt: Verlag für Polizeiwissenschaft.

Mackay, R.E. 2007b. Ethical justification for the theory of Law as Peacemaking. *Acta Juridica*, edition 'Restorative Justice: Politics, Policies and Prospects', pp. 73–90.

Mackay, R.E. 2010. Viewpoint: Christian social worker reflects on Church and child abuse. *Independent Catholic News*. Available at http://www.indcatholicnews.com/news.php?viewStory=16835 [accessed: 26 November 2012].

Mackay, R.E. 2013. 'Restorative Justice And The Churches – Options Paper'. Submission to Victorian Parliamentary Inquiry into *The Handling of Child Abuse by Religious and Other Organisations*. http://www.parliament.vic.gov.au/images/stories/committees/fcdc/inquiries/57th/Child_Abuse_Inquiry/Submissions/Mackay_Robert.pdf.

Marquette University Law School 2011. Restorative Justice Initiative. *Supporting Victims and Communities in the Healing Process*. Available at http://law.marquette.edu/rji/ [accessed: 26 November 2012].

McCold, P. 2010. Overview of Mediation, Conferencing and Circles. Paper presented to the *Tenth United Nations Congress on Crime Prevention and the Treatment of Offenders*, Vienna, April 10–17. International Institute for Restorative Practices. Bethlehem PA, USA.

McGrade, A.S. 1992. 'Introduction', in William of Ockham. *A Short Treatise on Tyrannical Government*, edited by A.S. McGrade, translated by J. Kilcullen. Cambridge: Cambridge University Press.

New Zealand Court of Appeal. 1998. *R. v Clotworthy* (1998) 15 CRNZ 651 (C.A.) (summary). Available at http://www.restorativejustice.org/articlesdb/articles/2354 [accessed: 26 November 2012].

Orts, E.W. 1993. Positive Law and Systemic Legitimacy. *Ratio Juris*. 6/3.

Shoebridge, D. 2011. Catholic church and Child Sex Abuse: Statement to the NSW Parliament. Available at http://parliament.nsw.gov.au/Prod/parlment/hansart.nsf/V3Key/LC20110914047?open&refNavID=HA8_1 [accessed: 26 November 2012].

Singer, P. 1986. Introduction, in *Applied Ethics*, edited by P. Singer. Oxford: Oxford University Press.

Tsunoda, R., de Bary, W.T. and Keene, D. (editors). 1964. *Sources of Japanese Tradition*. Volume 1. New York: Columbia University Press.

United Nations 1989. Convention on the Rights of the Child. Available at http://www2.ohchr.org/english/law/crc.htm [accessed: 26 November 2012].

Vatican City. *Canon Law*. Available at http://www.vatican.va/archive/ENG1104/_INDEX.HTM [accessed: 26 November 2012].

Vatican City. Post-synodical Apostolic Exhortation *Africae Munus*. Section C. 'The good governance of states', para. 83.2011. Available at http://www.

vatican.va/holy_father/benedict_xvi/apost_exhortations/documents/hf_ben-xvi_exh_20111119_africae-munus_en.html [accessed: 26 November 2012].
Weil, S. 1959. The Love of God and Affliction, in *Waiting on God*, translated by E. Crawford. London: Fontana.
Weil, S. 2003 (written 1942–3). Human Personality in *Simone Weil: An Anthology*, edited by S. Miles. London: Penguin.
Weil, S. 2006a (published posthumously 1949). *The Need for Roots* translated by A. Willis. London and New York: Routledge.
Weil, S. 2006b (published posthumously 1947). *Gravity and Grace*, translated by E. Crawford and M. von der Ruhr. London and New York: Routledge.

APPENDIX – QUESTIONS FOR THE SYMPOSIUM

A – Rights and Restorative Justice

1. Are rights a necessary but insufficient ingredient in the recipe for achieving justice?
2. Can we practice restoratively in the face of denial of rights?

B – Restorative Justice and Peacemaking

1. Is restorative justice a sufficiently robust concept in the face of unresolved debates about what is does?
2. Does law as peacemaking and a concept of practice focused on the parties' present experience, drawing upon their past and future concerns provide a convincing agenda for what we call restorative justice?

C– Law and Morality

1. Do we need to find a way to reconcile the goals of law and social morality?
2. Can a theory of moral and spiritual injury help us to bridge the gap between law and social morality, and thereby help us make sense of the nexus between restorative justice and rights?

Chapter 7
Global Justice, Restorative Justice and Universal Peace in the Reality of International Politics and State Power

Christodoulos K. Yiallourides and Mersilia Anastasiadou

Introduction

Justice, peace, equality, security and democracy have informed social discourse in every age. We also find notions of restorative justice in the work of Plato and Aristotle (Artinopoulou and Gavrielides, Chapter 2, Artinopoulou 2010: 5–14). Contemporary understanding of restorative justice may, however, be considered controversial and ambiguous, where we view power as a key factor that restorative justice depends and relies upon for its application. We view this to be a more important factor than the issues related to the procedural substance of restorative justice.

Realism defines power as a capability to impose, enforce or exercise influence and dominance (Mearsheimer, 2001: Waltz, 1979: Morgenthau, 1954; Dunne and Schmidt, 2001, pp. 141–7). It views power as a necessary ingredient in pursuit of goals and aims (Thucydides, 1972). It is power that gains breakthroughs and results with a realistic approach. This view is contrasted with the idealistic or liberal conception which identifies power with law and order (Doyle, 1997, 1983; Howard, 1978; Keohane and Nye, 1977; Moravcsik, 1997; Baldwin, 1993). According to this perspective, it is the institutions that are mandated to exercise power in maintaining law and order and a state of justice. Power according to this view does not necessarily reside with states but with the international institutions that promote justice, such as the United Nations and the International Court of Justice (Knapp, 2004, pp. 514–49; Frangonikolopoulos and Proedrou, 2010, p. 476). However, both schools do recognize that power undeniably influences global politics and therefore, restorative justice must be sought through an appropriate framework that takes into consideration the balance of power.

Furthermore, globalization has opened up possibilities for restorative justice to be applied on a larger scale by turning the world into a global village. The First International Symposium on Restorative Justice at Skopelos, Greece, provided the stepping stone/starting point to explore and research further the concept of restorative justice from a philosophical perspective. It was attended by scholars from various fields and from various parts of the world, which made for a rich exchange of multidisciplinary ideas regarding the concept of justice. We observed a plurality of approaches regarding justice which gave added value for exploring the topic of restorative justice. This drew us towards the cosmopolitan endeavour of shaping a widely acceptable conception of justice in international relations.

This chapter, therefore, intends to contribute to the subject of international relations by providing a framework for exercise/practical implementation of restorative justice in the international system of states. It seeks to enlarge the concept and take it further from its origins as a domestic procedure limited to the internal governance of states. The chapter is realistic in its approach in giving a pragmatic framework for justice rather than an aesthetic vision of the idea.

The Reality of the World Today

Poverty, despair, inherent instability, escalating tensions and conflict have characterized human society from time immemorial and have underlined the ever present threat of an uncontrollable war of all against all (Hobbes, 1996). In our contemporary experience too, no one seems to be in a position to devise a comprehensive political solution for halting and reversing this route towards social and global injustice (Chila, 2009, pp. 277–96). Our traditional and ever present dilemma, between freedom and justice – or more accurately perhaps, equal distribution of global welfare, capitalism (Smith, 1999) versus socialism (Kondylis, 2000, pp. 13–37), liberalism (Kondylis, 2000, pp. 45–67) versus social and economic equality or justice – defined the ideological and political agenda as well as the struggles, rivalries and conflicts of the nineteenth and twentieth centuries.

The world seems to have changed radically since the collapse of the Union of Soviet Socialist Republics in 1991, the dissolution of the Soviet-led socialist world system and its attendant ideology seeking a revolutionary transformation of the world into a communistic, classless global society (Fukuyama, 1989, 2006; Yiallourides, 2010, 2009, pp. 225–44 and,1989, p. 161). And yet, today, we may be witnessing a revival of the bipolar scheme of social justice versus civil justice which dominated the twentieth century.

Jurgen Habermas poignantly observes that we are living in the crisis of a 'post democratic' era which is characterized by a more capitalist and market oriented functioning of democracy (Habermas, 2012). This has taken democracy away from its roots as a form of governance seeking a more representational and equal political system to one where financial clout increasingly dominates the democratic system and political success. This system has led to a financial calamity and to despair in the developed world.

If Western man feels his future in a deadlock with despair replacing hope, then the rest of the world's populations may be considered as living their lives without any prospect of survival considering the deprivation of essential commodities and basic amenities afflicting them. While the moribund populations of the developed countries still demand their aspirations and hopes and resist the squelching of their ambitions, the people of the third world seem to have stopped reacting and given in to fate owing to a paucity of hope. It is the people of the 'developed' countries of the Western world who now feel the threat of the loss of their rights and the way of life that was based on the mass material prosperity of the past decades they had taken for granted.

We suggest that the western human specimen is reacting not to loss of culture or values but, primarily, to the loss of a materialistic way of life characterized by widespread consumerism and material prosperity. The twentieth century witnessed confrontation and conflict without defined rules, terms or conditions. This feature alone may largely account for the current dominance of a globalized and uncontrollable intervention of markets in politics and of the huge emerging problem of the demarcation of countries (Spiegel, 2011; Schmidt, 2012). It has also impeded efforts to outline a framework of conflict resolution and establishment of justice as a global good inherent in a universal approach to a world of rule of law. The conception of peace as a demand for freedom, justice, equality and independence has lost its historical meaning, its essence and substance and is once again proving elusive.

Thomas Hobbes provided an approach in his *Leviathan* to address this old and revitalized issue of the meaning of peace. He stressed the importance of a force of power or authority in imposing compliance with treaties or agreed terms. In his view, justice or injustice depends on a political force without which nothing can be classified as just or unjust (Metaxopoulos, 1989, p. 213; Kersting, 1992, pp. 59–62). His views do find parallels in the reality of international and national politics. We observe that, contrary to the international system where the political structure is anarchical, states maintain a hierarchical structure of power in their domestic affairs and internal structures (Kersting, 1992, pp. 62–3).

The international community, with its competitive system of states, cannot expect to form a parallel to a hierarchically structured state authority. In view of that and Thomas Hobbes' arguments, it is the states and the political structure within them that can best serve the cause of security and safety of its citizens. At the same time, we also need to be on guard against the possibility of a decline in respect for the historical, religious and cultural traditions and values that can arise in a state of weakened political strength, as is facing Europe at the moment. Such developments can influence the course of a society as it goes forward. History in this sense is not being made in the past but stretches horizontally to the future.

Infamy, pauperization, income inequality, injustice, warfare and deprivation of liberty that afflict many societies represent a global crisis with worrying concerns for development. They are also signs of an ungoverned structure of international administration of justice, order and security (Waltz, 1979, p. 88). Whatever order we do observe arises at a national level and in cases where there is a hierarchy within political systems. The wider global arena continues to be characterized by injustice.

The benefits arising from technological progress in the twentieth century – which has momentously transformed human life – have not reached the masses uniformly. To date, a vast majority in the third world has remained largely bereft of these benefits. It has been the rich countries, and the materially well-off populating the upper strata of society, who have benefited from technological developments and to whom it has provided the most prosperous conditions. The vast majority of the human population lives in what Johann Galtung called 'structural violence' – which is a state characterizing inequality, poverty, desperation, malnutrition, lack of basic amenities of life and unavailability of medical care (Galtung, 1980, 1975, 1969). Structural violence forces populations to migrate into the materially prosperous and politically stable parts of the world as they engage in a desperate search for survival.

Peace cannot be classified as a static or a fixed concept. Rather, it is fluid and dynamic with many permutations, orientations and perceptions. However, it is a concept that goes naturally with the conception of freedom, justice, equality, cooperation and dialogue. We can approach the question of how to achieve peace using a dialectical approach. Peace is not to be understood in its negative connotation as an absence of war; rather, it is a continuous struggle for freedom, justice and equality in order to eliminate poverty, pauperization and to undo structural violence (Galtung, 1975). The dialectical approach demands the treatment of conflict within social sciences and international relations as a struggle and demand for development, progress and justice (Dahrendorf, 2004, pp. 230, 235) rather than as a pathogenic phenomenon as understood in the past (Parsons, 1991, p. 30).

The period of colonization in the twentieth century symbolizes this demand for freedom and self-determination. The colonized states identified freedom with justice or, more accurately, with restoration of justice. From their perspective, restorative justice gained them the right of self-determination and an ability to decide their future freely and without any constraints. The United Nations fortified and guaranteed this right in its decisions as *jus cogens*, which is a peremptory norm and a fundamental principle of international law accepted by the international community of states and as a norm for which no derogation is ever permitted. The populations thus gained a right to vote democratically based on the principle of one man, one vote. In this way, the concept of restorative justice translated itself in the form of gaining freedom and human rights for populations living under occupation, in a state of deprivation of freedom and equality (Yiallourides 1981: 56). International law recognized their right to use armed force in order to regain freedom. A similar situation defines cases where people have demanded freedom, self-determination and, more specifically, a democratic right to self-govern against an authoritative or dictatorial regime.

Twentieth to Twenty First Century: Peace, Democracy and Justice

The twentieth century has been typified by great revolutions, destructive wars and exponential technological progress. Technological progress contributed monumentally to the quality of human life and changed the way we live; however, it may also contain the seeds of its own destruction if it falls into dangerous hands. It also witnessed a movement towards improving the social conditions around the globe by combating poverty, inequality, life threatening diseases and epidemics and in rectifying political grievances by promoting democracy. The world witnessed massive movements for civil democracy.

The major political powers established the United Nations as an institution for regulating the international system of states after the Second World War (Christodoulides and Bourantonis, 1998). The United Nations was mandated to promote freedom and equality in the world. However, it could not wholly succeed in this endeavour in imposing its hierarchical power over the ungoverned system symbolizing global politics (Czempiel, 2002, p. 124). Opinions differ as to whether the United Nations has succeeded in achieving its mission and aims for promotion of peace and security at a global level.

The Cold War era lasted from 1947–1991, during which time justice and freedom became ancillary issues to the struggle for global dominance between competing systems of international governance (Mearsheimer, 2007, pp. 630–45). The era was marked by a confrontation between socialism and capitalism and between liberalism and communism. Justice, during this period, was chiefly the domain of nation states, with the United Nations appearing incapable of establishing a universal system of collective justice or security. There were, of course, major occasions where justice prevailed, including the end of the South African Apartheid regime. The European Court of Human Rights also ruled on a number of individual cases. Cyprus's appeal to the European Court of Human Rights to restore justice after the Turkish invasion of 1974 is one such major case (Gavrielides, 2005). In the same vein, the Conference for Security and Cooperation in Europe (former Organization for Security and Cooperation in Europe) also set up a post for a High Commissioner in order to mediate for minorities and guarantee them their rights and freedoms (Heraclides, Kostakos and Frangonikolopoulos, 1994, pp. 181–2). The International Criminal Tribunal also administered justice in a few instances, most notably in the case of Yugoslavia. However, the international bodies administering justice continue to be mired in the complex web of national interests and the self-interest of powerful nations which can inhibit or support their role in administering justice. Finally, the role of technological progress and globalization cannot be discounted in the establishment of human rights and this is a topic we turn to in the following pages.

The Complex Grid of Globalization

Globalization refers to 'a set of processes that have increased interconnectedness across the globe and where, crucially, these connections in many respects transcend the narrow boundaries of the nation-state' (Kiely, 2005, p. 1). It is a phenomenon that is seen as, 'widening, deepening, and speeding up the worldwide interconnectedness in all aspects of contemporary social life, from the cultural to the criminal, the financial to the spiritual' (Held et al.,1999, p. 2).

David Harvey argues that globalization is a 'time-space compression', by which he refers to the increasing pace of contemporary life and free flow of capital across borders. The boundaries of time and space have been annihilated by globalization (Harvey, 1989, pp. 238–9). The world according to Harvey has become a smaller place as it has shrunk the boundaries of time and space and has brought markets, consumers and producers closer to one another. He argues that 'time and space are social powers' by which he means that people who have the capability to manipulate time and space are the ones who will exercise power (Harvey, 1989, p. 238).

These definitions capture the phenomenon of increasing interdependence beyond borders (Held, 1995, p. 78; Teschke, 2003). In this way, globalization as a phenomenon can potentially decrease the importance of national borders (Scholte, 1990, p. 60; Ohmae, 1995, p. 5). Countries and states are no longer insulated against events taking place outside their borders and in other parts of the world. This has created the need for coordinating policy and action across the world to deal with issues that are taking on transnational significance. Globalization has been accompanied by a rise in the influence of non-state actors who have proliferated at various levels around the world (Ataman, 2003, pp. 42–66). It has empowered these non-state actors to take on global ambitions transcending national borders (Cohen, 2006, pp. 6–12). These actors now have a bearing on the internal dynamics and politics of a state. At times, they have also influenced the external relations between states.

Mass media and communication technologies have shrunk the physical constraints of time and space (Masek, 1992, p. 57). These technologies allow non-governmental organizations, social workers and activists around the world to connect and raise issues on a global platform (Arts, Noortmann, Reinalda 2001). This connectivity has also homogenized the global culture to an extent. The prominence of these non-governmental organizations, social actors and human rights bodies in the international arena allows them to act as neutral mediators for resolving conflicts and restoring justice. It is their global reputation that prepares them for this role. At the same time, the citizenry in places afflicted with conflicts and injustice now have an international platform for airing their grievances, which can also be done through human rights bodies and non-governmental organizations. Thus, the developments accompanying globalization can also serve the cause of restorative justice.

Globalization is assumed to have undermined the centrality of the state by empowering non-state actors and supranational structures to regulate a state's external policies. Supranational structures and non-state actors can question and challenge the foundations of governing institutions in a state and have a bearing on how a state addresses transnational and other issues (Arts, Noortmann, Reinalda, 2001).

Non-state actors are increasingly rising to the forefront of global politics, aided by the power of connectivity (European Environmental Agency, 2011). The 'Arab Spring' demonstrated their potential for challenging the ruling structures of power, thereby attacking the centrality of the state (Travis, 2012, Florida International University Legal Studies Research Paper). However, the influence of non-state actors and supranational structures, which characterizes the interventionist aspects of globalization, has not been uniform across the globe. Stronger states can neutralize the influence of non-state actors and supranational institutions in their affairs, whereas weaker states may witness a greater intrusion from these same players. Herein lies the potential for restorative justice mediation in cases of conflicts among weaker states, a potential that increases along with the extent of international support for such mediation, which in its turn is related to the moral authority acknowledged in mediators.

While it may appear that international (and supranational) institutions may be weakening the centrality of the state and gaining a governing role in their internal and external affairs, a closer look at the decision-making structures in these institutions reveals that it is still the Great Powers who play a key role in building consensus within these institutions and in mandating an action. This is most evident in the case of the United Nations Security Council, where a single veto by one of the five permanent members can block any resolution (Debusmann, 2012; Kelsen, 2000, pp. 275–7). Without the involvement of the Great Powers, the United Nations may not have been very effective in resolving the crises affecting the world, especially the political crises (United Nations News Centre, 4 February 2012 and 19 July 2012). Thus, we can surmise that the state in the form of Great Powers still continues to shape our world today, in spite of supranational institutions and governing laws (Papasotiriou, 2007, pp. 60–72). The origins of power remain the same and lie with the strong states although the way power manifests itself in our globalized world may have changed. In this regard, we can take note of the fact that the supranational structures that provide a governing framework for the world at large were established by the Great Powers themselves.

Globalization has altered the international political arena by underlining the imperative support of supranational structures which is needed for any coordinated response to global crises. But while the response to these crises may depend on consensus at these supranational structures, it is still the Great Powers who play a prominent role in building that consensus. Globalization may have changed the platform from which the Great Powers exercise dominance but not their role. Consequently, the Great Powers can play an important role in promoting restorative justice by seeking a coordinated response to the various conflicts in the world through their representation in supranational institutions.

On the other hand, the phenomenon of globalization has transcended national boundaries and brought people and societies closer to one another. The removal of restrictions posed by territorial boundaries has unleashed possibilities for communication, collaboration and the development of common initiatives. This development bodes well for the cause of restorative justice, promotion of human rights, freedoms and equality. It offers a parallel route to the pursuit of justice and equality by allowing social groups in different countries to come together and pursue activities of common interest that also serve to protect their interests. The power to communicate has allowed the populations affected by the crises in Southern Europe to voice their discontent at the policymakers and to demand more equitable treatment. Social groups are now also powerful enough to overhaul or overturn the governing structures of states and to demand increasing participation in the political process, as evident in the so-called Arab Spring. Globalization has thus worked in the favour of societal forces by giving them more weight and influence in political matters of a state, especially in the politically free states of Europe and the West.

Even in other parts of the world, such as the Middle East, we have witnessed revolutionary forces that have overturned regimes in a few countries. It was a desire for a political change after years of economic hardship and inequality suffered by the common citizenry which propagated these forces of upheaval. However, now that the upheaval has occurred, there is a possibility of seeking a state of justice by means of restorative justice. This is especially true for other restive parts of the Middle East (such as Syria) where this model of restorative justice can provide a framework for integrating human rights and freedoms; however, this would require the support and approval of both the state and the citizenry or social groups to accept mediation by institutional or non-institutional players.

The United Nations has established the framework to govern mediation institutionally and at an international level for intervening in conflicts. This is a sort of a restorative justice, or a model for restorative justice, that can take many forms, such as arbitration, mediation or goodwill services. However, these models require the cooperation and approval of all parties concerned and affected by injustice. They also enable the Great and emerging powers to pursue their incentives and aims in a politically expedient manner. This model, however, differs from a localized or a domestic model of restorative justice in its practicalities.

At present, this model is in an evolutionary stage in meeting the demands of international society for more justice. It would undoubtedly benefit from a more robust participation by non-governmental organizations and other institutions and in the strengthening of their role as parties that can intervene successfully to mediate in international affairs and in a way that is deemed just by all the parties involved. This poses and has posed a key challenge for the international community from the era of Kant and Rousseau until its current expression as found in Rawls.

The next part of this chapter discusses the theoretical approaches for understanding the function of states in the international system and their relationship with the rule of law and justice.

International Politics as Seen Through the Prism of Realism and the Lenses of the Liberal School of Thought

Realism states that individuals' interests are not a primary force of influence and may not even count in international relations (Jackson and Sorensen, 1999, p. 97). It is an ideology that elevates a state's interests as the defining force in international relations and views each state as acting in accordance with its own interests. The phrase 'national interest' captures the true incentives, motives and orientation of states in an eloquent way (Wight 2002:97).

In the international arena, states operate in an anarchic environment. Realist writers use 'anarchy' in a metaphorical way in order to characterize the reality of the international arena (Stein, 1990, pp. 4–5). Their definition of anarchy stands for an absence of a central supranational structure or authority that can impose a singular political, economic and military agenda on the global stage and implement the rule of law in international society (Waltz, 1979, p. 88; Milner, 1993, pp. 143–65; Axelrod and Keohane, 1985, p. 226). Anarchy is a main characteristic of international politics and the interaction of states at a global level is primarily anarchical (Mearsheimer 2001; Dunne and Schmidt 2001, pp. 143, 158; Donelly 2005, pp. 32–3). Hobbes claimed, '*bellum omnium contra omnes*' (the war of all against all) (Jackson and Sorensen, 1999, pp. 74–6). Self-interest is the only reality according to Hobbes (Hartmann, 2001, p. 26).

Machiavelli argues that 'it must be taken for granted that all men are wicked and that they will always give vent to the malignity that is in their minds when opportunity offers' (Machiavelli, 1970, Book I, Chapter 3; Flyvbjerg, 1998, pp. 210–33). When Hans Morgenthau refers to Thomas Hobbes, he underlines that the laws rule only in the internal structure of states for peace, prosperity and symbiosis (Jackson and Sorensen, 1999, pp. 76–80). Also, he stresses that 'universal moral principles cannot be applied to the actions of states' (Morgenthau, 1954, p. 9). 'The actions of states are determined not by moral principles and legal commitments but by considerations of interest and power' (Morgenthau, 1967, pp. 3–6). What rules among the states is the 'law' of the strongest (Thucydides, The Melian Dialogue). Realism considers that the rule of law in international relations exists only when it is based on power. The relation of states with each other reflects their relative power hold over each other. The capability to use that power could be defined by the successful pursuit of their aims (Dunne and Schmidt, 2001, pp. 141–7). Political realism, as Morgenthau underlines, begins with man's inherent desire to gain power. That tension reflects the attitudes of groups and states to strength through alliances that seek to obtain a reconciliation to avoid being dwarfed by the power of an opponent (Waltz, 2003, p. 14). This condition is better described as external balancing (Collard-Wexler, 2006, pp. 397–432).

The developments of the twentieth century, and heralding the beginning of the twenty-first in the form of the emergence of regional blocs such as the European Union, suggest that the state may be losing its primary role in international affairs and ceding it to other bodies with a multilateral representation. However, an individual state's decision to participate in these regional blocks and supranational governing organizations is taken out of self-interest. Countries sign up for common markets because they perceive it to be in their own interests – for instance, by eliminating hostilities and enhancing trade through common markets to improve their own economic and political strength. War is costly; therefore, a reversion to diplomacy to resolve conflicts can be in a state's interest.

Furthermore, the rules of engagement within these governance structures and regional blocs are rewritten if they fail to serve a state's interests. For example, a lack of progress on climate change issues can be attributed to the non-uniform impact of regulation on individual states. Thus, not all states view climate change legislation in their favour. The European Union, if it survives, will be shaped by Great Powers within the bloc such as Germany and France. Recent developments within the European Union stand in stark contrast to what the movement for regional integration initially stood for. It has now become acceptable to consider suspending member states that are seen as a financial and economic liability for the union. The state, as evident by the preceding examples, is still a powerful player in the global arena and holds the power to rewrite and revise the terms of engagement within political and economic unions.

In contrast to realpolitik, liberalism regards the state as a 'necessary evil' and does not view all states as being governed in a similar fashion (Stearns and Pettiford, 2001, p. 57). According to this view, the state can be viewed as a vehicle that permits and guarantees a framework of cooperation and competition not only with other states but also with influential non-state actors in the realm of international, interstate and intra-state relations.

This approach gives space to non-state actors in social and economic fields to discover and develop their role and function within the political system (Cerny, 2010, pp. 18–9). The state in this view is mandated to transfer limited power to self-governing bodies or to supranational/international governing structures, such as the United Nations or the European Union, which have the responsibility or obligation to intervene in crises, problems and conflicts for their resolution and prevention, based on international law and rules governing interstate affairs. (Lamy, 2001, pp. 188–91)

The liberal school of thought gives emphasis to the role of international institutions, international law and human rights (Russett, 2010, pp. 103, 107–11). It does not necessarily diminish the role a state exercises in its affairs; rather, it views the state as one among many other players in the global arena who have an influence on matters concerning a state's economy, security and independence in foreign policy (Lamy, 2001, p. 193). The implication of this view, however, is that politics may be secondary to economics as a force in giving a state an ability to exercise independence in the aforementioned three areas of policy making, that is, foreign policy influence, security and economics.

In the liberal school of thought international law is considered implementable, countries as capable of cooperating with each other and a state is viewed as being capable of rising above self-centredness and self-interestedness (Lamy 2001: 193). Competition is viewed under an economic lens which translates into progress. Under the liberal approach, states transfer some of their powers to multiple supranational structures in order to facilitate a framework of global collaboration for finding solutions to problems facing the entire world – especially in this era of hyperconnectivity where no country is immune to what is happening in another part of the world (Stein, 1990, pp. 7–12). In this regard, economic interdependence is taken to bring states closer to one another and to reduce hostilities (Stearns and Pettiford, 2001, pp. 60–5).

Liberalism also views non-state functionaries as playing an influential role in the affairs and mechanisms of the state (Clark, 2001, p. 646). The power of the state is vulnerable to the power exercised by society, that is, by the population of the state, including its intellectuals and ideologues (Hawthorn, 1999, pp. 146–7). Liberalism defines the state, international organizations and markets as units of analysis for the purpose of resolving conflict and fostering cooperation in a world of competitive social and political pluralism. It is an approach that is global in its ambitions and believes that the power of the state will reduce in due course (Stearns and Pettiford, 2001, p. 54). The state, according to liberalism, is primarily a platform for negotiating interdependence within the global community.

Models of Democratic Theory

Democracy is considered to be the most practical political system for human nature by virtue of its inclusive and representational nature. Throughout history, from classical Greece to the movements for democratic right to self-government in the eighteenth and nineteenth centuries, this system has played a key role in establishing equality, individual independence, representation in the political system and self-fulfilment. These possibilities emerge from the nature of its practical application, which relies on building consensus and collaboration although we can observe differences in the ways it has worked in different times and places (Held, 1995, pp. 58–66, 100–30). Nevertheless, the promotion of a democratic model of governance dominates the global agenda, underpinned by its ability to reconcile freedom and justice in achieving equality of citizenry.

However, contemporary civil democracy has been unable to resolve the rising inequality in availability of material goods around the globe and in promoting global or regional welfare. At its core, democracy is predicated on dialogue as a means for resolving political differences, disputes and conflicts. It elevates the rule of law as a governing norm.

Mediation, which utilizes dialectical thought, is another mode of intervention in governing the structures of a political entity and relies on the possibility of dialogue, which is a democratic value (Chapter 1, Gavrielides and Artinopoulou). What is notable about alternative approaches such as mediation is a reliance on the existence of democratic principles and norms as a way of resolving disputes. Our contemporary notion of democracy is based on Joseph Schumpeter's conception as legitimation of authority and does not find parallels in the historically recorded experience of democracy of the fifth century BC (Becker, 2006, pp. 77–90).

Schumpeter followed the 'realist theory on democracy' and viewed it as the method of legitimation of power in state structures and of those setting the political agenda by virtue of their economic clout and ability to advertise their manifestos (Schumpeter, 1942). The manifestos and agendas appear as marketing campaigns to the citizenry who then vote for the political package more suitable to their perceived needs and desires. This view discounts the participatory nature of democratic politics and views it as a manipulative tool for gaining and legalizing power. This view, however, does cogently point out the weaknesses of the modern democratic system. The nature of politics and our evolution towards nation states from city states makes it difficult for the citizenry to take an active role in politics (Connolly, 1995). There is also an inequality which arises due not to differences in levels of education but to the distribution of welfare and power. The real dimensions of democracy as practiced in contemporary societies are revealed in this mode.

Jurgen Habermas (Habermas, 1996, 2006, pp. 90–106) and John Rawls (Kersting, 2001, pp. 31–53) by contrast proposed the deliberalization theory. Habermas stresses that participation, equality and equitable distribution of welfare or goods is only possible on a limited scale in any society and in the framework of the objective, not a manipulated function of publicity. Rawls's idealistic model of the democratic system follows the same path as Immanuel Kant's. His vision of a democratic society is free from violence and conflict. Justice, fairness and a demand for social equality in such a society exists at all three levels. John Rawls provides further strength to this theory using Rousseau's theory of social contract, which is based on the willingness and the demand of all the citizens to participate (Rousseau, 2011).

According to Jurgen Habermas, it is the capability and willingness to participate by the populace in a territorially limited framework of political action and participation that is a crucial issue in democracy. He notes with critical interest the issue of how autonomous local bodies or areas can develop a democratic system at an economic or any other level (Habermas, 2006, pp. 90–105). The objective publicity and information is a necessary precondition for participation in a democratic framework. He opines that the prevailing democratic structures are more procedural and less participatory, which is denigrating to the real spirit of democracy and denervates the citizenry.

Promotion of justice in society is a key concern of both Rawls and Habermas. Given their views on democracy, the existence of politically autonomous and small state entities can be viewed as a natural precursor to the cultivation of restorative justice as a phenomenon of everyday life. The discourse between the citizenry develops more fluently and naturally in smaller territorial entities. In this framework, Habermas insists on the necessity of a free and objectively informed public and an international society which bases its opinions on the strength of knowledge. These face-to-face interactions are effective in creating an environment where conflicts can be mitigated and mediation can be facilitated. While the rule of law is a necessary precondition in any democracy, the ability of the people to communicate and discourse on the issues affecting them also offers the possibility to restore and resolve injustice in varying cases.

The Role of Mediation

This chapter discusses the concept of restorative justice in a global state of affairs composed of an international system of states operating without an institutionally organized system of justice. This leaves room for mediation as an alternative for imposing justice and which has been identified as one of the ways under which restorative justice can take place.

Mediation stands for intervention by a third party in order to manage and/or resolve various types of conflict, including interstate or intra-state conflict, or communal conflicts. With mediation, we mean the intervention of a third party in an interstate and intra-state conflict or in the disputes between ethnic groups and communities or/and minorities, an intervention that is usually sought by and/or takes place with the consent of the parties to the conflict. Justice, in the context of mediation, may manifest itself in conflict resolution and the maintenance of peace.

Restorative justice can be perceived as a supplementary undertaking to mediation, as a process of moving beyond conflict resolution towards harmonizing relations between discordant groups, achieving the necessary conditions for a peaceful, prosperous and progressive symbiosis and coexistence in society. Developing a more democratic system of governance, may be a key to restorative justice. Another factor contributing to a pragmatic restoration of justice may be an emphasis on ethical or material compensation rather than an imposition of punishments or penalties. This ensures that those adversely affected by injustice feel they have obtained justice while other groups do not feel unduly victimized and society at large finds a way to move towards political reconciliation. It also maintains a consciousness of justice within societies and its communities that creates possibilities for relying on this method to resolve conflicts in the future. However, the conditions are vastly different and marked by opacity in the anarchical international system of states where there is no vertical or hierarchical power base or authoritative structure to impose the rule of law (Papasotiriou, 2012, pp. 207–22).

Martin Wight argues that 'if anarchy (in international relations) is understood to mean the absence of common government, then this is indeed precisely the feature in which international politics differ from domestic politics. In the domestic politics of states the central government, rule of law and public order do exist' (Wight, 2002, p. 105).

However, the anarchic model for explaining the political structure of international relations captures a reality that is being changed by the forces of globalization. The emerging political structure is marked by an increasing interventionist role by societies as groups and of individuals as persons. This has coincided with a proliferation of non-governmental organizations that have become increasingly influential given their interventions and successful resolution of issues and conflicts. Non-governmental organizations are a new force that can take up the role of mediators between states and between social groups and societies. Intervention by non-governmental organizations also benefits individual states. Even if we discard the ethical and moral imperatives for intervention, states have a lot to gain by mediation and the promotion of restorative justice since it allows them to pursue their economic and political interests at a lower cost compared to direct military or economic intervention.

Restorative justice and the practice of mediation could be transformed into a bidirectional force for implementing justice at various levels, as between individuals–social groups–society–state–supranational institution–interstate organization. The informed nature of the citizenry provides opportunities for restorative justice to manifest as a phenomenon for dealing with conflict. These developments are forcing states to move towards compliance with international law and towards a more humanized view of interstate relations. This is, at the moment, an idealist theme and a vision of the future or a model that could lead in that direction.

However, according to Ralph Dahrendorf, humanity is potentially heading towards building a global civil society whose foundations will be based on values of enlightenment, values of freedom and protection of individual rights (Dahrendorf, 2004, p. 247). In response to this, we would stress that we are facing an international system that is still composed of states as units of interaction.

Cases of the Practice of Restorative Justice and Mediation in International Relations

Politics at a global level is distinct from politics at the level of an organized society. States develop external relations with each other in a global arena, which are further regulated by the United Nations and international law. However, while states govern rules of law and political centres of power in their internal affairs, they interact in an anarchical manner with each other on the international scene (Ifestos 2009, pp. 155–200). International law has often depended on a power base for its implementation, which is where possibilities for restorative justice also lie.

Strong, powerful and large functional democracies and states rely on their political clout and power to achieve their foreign interests. The instances of mediation that we do observe, such as the 1998 Yugoslav crisis, also depend on the exercise of power and self-interest by these states. The United Nations commonly adopts mediation for resolving conflicts of an international nature. The use of mediation in this regard departs from its classical conception as a form of restorative justice which was mainly effective in resolving conflicts and disputes in a state's domestic domain.

This is because states have existing rules of law which are exercised or are expected to be exercised regardless of the interests or political clout of the ruling class. This is not possible at a global level where anarchy, self-interest and political dominance by the Great Powers can hinder the implementation of international law. We also observe political clout at play in international relations in cases where prominent personalities with fame and prestige offer their services to intervene and mediate between states in order to find a resolution to a state of injustice and pave the way for justice to rule again. Bishop Abel Muzorewa symbolized this during the cold war in the case of Zimbabwe (Levine, 1996, p. 358). John A. Scali, ABC journalist and Alexandr Fomin, KGB agent, during the 1962 Cuba nuclear world crisis functioned as mediators or backchannels and contributed decisively to the resolution of the crisis by achieving an agreement between the two superpowers, the United Nations and Union of Soviet Socialist Republic (Miller, 1991, pp. 346–49; McElrath, 2008, p. 205). In early 2013, the Former United Nations' Ambassador and New Mexico Governor Bill Richardson went to North Korea in order to intervene and appeal for the liberation of American prisoners (Richardson, 2013). These are few of the many examples where prominent and widely respected personalities have used their own personal clout in the cause of mediation. Another development in this regard is the role of non-governmental organizations. These are a product of globalization and have become increasingly vocal in mediation efforts around the globe. They have assumed a key role in promoting justice and fairness for global populations and in offering mediation services for the same causes. This role is only expected to grow in the intermediate future.

Non-governmental organizations also open up the possibility for collaboration in restorative justice and in bringing the key actors, or those who are facing injustice, closer to those who able to administer justice. Social media platforms, the internet and emerging yet unforeseeable technological progress are another force with a potential bearing on restorative justice as they enable the citizenry to bypass national borders and appeal for their case directly to non-governmental organizations and human rights bodies. The non-governmental organizations aim to intervene in the resolution of humanitarian, economic and social issues and in disaster relief activities. They also allow people to people contacts without the approval of a state to deal with natural disasters, food scarcity and other crises. Their position and international linkages allow them to take up the role of mediator in social and national disputes by default. They can function as intermediaries between supranational and national structures. They have won international prestige and recognition as a result of their activities in several cases. This further strengthens the case for them to mediate and provides an opportunity to add another force for intervention in cases where there has been a violation of law when a mediating role is required to restore justice at the level of both state and societal group. The European Union could perform a similar role in its position as a mediator for issues affecting its member states and non-EU countries (Gentz, 2007; Herrberg, Gündüz and Davis, 2009).The European Union intervenes, mediates and restores justice in instances involving violations of law by individuals and groups within the European Union. In the same vein, non-governmental organizations, by virtue of their linkages, prestige outreach and position are placed in an advantageous position to act as mediators in the framework of restorative justice. Restorative justice could also take place in many countries of the Middle East which are in the middle of a confrontational revolutionary development and where the internet intervenes at the level of ideas and values and also at the level of remedying injustices born from the actions of authoritative regimes.

Conclusion

If we seek to elevate restorative justice as a mechanism for fairness in international relations, we would do well to take into account the realistic account of how states manage their external relations. The exercise of restorative justice depends on factoring in this realistic perspective without which it may remain only a work in progress. A realistic model goes hand in hand with a pragmatic approach, which can further assist in improving the human condition.

Towards this direction, excluding the theoretical approaches, we have to take into account the global dimension of the role of technology that connects people. (Terry, 2007; White, 2005; Artz and Kamalipour, 2003; McChesney and Herman, 1998). In passing, we do note that restorative justice is a concept that has emerged in politically advanced societies and democracies where both state and citizens understand the necessity of the model of restorative justice as being in the interests of the state and not against it. States with authoritarian structures are often noted by an absence of justice for the whole of the population and rule of law, conditions under which restorative justice cannot take hold of social consciousness and materialize. Rule of law is a precondition for the development of complementary and alternative systems such as restorative justice.

This chapter focused on opportunities and possibilities for using restorative justice as a framework for implementing justice in the international system, international politics and interstate affairs. We discussed how the implementation of justice differs in the context of a state's internal affairs from its external affairs owing to the anarchic and chaotic nature of politics at a global level and the systematized nature of domestic politics. We dwelt upon the theoretical underpinnings of these differences and the implications of globalization on the same, considering that globalization is the dominant model of societal organization in our age and has markedly influenced how politics is organized on an international level via a combination of technology and empowerment of citizenry (or people power).

We conclude by saying that this development points towards an optimistic scenario where we can change how states relate to each by building a common civil society at a global level. This civil society can bring individuals, societies and groups closer to one another in the pursuit of their common interests and establish restorative justice as a way of solving conflicts within and beyond national borders.

References

Artinopoulou, V. 2010. *Restorative Justice. The Challenge of Current Legal Systems*. Athens: Nomiki Vivliothiki.

Arts, B., Noortmann, M. and Reinalda, B. 2001. *Non-state actors in international relations*. Aldershot: Ashgate.

Arzt, L. and Kamalipour, Y.R. 2003. *The Globalisation of Corporate Media Hegemony*. New York: State University of New York Press.

Ataman, M. 2003. The Impact of Non-State Actors on World Politics: A Challenge to Nation-States. *Alternatives: Turkish Journal of International Relations*, 2(1), pp. 42–66.

Axelrod, R. and Keohane 1985. Achieving Cooperation under Anarchy: Strategies and Institutions. *World Politics*, 38 (1).

Baldwin, D.A. 1993. *Neorealism and Neoliberalism: The Contemporary Debate*. New York: Columbia University Press.

Becker, M. 2006. *Sittlichkeit und Staat in Politische Philosophie*. Edited by M. Becker, J. Schmidt, R. Zintl. Schoningh: UTB.

Bull, H. 1977. *The Anarchical Society*. London: Macmillan.

Cerny, P. 2010. *Globalisation and Statehood in Issues in 21st Century World Politics*. Edited by M. Beeson and N. Bisley. Basingstoke: Palgrave Macmillan.

Charles, C. 1990. *The Block that Failed. Soviet–East European Relations in Transition*. Indianapolis: Bloomington.

Chila, I. 2009. Issues of International Politics in the era of Globalisation – A First Approach. In *Globalisation, European Union and Greece, Political and Economic Aspects*, edited by P. Siousiouras and C. Hazakis. Athens: Piotita, pp. 277–96 (in Greek).

Christodoulides, T. and Bourantonis, D. 1998. *The UN in the Doorstep of the Post-Cold War Era*. Athens: I. Sideris (in Greek).

Clark, I. 2001. Globalisation and the post-Cold War order. In: *The Globalization of World Politics*, edited by J. Baylis and S. Smith. Oxford: Oxford University Press.

Cohen, S. 2006. *The Resilience of the State, Democracy and the Challenges of Globalization*. London: Hurst and Company.

Collard-Wexler, S. 2006. Integration Under Anarchy: Neorealism and the European Union. *European Journal of International Relations*, 12, pp. 397–432.

Connolly, W.E. 1995. *The Ethos of Pluralization*. Minneapolis: University of Minessota Press.
Czempiel, E.O. 2002. *Die Pax Americana, der Terrorismus und die Zukunft der Internationalen Beziehungen*. München: C.H. Beck.
Dahrendorf, R. 2004. *Der Wiederbeginn der Geschichte – Vom Fall der Mauer zum Krieg im Irak*. München: C.H. Beck.
Debusmann, B. 2012. The UN Security Council shows its weakness (again). *Reuters*. Available at http://blogs.reuters.com/bernddebusmann/2012/03/02/the-un-security-council-shows-its-weakness-again/ [Accessed: 26 January 2013].
Donelly, J. 2005. *Realism in Theories of International Relations*, edited by S. Burchill, A. Linklater, R. Devetak, J. Donelly, M. Paterson, C. Reus-Smit and J. True. Basingstoke: Palgrave Macmillan.
Doyle, M.W. 1983. Kant, Liberal Legacies, and Foreign Affairs. *Philosophy and Public Affairs*, 12(3), pp. 205–35.
Doyle, M.W. 1997. *Ways of War and Peace*. New York: W.W. Norton.
Dunne, T. and Schmidt, C. 2001. *Realism in The Globalization of World Politics*, edited by J. Baylis and S. Smith. Oxford: Oxford University Press.
European Environmental Agency 2011. *Global governance – the rise of non-state actors, A background report for the SOER 2010 assessment of global megatrends*. 4. Available at: http://www.eea.europa.eu/publications/global-governance [Accessed: 26 January 2013].
Flew, T. 2007. *Understanding Global Media*. Basingstoke: Palgrave Macmillan.
Flyvbjerg, B. 1998. Habermas and Foucault: Thinkers for Civil Society? *The British Journal of Sociology*, 49(2), pp. 210–33.
Frangonikolopoulos C.A. and Proedrou P. 2010. The democratization of global politics. In: *The Cosmopolitan Democracy in Directions in the Study of International Relations* edited by C. Lavdas, D. Xenakis, D. Chysochoou. Athens: I. Sideris, pp. 463– 93 (in Greek).
Fukuyama, F. 1989. The End of History. *The National Interest*. [Online]. Available at: http://www.wesjones.com/eoh.htm [accessed: 26 January 2013].
Fukuyama, F. 2006. *The End of History and the Last Man*. New York: Free Press.
Galtung, J. 1969. Violence, Peace and Peace Research, *Journal of Peace Research*. 6(3), pp. 167–91.
Galtung, J. 1975. *Strukturelle Gewalt*. Rowohtl Reinbek.
Galtung, J. 1980. *The True Words. A Transnational Perspective*. New York: The Free Press.
Gavrielides, T. 2005. Human Rights vs. Political Reality: The Case of Europe's Harmonising Criminal Justice Systems, *International Journal of Comparative Criminology,* 5(1), pp. 60–84.
Gentz, S. 2007. *EU Influence in Conflict: Power to Mitigate or to Mediate?* Oslo Forum, pp. 54–62.

Habermas, J. 1996. The Normative Models of Democracy. In: *Democracy and Difference. Contesting the boundaries of the political*, edited by S. Benhabib. New Jersey: Princeton University Press.

Habermas, J. 2006. *Deliberative Demokratie und Zivilgesellschaft in Politische Theorie der Gegenwart in funfzehn Modellen*. Edited by W. Reese-Schafer. Munchen–Wien: Oldenbourg.

Habermas, J. 2012. Politik und Erpressung. *DieZeit*, [Online], available at: http://www.zeit.de/2012/37/Habermas-Krise-Europa-Rede-Georg-August-Zinn-Preis/seite-1,<http://www.zeit.de/2012/37/Habermas-Krise-Europa-Rede-Georg-August-Zinn-Preis/seite> [Accessed: 26 January 2012].

Hartmann, J. 2001. *Internationale Beziehungen*. Opladen: UTB.

Harvey, D. 1989. *The condition of postmodernity*. London: Blackwell.

Hawthorn, G. 1999. *Liberalism since the Cold War* in *The Interregnum – Controversies in World Politics 1989–1999*, edited by M. Cox, K. Booth and T. Dunne. Cambridge: Cambridge University Press.

Held, D. 1995. *Democracy and the Global Order*. Cambridge: Polity Press.

Held, D., McGrew, T., Perraton, J. and Goldblatt, D. 1999. *Global Transformations: Politics, Economics, and Culture*. Palo Alto: Stanford University Press.

Heraclides, A., Kostakos, G. and Frangonikolopoulos, C. 1994. *International Conflicts – Dealing and Resolution*. Athens: I Sideris (in Greek).

Herrberg, A., Gündüz, C. and Davi, L. 2009. *Engaging the EU in Mediation and Dialogue. Initiative for Peacebuilding*. Available at http://www.initiativeforpeacebuilding.eu/pdf/Synthesis_Engaging_the_EU_in_mediation_and_dialogue.pdf [Accessed: 26 January 2013].

Hobbes, T. 1996. *Leviathan*. Edited by J.C.A. Gaskin. Oxford: Oxford University Press.

Howard, M.E. 1978. *War and Liberal Consciousness*. Oxford: Oxford University Press.

Ifestos, P. 2009. The Sociopolitical structure of the international system, the role of collective security and the issue of international governance. In: *The Role of the United Nations in the Twenty-First Century*, edited by C.K. Yiallourides. Athens: Livanis, pp. 155–200

Jackson, R. and Sorensen, G. 1999. *Introduction to International Relations*. Oxford: Oxford University Press.

Kant, I. 2007. *Perpetual Peace*. Minneapolis: Filiquarian Publishing.

Kelsen, H. 2000. The Law of the United Nations: A Critical Analysis of Its Fundamental Problems. New Jersey: The Law Book Exchange – LTI Union.

Keohane, R.O and Nye, J.S. 1977. *Power and Interdependence: World Politics in Transition*. Boston: Little Brown.

Kersting, W. 1992. *Thomas Hobbes zur Einfuhrung*. Hamburg: Junius.

Kersting, W. 2001. *John Rawls zur Einfuhrung*. Hamburg: Junius.

Kiely, R. 2005. *Empire in the age of globalisation, US hegemony and neoliberal disorder*. London: Pluto Press.

Knapp, M. 2004. Internationale Organisationen als Instrumente globaler Friedenssicherung, in *Einfuhrung in die Internationale Politik*, edited by M. Knapp and G. Krell. München: R. Oldenbourg, pp. 514–49.

Kondylis, P. 2000. *From the Twentieth to the Twenty-First Century*. Athens: Themelio (in Greek).

Lamy, S. 2001. Contemporary mainstream approaches: neo-realism and neo-liberalism. In: *The Globalization of World Politics*, edited by J. Baylis and S. Smith. Oxford: Oxford University Press.

Levine, A. 1996. Political Accommodation and the Prevention of Secessionist Violence. In: *The International Dimensions of an Internal Conflict*, edited by M.E. Brown. Center for Science and International Affairs. Massachusetts: Harvard University Press.

Machiavelli, N. 1970. *The Discourses Book*. Edited by B.R. Crick. Penguin.

Masek, K. 1992. An der Schwelle des dritten Jahrtausends. *Conturen*, 7.

McChesney, R.W and Herman, E.S. 1998. *The Global Media: Missionaries of Global Capitalism*. London: Cassell.

McElrath, J. 2008. *Everything John F. Kennedy Book: Relive the history, romance, and tragedy of America's Camelot*. Massachusetts: F+W Publications.

Mearsheimer, J.J. 2001. *The Tragedy of Great Powers Politics*. New York: W.W. Norton.

Mearsheimer, J.J. 2007. *The Tragedy of Great Power Politics*. Athens: Piotita – W.W. Norton and Co. (in Greek).

Metaxopoulos, E. 1989. (Introduction) in *Leviathan*. Translation by G. Paschalides and E. Metaxopoulos, Athens: Gnosi (in Greek).

Miller, L.R. 1991. *Under the Cloud: The Decades*. New York:The Free Press.

Milner, H. 1993. 'The Assumption of Anarchy in International Relations Theory: A Critique' in *Neorealism and Neoliberalism: The Contemporary Debate*, edited by D. Baldwin. New York: Columbia University Press.

Moravcsik, A. 1997. Taking Preferences Seriously: A Liberal Theory of International Relations. *International Organization*, 51(4), pp. 513–53.

Morgenthau, H.J. 1948/1954. *Politics Among Nations: The struggle for power and peace*. New York: Alfred Knopf.

Morgenthau, H.J. 1967. The U.S. and the Mideast. *The New Leader*, 13.

Ohmae, K. 1995. *Borderless World*. London: Fontana.

Papasotiriou, H. 2007. Hegemonic Orders in an Anarchical Society: Conditions for Stability. *Defencor Pacis*. Athens: The Defence Analyses Institute (IAA) Review.

Papasotiriou, H. 2012. *The Problem of Order in an Anarchical Society in International Politics in Times of Change*, rdited by N. Tzifakis. Athens: Springer.

Parsons, T. 1991. *The Social System*. London: Routledge.

Richardson, B. 2013. Bill Richardson Explains North Korea Trip. *CNN News* 13 January 2013. Available at: http://www.youtube.com/watch?v=oe3GqllMao8 [Accessed: 26 January 2013].

Rosenau, J.N. 1992. Governance, Order and Change in World Politics. In: *Governance without Government: Order and Change in world Politics*. Edited by J.N. Rosenau and E.O. Czempiel. Cambridge: Cambridge University Press.

Rousseau, J.J. 2011. *The Social Contract*. Aziloth Books.

Russett, B. 1993. *Grasping the Democratic Peace: Principles for a post-Cold War World*. Princeton: Princeton University Press.

Russett, B. 2010. *Liberalism*. In: *International Relations Theories, Discipline and Diversity*, edited by T. Dunne, M. Kurki and S. Smith. Oxford: Oxford University Press.

Schmidt. H. 2012. It is ridiculous the world to be governed by the markets. *Skai*, [Online], Available at : http://www.skai.gr/news/world/article/211012/smit-geloio-na-kuvernatai-o-kosmos-vasei-ton-diatheseon-ton-agoron/ [Accessed: 26 January 2012].

Scholte, J.A. 1990. *Globalisation: Prospects for a Paradigm Shift in Politics and Globalisation*, edited by M. Shaw. London: Routledge.

Schumpeter, J.A. 1942. *Capitalism, Socialism and Democracy*. Abingdon: Taylor and Francis.

Smith, A. 1999. *The Wealth of Nations*, edited by A. Skinner. Harmondsworth: Penguin Books.

The Destructive Power of the Financial Markets. *Der Spiegel* [Online], Available at: http://www.spiegel.de/international/business/out-of-control-the-destructive-power-of-the-financial-markets-a-781590.html [Accessed: 26 January 2012].

Stearns, J. and Pettiford, L. 2001. *International Relations: Perspectives and Themes*. London: Pearson Education.

Stein, A.A. 1990. *Why Nations Cooperate, Circumstance and Choice in International Relations*. Ithaca and London: Cornell University Press.

Teschke, B. 2003. *The Myth of 1648, Class, Geopolitics, and the Making of Modern International Relations*. London; New York: Verso.

Thucydides. 1972, *History of the Peloponnesian War*. London: Penguin Books Ltd.

Travis, H. 2012. Wargaming the 'Arab Spring': Predicting Likely Outcomes and Planning U.N. Responses. *Cornell International Law Journal*, 45. Florida International University Legal Studies Research. 12–07. Available at: http://ssrn.com/abstract=2062578 [Accessed: 26 January 2013].

United Nations News Centre. 2012. 4 February. Syria: Ban voices deep regret after Security Council fails to agree on resolution. Available at: http://www.un.org/apps/news/story.asp/www.fao.org/story.asp?NewsID=41144&Cr=Syria&Cr1 [Accessed: 26 January 2013].

United Nations News Centre. 2012. 19 July. Security Council fails to adopt resolution on Syria, Available at: http://www.un.org/apps/news/story.asp?NewsID=42513&Cr=Syria&Cr1 [Accessed: 26 January 2013].

Waltz, K. 1979. *Theory of International Politics*. Michigan: The University of Michigan Press.

Waltz, K. 2003. *History as Perennial Structure in The Myth of 1648, Class, Geopolitics, and the Making of Modern International Relations*. Edited by B. Teschke. London; New York: Verso.

White, J.D. 2005. *Global Media: Television Revolution in Asia*. London: Routledge.

Wight, M. 2002. *Power Politics*. Continuum International Publishing Group.

Yiallourides, C.K. 1981. *Minderheitenschutz und Volksgruppenrecht im 20. Jahrhundert unter besonderer Berucksichtigung der Verhaltnisse auf Zupern*. Bochum: Studienverlag Dr. N. Brockmeyer.

Yiallourides, C.K. 2009. *The Incomplete Revolution in Globalisation, European Union and Greece, Political and Economic Aspects*. Edited by P. Siousiouras and C.Hazakis. Athens: Piotita. pp. 225–44 (in Greek).

Yiallourides, C.K. 2010. Incomplete Revolution and Globalised Crisis. *Geostrategics*, pp. 18–19; 23–45.

Chapter 8
Institutionalizing Restorative Justice: Paradoxes of Power, Restoration and Rights

Mara Schiff

Introduction

This chapter arises from my participation in the First International Symposium on Restorative Justice and Human Rights held in Skopelos, Greece in June, 2012. Prior to the event, my intention was to discuss the rights of minority youth disproportionately marginalized by increasingly harsh and punitive school disciplinary policies and the possibilities of restorative justice to help repair and restore such rights (Bazemore and Schiff, 2005). However, once in Skopelos, I elected to recontextualize my discussion to reflect upon important points made by previous presenters. My experience at the Symposium thus far had led me to ponder the possibility that the success of restorative justice in educational, juvenile or criminal justice institutional contexts may be intrinsically limited by the broader complex power structures within which such reform is situated. That is, Western culture's delicate economic, social and political bases of power require the existence of corresponding class and status imbalances. So, informed by a critical criminological approach (Sykes, 1974), alongside elements of critical race (Bell, 1980, 2000) and structural violence (Gil, 2004, 2008) theories, I revised my presentation and subsequent paper to suggest that any possibility for restorative justice to offer more than a marginalized alternative approach for dealing with complex justice issues may be quite limited without considerable systemic overhaul addressing inherent race and class biases in our institutions. While I am increasingly demoralized about the possibilities of such reform in light of recent tragic events (such as the Trayvon Martin shooting in Florida and other similarly racialized criminal and educational events), perhaps some less apocalyptic approach to reforming justice and educational institutions may exist, and I explore that possibility in this paper.

While I am not a critical criminologist, critical race or structural violence theorist and make no claims to be expert in these areas, my thoughts during this Symposium pushed me to dance briefly in this arena as I reflected on the continued marginality of restorative justice. I suspect this condition may have less to do with the philosophy's own intrinsic merits or faults, and rather more to do with the degree to which: 1) its non-adversarial, dialogue driven and collaborative structure threatens existing definitions and understandings of law and the implementation of justice; and 2) there is inadequate recognition of the justice structures it seeks to alter and within which it must be implemented.

During and since the Symposium, I have increasingly wondered if restorative justice's inability to achieve a level of mainstream acceptance is less about what it actually *does*, and more about failing to understand and insinuate itself within the political and organizational environments upon which it depends for its political and economic survival. That is, the guiding and inalienable values and principles of restorative justice (inclusion, respect, fairness, tolerance, acceptance and so on) stand virtually in diametric opposition to the values of retributive systems (such as punishment, isolation, deprivation, proportionate infliction of harm) which characterize both our justice and school disciplinary approaches. Retributive philosophy and its corresponding legal structures fundamentally differ from a restorative vision based on values consistent with social justice ideals. According to Pavlich (2009), restorative justice is inherently limited by its implementation through 'programs that complement, are located within, or even carried out under the auspices of state justice agencies' (p. 24). As I will explore in this paper, that also means inherently racialized, unequal and unfair systems that cannot embrace a concept like restorative justice, which necessarily challenges the structural foundations of such institutions.

I propose here that perhaps the success of restorative justice depends on its ability to create 'learning organizations' (Senge, 1990) within justice and educational institutions. Restorative justice advocates must collectively shift institutional conceptions of power such that sustainability depends *less* on criminalizing the behavior of marginalized populations and *more* on the capacity to embrace such others as essential contributors to crafting socially, politically and fiscally responsible models of justice. One way to do this may be by creating learning organizations (Senge, 1990) that simultaneously transform the thinking of their members and the organizations themselves toward a more responsible and restorative conception of justice. While I have no idea how to actually *do* this, fortunately the obligations of this chapter and book do not require that conclusion, instead I propose simply to begin a dialogue about its potential feasibility and then let others consider if this is a conversation worth pursuing. I hope to reflect both the spirit and the nature of the symposium that encouraged such mental meandering without either judgment or the need to be right.

The purpose of this paper is to: 1) explore the complex relationship between restorative justice and the theoretical and cultural contexts that characterize institutional power structures inherent within and surrounding its implementation; 2) propose that its ability to survive the twenty-first century intact may be, ironically, by embracing and gradually changing the very same institutions that currently limit its success. After discussing some of the literature on justice and forms of power, I will consider the capacity of restorative justice to emerge from its status as a marginalized alternative to existing punitive school discipline or criminal/juvenile justice sentencing strategies. I consider whether such mainstreaming of restorative justice may require recreating justice and educational institutions as learning organizations that embrace restorative values and principles. Ultimately, I believe that restorative justice advocates are faced with a dilemma; either be co-opted by retributive and punitive legal institutions, or co-opt the co-opters into believing that the future of the justice process lies in an inclusive, collaborative, participatory, restorative approach.

Problem Statement

A friend called me today with a horrific story about her 12-year-old honors student daughter who had been charged with class D terrorism following public disclosure of a private paper she wrote and published on a private Facebook page. The paper detailed a fantasy murder mystery in which a disliked teacher is murdered by one of a group of phantasmagorical Disney-like animals. While the paper is certainly inappropriate in trivializing a violent crime and its potential hurtfulness to another human being, it was hardly a terrorist threat worthy of police attention. This student was lucky enough to have a highly educated, street and system savvy, white mother who knew what to do and who to address to make this ridiculous charge disappear. Though not, however, the ostracism engendered by an adolescent co-conspirator turned adversary to gain advantage among her socially conscious pre-teen peers. Sadly, this former honors student was removed from school to be home schooled by her sensitive, self-employed and available mother.

While both mother and daughter were left shell-shocked by the unforeseen consequences of a single thoughtless act and with a lingering sense of injustice, I am left wondering what would have happened had this child been black, poor and the daughter of a undereducated mother afraid or incapable of fighting charges from an unjust education and justice system (Fikes, 2012)? What if this had been a simple case of one child threatening another in the chest-puffing way that kids of this age will do? What if this had not occurred in a relatively privileged, mostly white community but in a poor, mostly minority, understaffed and under-resourced school district? From a restorative justice perspective, this case was a perfect opportunity for the school to gather the affected adults and youth, sit them down together in a restorative circle and simply ask:

- What happened?
- What harm occurred and what was the impact?
- Who is responsible?
- What needs to happen to repair the harm? (Zehr, 2002)

Restorative justice is a simple and rather obvious way to deal with an act that had limited, if any, seriously harmful consequences for those involved, but which did have significant social and relationship impacts. However, the intersection of the education system that reported the incident and the justice system that responded suggests what may happen to (often poor and minority) youth when adults in charge fail to consider the context in which such behavior occurs, and when such behavior (even of honors students) threatens the delicate balance of power that adults maintain over youth in their care and, correspondingly and similarly patronizingly, that governmental justice systems maintain over their subjects. In an adversarial legalistic power structure the position of winner or loser is too often dictated by skin color, socioeconomic status and access to resources of power. So, in the spirit of the Symposium's informed and rambling dialogue that did not require organized or documented thought, I am left to consider:

> Given the nature of the United States' socially unjust, structurally violent criminal justice, juvenile justice and education enterprises, is it possible for restorative justice to survive and transform such systems to produce socially just results, or is restorative justice more likely to get compromised and co-opted by the overwhelming dominant cultural ethos (and corresponding power structures) of the organizations it seeks to transform? Ultimately, is restorative justice strong enough to co-opt the co-opters?

Literature Review

Basic Overview of Restorative Justice and its Relationship to Justice and Educational Institutions

Some decades ago, Platt (1977) suggested that the juvenile justice system was primarily a middle-class mechanism invented for the purpose of controlling lower-class immigrant youths. Bortner (1988) later contended that the juvenile justice system was created to imbue youths with middle-class societal values and behaviors that essentially extended state control and oppression by those with power and privilege. Petersen (1995) proposed that policies directed at youth are designed and implemented by political and other public officials who create punishment-oriented policies 'to demonstrate that they are "getting tough" on crime' (ibid., p. 638). By extension, getting tough on crime suggests that those who do not accede to formal legal structures and corresponding social control will be penalized for their transgressions against the social order.

Over the last 25 years, restorative justice has emerged as an internationally recognized response to crime, delinquency and school rules violations. In the justice system, Van Ness (2005) reports that approximately 100 countries now utilize restorative justice, while Umbreit (2008) estimates that there are over 300 victim–offender mediation programs in the United States of America and over 700 in Europe. Bazemore and Schiff (2005) estimated there were over 700 juvenile conferencing programs in the US around 2001. Moreover, supranational organizations including the Council of Europe (2006), the European Union (2001) and the United Nations Economic and Social Council (1999, 2002) have publicly commended and encouraged the use of restorative practices (Richards, 2010).

Restorative practices have been incorporated in nearly every stage of the criminal justice and education systems, including disciplinary and other behavioral issues in schools (Morrison, Blood and Thorsborne, 2005; Schiff and Bazemore, 2011; Reistenberg, 2012). Richards (2010) reports use of restorative approaches in first-offender diversion programmes in both criminal and juvenile courts (Rodriguez, 2007), alternative sanctioning options for adult offenders (Bonta et al., 2002), use in crimes of violence such as sexual assault and sexual abuse (Cossins 2008; Daly 2006; Daly and Stubbs 2007), domestic violence (Coker 2006; Stubbs 2007; Gavrielides and Artinopoulou 2012), homicide (Eschholz, Chiricos and Gertz, 2003; MacGregor 1996; Molhan 1996; Pranis 2001; Swift 1994; Tillis, 2013), other acts of severe violence (Umbreit, Bradshaw and Coates, 1999, 2003; Gavrielides, 2012a; Gavrielides, 2012c) including hate crimes (Dixon and Ray 2007; Umbreit, Coates and Vos, 2002; Umbreit, Lewis and Burns, 2003; Volpe and Strobl 2005; Gavrielides, 2012b) and with prisoners on death row (Beck, Britto and Andrews, 2007; Umbreit and Vos 2000). Shapland et al. (2006) suggest 'that restorative justice is among the most ubiquitous new approaches for dealing with offending in the West (ibid., p. 505).'

According to Howard Zehr (1990), the use of restorative justice requires a fundamental 'paradigm shift' away from a justice response where crime and deviant behavior is located within individuals who are blamed for such behavior – as in a retributive justice model – to an inclusive, participatory, dialogue driven and empowering community-based justice (Zehr, 1990; Pavlich, 2009). Restorative dialogue models all generally require that offender(s), victim(s) or a victim representative, a facilitator, and other family and/or community members sit face-to-face in an informal meeting to consider the impact of a crime or harm on victims and communities and then to develop a plan to repair this harm. The dialogue process is not intended to establish guilt or innocence, affix blame, or impose punishment, and participants do not rely on formal legal procedures or attorneys to reach decisions. What makes the specific encounter and the process itself 'restorative' is the extent to which the process *adheres to a set of core principles and a focus on the overall goal of repairing the harm* crime causes (Van Ness and Strong, 1997, 2001; Bazemore and Walgrave, 1999). As suggested above, restorative justice practices have been implemented in a range of organizational and community contexts (Braithwaite, 2002; Bazemore and O'Brien, 2002) and – based on hundreds of studies, including a number of randomized experiments – restorative approaches have achieved the status of an evidence-based practice (see Sherman and Strang, 2007; Bonta et al., 2002; Latimer, Dowden and Muise, 2005; Umbreit, Coates and Vos, 2002).

The principles of restorative justice consider crime a violation of individuals, relationships, and communities that 'creates obligations to make things right' (Zehr, 1990, p. 181) in a process wherein justice is more than simply punishing, or *treating*, lawbreakers. Instead, a *restorative* response to crime, harm, and/or conflict seeks to do justice by repairing the harm caused to victims, offenders and community and, to the greatest extent possible, rebuilding the relationships damaged by crime and other conflicts. Achieving justice, and meaningful school discipline, in a restorative way invites stakeholders to hold offenders or rule-breakers accountable, not by asking them to take the punishment, but by ensuring that they take *responsibility* by making amends to their victims and the community. A restorative justice response includes two primary components: 1) a non-adversarial decision-making process that allows stakeholders to discuss the harm done to victims, while considering needs of all participants; and 2) an agreement for going forward based on the input of these stakeholders about what is needed to repair the harm.

The strength and integrity of a restorative intervention is determined by the degree of adherence to *core principles* which prioritize the extent to which: 1) the response repairs the harm to victim, community, offenders and their families; 2) each stakeholder is involved in the discussion of the incident and is given input into the plan for repair; and 3) community and government roles (including the criminal justice and education systems) are transformed to allow communities a greater voice and increased responsibility for responding to community conflict, while criminal justice and other enforcement systems (like school discipline) assume a more facilitative role (Christie, 1977; Pranis, 2001; Van Ness and Strong, 1997).

Why then, despite the widespread international adoption of restorative practices and the increasing evidence of its effectiveness, has the idea remained marginalized and failed to produce the fundamental overhaul of criminal justice envisioned by the movement's early advocates (Bazemore and Maruna, 2009)? Maruna (2011) contends that 'the ghettoizing of restorative ideas into interventions designed for adolescents caught committing misdemeanor or very low-level criminal offenses (shoplifting, unsafe driving) in so many jurisdictions has tarred the "restorative" brand and raised the serious risk of 'net-widening' (Cohen, 1985, p. 667).' However, perhaps such marginalization is not by accident, but is actually part of a larger and more endemic rejection of restorative values that would tend to increase social justice, share power with unpopular groups, question the legalistic status quo that criminalizes the behavior of poor minority citizens, and reduce reliance on established mechanisms of criminal and juvenile justice that fuel an established order of economic and political power? The following sections explore this possibility.

Critical Criminology, Critical Race Theory and the Production of Justice

A critical criminological perspective suggests that the law has been designed specifically for the purpose of preserving the rights and privileges of the powerful at the expense of more vulnerable classes (Sykes, 1974). The underclass is further deluded into thinking that they have a stake in preserving this structure which either protects their interests or offers a career path necessary for their economic well-being (ibid., 1974). From this vantage point, the poor may break the rules no more often than the privileged, but are more likely to be caught and captured because:

1) their lives are more visible to public surveillance on the street; 2) they are more expendable for the purpose of deterring others from such behavior; 3) they fuel the economy not by their labor but rather by their role as 'inputs' into the criminal justice machine; and 4) their 'obedience' is necessary to preserve the institutions that provide the jobs that employ much of the middle class. Moreover, the rules imposed to control their 'illegal' behavior may contradict their own normative subcultural values, thus criminalizing the acts made necessary (for instance, drug sales – a major cause of incarceration in the US) to obtain a decent and desired middle-class existence. This vulnerability is exacerbated by the hostility felt at being subject to a social order they had little hand in creating and are excluded from participating in fully (ibid., 1974).

Consistent with critical criminology, critical race theory (CRT) argues that law in modern Western societies reflects the subjective perspective of the dominant white, affluent, adult, male (Hudson, 2006). Critical race theorists (such as Bell, 1992, 1995, 2000; Ladson-Billings and Tate, 1995; Simson, 2012) purport that racial disproportionality is the result of a centuries long process of 'negative racialization of non-white groups in the United States as racial "others" who do not "truly" belong to the US social fabric and can be treated accordingly' (Simson, 2012, p. 11). CRT further suggests that the liberal agenda of civil rights, integration, affirmative action, and other measures is insufficient to address deeply rooted beliefs and impacts of racism. Standards and institutions created by and fortifying white power mask an inherently white supremacist organization of power, whether consciously or not. In this way, what are promulgated as rational or objective truths in fact both simultaneously conceal and promote the manner in which the privileged objectify their claims and thus promote them as universal veracities. CRT organizes a body of science wherein 'people of color have deliberately chosen race-conscious orientations and objectives to resolve conflicts of interpretation in acting on the commitment to social justice and antisubordination' (Bell, 1995, citing Calmore, 1992).

According to this analysis, codified racism in law and legal systems leaves people of color, 'especially African Americans, subject to unequal protection of the laws, excessive surveillance, extreme segregation, and neo-slave labor via incarceration, all in the name of crime control' (Brewer and Heitzog, 2008, p. 626). Hudson (2006, citing Naffine, 1990) contends that criminal justice discourse and its practices further invoke and reproduce the male, white subjectivity of law. Prominent in education literature and bleeding into justice arenas, CRT suggests that such racial exclusion is not an accidental oversight, but is in fact the inevitable result of liberal political philosophy.

Social Justice and Structural Violence

Consistent with Bell's (1995) CRT, Gil (2004) argues that socially unjust societies, such as the US, create forms of structural violence that, intentionally or not, maintain economic, social and political forms of domination and control over less well-off citizens. Such structural violence preserves inequalities of 'rights, responsibilities and opportunities' that institutionalize existing discriminatory power structures in public schools and justice systems (ibid., 2004, p. 3). Whereas socially just societies promote values consistent with restorative justice, such as equality, liberty, individuality and cooperation, socially unjust societies tend to promote values of inequality, domination, selfishness, disregard for community, competition (ibid., 2004). This set of socially unjust values promotes a subtle structural violence that develops and sustains such institutionalized injustices as poverty, hunger, racism, homelessness and unemployment. As such, the socially unjust and violent society creates victims of its citizens who are simultaneously blamed for their dire circumstances (like poverty and underemployment) and systematically prevented from escaping them (through adequate public education, a living wage, sufficient jobs or available health care). In such a culture, underprivileged individuals are responsible for their unfortunate experiences, while the privileged are rewarded and congratulated for theirs. The collective is nowhere held responsible for the conditions that allow and promote either experience, nor the disparity between them, causing a collateral structural victimization as well.

At some point, such contrivances of social injustice become embedded in a culture that promotes, and whose recipients begin to accept, these consequences as normal and acceptable. The violence resulting from such inequity is both blamed and perpetrated on *individuals* who are *individually* held responsible for society's inability to uphold their rights to a decent life. The culture that allows such conditions to fester is *not* held accountable for injustices such as intolerably high crime rates, inadequate education, pervasive homelessness, inescapable poverty, inadequate health care and so on. Government institutions are thus seen as rational and justified in their use of repressive force to control the actions of individuals, and such cultural and structural violence is promoted as a necessary means to control the unacceptable actions of the oppressed and reinforce adherence to the status quo order.

When integrated with CRT and critical criminology, structural violence theory suggests that unjust societies must define and criminalize the behavior of racial minorities to preserve the illusion that crime, school rules violations or other aberrations in the established social order are 'normal,' and thus can and should be punished with additional and corresponding violence. In this worldview, the violence perpetrated on those defined as criminal or delinquent is both justifiable and necessary to preserve the social order and prevent consequential chaos. By this standard, denying rights to such rule violators is both acceptable and laudable as it preserves the standard of living rightly due to middle and upper class citizens who maintain the status quo through their law-abiding behavior, taxes and acquiescence. In this model, a defensible response to breaking the law is *not* to teach socially conscious behavior, nor shower the violator with love and compassion, nor to question the societal conditions that breed crime, indignity and disrespect to others, but rather to punish the offender to teach him a lesson. Despite significant evidence to the contrary, the idea that punishment will result in law-abiding behavior and will deter others is prominently touted not because it works, but because it maintains a necessary social, political and economic class order.

Disproportionate Minority Contact (DMC) in Justice and Educational Institutions

The system's differentially unjust treatment of minorities is reflected in the concept of disproportionate minority contact (DMC), which documents the extent to which minorities, and especially African Americans, are disproportionately represented at all levels of the criminal and juvenile justice systems (Cabanis et al., 2006). DMC has seeped dangerously into public education systems where disciplining children in school and turning their behavior into punishable delinquency is the predicable outcome in the context of a larger *cultural intention* to maintain the superiority of powerful white citizens at the expense of less privileged black others (Skiba, 2012; Losen and Gillespie, 2012; Osher, 2013). For example, national data in the US showed that in 2000, black students represented only 17 per cent of public school enrollment but accounted for 34 per cent of suspensions (Advancement Project, 2005); special education students (mostly black and minority) represented 8.6 per cent of public school students, but 32 per cent of youth in juvenile detention nationwide (NAACP, 2005); and black students with learning disabilities were three times more likely to be suspended than similarly situated white students and four times more likely to end up in correctional facilities (Poe-Yamagata and Jones, 2000). Other data show that nearly 1 out of every 6 African American students is suspended, as compared with 1 out of 20 for white students (1 in 12 Native American and 1 in 14 for Latinos). The number increases to 1 in every 4 for African American students with learning disabilities, a full 16 percentage points higher than for white students with comparable disabilities (Losen and Gillespie, 2012). This cannot be simply by accident.

Recent data from Texas shows that white students were typically disciplined for mandatory offenses like truancy, fighting on school grounds or other physical assault, while black students had a 31 per cent higher chance of removal from the classroom for discretionary offenses, such as disrespecting a teacher, offensive language or classroom disruption (Fabelo et al., 2011). Moreover, students suspended or disciplined for discretionary offenses were more likely to encounter the juvenile justice system, and students who were suspended or expelled (for any reason) had a greater likelihood of contact with the juvenile justice system in their middle or high school years, particularly when they were disciplined multiple times (ibid., 2011). Tragically, the alarming and disproportionate rate at which minority students who are subject to school disciplinary violations end up in the juvenile justice system is now referred to as the 'school-to-prison pipeline' because of the disarmingly high rate at which such students are transferred from classrooms to courtrooms (Advancement Project, 2011).

While the recognition of DMC is critically important, it is also an example of what Peterson (1995) calls 'experts' constructing both social problems and their solutions, while powerless or marginalized outsiders are relegated to passive roles as recipients of, in this case, 'justice,' with limited capacity to participate in effectuating the policies that govern their lives (ibid., 1995). From the CRT perspective, policies designed to respond to DMC will still reflect the interests of elite policymakers rather than policy recipients, and such 'experts' will retain exclusive domain over the problem's definition and solution that continue to put both the problem and its solution in polarizing racialized terms.

As suggested in previous sections of this paper, cultures such as in the US will continue to regulate and criminalize poor people's problems where racial minorities (and especially youth) are more likely to be poor and therefore subject to increasing government control and surveillance.[1] Governmental control over social problems such as delinquency will breed ongoing racial disparity and discrimination in the juvenile justice and education systems where policymakers, unlikely ever to be the recipients of their own policies, have no real investment in empowering such others. In this scenario, professional policymakers, intentionally or not, support an existing social order with its corresponding balance of privilege and deprivation. Rather than challenging the disparities and coercion of the juvenile justice system, the status quo typically remains unchecked under the guise of new public policies labeled as 'reforms.'

An example of this occurred with the tragic school shooting in Newtown, Connecticut sensationalized in detailed 'infotainment' media accounts (Buckingham, 2004). As followed Columbine and other horrific acts of violence in schools that criminalize deranged shooters who somehow gain unauthorized access to school grounds, subsequent policy focuses on increased surveillance, restriction and security rather than the underlying violent conditions that breed such responses. Following the Columbine shooting, the US initiated zero tolerance policies in schools in an attempt to limit weapons and guns in schools. Following Newtown came cries for increased gun control and security measures in schools, including placing armed police patrols in every school and militarized practice drills for teaching young students (as young as 5 or 6) how to hide or escape from such events. While these 'reforms' may not necessarily be wrong or bad in themselves (though I have grave concerns about traumatizing young children with drills ostensibly for their own welfare), the unintended consequences are an increasingly militarized public school system, and a detour from the more difficult problems of the anger and frustration bred in increasingly unequal and inattentive school and justice systems.

1 According to the 2010 US Census report, 12.4% of white youth live in poverty, as compared with 38.2% black and 35% Hispanic youth (SOURCE: U.S. Bureau of the Census, Income, Poverty, and Health Insurance Coverage in the United States: 2010, Report P60, n. 238, Table B-2, pp. 68–73.)

The Intersection of Western Justice Systems and the Restorative Justice Ideal

As suggested by Pavlich (2009) and others, restorative justice is in the strange and paradoxical position of trying to breach the social order of governmental justice and educational systems while also trying to simultaneously integrate within those same institutions. As restorative approaches find tenuous footing in both justice and educational policy arenas where many local and international jurisdictions are implementing some form of restorative practice, they find increasing favor with both liberals and conservatives. Liberals contend that restorative justice serves as an effective alternative to punitive and destructive models of imprisonment, school suspension, expulsion and disciplinary referral, and enhances social justice while offering a way to heal or rehabilitate salvageable offenders or school miscreants. Conservatives are increasingly arguing that it can be an effective alternative to costly forms of imprisonment that still holds offenders accountable to victims and communities (Richards, 2011; Right on Crime, 2011).

Non-partisan 'justice reinvestment' strategies (Maruna, 2011; Fox, Alburtson and Warburton, 2011) argue that the level of crime can and should be reduced in the most efficient way possible 'to create a more law-abiding society at a lower cost than the traditional detect/convict/punish approach (Fox et al., 2011, p. 122)' and that restorative justice is precisely the means to accomplish this (Maruna, 2011). However, while national and international calls for increased use of restorative justice are slowly emerging, the average citizen has still never heard of it. He has, however, heard of such policies as 'three strikes and you're out,' 'zero tolerance,' 'mandatory sentencing,' or 'stand your ground' gun laws, to name a few retributively-oriented laws.

However, is it possible that restorative justice remains limited because, as CRT would contend, even a liberal conception of justice requires the presence of an established other in order to define right/wrong or good/bad? These others are defined by their lack of that which distinguishes them from the powerful majority they stand in contrast to, specifically power, money and generally white skin (Hudson, 2006). In other words, even well-meaning and socially conscious liberals must 'constantly reproduce divisions and constitute new divisions between the rational and the irrational, the civilized and the barbaric (Hudson, 2006),' which results in isolating, disparaging and demonizing the lifestyles and behavior of poor, black and female identities. Hudson (2006), Maruna (2011) and Simson (2012) all argue that restorative justice stands the best chance of resolving such disparity, however none offer a systematic, operational mechanism by which to do so.

Moving Restorative Justice from the Margins to the Mainstream

The above discussion suggests that the justice structure produced in western, postindustrial, postmodern (Miller and Fox, 2007) societies necessarily marginalizes minority populations and dictates disproportionate outcomes, whether intentionally or not. In this analysis, justice systems must reflect the socially unjust, structurally violent societies within which they operate, and there will always be losers in a justice system whose existence requires a criminalized underclass that feeds the production of justice.

Restorative justice, or any social justice reform initiative for that matter, can only topple this machine by: 1) implicitly acknowledging and confronting its threat to the status quo and the structural and real violence inherent in that order (as in Bell, 1995; Gil, 2008, 2004; Hudson, 2006); 2) learning to speak and then subvert the language and practices inherent in such justice systems to a language that Hudson (2006) calls a language of 'discursiveness, relationalism and reflection;' 3) using this understanding to create 'learning organizations' (Senge, 1990) of justice institutions. Moving restorative justice from the margins to the mainstream is a far greater challenge than implied by the mere presence or absence of restorative justice programs, policies and procedures within existing unjust criminal justice, juvenile justice, or educational environments, or by the existence of evidence-based empirical and scientific support. It requires attending to the sociostructural environments within which such reform is implemented.

This suggests that without addressing the balance of power inherent in and necessary to sustain Western sociopolitical and legal institutions, the open, flexible, inclusive approach proffered by restorative justice may be quite unwelcome. If even a liberal social order depends on the presence of a demonized other in order to maintain and justify elements of social control, and restorative justice circumvents that order by promoting dialogue based on equality and fair hearing of ***all*** a participant's narratives – irrespective of race, origin, orientation or other distinguishing characteristic – it may thus create a subtle (or not-so-subtle) backlash of resistance. In order for restorative justice to succeed, perhaps it must include attention to the environmental conditions that preclude its success and limit its widespread application. Moreover, in a structurally violent and racist society, the means of implementing justice must also be necessarily violent and racist, as first evidenced by unconscionably high incarceration rates for even minor and non-violent crimes and, second, by the disproportionately high number of minorities included in that population. A compassionate and inclusive vision of justice would have to be minimized, or even ridiculed, as a weak and unfeasible strategy for producing justice.

Whether the successful implementation and exercise of restorative justice can ever be divorced from the political, social, economic and cultural context within which it is designed, operated and is implemented is questionable (Pavlich, 2005, 2009). Pavlich (2005) suggests that restorative justice has created a somewhat schizophrenic identity by characterizing itself as a philosophical approach distinct from existing justice institutions but which is 'undermined by the manner in which [it] positions itself as supplementary and ultimately subordinate to state justice enterprises (p. 21).' Some advocates argue that restorative justice can only successfully operate once disengaged from the existing power structures within which its inherent 'restorativeness' is necessarily compromised (see Sullivan and Tifft, 2001). However, Gil (2008) contends that the successful operationalization of restorative justice can occur through conscious, systematic and long-term integration within governmental organizations that may, over time, enable successful reform of socially unjust values and corresponding institutional practices. According to Gil (2008), it is both possible and preferable to create structurally just societies through non-violent and strategic means rather than radical and revolutionary ones, and such change requires:

> pos[ing] challenging questions and engag[ing] people in reflection and dialogue concerning the consequences of prevailing social, economic, political and cultural realities for the quality of their lives and their beahviours … One cannot help others to extricate themselves from the dominant ideology and culture unless one is no longer afraid to acknowledge one's alternative perspective (ibid., p. 509).

Given the nature of the criminal justice, juvenile justice and education enterprises, the question becomes whether such institutionalization is more likely to produce the desired, transformative socially just results that Gil (2008) suggests, or is the integrity of restorative practices more likely to be compromised and co-opted by stronger and more powerfully currents, as Pavlich (2005) suggests? *Is restorative justice ultimately strong enough to co-opt the co-opters?* Below, I explore the possibility that maybe one part of the answer may lie in adopting a business strategy popularized two decades ago by Peter Senge (1990) in his identification and description of learning organizations. I have, at this time, no answers for how such implementation may occur, but rather am simply considering the idea as a possible strategy for more fully introducing and integrating restorative concepts within existing justice and educational institutions.

Learning Organizations, the Five Disciplines and Restorative Justice

One of restorative justice's great strengths is the passion and commitment of its advocates. In that respect, it is unlike any other branch of juridical thought. Advocates are attracted and committed to restorative justice because it resonates with their own deeply held beliefs in the rightful order of people, things and relationships. I have never been in a room full of restorative justice advocates where I was not moved by the power of their passion, conviction and commitment, and gratified to be among them. This was true in Skopelos and a large part of what made it such a powerful and dynamic event. Restorative justice is never just what we do, it is who we are, and in that respect it is different from other justice approaches. That said, we are now obligated to identify, characterize, organize and act upon that passion and shared vision to develop ways of systematically shifting justice thought and action in institutions that may not simply resist restorative justice, but may have considerable reason to suppress it, as suggested above.

Somewhat ironically, the sustainability of restorative justice may perhaps benefit by borrowing from a decades-old business model. Peter Senge's (1990) learning organizations model may offer a broad strategy for addressing some of the issues that confront restorative justice in its quest to integrate a socially just, restorative approach within existing discriminatory justice and educational institutions. Senge's model may provide a structure by which to do what Gill (2008) suggests by systematically changing the nature and implementation of what is considered justice and within justice organizations. According to Peter Senge (1990: 3) learning organizations are:

> organizations where people continually expand their capacity to create the results they truly desire, where new and expansive patterns of thinking are nurtured, where collective aspiration is set free, and where people are continually learning to see the whole together.

While Senge did not design his conversation to address structural social inequity, his model can perhaps be appropriately diverted to address some of the concerns raised in this chapter. Senge (1990) presents 'the Five Disciplines' necessary to create a learning organization, which are described and related to restorative justice and social inequality below. For restorative justice to succeed, it must confront current sociostructural and cultural obstacles that impede its progress as a fully-fledged justice model (Walgrave, 1999; Schiff and Bazemore, 2001), and perhaps one strategy is to begin at the organizational level. I use the term organization quite broadly here to include governments, their institutions, their agents and the communities they serve. Addressing the broader inequalities that pervade justice systems and prevent fully exercising the potential of restorative justice may require a clear and consistent platform that: 1) is consistently promoted across cultures, countries, and jurisdictions; 2) sets a broad strategy for implementation across this variety of cultural contexts; 3) considers the degree to which restorative justice and social justice are entwined and then takes a firm position on it. While a primary premise of restorative justice is flexibility and adaptability to different cultural contexts, and I do not mean to minimize this, success may also require promulgating specific and viable operational goals, values, objectives and principles that translate clearly across any cultural divide and that include clear and consistent operational strategies. Most importantly, there must be some agreement among restorative justice advocates that issues of social justice, addressing racial and other forms of discrimination and promoting tolerance are central and critical elements of all restorative endeavors. Perhaps by considering the learning organization model, restorative justice can begin to characterize a flexible, though universal, implementation strategy to slowly and subtly insinuate social and racial consciousness within governmental and non-governmental organizations across individual jurisdictions and cultures.

The Five Disciplines and Restorative Justice

Discipline 1: Systems Thinking

Senge defines systems thinking as a framework for seeing patterns and interrelationships where people shift from feeling like powerless individuals in powerful organizations where individual actions have no consequences, to a broader vision in which larger systemic patterns can be identified and either minimized or reinforced to gain and sustain a competitive advantage. Restorative systems thinking would require a collective capacity to identify local and international patterns and interrelationships that either promote social injustice or confront it, and then empower individuals to use restorative justice as a means to disable perceptions of individual powerlessness in the face of overarching justice and educational organizations. In this larger world view, advocates might devise systemic strategies for implementing restorative values that promote equal justice, and communicating that these are indispensable for longer term sustainable justice. This might require mobilizing a large base of international academic, policy, institutional and practical restorative justice supporters to collectively overcome our fragmentation, and a corresponding failure to adequately emphasize the importance of social justice in systemic restorative justice implementation.

Perhaps this would require creating a 'restorativist' professional ideology that explores the importance of social justice in criminological interventions generally, how these are addressed by restorative interventions specifically, and how these might be more fully integrated into justice institutions and research (Cullen and Gendreau, 2001). A restorativist ideology would outline core values, beliefs and principles where social justice is an essential element of criminal justice, and where justice is measured and defined as more than simply producing harm in response to harm. The object might be to demonstrate the effectiveness and efficiency of generating restorative outcomes that increase productivity, improve relationships and enhance communities in response to harm, rather than the opposite.

Discipline 2: Personal Mastery

Senge characterizes personal mastery as a series of practices and principles that include three important elements: personal vision, creative tension and commitment to truth. According to Senge, mastery is never something that can be achieved, but is rather a lifelong learning journey toward increasing awareness. 'People with a high level of personal mastery are acutely aware of their ignorance, their incompetence, their growth areas' (Senge, 1990, p. 142). Personal vision involves aligning goals and objectives with a sense of a real vision to create a clear picture of a desired future. For restorative justice, this vision may first mean clarifying restorative values and principles in some universally accepted structure and corresponding organizing document that can inform international restorative initiatives and standards at the programmatic, policy and legislative levels. It may require a clear vision of what restorative justice would actually look like when implemented on a global scale.

More importantly, this may involve establishing some concurrence on a set of restorative social justice goals to which advocates commit and to which all restorative initiatives adhere. Social justice is inherently and intrinsically linked to racial justice, and thus we cannot consider restorative justice on a worldwide scale without acknowledging its impact, both direct and indirect, on social and racial objectives. That is, restorative initiatives must all contribute in some fashion to the production of social justice and racial equality, implicitly or explicitly. While to some degree this already occurs, and is implied in any restorative initiative, it is not overtly acknowledged in any systematic fashion that recognizes the overarching specific and measurable social justice goals inherent in restorative justice. As suggested by personal mastery, this may not be something we ever achieve, but it must always be something we systematically strive toward.

Senge's *creative tension* involves identifying gaps between vision and current reality, which in turn should provide a source of creative energy to achieve organizational vision. The vision will either pull the reality toward it, or the reality will pull the vision downward. This is at the heart of the this chapter's central question; is restorative justice strong enough to co-opt its retributive co-opters, or can it pull toward its own vision of a reparative, healing and just system?

Commitment to truth is a relentless willingness to uncover limiting and deceptive beliefs alongside a quest for truth causing a deep awareness of the structures that underlie and generate events, and then using this awareness to change the structures and produce the different, and intentional, results. This is central to this chapter's contention that looking deeply at the underlying social, economic and political structures that preclude a restorative justice system is essential. As Pavlich (2009) suggests and others imply, it may be virtually impossible to impose true justice in an unjust system. As suggested by Maruna (2011) and others, restorative justice has fallen far short of its original justice system transformative goals. Restorative justice advocates often fail to honestly and relentlessly identify what is being missed in comparison to desired goals, and to develop systematic strategies for moving closer to that vision. That is, we may tend to live inside a box of our own making. The tension between the reality of trying to define and implement socially just restorative processes within socially unjust retributive societies, as well as the tension of trying to define what restorative justice *is,* while maintaining its flexible and adaptive principles, must be acknowledged and confronted. Articulating such definition and distinction must be an open and explicit element of all restorative work, and an essential element in transforming discriminatory justice and educational systems.

Discipline 3: Mental Models

Mental models rely on understanding the world and taking action based on assumptions that may sub- or unconsciously motivate behavior and either move us forward or hold us back. Our mental models constrain us to familiar ways of thinking and acting, and limit our ability to either perceive opportunities that seem inconsistent with our preconceived notions or to develop them. Restorative justice advocates have been satisfied with finding niches in existing governmental systems from which to implement programs and with meeting the needs of limited numbers of juveniles and students. These are constraints imposed by limited mental models of what's possible and how to achieve it.

In some counties and US states, legislation has promoted restorative responses in both education and juvenile justice. However, such initiatives are intrinsically limited by the inherently racist governmental and policy systems within which they are designed and implemented, the limited perspectives of those designing the policies, and the assumption that restorative justice must work within these to make progress. It is virtually impossible to promote socially and racially just initiatives in societies that thrive on injustice. As such, restorative advocates must consider how to expand the limited and inherently discriminatory mental models that currently dominate the justice and educational systems, and consider how such models can be transformed to include values, principles and practices consistent with a restorative vision. Moreover, as suggested by Gil (2008), this monumental task requires confronting systems that paradoxically promote fairness and equity while thriving on the injustice required for their continued existence, and doing so by 'pos[ing] challenging questions and engag[ing] people in reflection and dialogue' (ibid., p. 509). As I stated earlier. I have no idea how to do this, but I think it is a goal worthy of pursuit and a vision worthy of admiration. Restorative justice advocates must envision a mental model of the future that addresses the imbalances in current systems and makes a just model profoundly preferable to an unjust one.

Discipline 4: Shared Vision

Clear and shared goals, values, and missions inspire others to want to contribute and breed commitment. Shared vision requires creating and building a joint mission, and demands identification of commonly shared purposes and coherent activities. Restorative justice has perhaps managed this on a broad scale, but not a specific and well-defined one (Gavriliedes, 2008). Learning organizations require a shared vision that encourages commitment, new ways of thinking and acting, risk-taking, experimentation and long-term commitment. While restorative justice practitioners and researchers are typically highly committed, experimental and visionary thinkers and actors, they do not always share a common vision for how to develop and implement restorative practices and policies nor, more importantly, how to create organizational environments that might welcome such a vision. In addition, there is not a shared sense of the extent to which social and racial justice is an essential element of the restorative mission, and some might argue that restorative justice is explicitly *not* about changing class and power structures, but simply about resolving individual cases fairly and equitably. I think the two are inseparable and that, ultimately, just case outcomes cannot occur in unjust systems. A clear commitment to overcoming inbred structural inequalities that breed criminal injustice as well as racism, classism and sexism is essential to overcoming the structural inequities that preclude acceptance of restorative practices.

Perhaps restorative justice alone cannot be exclusively expected to rectify such social inequalities, but it can and should help to create an environment that supports tolerance, inclusion, and respect, all necessary precursors to justice. At some point, restorative vision and corresponding practices must coalesce to overcome systemic institutional tolerance for structural injustice. While admittedly, again, I have no idea how to achieve this, I do believe it is possible to envision a system that holds people in honor and respect rather than in scorn and contempt and that it is undoubtedly impossible to achieve this without first holding a vision of such a system.

Discipline 5: Team Learning

Finally, restorative advocates must be encouraged to trust one other, complement each other's strengths, compensate for each other's weaknesses, and aim for higher goals than possible to achieve individually. Restorative justice has suffered from the lack of a team mentality that has, in some cases, created an individualistic rather than a collective approach and a divisiveness rather than inclusiveness (Gavriliedes, 2008). Restorative justice cannot survive without a shared team mentality that promotes the kind of systemic change required to eliminate disparity and produce social, criminal, juvenile and educational justice. It is essential to marshal the individual and collective strengths of restorative advocates into some form of a unified strategy. Perhaps this is through an inclusive international accrediting, training and/or research organization, or some other strategy. But there is, in this age of instantaneous electronic communication, no reason we can or should not be easily connected and in regular communication and be able to formulate shared vision, goals and strategies.

Conclusion: The Possibility of the Learning Organization Model for a Sustainable Restorative justice

In the spirit of the Skopelos symposium, I have explored here the idea that restorative justice offers a possible solution to extant social justice ills, but is limited both by the institutional culture within which it operates as well as its own internal limitations. I have reviewed a variety of theories on social injustice that characterize current justice and educational institutions and that make the implementation of restorative justice exceptionally challenging and politically unfavorable. Some theorists and researchers (Maruna, 2011; Hudson, 2006; Simson, 2012; Shapland et al., 2006), suggest that restorative justice holds promise for overcoming some of the structural obstacles that preclude a more rational and just response to harm, and I think it is time to undertake that challenge.

I don't know if overcoming injustice through restorative approaches is possible or not. It may be that we, as restorative advocates, must content ourselves with small wins that grow increasingly more popular and promising over time and across jurisdictions, but which can never really alter the structure of systematic cultural and social injustice. Perhaps, as Aristotle suggested, injustice as a broad abstract concept can never be fully overcome, eradicated or even identified. Rather, injustice can only be addressed time after time, once and again, in each of the small efforts individuals undertake to make the world a better and more tolerant place (Nicomachean Ethics). Perhaps this is what restorative justice is about and the best, and worst, it can hope to achieve. As I was finishing this chapter, a major article appeared in the New York Times magazine in which restorative justice was utilized of a tragically murdered teenager. In weighing the benefits and costs of the process, the author reflected, 'In hindsight, Kate [the victim's mother] sees the restorative justice process as a sort of end in itself. "Just being able to have the circle made it a success" Kate said.' (Tillis, 2013). That this article appeared in a major and reliable news publication perhaps indicates a not so small victory. The nearly 500 comments on the article are mixed in their response, but as a whole at least indicate the possibility of restorative justice entering US national public discourse in 2013 and being used as something other than an ancillary alternative to traditional justice processes.

In suggesting that restorative justice advocates might consider lessons from a learning organization strategy to begin systematically addressing the social, racial and other inherent injustices systematically perpetrated by our social welfare systems, I have tried to integrate a multidisciplinary approach to look outside our sometimes myopic criminal justice lens and consider lessons from other, unexpected disciplines. I don't know if this idea makes sense or not, and I certainly don't know how to operationalize it. But, fortunately for me, my task here was simply to think about some interesting ideas and present them for others to consider, not to have the answers or know what to do about the questions. In the end, the question remains for you to consider: *Is it possible for restorative justice to transform the systems upon which it depends for survival to produce socially just results, or will it be compromised and co-opted by the inherently racist and discriminatory organizations it seeks to transform? Ultimately, is restorative justice strong enough to co-opt the co-opters?*

References

Advancement Project. 2005. *Education on Lockdown: The Schoolhouse to Jailhouse Track.* Available at http://www.advancementproject.org/sites/default/files/ publications/FINALEOLrep.pdf

Bazemore, G. and Maruna, S. 2009. Restorative justice in the reentry context: Building new theory and expanding the evidence base. *Victims & Offenders*, 4, pp. 375–84.

Bazemore, G. and O'Brien, S. 2002. The Quest for a Restorative justice Model of Rehabilitation: Theory-for-Practice and Practice-for Theory. In: Lode Walgrave (ed.), *Restorative Justice and the Law*. Cullompton: Willan Publishing. pp. 31–67.

Bazemore, G. and Schiff, M. 2005. *Juvenile Justice Reform and Restorative Justice: Building Theory and Policy from Practice*. Cullompton: Willan Publishing.

Beck, E., Britto, S., and Andrews, A. 2007. *In the shadow of death: Restorative justice and death row families*. New York: Oxford University Press.

Bell, D. 1980. 'Brown v. Board of Education and the interest convergence dilemma.' *Harvard Law Review*, 93, pp. 518–33.

Bell, D. 1992. *And we are not saved: the elusive quest for racial justice*. New York: Basic Books.

Bell, D. 1995. '1995 commencement address—Howard University School of Law.' *Howard Law Journal* 38, pp. 463–71.

Bell, D. 2000. 'Brown v. Board of Education {74 S. Ct. 686 (1954)}: forty-five years after the fact.' *Ohio Northern University Law Review* 26(2), pp. 171–81.

Bonta, J., Wallace-Capretta, S., Rooney, J. and McAnoy, K. 2002. 'An outcome evaluation of a restorative justice alternative to incarceration.' *Contemporary Justice Review* 5(4), pp. 319–38.

Bortner, M.A. 1988. *Delinquency and justice: An age of crisis*. New York: McGraw-Hill.

Braithwaite, J. 2002. 'Setting Standards for Restorative justice', *British Journal of Criminology* 42(3), pp. 563–77.

Brewer, R. and Heitzog, N. 2008. 'The Racialization of Crime and Punishment: Criminal Justice, Color-Blind Racism, and the Political Economy of the Prison Industrial Complex.' *American Behavioral Scientist* 51, p. 625.

Buckingham, J. 2004. 'Newsmaking' criminology or 'Infotainment' criminology?' *Australian and New Zealand Journal of Criminology*, 37(2), pp. 253–75.

Cabanis, E.R., Frabutt, J.M., Hendrick, M.H. and Arbuckle, M.B. 2006. 'Reducing disproportionate minority contact in the juvenile justice system: Promising practices.' *Aggression and Violent Behavior* 12 (2007), pp. 393–401.

Calmore, J. 1992. Critical Race Theory, Archie Shepp, and Fire music: Securing an Authentic Intellectual life in a multicultural world. *Southern California Law Review*, 65, pp. 2, 129–231.

Christie, N. 1977 'Conflicts As Property.' *British Journal of Criminology* 17(1), pp. 1–15.

Cohen, S. 1985. *Visions of Social Control: Crime, Punishment, and Classification*. Cambridge,: Polity Press.
Coker, D. 2006. Restorative justice, Navajo peacemaking and domestic violence. *Theoretical Criminology* 10(1), pp. 67–85.
Cossins, A. 2008. Restorative justice and child sex offences: The theory and the practice. *British Journal of Criminology* 48(3), pp. 359–78.
Council of Europe. 2006. *Recommendation of the committee of ministers to member states on assistance to crime victims*. Paris: Council of Europe.
Cullen, F.T. and Gendreau, P. 2001. 'From nothing works to what works: Changing professional ideology in the 21st century.' *The Prison Journal* 81(3) (2001), pp. 313–38.
Daly, K. 2006. Restorative justice and sexual assault: An archival study of court and conference cases. *British Journal of Criminology*, 46, pp. 334–56.
Daly, K. and Stubbs, J. 2007. Feminist theory, feminist and anti-racist politics, and restorative justice. In G. Johnstone and D. Van Ness (eds), *Handbook of Restorative Justice*. Cullompton: Willan Publishing, pp. 149–70.
Dixon, L. and Ray, L. 2007. Current issues and developments in race hate crime. *Probation Journal* 54(2), pp. 109–24.
Eschholz, S., Chiricos, T. and Gertz, M. 2003. Television and Fear of Crime: Program Types, Audience Traits, and the Mediating Effect of Perceived Neighborhood Composition. *Social Problems* 50, pp. 395–415.
European Union. 2001. *Council Framework Decision of 15 March 2001 on the standing of victims in criminal proceedings*. Brussels: European Union.
Fabelo, T., Thompson, M.D., Plotkin, M., Carmichael, D., Marchbanks III, M.P. and Booth, E.A. 2011. *Breaking Schools' Rules: A Statewide Study of How School Discipline Relates to Students' Success and Juvenile Justice Involvement.* The Council of State Governments Justice Center. New York, NY.
Fikes, R. 2012. Breathing while Black: rude and frightful encounters with the police recalled by distinguished African Americans, 1860–2012. *Journal of Pan African Studies*, 5(5), p. 41.
Fox, C., Albertson, K. and Warburton, F. 2011. Justice reinvestment: Can it deliver more for less? *The Howard Journal*, 50(2), pp. 119–36.
Gavrielides, T. 2008. 'Restorative justice: the perplexing concept. Conceptual fault lines and power battles within the restorative justice movement' *Criminology and Criminal Justice Journal* 8(2), pp. 165–83.
Gavrielides, T. 2012a. *Rights and Restoration within youth justice*, Whitby, ON: de Sitter Publications.
Gavrielides, T. 2012b. Contextualising Restorative Justice for Hate Crime. *Journal of Interpersonal Violence*. http://jiv.sagepub.com/content/early/2012/05/28/0886260512447575.abstract.
Gavrielides, T. 2012c. Clergy Child Sexual Abuse & the Restorative Justice Dialogue, *Journal of Church and State*. http://jcs.oxfordjournals.org/content/early/2012/04/23/jcs.css041.extract.

Gavrielides, T. and Artinopoulou, V. 2012. Violence against women and restorative justice, *Asian Journal of Criminology.*

Gil, D. 2004. Perspectives on social justice. *Reflections*, 10(4).

Gil, D. 2008. Toward a Radical Paradigm of Restorative justice. In: *Handbook of Restorative Justice: A Global Perspective* (eds), Dennis Sullivan and Larry Tifft. London: Routledge.

Hudson, B. 2006. Beyond white man's justice: Race, gender and justice in late modernity. *Theoretical Criminology* 10(1), pp. 29–47.

Ladson-Billings, G. and Tate, W.F. (1995) Toward a critical race theory of education, *Teachers College Record*, 97, pp. 47–68.

Latimer, J., Dowden, C. and Muise, D. 2005. The Effectiveness Of Restorative justice Practices: A Meta-Analysis. *The Prison Journal* 85(2), June 2005, pp. 127–44.

Losen, D. and Gillespie, J. 2012. *Opportunities Suspended: The Disparate Impact of Disciplinary Exclusion from School.* Civil Rights Project/Proyecto Derechos Civiles: Los Angeles, CA.

Maruna, S. 2011. Lessons for justice reinvestment from restorative justice and the justice model experience. *Criminology & Public Policy* 10(3), pp. 661–9.

MacGregor, S. 1996. *Switch on to your inner strength.* Crows Nest: CALM Pty Ltd.

Miller, H. and Fox, C.T. 2007. *Postmodern Public Administration.* Armonk, NY: ME Sharpe.

Molhan, S. 1996. *A mother's mission: The Sue Molhan story.* South Bend: Diamond Communications, Inc.

Morrison, B., Blood, P. and Thorsborne, M. 2005. Practicing restorative justice in school communities: Addressing the challenge of culture change. *Public Organization Review* 5(4), pp. 335–57.

NAACP Legal Defense and Educational Fund, Inc, 2009. *Annual Report of the NAACP Legal Defense and Educational Fund, Inc. (2007–2009) 43[hereinafter Legal Defense Fund]*, available at http://naacpldf.org/files/publications/NAACPLDF_2007-2009_Annual_Report.pdf.

Naffine, N. 1990. *Law and the Sexes.* Sydney: Allen & Unwin.

Osher, D. 2013. It Is Not About Simple Solutions and Quick Fixes: Lessons Learned from a Comprehensive Districtwide Approach to Improving School Safety and the Conditions for Learning. Presentation at the '*Closing the School Discipline Gap' conference.* Washington, DC.

Pavlich, G. 2005. *Governing paradoxes of restorative justice.* London: The Glasshouse Press.

Pavlich, G. 2009. Critical policy analysis, power and restorative justice. *Criminal Justice Matters* 75(1), pp. 24–5.

Peterson, R. (ed.). 1995. *Crime and Inequality.* Palo Alto: Stanford University Press.

Petersen, R. D. 1995. Expert policy in juvenile justice: Patterns of claims making and issues of power in a program construction. *Policy Studies Journal* 23(4), p. 636. Retrieved from http://ezproxy.fau.edu/login?url=http://search.proquest.com/docview/210562516?accountid=10902.

Platt, A. 1977. *The Childsavers: The Invention of Delinquency*. Chicago, IL: University of Chicago Press.

Poe-Yamagata, E. and Jones, M.A. 2000. *And Justice for Some*. Washington, DC: Building Blocks for Youth. Web site: http://www.buildingblocksforyouth.org/justiceforsome/jfs.html.

Pranis, K. 2001. A cry for love. http://www.restorativejustice.org/resources/docs/cry.

Reistenberg, N. 2012. *Circle in the Square.* St. Paul, MN: Living Justice Press.

Richards, K. 2010. Restorative justice and 'empowerment': Producing. *Critical Criminology*, 19, pp. 91–105.

Right on Crime. 2011. http://www.rightoncrime.com/?s=restorative.

Rodriguez, N. 2007. Restorative justice at Work: Examining the Impact of Restorative justice Resolutions on Juvenile Recidivism. *Crime & Delinquency* 53(3), pp. 355–79.

Schiff, M.F. and Bazemore, G. 2001. Exploring and shaping the future. In: *Restorative community justice: Repairing harm and transforming communities*, G. Bazemore and M. Schiff (eds), pp. 333–47.

Senge, P.M. 1990. *The fifth discipline: The art and practice of learning organization*. London: Century Business.

Shapland, J., Atkinson, A., Atkinson, H. and Colledge, E. 2006. Situating restorative justice within criminal justice. *Theoretical Criminology* 10(4), pp. 505–32.

Simson, D. 2012. Restorative Justice and its Effects on (Racially Disparate) Punitive School Discipline (May 12, 2012). *7th Annual Conference on Empirical Legal Studies Paper*. Available at SSRN: http://ssrn.com/abstract=2107240 or http://dx.doi.org/10.2139/ssrn.2107240.

Skiba, R. 2012. Reaching a Critical Juncture for Our Kids: The Need to Reassess School-Justice Practices. *National Leadership Summit on School-Justice Partnerships: Keeping Kids in School and Out of Court*. New York: New York State Permanent Commission on Justice for Children.

Sullivan, D. and Tifft, L. 2001. *Restorative Justice: Healing the Foundations of our Everyday Lives*. Foreword by H. Mika. Monsey, New York: Willow Tree Press. Second edition 2005.

Swift, J. 1994. *A cry for justice: A mother's journey to confront the killer of her children*. Boca Raton: Cool Hand Publications, Inc.

Sykes, G.M. 1974. *The Journal of Criminal Law and Criminology (1973)*. Vol. 65, No. 2 (June, 1974), pp. 206–13. Northwestern University. Article Stable URL: http://www.jstor.org/stable/1142539.

Tillis, P. 2013. Can Forgiveness Play a Role in Criminal Justice? *New York Times Magazine*. 4 January, 2013. http://www.nytimcs.com/2013/01/06/magazinc/

can-forgiveness-play-a-role-in-criminal-justice.html?pagewanted=all&_r=0.

Tyler, T., Sherman, L., Strang, H., Barnes, G. and Woods, D. 2007. Reintegrative shaming, procedural justice, and recidivism: The engagement of offenders' psychological mechanisms in the Canberra RISE drinking-and-driving experiment. *Law and Society Review*, 41(3), pp. 553–85.

Umbreit, M., Bradshaw, W. and Coates, R. 1999. Victims of severe violence meet the offender: Restorative justice through dialogue. *International Review of Victimology* 6(4), pp. 321–43.

Umbreit, M., Bradshaw, W. and Coates, R. 2003. Victims of severe violence in dialogue with the offender: Key principles, practices, outcomes and implications. In E. Weitekamp and H.-J. Kerner (eds.), *Restorative justice in context: International practice and directions*. Cullompton: Willan Publishing. pp. 123–44.

Umbreit, M.S., Coates, R. and Vos, B. 2002. The impact of restorative justice conferencing: A multi-national perspective. *British Journal of Community Justice*.

Umbreit, M. Coates, R and Vos, B. 2007. Restorative justice Dialogue: A Multi-Dimensional, Evidence-Based Practice Theory. *Contemporary Justice Review: Issues in Criminal, Social, and Restorative justice* 10(1).

Umbreit, M., Lewis, T. and Burns, H. 2003. A community response To a 9/11 hate crime: Restorative justice through dialogue. *Contemporary Justice Review*, 6(4), pp. 383–91.

Umbreit, M. and Vos, B. 2000. Homicide survivors meet the offender prior to execution. *Homicide Studies*, 4(1), pp. 63–87.

United Nations Economic and Social Council. 1999. *Development and implementation of mediation and restorative justice measures in criminal justice*. United Nations Economic and Social Council.

United Nations Economic and Social Council. 2002. *Basic principles on the use of restorative justice programmes in criminal matters*. United Nations Economic and Social Council.

Van Ness, D. 2005. An overview of restorative justice around the world. In: Paper presented to the *Eleventh United Nations Congress on Crime Prevention and Criminal Justice*. Bangkok, Thailand.

Van Ness, D. and Strong, K. 2001. *Restoring Justice*. (second edition). Cincinnati, OH: Anderson Publishing Company.

Volpe, M. and Strobl, S. 2005. Restorative justice responses to post-September 11 hate crimes: Potential and challenges. *Conflict Resolution Quarterly* 22(4), pp. 527–35.

Walgrave, L. 1999. Restorative juvenile justice: In search of fundamentals and an outline for systemic reform. In: *Restorative juvenile justice: Repairing the harm of youth crime* (ed. G. Bazemore and L. Walgrave) pp. 45–74. Monsey, NY: Criminal Justice Press.

Zehr, H. 1990. *Changing Lenses: A New Focus for Crime and Justice*. Scottsdale, PA/Waterloo, ON: Herald Press.

Zehr, H. 2002. *The Little Book of Restorative Justice.* Intercourse, PA: Good Books.

Chapter 9
Relationality in Justice and Repair: Implications for Restorative Justice

Susan Sharpe

Introduction

In the seminal book *Changing Lenses*, Howard Zehr pointed out that a photographer's choice of lens affects what is captured in the photo taken, and also affects the relationships and proportions of the elements that appear (Zehr, 2005, p. 178). In the same way, he said, 'The lens we use to examine crime and justice affects what we include as relevant variables, what we consider their relative importance to be, and what we consider proper outcomes' (ibid. p. 178). He was arguing that our conventional view was shaped by the habit of seeing things in terms of lawbreaking, legal guilt, and punishment. He argued that a restorative lens would capture a more realistic picture, one where the violation of crime would figure more prominently, so that the resulting harm would be more visible, accountability would look different, and the prospect of healing would be included in the frame.

Zehr's central claim was that, 'Crime is a violation of people and relationships' (ibid, p. 181). The first part of the claim is very clear; it rings true when we hear it pointed out that crime harms persons, not the state, and much of the appeal of restorative justice lies in this redirection of attention to those most directly involved in and affected by crime. Yet the second part of this claim gets less attention. The phrase 'and relationships' seems to be considered an obvious extension, something that naturally will be looked after as we include the stakeholders involved in and affected by crime.

This chapter gives more explicit attention to that phrase 'and relationships', thus joining the growing number of scholars who are taking a relational orientation to law, to justice, and to restorative justice (see Downie and Llewellyn, 2012: Harris, 1987; Lederach, 2005; Napoleon, 2004; West, 1997; also Gavrielides and Zellerer in this volume). In writing this I am especially grateful to Theo Gavrielides and Vasso Artinopoulou for inviting me to participate in the Symposium behind this book, because that invitation encouraged me to explore a question that had nagged at me for a decade: might restorative justice be pointing to an unrecognized dimension of human rights? That's a suggestion I have been nervous about making, but when invited to join an exploration of restorative justice and human rights, I could not resist sketching out the claim. Because the Symposium co-hosts fostered such a spirit of inquiry and camaraderie, and because my fellow Symposiarchs were intrigued by the idea, I have taken courage in exploring it further. I hope that readers will also take up the question and consider it with me: might restorative justice be pointing us not only to the need for relational repair, but also to the need for a right to relational repair?

To clarify the question and propose initial considerations, this chapter sets out to do three things. First, it points to the relationality of justice and calls for a shift in the restorative justice world view. Second, drawing on Jennifer Nedelsky's relational approach to rights, it suggests that we might think differently about restorative justice in relation to due process rights. Third, the chapter argues that co-created narrative is an important way of meeting core justice needs, such that opportunities for restorative justice dialogue ought to be considered and protected as a human right.

Relationality: The Missing Ground

Relational theory is a feminist perspective importantly spurred by Jean Baker Miller's work on psychological development (Miller, 1976) and by Carol Gilligan's work on moral development (Gilligan, 1982). As Koggel puts it, 'Relational theory uses as its starting point the fact that human beings exist in relationships' (Koggel, 2012, p. 70).

On the face of it, such a starting point seems unremarkable. It is obvious that humans are importantly connected to others; we live, work, and play in relation to others throughout our lives. But it is not the fact of relationship that is key to relational theory; rather, it is the centrality of relationship that draws the attention of relational scholars (Nedelsky, 2011, p. 19). And for those of us steeped in Western views of human nature, that centrality is easy to miss.

Biologist Mary E. Clark points out that 'every society, every culture has its own theory of human nature, which it takes as *the* truth' (Clark, 2002, p. 2; emphasis in original) and that 'how we humans "see" reality, what we comprehend, is always constructed. Our world view – the working "truth" we use as a map for living – is always culturally created, and it is always a selected and partial understanding' (ibid., p. 2).

We construct such world views because the whole of reality is so complex. We need a working model of reality – a hypothesis to identify what matters and explain how things work – to organize our experience and help us navigate our way (ibid., p. 11). (For discussion of this point in relation to paradigms and restorative justice, see Zehr, 2005, pp. 83–94 or Gavrielides' Chapter 15 in this volume.) The gestalts we use – the working models we inherit or construct – matter in the same way that photographers' lenses do: they govern what is included in the viewing frame, what is foreground and what is background in that frame, and what is in focus and therefore attended to.

In the West, Clark says, our primary world view is an atomistic one where the focus is on individual units who move in reaction to each other, much as billiard balls do. She says, 'In the standard tradition of the Billiard Ball (or "atomistic" or "individualistic") universe, human beings are imagined very much like independent, isolated, bounded objects having a variety of cause and effect "collisions" with each other' (Clark, 2002, p. 8).

That gestalt shapes our institutions too, including our system of criminal justice (ibid., p. 12). We can see this atomistic perspective in the Western legal focus on criminal offenders,[1] in the practice of holding them individually responsible for their actions, and in our habit of leaving victims, families, and communities on their own to recover as best they can from the effects of crime; we can see it in a reliance on punishment, which assumes that offenders will make rational choices to reduce their own pain, and which assumes that an offender can be punished without regard for the effect on his or her family; we can see it in rehabilitation, which seeks to change offenders' motivations and behaviours, without changing systemic factors that influence both; we can see it in an assumption that justice can be a matter of dealing with one dimension of criminal harm – that of the offender's behaviour – and leaving other justice needs (like victims' recovery) to be dealt with separately.

A very different gestalt, a relational world view, governs perceptions in non-Western parts of the world where 'everything in the universe is seen to belong to a single, interconnected whole' (ibid., p. 8). This gestalt sees:

> a world of connectedness, of interacting, interdependent entities, whether they be human bodies, an economy or other social arrangement, an ecosystem, or a galaxy. Within each entity, the parts are likewise interdependent, and it is their reciprocal interactions that keep the whole universe functioning. Indeed, each part, each entity *contains* the whole, *is* the whole, and nothing can survive apart from the whole. No entity is unconnected to, unaffected by, all the others. There are no discrete 'billiard balls'. (ibid., p. 9)

From a relational perspective, humans not only *are* in relationship; we also *are constituted* in relationship, not only as children being formed by our families, communities, and cultures, but also throughout our lives (Nedelsky, 2011, p. 19). We humans exist not only in the material world – on the earth, in the air, in our bodies – but also in interconnection. Our interconnections not only describe us (as in, He has three children, or She is a project manager) but also define us (for example, the spouse I am is shaped by the spouse I have, and the spouse I have is shaped by the spouse I am). The fact that we are fundamentally relational beings is part of what makes violation so potentially damaging, and not only because it can

1 This chapter focuses on the criminal context, because that is the arena where relationality is most circumscribed by the law. However, the point of this discussion would apply equally well to other restorative justice arenas.

disrupt whole constellations of interconnection, but also because it can distort the very ways we are constituted in the world and help constitute the world.

Clark points out that neither the atomistic nor the relational world views offers a complete view of the world. Each contains aspects of the other. Relationships obviously are present and important from an atomistic perspective, and individuals have agency and autonomy in a relationally drawn world. The two gestalts differ in how they organize people's perceptions of the world – as in the famous Rubin goblet, a figure-ground puzzle that invites viewers to see an image as being either a goblet or two faces almost nose to nose. In the Western legal tradition, with its focus on individual rights and responsibilities, we might say that the person is figure and relationship is ground.

Restorative justice, while claiming that crime violates people and relationships, has remained caught in an atomistic world view (Napoleon, 2004, p. 37). We have done a good job of bringing more stakeholders into the picture and even sometimes into the centre of the frame. But we have not changed our lens so as to bring relationality into clearer focus. We have kept individuals as figure and left relationship to ground. We have pointed the camera at relationship, but have not changed the lens so as to bring it into proper view.

We can see a continued atomistic world view in ways that restorative justice echoes the offender focus of the criminal justice system, such as by working only on cases referred by the courts, which means being accessible only in cases where offenders have been caught and, usually, charged. We are focused on offenders as isolated individuals when we argue that restorative justice is effective because it reduces recidivism, or when we routinely deal with offenders individually because our programmes are not of interest to victims. An atomistic view is evident in the restorative justice field's focus on youth crime because young people are still malleable and therefore still deserving of a second chance.

We also can see an atomistic world view in the extensive literature arguing that restorative justice theory and practice potentially conflict with due process rights, including the right to trial, the right to counsel, and the right to proportional sentencing (see, for example, McEvoy and Eriksson, 2006, p. 329; Skelton and Sekhonyane, 2007, pp. 581–85). With few exceptions,[2] restorative justice scholars recommend resolving this conflict in favour of established rights. On proportionality, for example, John Braithwaite says, 'Within the social movement for restorative justice, there is and always has been absolute consensus on one jurisprudential issue. This is that restorative justice processes should never exceed the upper limits on punishment enforced by the courts for the criminal offence under consideration' (Braithwaite, 2002a, p. 150). Johnstone reaffirms the rightness of that consensus:

---

2 Skelton and Sekhonyane (2007, p. 591) suggest that a concern over due process rights is too narrow, and Walgrave says that proportionality and other due process principles 'remain respectable, but they must be critically checked as to their meaning in a restorative justice context, and possibly be reformulated, rejected or replaced' (2002, p. 216).

> The restorative justice process, no matter how benevolent the intentions behind it and no matter how different it is in its objectives from a punitive process, is still a *criminal justice* process. Hence, arguably those subject to it should be entitled to much the same level of procedural protection as defendants who are prosecuted and tried in the courts' (Johnstone, 2002, p. 31; emphasis in original).

It is noteworthy, though, that discussions of restorative justice in light of due process rights, generally are framed in terms of how restorative justice outcomes compare to those of the courts – that is, whether the rights one would have in the conventional forum are compromised by that same person's participation in the restorative justice forum. A relational gestalt brings into view a question we have not been asking, that is, whether rights attached to the legal forum might compromise rights attached to the restorative justice forum. In other words, are there other rights, relational rights, that we have been overlooking and ought to be considering?

The question can be seen in a 2001 court case (R. v. A.J.R., 2001) in which two youths and an adult were co-accused of robbery with the use of a firearm. For two years the Youth Court had been referring cases to Calgary Community Conferencing (CCC), a local restorative justice programme, for community conferencing; agreements that participants reached at those conferences had been forwarded to the Court and incorporated into its dispositions. In R. v. A.J.R., one youth had pleaded guilty and received disposition; the second youth had pleaded guilty and been referred to CCC; the adult accused had entered a plea of not guilty and was awaiting a preliminary inquiry.

The prospect of a community conference including the victim and one of the offenders, both key witnesses in the case, raised the question of due process rights for the adult co-accused and prompted a hearing on the question of whether a Youth Court should refer to a restorative justice programme any case in which there are unresolved criminal charges pending against co-accused persons (ibid., p. 2). The judge, herself a strong supporter of restorative justice, ruled that a referral in such circumstances would be inappropriate because of the risk of witness taint. She saw a reasonable possibility that the community conferencing discussion might lead one or both witnesses to change their testimony from what was in their original statements, thus undermining their credibility as witnesses and creating an unfairness to the Crown (ibid., p. 16).

The ruling was thoughtful and fair, acknowledging that a change in testimony would not have been the intention behind the community conference. Still, the judge concluded, encouraging these people to discuss the event for which they were both witnesses had the real potential to cause problems for a future prosecution, making it an undue risk. The final ruling read, 'The risk of witness taint is real. This risk and the consequent potential for negatively affecting the prosecution of a co-perpetrator outweigh the benefits which the young person A.J.R. would potentially derive from participating in the program. Accordingly I decline to make the referral' (ibid., p. 23).

From a conventional, atomistic perspective, this ruling is unremarkable. From a legal perspective, the Court had no other choice. But from a relational perspective, we might question it. Is there no possibility that the potential benefits of community conferencing for the young person, or for the victim (who was not mentioned in the judge's reasons), or for both of them, might at least equal the potential for negatively affecting the prosecution of a co-perpetrator?

Readers are likely to find this an absurd question. The importance of a fair trial is so fundamental in Western law that even to consider jeopardizing it for the sake of another person's benefit seems preposterous. The Western mind recoils at the prospect. But why? What makes it axiomatic that an offender's due process needs outweigh others' justice needs? It may be that the strength of an atomistic gestalt is what makes the question seem absurd.

The point here is not to challenge the decision reached in this case or to minimize the profound importance of protecting due process rights. I wholeheartedly agree that the UN Human Rights instruments offer important 'guidance on the foundational values and rights restorative justice processes ought to observe' (Braithwaite, 2002b, p. 567). Certainly, I do not advocate putting at risk anyone's right to a fair trial. Nor do I mean to criticize the Court's priorities, which in this case were shared by the restorative justice programme in question. In fact it was a community conferencing programme coordinator who flagged the witness taint concern for the Court and helped the lawyers think through their arguments on the question (R. v. A.J.R., 2001, p. 3).

The aim here is only to point out that a reflexive, unquestioned deference to due process rights reflects an atomistic world view and the priorities that such a world view privileges. As Jennifer Llewellyn explains:

> Prevailing conceptions of justice that underlie and animate contemporary justice systems (at least in the West and increasingly exported throughout the world) are rooted in a particular set of assumptions about selves and ideal social conditions drawn from the liberal tradition. As a result, these theories privilege the protection of individual independence through separation as the animating ideal of justice. (Llewellyn, 2012, pp. 90–91)

If we find it anathema even to ask about relational rights having the same weight as due process rights, then we are consigning relational concerns to the background and giving them secondary status. Failing to even engage with the question would seem to classify relational repair as a luxury, a benefit to be appreciated when it is available, but not something to insist on or fight for. Is that what we intend?

The point here is simply to invite a closer examination of restorative justice philosophy and its implications for theory and practice. I argue that it is not enough to recognize that it is persons rather than the state who are violated by crime and then to include them in a process of redress; including additional stakeholders makes limited difference if we still view them atomistically. My claim, echoing Jennifer Llewellyn, is that to realize the potential of restorative justice, we must understand it as a relational theory of justice. And understanding it this way 'compels us to take the fact of relationship, of connectedness, as our starting assumption' (ibid., p. 90).

Relationality: Making It Figure

What difference might it make to take connectedness as our starting assumption? Several things might change. Certainly it might prompt us to examine practice patterns to see whether we're tending sufficiently to parties' relational concerns, or to enough of the relationships affected by crime. It might encourage us to respond with restorative justice in all cases of crime, not only in cases where offenders are apprehended and deemed malleable. It might prompt us to distinguish violation from discipline and focus our energy on the former rather than the latter.

An important effect might be to shift our thinking on controversial issues. In some cases that shift might be to redirect our attention; the controversy about punishment, for example, might shift from a definitional debate about pain vs. punishment (for instance, see Gavrielides, 2005 or Sharpe, 2007 for discussion of this debate) to a question of whether or how punishment affects key relationships. A relational focus might shift some of our boundaries, such as by challenging the idea that relationships can be severed by violence or should be severed by redress (such that sexualized assault and domestic violence cases should never be eligible for restorative justice dialogue). Or, the essential point of this chapter, that starting with the fact of our connectedness might shift the priorities we bring to a question of rights.

Legal scholar Jennifer Nedelsky points out that human rights have always dealt with relationship. 'What rights do and have always done is construct relationships – such as those of power, responsibility, trust, and obligation' (Nedelsky, 2011, p. 236). Relationship, however, has not been focal to human rights, and Nedelsky argues that it should be. She says,

> What I propose is that this reality of rights structuring relationships become the central focus of the concept itself and, thus, of all discussion of what should be treated as a right, how rights should be enforced, and how they should be interpreted. It is really a matter of bringing to the foreground of our attention what has always been the background reality. (ibid., pp. 238–9)

Nedelsky also notes that rights are always in contest, always necessitating difficult decisions. In her view, people will do a better job of making those decisions 'if they focus on the kinds of relationships they actually want to foster, what the values at stake in that fostering are, and how different concepts and institutions will best contribute to that fostering' (ibid., 238–9).

More explicitly, Nedelsky proposes that a relational approach would examine rights conflicts by asking a series of four questions: How is law structuring the relevant relations, and how is that structuring related to the conflict? What are the values at stake? What kinds of relationships would foster those values? How would competing versions of a right structure relations differently? (ibid., p. 236). Her questions offer a helpful way to think about the question of rights in relation to conventional vs. restorative justice. The responses offered here are a first pass at relevant considerations and an invitation to further exploration.

First, *how is law structuring the relevant relations, and how is that structuring related to the conflict?* At root, criminal law has defined the offender's relationship to the state as being *the* relevant relation.

Thus, in the court case described earlier, what takes primacy is that one offender has chosen to contest the State's charge. What is foreground (or figure) is the risk created by the State's relationship of power over the accused person who denies the charge against him. Officially relegated to the background are the relationships created and altered by the co-accused who has admitted responsibility in the robbery. Again, the Court's ruling was that the 'potential for negatively affecting the prosecution of a co-perpetrator outweigh the benefits which the young person A.J.R. would potentially derive from participating in the program' (R. v. A.J.R., 2001, p. 23)

Further, criminal law structures relations by distancing victim and offender (and their families or supporters) from each other. In the courtroom, the law structures their relations by controlling what they hear from each other, whether through testimony at trial, victim impact statements, or offender apologies at the time of sentencing – all of which are vetted as lawyers plan their cases and judges determine admissibility (Bibas, 2012, p. 17; Branham and Burr, 2008, p. 1,022; Hayner, 2002, p. 28; Moroney, 2010, p. 94).

The growth of victims' rights legislation has granted some relevance to the relationship between victim and state, and restitution orders acknowledge a debt relationship between victim and offender. However, this does little to challenge the notion of the state–offender relationship as primary. Legal scholar Stephanos Bibas notes that some victims rights measures – including counselling rape victims, sheltering battered women, awarding restitution, or notifications about bail or conviction – are uncontroversial because they do not threaten the state's monopoly of criminal justice (Bibas, 2012, p. 90).

Second, Nedelsky asks *what values are at stake* in a question of which rights should have priority. Answering this question comprehensively could create a long list, but at minimum it would include safety, accountability, denunciation, truth, dignity, and satisfaction. In the list below, I sketch how each of these values might be claimed by the conventional justice system, followed by terms that are also aligned with a restorative justice philosophy.

- Safety: keeping people (both present and potential victims) protected from someone who has shown him/herself to be a danger, whether by threatening or committing harmful behaviour. But safety also means regaining a sense of safety in the world, for example, such that one can relax again in a public setting.

- Accountability: answering to the state for violating its criminal code; suffering some loss at least symbolically commensurate with the loss one has caused someone else. But accountability also means explaining one's behaviour, acknowledging that it was wrong, and taking responsibility for its effects.
- Denunciation: clarifying that harmful behaviour will not be tolerated by the community. But also clarifying why that behaviour is intolerable and affirming the kind of behaviour that is expected instead.
- Truth: building an accurate understanding of what happened, so that decisions about outcomes are sound ones. But truth also calls for a layered understanding of complex events; it needs to reflect emotions, motivations and interpretations, and include the various perspectives from which those events and their after-effects have been experienced.
- Dignity: treating each person with respect and ensuring fair treatment in any processes affecting them. But also the dignity of full personhood, being treated and engaged with as a complex and relational person having complex qualities, needs, and motivations.
- Satisfaction: feeling confident that the violation as been denounced and a price has been paid. But also being able to integrate into one's life the pain and loss stemming from the violation, and being able to move on in healthy ways.

Third, Nedelsky asks *what kinds of relationships would foster those values.* Here too a full response would be more extensive, but it seems that fostering such values might at least require relationships that are:

- Inclusive: involving not only those relationships that law or policy deems relevant, but also other interconnections that are affected by what has happened, that would be affected by the process or the outcomes of redress, or both.
- Voluntary: respecting people's right to engage with those who are importantly connected to them and people's right to set limits on any such engagement.
- Dialogic: allowing for open communication between and among the interconnected parties; communication that is informally structured and that makes space for their stories, questions, and differences.
- Supported: building emotional as well as physical safety by assisting some connections (such as providing accompaniment at difficult times, or advocating for the vulnerable) and protecting against other connections (such as by no-contact orders when desired), in order to help parties prepare carefully for dialogue that is sought and appropriate and to help them participate effectively when it does occur.

Finally, Nedelsky asks *how would competing versions of a right structure relations differently?* Western law has structured relations as an adversarial contest between the state and the accused (along with the lawyers who represent them and the judges who referee and who designate winners). Due process rights (along with other with rules and processes) help to level the playing field between the two contestants, and play is restricted to those two or to others brought in (as witnesses) to assist their competition. People who have relevant information or perspectives are invited to present only the information that prosecution and defence have already gathered and organized into stories that advance their claims. Such information therefore needs to be protected – kept from the contamination of competing information – until it can be officially presented in court.

When interconnection is the priority instead, such as in victim–offender dialogue for the sake of repairing harm, then relations are structured so as to encourage interaction, rather than to limit it, and to help people engage directly with one another. The purpose of the interaction is not to prove a claim and discredit counterclaims, but rather to build shared understandings that reflect all relevant perspectives and incorporate all relevant priorities, and then to share responsibility for making decisions that best meet the greatest number of related needs. Here, structures allow for co-created narrative, wherein each person can tell his or her own story in his or her own terms and highlight its personal significance; each person can also hear each other person's story of the event that connects them and can understand the significance it holds for that other person. As Van Ness and Strong put it, 'This is a subjective rather than objective account; consequently, it has integrity both to the speaker and to the listener' (Van Ness and Strong, 2010, p. 74). Each person's story is informed and potentially changed by each other person's account; together they create a shared understanding larger than either had before they talked about it together.

To clarify the importance of narrative and of its being co-created, it will help to look more closely at the violation of relationship and the significance of relational repair.

Violation and Repair

Violation can harm persons and possessions and restitution can help redress injury or loss. But violation also harms the quality of our relatedness to others, and the greater the violation the more extensive that relational harm is likely to be. This occurs because, as stated earlier, we are constituted in relationship (Nedelsky, 2011, p. 19). Identity is neither formed nor sustained in isolation. Rather, Françoise Baylis says, one's identity is largely a collection of stories that one constructs and maintains over time in relation with others, through a series of actions, interactions, reactions and transactions (Baylis, 2012, p. 110). She points out that identity is fluid, being created and recreated 'at the intersection of what a person claims about herself and what others claim about her. On this view, identity is a balance between self-ascription and ascription by others' (ibid., p. 110).

Violation can be devastating when it seems to signal a frightening imbalance between self-ascription and ascription by others. This may explain why the question of Why me? is so potent in the aftermath of a stranger crime, or How could you do this to me? in cases where a violation feels like the betrayal of an existing relationship. In either case the victim is asking, What was it about me – my person, my bearing, my behaviour – that led you to choose me as the target of your action, or to choose such an action in relation to me?

The need for balance between self-ascription and ascription by others may also explain why it is so important for victims of incest to be believed and protected once they disclose the abuse. Being called a liar, or simply seeing no action taken to intervene, can be understood as a statement about a victim's identity and worth within a family or community. The majority of victims in a study by Judith Herman reported that what they wanted most was to see their abusers deprived of undeserved respect and privilege. 'For those who had been abused by family members, ceremonial gatherings such as holiday celebrations, weddings, and funerals were an important barometer of the perpetrator's standing in comparison to their own' (Herman, J., 2005, p. 594).

Violation can be powerful when it disrupts the story of one's life. As Howard Zehr says, being victimized calls into question our most fundamental assumptions about the orderliness of the world, our sense of autonomy or personal control, and our sense of relatedness – where we fit in a web of social relationships. He says, 'Our lives rest on these three pillars. We built these pillars as we built our lives, from childhood to adulthood, and now they have been knocked out from under us. The core trauma of victimization might be called the "three ds" – disorder, disempowerment and disconnection' (Zehr, 2002, p. 23).

These kinds of disruption are evident in the wake of serious crime, where the emotional aftermath can last months or years (Gustafson, 2005, p. 202–4). Victims of violent crime have an increased risk of PTSD and major depression; victims of domestic violence are more likely to attempt suicide, abuse alcohol or drugs, or be diagnosed as depressed or psychotic (Herman, S., 2010, p. 19). The aftermath can also include a vicious cycle of destruction, as childhood victimization is a critical risk factor for later becoming a violent offender (ibid., p. 20). Zehr explains that childhood victims of trauma may 'establish a sense of autonomy by domination over others, an order based on violence and force, and a sense of relatedness rooted in distrust of others and kinship with fellow "outsiders"' (Zehr, 2002, p. 24). As Gustafson says, trauma interferes with a person's ability to move successfully through the developmental stages of the human life cycle. Thus, 'the experience of both crime victims and criminal offenders is often replete with earlier layers of traumatic experience, complicating the recovery journey for both and, though this is never deterministic, often proving to be criminogenic across generations' (Gustafson, 2005, p. 203).

Being responsible for violation, or accepting responsibility for it, can also disrupt the story of one's life. Gustafson reports that offenders often have complex questions about their own behaviours, asking, essentially, 'How did I allow my life to get so far out of control that I acted in the way I did, creating such painful consequences for my victims, for myself, for our families and loved ones? … How did I get so "bent" that I could believe that shaming and degrading someone else would rid me of my own sense of shame and degradation?' (Gustafson 2005: 202).

For both victims and offenders, then, violation disturbs identity and damages relatedness, often reaching deep into a person's network of interconnection. Recovery requires incorporating the violation into a revised understanding of self, and the process of doing so can allow one to reclaim or reconstitute the meaning, power and connection that were distorted by violation. That reclamation can be a long and complex process involving many paths; one important pathway is narrative.

Renowned trauma specialist Judith Herman says, 'Victims need an opportunity to tell their stories in their own way, in a setting of their choice; the court requires them to respond to a set of yes or no questions that break down any personal attempt to construct a coherent and meaningful narrative' (Herman, J., 2005, p. 574). Victims advocate Susan Herman says that articulating what they experienced and what they need helps victims to regain a sense of control over their lives. She argues that

> These opportunities for victims to talk about their experiences should exist within government and at the community level. In appropriate circumstances, victims should also be afforded opportunities to communicate with offenders, both to impart information about the impact of the crime and to learn more about the crime from the offender. (Herman, S., 2010, p. 62)

Because our identities are embedded in our stories, recreating meaning requires that one re-story one's life in order to incorporate a violation (Zehr, 2002). Healing, Zehr says, comes 'by facing one's past, coming to terms with it, drawing boundaries around it, incorporating experiences of hurt and wrongdoing into a new story' (ibid., p. 24). He says, 'Whether we have victimized or have been victimized, the journey from brokenness and isolation to transcendence and belonging requires us to re-narrate our stories so that they are no longer just about shame and humiliation but ultimately about dignity and triumph' (ibid., p. 28).

Yet being heard is not all that matters. It is important also to hear others' accounts of a shared event. And it is in part because one's own account of an event is never the whole story; as important as it is to define one's own experience, it is equally important to hear others' experience of the same event. It is also because one person cannot possibly see an event from all perspectives; any one person's point of view necessarily misses others. This is in part because memory itself has a relational dimension. Sue Campbell says, 'While sometimes experienced as a feature of our interiority, human remembering also takes place through action, narrative, and other modes of representation in public space and in the company of others' (Campbell, 2006, p. 362). It is with others, Campbell says, that:

> we forge, maintain, and share an accurate view of the past or fail to do so. Reliving and re-appropriating the past in memory is also continuously self-constituting, and our evolving self-conceptions, the shifting lenses through which we re-experience the past, are sensitive to how others affirm, correct, or doubt our interpretations. (Campbell, 2012, p. 135)

Judith Herman says that people in a trauma survivor's social world can influence the outcome of that person's trauma. 'A supportive response from other people may mitigate the impact of the event, while a hostile or negative response may compound the damage and aggravate the traumatic syndrome' (Herman, J., 1997, p. 61).

Susan Miller describes the journeys of two rape victims who for years had carried the sting of victim blaming messages (such as, Did you try to fight him off? Why did you open the door that night?), messages that came from their own loved ones as well as from strangers. She says that both of these rape victims:

> discovered that they fought back incredibly hard against their rapists, accounts that not only surprised the women but also empowered them. Although they remembered some of the things they had said to deflect or defuse the rapist's anger, the additional knowledge the women gleaned during the face-to-face dialogues with the rapists reinforced a sense of courage and competence in saving their own lives. (Miller, 2011, p. 165)

These same victims also were relieved to learn that their rapists had chosen them randomly, which erased the victims' lingering worry that they might have unknowingly done something that resulted in becoming a target (ibid., p. 165). Being relieved of blame can be especially important when violation occurs within the context of an ongoing relationship. In addition to hearing their offenders shoulder full responsibility for abuse that betrayed a trust, such victims can gain something else crucial from dialogue with their abusers. Miller reports that the child sexual assault victims she interviewed 'wanted to demonstrate to the offenders that they were no longer passive or helpless victims; rather, they were in control of their lives and were not going to permit the offenders to (figuratively) overpower them again during the dialogue process and beyond' (ibid., p. 165).

Thus, recovery for these victims was not only about understanding or coming to terms with what had happened to them; it was also about being someone different in the world, and being seen as different by the former abuser. It was about transformed relationship. Taking control of her life had been a gradual process for one young woman who had been abused by her father, and she had accomplished that transformation elsewhere in her constellation of interconnections, outside the relationship with her abuser (with whom she had not had contact for years).

Yet it wasn't quite enough for her to have become a different person. In order to fully integrate the violation and move beyond it, she needed to reconstitute the relationship that had constituted her as a victim. She needed for her abuser to see that she was different from the girl he had been able to manipulate and harm. She needed to say to him, 'I'm not afraid of you. You don't control me' (ibid., p. 90). In other words, she needed to be different *in* that relationship, in the presence of her abuser, in order to loosen its grip on her and to move on freely. Afterwards she said, 'I'm so glad I did it. I'm a different person' (ibid., p. 91).

None of this is to claim that recovery from trauma depends on victims and offenders sitting down together to dialogue. Many victims want no part of talking with people who have harmed them; many offenders would be unwilling or unable to engage with their victims at the level of honesty, responsibility, and remorse that would make such communication safe or productive.[3] But insofar as we are relational beings, violation is relational too, and redress cannot be sufficient if it makes no space for the possibility of relational repair.

Implications

The foregoing is meant to provoke consideration, not to argue a position. But before closing it is reasonable to name some implications.

If indeed relational harm is significant, such that its repair is essential to the work of justice, then avenues for repair must be open on the other side of any crime that violates. That is, if we are fundamentally relational beings, then human rights must include relational rights, including a right to assistance with relational repair.

This is not a claim that existing restorative justice programmes should dramatically expand; how best to protect such a right is no doubt a complicated question to be approached carefully. Nor is this a claim that the courts or other criminal justice institutions should take on responsibility for relational repair; this is proposed not as a positive right that governments should be obliged to provide, but as a negative right that no government should be able to preclude. That is,

3 To be clear, victim–offender communication must be safe on every level, and the more serious the violation the more risky such communication can be. Trauma victims are at risk of having their trauma retriggered; victims of gendered violence are at risk of being further victimized by community members who help abusers deny responsibility; victims of ongoing abuse risk being threatened and controlled even in the midst of apparently non-violent discussion. For all these reasons, the majority opinion has been that victim–offender dialogue is not appropriate for sexualized assault or family violence, and many remain vociferously opposed. Still, as Julie Stubbs notes, the debate has become more nuanced (Stubbs, 2010, p. 103), which is to the good. We all have much to learn about how to respond effectively to these kinds of deeply relational violations.

a claim that, at minimum, no one should be able to block relational work that victims, offenders, or their families or supporters wish to do with each other.

More specifically:

- Referrals for exploring the option of victim–offender dialogue ought to be routine in all cases where offenders acknowledge responsibility for harms resulting from their crimes. The timing of such dialogue should be appropriate to the case and to the needs of the parties, including the responsibilities of the legal system; thus, such dialogue might sometimes be tied to diversion, might sometimes yield sentencing recommendations or have a role in plea agreements, and might sometimes take place post-adjudication, during a period of incarceration or as part of an offender's re-entry to the community. But the option should be open in all criminal cases where there is a guilty plea, rather than in the small subset of cases that get referred at this point.
- Support (from appropriately trained facilitators) for exploring the possibility of victim–offender dialogue ought to be available in all cases where victims are struggling with the aftermath of violence, including cases of family violence or sexualized assault.
- All states should provide for dialogue between interested victims and their incarcerated (or formerly incarcerated) offenders in cases of violent crime.

It is important to note that this proposal does not compromise the voluntariness that is a hallmark of good restorative justice practice. Nothing here claims that anyone should be required to participate in victim–offender dialogue. But they should have the option to do so. As John Braithwaite (2002b, p. 565) says, avoiding domination mandates 'institutional design that gives every stakeholder a meaningful opportunity to speak and be heard'.

Conclusion

This chapter began with a claim that restorative justice has remained caught in the same atomistic world view that defines most Western institutions, including its system of criminal justice, and that 'changing lenses' will require that we deliberately cultivate a relational world view. Taking relationality as a starting point might lead us to view differently a number of things in the restorative justice field; a key one would be to reexamine the restorative justice field's reflexive deference to due process rights. To initiate that re-examination, I suggested responses to four questions Jennifer Nedelsky poses for resolving contested rights and argued that co-created narrative is an important path toward recovery from the effects of violation. To clarify the value of co-created narrative, I highlighted some of the difference that interaction can make to reconstituting identity on the other side of serious violation. Finally, I suggested that relational repair is important enough to merit protection as a human right, such that the opportunity for victim–offender dialogue should be routine rather than subject to case by case referral, and that policies should not preclude on principle the exploration of appropriate communication between victims and their offenders.

Claiming that people have a right to relational repair is a bold one to make. It invites a host of thorny questions, and embracing the claim would further complicate already conflicted terrain. But Nedelsky is right that we can do a better job with those thorny questions if we pay attention to how we structure relations and if we choose structures that best foster the values our institutions are founded on. Therefore I am heartened by this book's invitation to revisit the philosophy of restorative justice, and I am hopeful that readers will examine this claim for its fit with that philosophy. Perhaps doing so will enrich both.

Lynn Hunt closes *Inventing Human Rights* with encouragement to continue improving on the eighteenth-century version of human rights (Hunt, 2007, p. 212). The cascade of rights continues, she says, always with great conflict and slowed down by courts and institutions. Still, 'The history of human rights shows that rights are best defended in the end by the feelings, convictions, and actions of multitudes of individuals, who demand responses that accord with their inner sense of outrage' (ibid., p. 213).

Many restorative justice practitioners know that sense of outrage. It is heartbreaking to hear from victims who for years have hungered for an apology for behaviour that ripped apart their lives. It is heartbreaking to hear from violent offenders who for years have wanted to apologize to their victims. It is heartbreaking to hear again and again of the profound difference it can make to dialogue in the wake of violation, yet still to hear court officials and policymakers say that victim–offender dialogue is out of bounds for the vast majority of cases. When we take relationality as our starting point, recalling that crime violates persons *and relationships,* that boundary becomes even more troubling. It is time to examine it through a new lens.

References

Baylis, F. 2012. The Self *in Situ*: A Relational Account of Personal Identity, in *Being Relational: Reflections on Relational Theory and Health Law*, edited by J. Downie and J.J. Llewellyn. Vancouver, Toronto: UBC Press, pp. 109–31.

Bibas, S. 2012. *The Machinery of Criminal Justice*, New York: Oxford University Press.

Braithwaite, J. 2002a. In Search of Restorative Jurisprudence, in *Restorative Justice and the Law*, edited by L. Walgrave. Cullompton: Willan, pp. 150–67.

Braithwaite, J. 2002b. Setting Standards for Restorative Justice. *British Journal of Criminology*, 42, pp. 563–77.

Branham, M. and Burr, R. 2008. Understanding Defense-Initiated Victim Outreach and Why it is Essential in Defending a Capital Client. *Hofstra Law Review*, 36, pp. 1,019–33.

Campbell, S. 2006. Our Faithfulness to the Past: Reconstructing Memory Value. *Philosophical Psychology*, 19(3), pp. 361–80.

Campbell, S. 2012. Memory, Reparation, and Relation: Starting in the Right Places, in *Being Relational: Reflections on Relational Theory and Health Law*, edited by J. Downie and J.J. Llewellyn. Vancouver, Toronto: UBC Press, pp. 132–60.

Clark, M.E. 2002. *In Search of Human Nature*. New York: Routledge.

Downie, J. and Llewellyn, J.J. (eds.) 2012. *Being Relational: Reflections on Relational Theory and Health Law*. Vancouver, Toronto: UBC Press.

Gavrielides, T. 2005. Some Meta-Theoretical Questions for Restorative Justice. *Ratio Juris*, 18(1), pp. 84–106.

Gilligan, C. 1982. *In a Different Voice: Psychological Theory and Women's Development*. Cambridge, MA: Harvard University Press.

Gustafson, D. 2005. Exploring Treatment and Trauma Recovery Implications of Facilitating Victim–Offender Encounters in Crimes of Severe Violence: Lessons from the Canadian Experience, in *New Directions in Restorative Justice: Issues, Practice, Evaluation*, edited by E. Elliott and R.M. Gordon. Cullompton: Willan, pp. 193–227.

Harris, M.K. 1987. Moving into the New Millennium: Toward a Feminist Vision of Justice. *Prison Journal,* Fall–Winter, pp. 27–38.

Hayner, P. 2002. *Unspeakable Truths: Facing the Challenge of Truth Commissions*. New York: Routledge.

Herman, J. 1997. *Trauma and Recovery*. New York: Basic Books.

Herman, J. 2005. Justice from the Victim's Perspective. *Violence Against Women*, 11(5), pp. 571–602.

Herman, S. 2010. *Parallel Justice for Victims of Crime*. Washington, DC: National Center for Victims of Crime.

Hunt, L. 2007. *Inventing Human Rights: A History*. New York: Norton.

Johnstone, G. 2002. *Restorative Justice: Ideas, Values, Debates*. Cullompton: Willan.

Koggel, C. 2012. A Relational Approach to Equality: New Developments and Applications, in *Being Relational: Reflections on Relational Theory and Health Law*, edited by J. Downie and J.J. Llewellyn. Vancouver, Toronto: UBC Press, pp. 63–88.

Lederach, J.P. 2005. *The Moral Imagination: The Art and Soul of Building Peace*. Oxford: Oxford University Press.

Llewellyn, J.J. 2012. Restorative Justice: Thinking Relationally about Justice, in *Being Relational: Reflections on Relational Theory and Health Law*, edited by J. Downie and J.J. Llewellyn. Vancouver, Toronto: UBC Press, pp. 89–108.

McEvoy, K. and Eriksson, A. 2006. Restorative Justice in Transition: Ownership, Leadership and 'Bottom-up' Human Rights, in *Handbook of Restorative Justice: A Global Perspective*, edited by D. Sullivan and L. Tifft. London: Routledge, pp. 321–35.

Miller, J.B. 1976. *Toward a New Psychology of Women*. Boston: Beacon Press.

Miller, S.L. 2011. *After the Crime: The Power of Restorative Justice Dialogues Between Victims and Offenders*. New York: New York University Press.

Moroney, S. 2010. Restorative Options for an Offender's Spouse, in *The Promise of Restorative Justice: New Approaches for Criminal Justice and Beyond*, edited by J.P.J. Dussich and J. Schellenberg. Boulder: Lynne Rienner, pp. 75–104.

Napoleon, V. 2004. By Whom, and By What Processes, Is Restorative Justice Defined, and What Bias Might This Introduce?, in *Critical Issues in Restorative Justice,* edited by H. Zehr and B. Toews. Monsey, NY: Criminal Justice Press, pp. 33–45.

Nedelsky, J. 2011. *Law's Relations: A Relational Theory of Self, Autonomy, and Law*. New York: Oxford University Press.

R. v. A.J.R., 2001 ABPC 120

Sharpe, S. 2007. The Idea of Reparation, in *Handbook of Restorative Justice*, edited by G. Johnstone and D.W. Van Ness. Cullompton: Willan, pp. 24–40.

Skelton, A. and Sekhonyane, M. 2007. Human Rights and Restorative Justice, in *Handbook of Restorative Justice*, edited by G. Johnstone and D.W. Van Ness. Cullompton, Devon, UK: Willan, pp. 580–97.

Stubbs, J. 2010. Restorative Justice, Gendered Violence, and Indigenous Women, in *Restorative Justice and Violence Against Women*, edited by J. Ptacek. NY: Oxford University Press, pp. 103–22.

Van Ness, D.W. and Strong, K. 2010. *Restoring Justice: An Introduction to Restorative Justice*. New Providence, NJ: Matthew Bender.

Walgrave, L. 2002. Restorative Justice and the Law: Socio-ethical and Juridical Foundations for a Systemic Approach, in *Restorative Justice and the Law*, edited by L. Walgrave. Cullompton: Willan, pp. 191–217.

West, R. 1997. *Caring for Justice*. New York: New York University Press.

Zehr, H. 2002. Journey to Belonging, in *Restorative Justice: Theoretical Foundations*, edited by E.G.M. Weitekamp and H. Kerner, pp. 21–31.

Zehr, H. 2005. *Changing Lenses: A New Focus for Crime and Justice* (third edition). Scottsdale, PA: Herald Press.

Chapter 10
Rights and Restoration in Canada: Reflections on Practice, Law and Theory

Brenda Morrison

> Where, after all, do universal human rights begin? In small places, close to home – so close and so small that they cannot be seen on any map of the world. Yet they are the world of the individual person: the neighborhood he lives in; the school or college he attends; the factory, farm or office where he works. Such are the places where every man, woman, and child seeks equal justice, equal opportunity, equal dignity without discrimination. Unless these rights have meaning there, they have little meaning anywhere. Without concerted citizen action to uphold them close to home, we shall look in vain for progress in the larger world.

Eleanor Roosevelt, 1958, on presenting *In Your Hands* to the United Nations, in response to a worldwide, year-long observance of the Tenth Anniversary of the Universal Declaration of Human Rights.

United Nations: Human Rights and Restorative Justice in Canada

It was with hesitation that Canada signed the Universal Declaration of Human Rights (UDHR) in 1948, due to discomfort within the Federal Cabinet on substantive norms enshrined in the Declaration (Schabas, 1998). Lester B. Pearson, who was the Canadian Minister of External Affairs at the time, abstained from the vote within the United Nations' General Assembly. Member States saw this as a 'puzzling and isolated position' for Canada, as every other state signed except for so-called Soviet bloc states (ibid.). Pearson prevailed in readjusting Canadian policy and signed three days later. Schabas (1998) argues that this sombre prelude begs the acknowledgement of challenges faced by Canada in recognizing human rights norms. After signing the UDHR, Pearson went on to be awarded the Nobel Peace Prize in 1958 and became Prime Minister of Canada in 1960. In 1982, the Federal Government modified Canada's Constitution in order to better reflect the human rights goals and standards set by the UDHR. There are now four key mechanisms to protect human rights: Canadian Charter of Rights and Freedoms; Canadian Human Rights Act, Human Rights Commissions and provincial human rights laws and legislation. More recently, Canada has played a key role in the negotiations of United Nations Convention on the Rights of the Child which was adopted by the Assembly in 1989 and signed by Canada and 193 other countries in 2010.

The United Nations has also played a part in the international development of restorative justice, beginning with the Working Party on Restorative Justice (1998):

> It is our belief that the United Nations has a unique opportunity to help shape a new model for criminal justice and crime prevention, one which will serve to restore peace in communities and societies throughout the world.

The working party endeavoured to use a Delphi process to come to a consensus definition of restorative justice. When successive iterations failed to produce consensus among scholars, the working party settled on adopting the definition put forward by Tony Marshall (1996):

> Restorative justice is a process whereby all the parties with a stake in a particular offence come together to resolve collectively how to deal with the aftermath of the offence and its implications for the future.

This was the definition presented to, and ultimately adopted by, the United Nations. In April 2000, Canada and Italy played leading roles at the UN Commission on Crime Prevention and Criminal Justice through introducing a resolution proposing the development of basic principles on the use of restorative justice. This resolution was approved unanimously, through the sponsorship of thirty-eight other countries, and referred to the Economic and Social Council (Van Ness, 2003). Canada again took the leading role, hosting a meeting of restorative justice scholars, practitioners and advocates in late 2001. In July 2002, the United Nations Economic and Social Council adopted 'Basic Principles on the Use of Restorative Justice Programmes in Criminal Matters', endorsing guidelines to encourage member states to implement restorative justice in the operation of their domestic juvenile criminal justice systems. In April 2005, at the UN Congress on Crime Prevention and Criminal Justice, a further declaration was adopted:

> To promote the interests of victims and the rehabilitation of offenders, we recognize the importance of further developing restorative justice policies, procedures and programmes that include alternatives to prosecution, thereby avoiding possible adverse effects of imprisonment, helping to decrease the caseload of criminal courts and promoting the incorporation of restorative justice approaches into criminal justice systems, as appropriate.

In December 2006, the United Nations Office on Drugs and Crime published the *Handbook on Restorative Justice Programmes* (Dandurand and Griffiths, 2006), which was developed to assist governments with criminal justice reforms, through providing practical information on the concept of restorative justice, types of restorative processes used throughout the world and how to create and manage those programmes. Many of the restorative justice programmes and practices highlighted in the handbook were developed in Canada and the handbook was written by two Canadian scholars, Drs. Yvon Dandurand and Curtis T. Griffiths, with the support of the Canadian government. The Handbook explains how restorative justice is different from traditional justice practices:

> Restorative justice programmes are based on the belief that parties to a conflict ought to be actively involved in resolving it and mitigating its negative consequences. They are also based, in some instances, on a will to return to local decision-making and community building. These approaches are also seen as means to encourage the peaceful expression of conflict, to promote tolerance and inclusiveness, build respect for diversity and promote responsible community practices (ibid., p. 5).

> Restorative justice programmes are based on the fundamental principle that criminal behaviour not only violates the law, but also injures victims and the community. … Restorative justice refers to a process for resolving crime by focusing on redressing the harm done to the victims, holding offenders accountable for their actions and, often also, engaging the community in the resolution of that conflict (ibid., p. 6).

In 2009, at the First World Congress on Restorative Juvenile Justice, deliberations took place on the UN Convention on the Rights of the Child (CRC); in particular, Art. 40(1) of the CRC, to treat children in conflict with the law in a manner consistent with the promotion of the child's sense of dignity and worth:

- to reinforce the child's respect for the human rights and fundamental freedoms of others;
- to promote the child's reintegration and the child's assuming a constructive role in society.

In summary, Canada has played a strong leadership role in the United Nations endorsement of human rights, children's rights and restorative justice, laying the foundation in changes within Canada's legal framework. The question remains, how important are these state-based agreements in leveraging support for restorative justice and upholding human rights in Canada, particularly at a community level?

Restorative Justice and Canadian Law

In 1996, the sentencing principles in the Canadian Criminal Code (CCC) were amended to encourage the use of community-based processes and a focus on restorative elements such as the need to promote a sense of responsibility in offenders and for offenders to acknowledge and make reparation for the harm they have done to their victims and to the community (see Daubney, 2010). These provisions arose out of a Royal Commission on Sentencing (1984–1987), who published their report, *Taking Responsibility,* in 1988. The report recommended significant research and development of restorative justice at all levels of the judicial system: federal, provincial and local (see Morrison and Pawlychka, 2010, for review).

In contrast to so-called tough on crime penalties, the CCC states that offenders should not be deprived of the human right to liberty if less restrictive sanctions may be appropriate in the circumstances [S. 718.2 (d)] and that all available sanctions other than imprisonment, that are reasonable in the circumstances, should be considered for all offenders, with particular attention to the circumstances of aboriginal offenders [S. 718.2 (e)]. In concert with the UN's declaration on restorative justice, the purpose and principles of sentencing are to provide reparations for harm done to victims or to the community [S. 718 (e)] and to promote a sense of responsibility in offenders and acknowledgement of the harm done to victims and the community [S. 718(f)].

In 1999, the use of restorative justice was supported by the Supreme Court of Canada in the case of *R. v. Gladue*. The Gladue decision clearly endorsed the normative value of healing within sentencing principles, based on the practice of circle sentencing and community-based diversion programmes (Turpel-Lafond, 1999). The Gladue decision gives particular attention to aboriginal peoples, as it acknowledges that the underlying roots of discrimination must be addressed if we are to lower the overrepresentation of aboriginal people within the correctional justice system. At the same time, it is an historical decision for all Canadians, as it speaks to the overutilization of prisons as a sentencing tool in all criminal cases. In cases where incarceration is deemed necessary, the principles and practices of restorative justice are also reflected in the *Corrections and Conditional Release Act (CCRA)*. The Act states that the purpose of the federal correctional system is to contribute to the maintenance of a just, peaceful and safe society by, (a) carrying out sentences imposed by the court through the safe and humane custody and supervision of offenders; and (b) assisting the rehabilitation of offenders and their reintegration into the community as law-abiding citizens through the provision of programmes in the penitentiaries and in the community.

Within Canada's juvenile justice system, the Youth Criminal Justice Act (YCJA) replaced the Young Offenders Act in April 2003, providing legislative direction to reduce the use of custody in all but the most serious and violent offences and providing legislative direction which recognizes that an effective response to youth crime must consider the limited developmental capacity of youth requiring integration of various factors affecting their lives, such as education, mental health, family and community. Specific restorative justice values underlying the legislation include the following:

- Addressing developmental challenges and needs of young persons in order to guide them into adulthood is a societal responsibility.
- Communities and families should work in partnership through multidisciplinary approaches to address crime prevention by looking at its underlying causes, and by providing guidance and support to young persons, particularly those at risk.
- Information regarding youth justice, crime and measures taken to address youth crime, should be publicly available.
- Young persons have rights and freedoms, including those set out in the United Nations Convention on the Rights of the Child, in the Canadian Charter of Rights and Freedoms and in the Canadian Bill of Rights.
- The youth criminal justice system should command respect, and should take into account the interests of victims.
- The youth justice system should foster responsibility and ensure accountability through meaningful consequences and effective rehabilitation and reintegration.
- The youth justice system should reserve its most serious interventions for the most serious crimes and reduce over-reliance on incarceration.

While these are general principles outlined in the Preamble of the Act, overall they reflect the acceptance of an approach that is consistent with restorative justice. For instance, the YCJA aims to prevent crime by addressing underlying circumstances of offending behaviours and by emphasizing rehabilitation and reintegration of young persons into society, with specific consideration for the reduced level of maturity and greater level of dependency of young persons on adults. Consequences resulting from crime are to be meaningful to the young person and must promote accountability while being fair and proportionate to the crime. The YCJA also makes specific provisions for young persons to be heard and involved in the processes that lead to decision-making. Finally, Sec. 3(1)(c) of the Act emphasizes that measures taken against young persons should:

> (i) Reinforce respect for societal values;
> (ii) Encourage the repair of harm done to victims and the community;
> (iii) Be meaningful for the individual young person given his or her needs and level of development and, where appropriate, involve the parents, the extended family, the community and social or other agencies in the young person's rehabilitation and reintegration, and
> (iv) Respect gender, ethnic, cultural and linguistic differences and respond to the needs of aboriginal young persons and of young persons with special requirements.

Thus, although the YCJA makes no direct reference to restorative justice, there is general agreement that it 'does seem to open the door to the development of initiatives generally associated with restorative justice' (Charbonneau, 2005,

p. 75). In particular, the Act requires police and Crown attorneys to consider extrajudicial measures, including informal warnings, police or Crown cautions, police referrals to community programmes or agencies, referrals to pre-charge screening programmes or youth justice committees, or conferences (Tustin and Lutes, 2010).

Further, the Act includes provisions for the inclusion of victims in the proceedings; specifically, Section 5 of the YCJA directs (in part) that extrajudicial measures must:

- encourage acknowledgement and reparation of harm to the victim and community;
- encourage families of young persons, including extended families, and the community to become involved in the design and implementation of those measures; and
- provide an opportunity for victims to participate in decisions related to the measures selected and to receive reparation.

Further, the YCJA Sec. 2(1), specifically authorizes the use of restorative justice conferences by a youth justice court judge, the provincial director, a police officer, a justice of the peace, a prosecutor or youth worker, or a youth justice committee.

Yet, despite these state-based legislative foundations restorative justice remains at the margins of Canada's justice system. The rule of law has failed to build a normative framework of practice, enshrined within Canada's justice system at all levels – youth justice, criminal justice and corrections. What are the systemic barriers to bringing restorative justice to practice? Why do the principles of restorative justice remain in the lofty towers and heavy books of the judiciary and are not brought to the citizens they are meant to serve?

Research and Development of Restorative Justice: Lack of Praxis

Within the extant literature on human rights and restorative justice, many have argued that there has been a fundamental lack of praxis in building understanding and engagement: in bringing law to practice and practice to law; in bringing theory to practice and practice to theory. Each lives in their own silo, where rhetoric builds gulfs, not bridges. Canada's role, on an international front, has been one of exporting restorative justice practice, rather than building understanding and capacity on the domestic front, as Morrison and Pawlychka (2011) conclude:

> The evidence that has emerged from this analysis suggests that Barry Stuart's (Balanced and Restorative Justice Conference 2007) reflections on his experience of restorative justice in Canada still ring true: 'Canada's role in the development of restorative justice is as an exporter. We invent it, and others develop it in a fuller capacity'. One of the common adages in the field of restorative justice is to

> create opportunities to learn from our mistakes. Canada has the opportunity, and the capacity, to learn from this international experiment in restorative justice to which it has so proudly contributed. Moreover, Canada has the capacity to renew the promise of restorative justice as a domestic import. The lesson learned is that we must engage in praxis locally, provincially, nationally, and internationally.

Likewise, Moore and Mitchell (2011) investigated the theoretical and practical intersection between the principles and provisions of the CRC and the UN's Basic Principles on the Use of Restorative Justice in Criminal Matters in Canada, concluding that:

> CRC implementation has been impeded by myopic disciplinary approaches that have dissolved its constituent principles by isolating them from its provisions. Young people's human rights are languishing within Canadian juvenile justice contexts, and thus, historical efforts to build an ecosystem of rights-respecting communities in [Canada] are being compromised.

One important bridge that needs to be built is bringing human rights to restorative justice and restorative justice to human rights:

> Otto Driedger of the University of Regina insisted that in order to come into compliance with the Convention, restorative justice models were imperative – not as an absolute alternative but as a parallel initiative, that will assist us to have a less polarized approach. But it will be a long process. (Senate of Canada, 2007: 93–4).

The same is true in the context of children's rights, where understanding power relations has been found to be central to implementation and development of the CRC (Moore and Mitchell, 2011, pp. 99–100):

> The re-constituted model and additional theoretical development from this study hold the construct of *power* as central (between and amongst disciplines, adult/child power relations, institutions, policy texts and practice) although it is clear that definitions of power continue to be highly contested (Bauman, 2010). In the context of this study's findings, we prefer the global/local context of the CRC that is also reflected in Hannah Arendt's definition of power: 'the human ability not just to act but to act in concert' (1970: 44). … This approach is neither a linear interpretation of childhood nor of the Convention, but a more organic episteme, a rhizomatic appreciation that allows space for considering and re-considering contradictory viewpoints from philosophy, cultural studies, justice, social work, education, mental health, and so on (Moore and Mitchell, 2008).

In other words, praxis needs to be at all levels of human and social development that bridge the domains of many institutional silos. Canada is not alone in this regard, Chris Cunneen (2010, pp. 184–5) points out that the same is true in Australia, in the context of the criminal justice system:

> Despite all the words that have been written on restorative justice over the last 25 years, one cannot escape the feeling that restorative justice is essentially a peripheral add-on to the main workings of the criminal justice system. In New South Wales, Australia, … there are clearly articulated legislative and administrative procedures for the use of conferences. The system has been in place since the later 1990s, developed after various trials of restorative justice for young people which date back to the early 1990s. ... So after nearly 20 years, what has been the net outcome? Depending on the year, between 2 and 4 per cent of police interventions involving young people result in referral to a youth justice conference. ... At the other end of the legal process – the courts – restorative justice has not fared any better. For every one young person who appears in a restorative justice conference, about 15 appear in court ... And this is in a jurisdiction viewed as one of the pioneers in the 1990s in developing restorative justice practices for young people.

Cunneen (2010) concludes that restorative justice does not actively engage in research and development of current restorative justice practices within the context of the broader justice system. To move beyond the margins of the justice system, there needs to be a constantly reflexive, dialectical relationship between theory and practice. In other words, restorative justice 'lacks an analysis of its own significant shortcomings; it lacks an analysis of political power and social power; it lacks a **transformative** politics' (p. 186). In particular, much like Canada, reduced to a marginal normative theory, Cunneen argues that restorative justice has failed indigenous youth in Australia.

Based on the evidence to date, these claims ring true for Canada as well. There has been no consistent support to engage in praxis, particularly in praxis that engages community- and state-based policy, programmes and practice. There is no good reason, other than political will, that the practice of restorative justice should remain relegated to a marginal normative theory when restorative justice's theoretical roots span both normative and explanatory theory (see Braithwaite, 2002; Walgrave 2008, for an overview) and when there are community groups willing to engage in research and development, that is, engage in praxis. Perhaps a return to the seminal roots of restorative justice in Canada will bring further insights?

Restorative Justice in Practice

To engage in praxis is to critically engage in the theory and practice of restorative justice. Many have argued that practice has led theory in the development of a restorative justice system. Many have also said that restorative justice values must ground any restorative justice process. Sharpe (1998) articulated one of the early visions for restorative justice in Canada:

> Restorative justice is a justice that puts its energy into the future, not into what is past. It focuses on what needs to be healed, what needs to be repaired, what needs to be learned in the wake of a crime. It looks at what needs to be strengthened if such things are not to happen again.

Her vision clarifies five principles of the practice of restorative justice:

1. Inviting full participation and consensus
2. Healing what has been broken
3. Seeking full and direct accountability
4. Reuniting what has been divided
5. Strengthening the community, to prevent further harms.

While the contemporary practice of restorative justice has evolved over the last 40 years the early models that Sharpe described are still the predominant forms (Victim Offender Reconciliation or Mediation; Community/Family Group Conferences; Peacemaking Circles) of restorative justice practiced in Canada, as a number of papers have illustrated (Cormier, 2002; Tomporowski et al., 2010; Morrison and Pawlychka, 2011).

Victim Offender Reconciliation and Mediation

The restorative justice movement in Canada traces its modern inception to a landmark juvenile justice case in 1974, where two young men destroyed the property of 22 victims in Elmira, Ontario. The decisions and actions of Mark Yantzi, a Mennonite probation officer, and Judge Gordon McConnell, set a precedent for a restorative response to young offenders in Canada. Officer Yantzi, with the encouragement and support of Dave Worth of the Mennonite Central Committee, attached an addendum to the back of the pre-sentence report recommending that the offending juveniles be ordered to knock on the doors of their victims, apologize for their crimes, listen to what the victims had to say to them, determine the amount of restitution and ask for forgiveness. Judge McConnell saw no legal precedence to order these actions by the juveniles. Officer Yantzi, weighing the benefits offered by the court with those of a face-to-face meeting with the victims, spoke with the juveniles, convincing them to volunteer to perform these acts of restoration; thus, the judge could include them as part of a probation order. Russ Kelly (2010) was one of those two young offenders:

> On that day, my life changed forever as I managed to overcome the challenges of a punitive society and turn my life around. Meeting my victims taught me a valuable lesson in humanity and I never damaged anyone's property after

> that, but I still had a problem. It took another 20 years to kick my addiction to drugs and alcohol. I was tired of waking up sick and tired. And, I was tired of going to funerals. I was on the road to nowhere. So, I had to make a choice. I moved, changed jobs, stopped going to hotels, and stopped hanging out with the people that could feed my established habit. Still, I was taking 2 steps forward and 1 step back. The journey ahead was a rough one as I tried to escape my self-destructive life. That is when I met Irene and we fell in love. She gave me purpose and reason. My life improved as I strive to be a better person. ... My circumstance led me down a dead-end road ... my courage allowed me to find another path. (Kelly, Correctional Services of Canada, 2010; see also Kelly 2009 for the full story)

This landmark case lead to the development of Kitchener's victim–offender reconciliation programme (VORP) and became a foundation programme for Community Justice Initiatives (CJI) in Kitchener-Waterloo, Ontario. As interest grew within Mennonite communities, this influence spread across Canada to Langley, in the Fraser Valley of British Columbia (see Morrison and Pawlychka, 2012, for a review of restorative justice and juvenile justice in British Columbia). Community Justice Initiatives in British Columbia now partner with the Correctional Service of Canada (CSC), offering Victim–Offender Mediation (VOM) for serious cases of crime, including homicide and sexual abuse (see the cases of: Hutchison, 2006; Virk, 2008). These voluntary processes involve a facilitated dialogue between victims and offenders, typically within a CSC correctional facility. There are now a host of transformational stories of powerful experience of forgiveness, healing and restoration (see Jenkins, 2012) through VOM; however, these stories are seen as exceptional on the Canadian narrative landscape of justice. When these stories appear in the headlines, these powerful stories are often relegated to the "exceptional" silo in the hearts and minds of community members. Is it possible to bring these exceptional stories to those small places, close to home, to influence systemic change at a local community level? Stories alone fail to drive critical reflection and engage praxis. In doing so, they fail communities in sustaining a normative theory of restorative justice. How can we better harness these powerful stories of hope, healing and restoration?

Family Group Conferencing

Family group conferencing (FGC) is probably the most internationally recognized model of restorative justice. Developed and legislated in New Zealand in the late 1980s with a range of other provisions, this judicial process flips the diversion process on its head. Rather than being diverted from court to restorative justice (as is the case in Canada), young offenders in New Zealand are directed from restorative justice to court when a FGC alone is not deemed appropriate (as in serious offences such as murder and sexual abuse). Like VOM, a FGC involves a facilitator; however, the range of participants is much broader and brings together the family and friends of the offender and victim. As part of the process, the offender's family is given private family time to collectively consider the restoration plan. From New Zealand, FGC jumped the Tasman Sea to Australia in the early 1990s. In some states the private family group time remained part of the FGC process, while in others it was dropped. For example, the well-known scripted Wagga Wagga (or Real Justice) model of a conference does not include private family time; instead, all participants (victims, offenders and their respective communities of care) remain together throughout the process as the emphasis is on the *encounter* between the parties affected by the harm (see McDonald et al., 1995). It was this latter conferencing model that was brought to Canada in the late 1990s and adopted by the Royal Canadian Mounted Police (RCMP) as a diversion process from court (see Chatterjee and Elliott, 2003). In Canada it is often referred to as a community justice forum or conference. As noted earlier, the Youth Criminal Justice Act [s. 19(20)] mandates conferences as a mechanism for advice on extrajudicial measures, sentencing and reintegration plans. Despite this, there is very little data on the use of conferences within Canada (see Morrison and Pawlychka, 2011); further, the model has been adapted by many other institutions (like child protection and education) and communities, without first building an understanding of the role of the process within a different institutional or community-based context. One question that has arisen is: under what conditions can this process be co-opted by the institution to be yet another mechanism of social control, rather than social engagement? In other words, are institutional needs trumping the restorative value of meeting individual and community needs?

Peacemaking Circles

The harsh realities of the justice system for aboriginal people in Canada began to be more fully recognized in the late 1980s and early 1990s, with disproportional representation and high recidivism and crime rates being widely recognized (see Dickson-Gilmore and La Prairie, 2005). A number of judges (in particular in the Prairie provinces and territories, where disproportional representation was particularly high) recognized that a shift in judicial practice needed to take place. A notable case was under the care of Judge Barry Stuart of the Yukon Territorial Court, who adjourned the proceeding of *R. v. Moses* (1992) – who pled guilty to carrying a baseball bat with the intention of assaulting a police officer – and convened the first sentencing circle, drawing on traditional aboriginal practice in the Yukon Territory (see Stuart, 1996). While sentencing circles are a judicial attempt to incorporate what are identified as aboriginal traditions and values, they are not the rediscovery of a traditional practice of aboriginal peoples in Canada; rather, they are an invention of the judiciary serving aboriginal communities (Crnkovich, 1995).

Sentencing practice is based on three guiding premises: (1) a criminal offence represents a breach of relationship between the offender and the victim/community; (2) the well-being of the community is dependent on healing these breaches; and (3) the community is the best resource to address these breaches. As such, a sentencing circle is a community-directed process that partners with the criminal justice system in an effort to build consensus on a sentencing plan (Griffiths and Hamilton 1996; Pranis, Stuart and Wedge, 2003). Sentencing circles include a wide range of community members in the process: victims, victim supporters, offenders, offender supporters, judge, prosecutor, defence counsel, police and court workers. In the early days, judges were the primary facilitators of circle hearings and this evolved to community members co-facilitating the circles (Crnkovich 1995).

As discussed earlier, in 1999 the use of sentencing circles was supported by the Supreme Court of Canada in the case of *R. v. Gladue* (along with *R. v. Wells*). As Rudin (2008) concludes, this decision:

> was a significant, and in many ways, unprecedented decision of the Supreme Court of Canada. ... By calling Aboriginal overrepresentation a crisis in the Canadian justice system, the court was locating the problem in the justice system itself. It was not the fact that Aboriginal people were committing crimes that was the crisis; rather it was the response to that offending behaviour that was problematic. And that response, as the court noted, was an undue emphasis on incarceration. This is an important point. The purpose of the sentencing reform amendments of Bill C-14, passed in 1996 and at the heart of the *Gladue* decision, was not necessarily to reduce rates of offending in Canada, but rather to lessen the country's reliance on incarceration as a response to such behaviour. (ibid., p. 54)

Despite the hoped for promise of this legislative position, the promise of *Gladue* has not been fulfilled in Canada. Rudin (2008) argues that:

> complacency is perhaps the biggest bar to change. ... Social change and law reform are not matters than can be left by those most involved in the system for others to do. Gladue does not relieve people of their responsibility to work for change but it does make that work both more necessary and easier (ibid., p. 469).

It seems that complacency has become the norm and that those in the judiciary answer to the government, opposed to the citizens they serve. For example, in the case of *Arcand*, the 'Alberta Court of Appeal essentially ignored the fact that the offender was an Aboriginal person, and thus never really turned their minds at all to the extent to which Gladue applied' (Rudin, 2010, p. 1007). In Rudin's (2010) analysis of the *Arcand* case he argues that the court was wilfully blind to legislative, judicial and circumstantial factors. Over and above this particular case, Rudin's overarching concern was the relationship between government and courts: 'It is not the role of courts to anticipate the direction that Parliament may or may not take' (ibid., p. 1,007). This evidence suggests that the power base of judicial process lies with the state, this is Canada's default stand. Why is this default mechanism the case? Perhaps Canada's history as a nation state has something to reveal?

While Canada has much to be proud about in the development of restorative justice nationally and internationally, we have certainly not attained all that was hoped for in those early days of practice and legislation. Tomporowski et al. (2010), for example, raise a number of challenges facing restorative justice in Canada: the need for adequate and ongoing funding for programmes; lack of comprehensive data collection, locally and nationally; need for research on suitability of cases for restorative justice; expanding the limited use (despite legislation) of restorative justice; determining the relationship between aboriginal justice and restorative justice, as well as transitional justice; increasing public awareness of restorative justice; engaging victims and victim support agencies in restorative justice; addressing the concern regarding qualifications for restorative justice practitioners and standards for restorative justice programmes. These challenges raise many questions, with most of them coming down to Canada's reluctance to engage in praxis. Why does Canada continue to not fully engage in funding research and development of restorative justice? Why does the state continue to hold back, despite the fact that there is more evidence that restorative justice works in reducing crime and increasing victim satisfaction, compared to traditional justice practices (see Sherman and Strang, 2007)? Yet, perhaps the empirical evidence of particular practices of restorative justice is not enough to establish a substantive normative framework, as Lewin (1951) notably stated: there is nothing as practical as a good theory. Perhaps we have failed to engage in substantive normative and explanatory theory?

Setting Standards for Restorative Justice: Theory Grounding Practice

Braithwaite (2002) has proposed three types of restorative justice standards that could be useful for a deeper analysis of restorative justice programmes. The argument for these sets of standards begins with an argument for pluralizing state power and grounding the standards in consensus UN Human Rights agreements and empirical findings on restorative justice. The argument is grounded in 'two philosophical positions: (a) top-down accountability of some form is needed, with top-down standards that are contestable bottom-up; (b) that human rights must be protected by restorative justice processes' (ibid., p. 563). The standards address some of the concerns raised in the overview of the Canadian context: non-domination of the state; developing public awareness; research and development that enhances the leading edge of programmes that heal, along with denouncing programmes that do further harm; enhancing the empowerment of victims and communities, along with denouncing programmes that exploit victims as props; safeguarding the right to appeal decision-making processes and outcomes. The foundation of these standards is grounded in the Preamble of the Universal Declaration:

> Whereas recognition of the inherent dignity and the equal and inalienable rights of all members of the human family is the foundation of freedom, justice and peace in the world …

Braithwaite (2002) singles out Article 5 as being the most interesting to restorative justice advocates:

> No one shall be subjected to torture or to cruel, inhuman or degrading treatment or punishment. … Of course, all states have interpreted Article 5 in a most permissive and unsatisfactory way from a restorative justice point of view. The challenge for restorative justice advocates is to take this tiny anti-punitive space this Article creates in global human rights discourse and expand its meaning over time so that it increasingly acquires more restorative interpretation (ibid., p. 568).

Besides the Universal Declaration, the Declaration of Basic Principles of Justice for Victims of Crime and Abuse of Power (adopted by the General Assembly in 1985) is also highlighted, as it includes restorative values less well illustrated in other human rights instruments: 'restoration of the environment' (Article 10); 'compassion' (Article 4); 'redress' (Article 5); 'restoration of rights' (Article 8); 'restitution' (various Articles); and 'Informal mechanisms for the resolution of disputes, including mediation, arbitration and customary justice or indigenous practices' which 'should be utilized where appropriate to facilitate conciliation and redress for victims' (Article 7). In Braithwaite's proposed standards for restorative justice programmes and practices must be based on a set of *foundational* (constraining) principles: non-domination; empowerment; legally specified upper limits on sanctions; respectful listening; equal concern for all stakeholders; accountability and appealability; respect for fundamental human rights as specified by UN Declarations and Covenants. A second set of standards focus on what the process aims to *maximize* in terms of restoration: dignity, property loss, safety/injury/health, damaged human relationships, communities, environment, emotional resilience, freedom, compassion and caring, peace, sense of duty as a citizen. The process should also maximize social support to develop human capital and maximize the prevention of future injustice. These two sets of values:

> Imply parsimony in the use of punishment; together they say there are many positive approaches to regulation that we can consider before we consider our reluctant willingness to resort to punishment (ibid., p. 570).

A final set of values, emergent values, are not found in the UN documents. It is here in the emergent qualities of human interaction that restorative process gives life to the 'better angels of our nature' (Pinker, 2011). These are the gifts that recognize our common humanity, which only have meaning when freely given to others: remorse over injustice; apology; censure of the act; forgiveness of the person;

and mercy. For example, we can encourage active listening and non-domination (constraining values) through using a talking piece in a Peacemaking Circle; participants can call for restoration of property and human dignity but it is in the relational space between us that the emergent values reside. Forgiveness can never be demanded, as this would violate the constraining value of non-domination and the maximizing value of human dignity. Forgiveness is a gift that one human gives to another. It is only in this context that forgiveness has full meaning for those at the heart of the injustice.

Braithwaite (2002) concludes his paper with a call for local communities not to wait for the UN, that local communities can begin with deliberating the grounding values, rights, principles and standards important to them as stakeholders. Contested standards need to be resolved through critical reflexive praxis among peers, in training sessions and with regulatory bodies.

> At the end of the day it is better that restorative justice learn from making mistakes than that it make the mistake of refusing to learn (ibid., p. 575).

The evidence in Canada, thus far, is that Canada has made the mistake of refusing to learn. What is it that Canada has to learn? What is the hidden resistance? Perhaps it is institutional design and culture that has failed us?

Institutions and Restorative Justice

State based institutions are challenged to meet the communal needs of individuals, particularly in the context of their human rights. When concerns of human rights and harms are framed as institutional problems that demand an institutional response, institutions tend to shy from opportunities for a community based response, often citing privacy concerns. The same concerns can also be framed as a community problem that offers an opportunity for the community to respond. How social problems are framed limits and opens opportunities for response. Communities cut across institutional domains, and can respond in ways that broaden the scope for achieving human rights, justice and dignity. The practice of restorative justice enables communities to tap into the rich ecologies of an individual's life by generating a relational inquiry and response through the ritual of creating a communal space of social engagement over control. Restorative justice draws on three broad leverage points that offer a distinct perspective to typical institutional responses of social control. First, rather than focusing on external sanctioning systems (reward and punishment) as a motivational lever, restorative justice focuses on relational ecologies as a motivational lever that foster rich value-based internal sanctioning systems. Thus, in responding to threats to social order, instead of asking 'who did it' and 'what punishment do the offenders deserve?', the questions centre around 'who has been hurt?', 'what are their needs?' and 'whose obligation is it to meet these needs?' (Zehr, 2002). Second, the process of answering these questions includes those closest to the harm and those closest to the community affected. This is distinct from current institutional practice, wherein the decision-making is often left to third parties, removed from the direct incident, particularly in the context of serious threat or harm. In the context of courts, the system has been characterized as stealing conflict from those most affected (Christie, 1977). Third, restorative justice does not trump emotion with reason, but finds reason for emotion (Sherman, 1999). This is distinct from most institutional responses that focus on establishing the facts, with little focus on the social, emotional and spiritual dimensions the make up the rich ecologies within the lives of individuals and communities. In answering Zehr's questions, restorative justice draws on a wide range of positions, rather than take a one size fits all punitive approach. Instead, restorative justice asks itself hard questions, making cases for optimistic and pessimistic accounts of restorative justice, in terms of theory and practice (Braithwaite, 2002).

The practice of restorative justice is theoretically eclectic, cutting across disciplinary silos, with a range of normative and explanatory theories making a case for restorative justice (ibid., 2002). Normative theories draw on a range of world views: from indigenous and faith-based to sociological, such as Durkheim and Foucault (see ibid., 2002). Explanatory theories draw on normative theory in different ways; such as, re-integrative shaming theory, which builds understanding of the role of the moral emotion of shame and the process of shaming (see Ahmed et al., 2001; Morrison, 2007); defiance theory (Sherman, 1993), which builds understanding of when punishment increases crime, decreases crime and has no effect; social identity theory (Tajfel and Turner, 1979) and self-categorization theory (Turner et al., 1987), which builds understanding of the social psychological mechanism that bridges the self and society. Building on this last theoretical analysis, Tyler (2006; see also Wenzel, Woodyatt and Hedrick, in press) in an article on rule breaking, procedural justice and restorative justice concludes that a shift from regulation by external sanctions, to self-regulation, is important:

> Sanctioning-based models, which dominate current thinking about managing criminals, have negative consequences for the individual wrongdoer and for society. It is argued that greater focus needs to be placed on psychological approaches whose goal is to connect with and activate internal values within wrongdoers with the goal of encouraging self-regulatory law-related behavior in the future.

This analysis resonates with that of Valerie Braithwaite (2009b) who brings together her work on social values and motivational postures, within a responsive regulation framework. In particular, her work identifies institutional practices that generate defiance, undermining the individual's capacity and willingness to cooperate in core facets of social life, from family and school to work and governance. Responsive regulation is contrasted with formalized regulatory responses (Braithwaite, J., 2002), which Valerie Braithwaite argues are institutionally siloed. Within a formalized regulatory system the implicit belief is that clear rules and laws within the architecture of the system, backed up by clear and consistent sanctions, will elicit the desired behaviour. The basic assumption is that at some level all actors are rational, assuming individuals and groups are uniformly programmed in the way they respond to rules and laws. In contrast, Braithwaite (2009) has identified five motivational postures: commitment, capitulation, resistance, disengagement and game playing. In summary, Braithwaite (2009) argues that traditional, sanction-based, rational actor models ignore the science of how individuals, groups and society function. Social identity and self-categorization theory offer further insights beyond standard rational choice theory. The conceptual shift can be framed through an understanding of the nature of power. Turner (2005) proposes a new theory of power emphasizing group identity, social organization and ideology, rather than dependence as the basis of power.

The theory proposes that processes of power, underlying basic mechanisms of social control – persuasion, authority and coercion – can account for more explanatory variance by reversing the causal sequence of the standard theory. The latter argues that control of resources produces power, power is the basis of influence and that mutual influence leads to the formation of the psychological group. The three-process theory argues that psychological group formation produces influence, that influence is the basis of power and that power leads to control of resources (ibid., p. 1).

This conceptual shift has implications for theories of social change, emphasizing that power is leveraged as a function of social relationships, in the context of 'definite social, ideological and historical content rather than reifying it as an abstract external force producing generic psychological effects' (ibid., p. 1). In other words, differential social engagement across ideology and context, as a basis for social identification, leads to enhancing the power base for access to resources.

Differential social engagement, beyond a one size fits all system, is a challenge for social institutions that represent many different individuals. To find a place for restorative justice within social institutions, they need to create the institutional space to do so, moving from a formalized regulatory framework to a responsive regulatory framework (Braithwaite, 2002). To move from institutions of social control to institutions of social engagement, the very power dynamics of an institution must be challenged (see Morrison, 2011). The maritime province of Nova Scotia stepped up to this challenge to become one of the oldest and by all accounts the most comprehensive province wide restorative justice programs in Canada.

The Case of Nova Scotia: Pluralizing State Powers

Conceived in 1997, and implemented in 1999, the Nova Scotia Restorative Justice Program (NSRJ) operates at all stages of the justice system (Archibald and

Llewellyn, 2006). Like many other restorative justice programmes across Canada, it is centred on youth justice and community-based programmes, operating through referrals by police, prosecutors, judges and correctional officials; in other words, at a range of intersections with the justice system. An extensive evaluation, comparing thousands of cases over five years (Clairmont, 2005), was only one step in a wider process of praxis and 'led to considerable rethinking of restorative justice theory and practice in relation to governing policies, standards for programme implementation and responses to controversial issues' (Archibald and Llewellyn, 2006, p. 299).

It is often noted that Nova Scotia's programme began with a conversation between two people – a Deputy Minister of Justice and a defence counsel – on a long flight back to Nova Scotia, following attendance at the first international conference on restorative justice held in Canada, hosted by the Centre for Restorative Justice at Simon Fraser University (ibid., 2006)). Yet perhaps the seed was planted earlier. Previous to this, in 1996, John Braithwaite had delivered the Dorothy J. Killam Memorial Lecture on Restorative Justice and A Better Future, arguing that:

> Few sets of institutional arrangements created in the West since the industrial revolution have been as large a failure as the criminal justice system. In theory it administers just, proportionate corrections that deter. In practice, it fails to correct or deter, just as often making things worse as better. It is a criminal *injustice* system that systematically turns a blind eye to crimes of the powerful, while imprisonment remains the best-funded labour market program for the unemployed and indigenous peoples. … The interesting question is why are they such failures. Given that prisons are vicious and degrading places, you would expect fear of ending up in them would deter crime. … A lack of theoretical imagination among criminologists has been one underrated reason for the failure of the criminal justice system. Without theorizing why it fails, the debate has collapsed to a contest between those who want more of the same to make it work and those who advance the implausible position that it makes sense to stigmatize people first and later subject them to rehabilitation programs inside institutions. With juvenile justice in particular, the debate throughout the century has see-sawed between the justice model and the welfare model. See-sawing between retribution and rehabilitation has got us nowhere. If we are serious about a better future, we need to hop off this see-saw and strike out in search of a third model.

The lack of data and theoretical imagination on restorative justice remains true, by and large, in Canada. Nova Scotia is the exception; they took Braithwaite's challenge to heart and engaged in Canada's largest experiment with restorative justice to date. The genesis of the programme rested on three theoretical levers that are integral to the operationalization of restorative justice (ibid., p. 302–4): (1) partnership between the state and various communities; (2) conceptualizing restorative justice as more than victim–offender mediation, which 'commonly misses or obscures the role of the state and the community'; (3) the programme aligned with a 'set of Canadian traditions and values through which restorative justice … is refracted'. Nova Scotia also took evaluation seriously, building on the vision of Susan Sharpe (1998), as cited above and being explicit about goals and objectives. The goals were to: reduce recidivism; increase victim satisfaction; strengthen communities; increase public confidence in the justice system. The objects of the programme were to: provide a voice and an opportunity to participate for the victims and the community; repair the harm caused by the offence; reintegrate the offender; hold the offender accountable in a meaningful way. Together these objectives and goals are significantly broader and offer more scope than the traditional system. As discussed previously, restorative justice is consistent with the rule of law in Canada, as established by statutory authority in the Criminal Code and the Youth Criminal Justice Act. In Nova Scotia the Youth Justice Act, also provides authority for provincial and municipal offences. In summary, the programme was comprehensive and integrated throughout the justice system; further, the programme explicitly embraced praxis through the transparency of goals and objectives, which were evaluated. As such, it provides a unique opportunity to explore challenges related to partnerships across and within the institutional and community domains of restorative justice.

A number of key challenges were recognized in institutionalizing comprehensive restorative justice across the province: politics of gender and restorative justice; agency cultures and the transition from alternative measures to restorative justice; restorative process and serious criminal harms; whether the process is upping the ante or just widening the net; equity, diversity and cultural difference; balancing community control with state superintendence. Once raised, these challenges were met through further research, development and evaluation of 17 projects, just as was called for in the House of Commons (1982) report, *Taking Responsibility*. In other words, Nova Scotia engaged in further praxis. Beyond the initial 17 projects, the research and development of restorative justice has now entered the domain of human rights, beginning with rethinking a normative framework of justice, based on relational values.

In reflecting on the research and development to date in Nova Scotia, Llewellyn (2011) articulated a relational theory of justice. The foundational assumption of the theory is that human beings are inherently relational in that we are not merely interdependent with one another, but that we understand each other, through each other. If the goal of justice is to achieve, protect and maintain just social relations, then we must practice and pursue the human rights of equal respect, concern and dignity. This foundational assumption resonates with the concept of Ubuntu in South Africa. It also resonates with the theoretical foundations of social identity theory (SIT) and self-categorization theory (SCT), as described by Hornsey (2008, p. 210):

> the social identity approach presented a new perspective on social influence, conformity, and power. From a SCT perspective, the norms of relevant ingroups are a crucial source of information about appropriate ways to think, feel, and act.

The theories have been influential in a number of areas related to restorative justice: group-based emotions, such as shame (Ellemers, Doosje and Spears, 2004); collective guilt (Doosje et al., 1998); and forgiveness and responsibility (Wenzel, Woodyatt and Hedrick). The work on intergroup forgiveness includes the first forays into examining the psychological meaning of the most inclusive level of identity proposed by SCT, the human identity (Wohl and Branscombe, 2005). Hornsey (2008, p. 217) concludes that 'at a time when theories are becoming increasingly "micro" in their scope, the social identity approach is a rare beast, a meta-theory that is ambitious in scope'. The question remains whether it is ambitious enough to test the many claims of restorative justice in upholding human rights.

In April 2012 the Nova Scotia Human Rights Commission published a draft framework and procedures for 'Restorative Boards of Inquiry: Fostering Dignity and Respectful, Responsible Relationships'. The first inquiry was held in September 2012. The CEO of the Nova Scotia Human Rights Commission, echoing Sharpe's touchstones of restorative justice, said the focus was on: 'rebuilding relationships, repairing emotional harms and developing a forward-looking plan that all the parties can take a role in creating and implementing' (HRC, 2012). In January 2013:

> The Nova Scotia Human Rights Commision, through its 2012 vision statement and strategic goals commits to building and strengthening relationships, which preserves and protects human rights. The Commission had at times struggles with the harms frequently created by the legalistic and adversarial traditional Boards of Inquiry processes. From this struggle a new model emerged: The Restorative Board of Inquiry is the Commission's answers to reducing those harms. The traditional Board of Inquiry is better suited for handling technical issues, and will still be available. Restorative Boards of Inquiry are offered to help resolve emotional harms, and will be the mainstay of the Commission's Board of Inquiry work.

From those early sombre beginnings of human rights in Canada, at least in Nova Scotia, there is a climate for the politics of hope (Archibald, 2008, p. 85).

The larger challenge is bringing restorative justice to an ailing criminal justice system, for it remains true that 'Western criminal justice institutions deter crime prevention (Braithwaite, 2005). Restorative justice has come to the human rights tribunals, in other words, to the state. The larger challenge is to bring human rights to restorative justice in those small places close to home; that is, in our communities.

In Llewllyn's (2011) relational theory of justice she addressed the larger challenge we must all face, as individuals, communities and members of nation states:

> This relational understanding of human beings challenges the prevailing story of who we are, how we are connected, and what we need and deserve from one another. This prevailing story, which underlines many of our social and political institutions and systems, is that of an independent, self-sufficient individual who seeks protection and security in rights that hold others at bay; who seeks safety in a justice system that lays blame and punishes the individual at fault; who finds success by pulling themselves up by their boot straps; and who sees freedom as acting without the involvement or interference of others.

Beyond this ideology there will be other challenges for Canada. To be a fair and just country, we must face our own past and own our own story as Canadians.

The Canadian Story of a Just Society

John Ralston Saul (2008) argues that Canadians:

> are a people of aboriginal inspiration organized around the concept of peace, fairness and good government. That is what lies at the heart of our story; at the heart of Canadian mythology, whether francophone or anglophone. If we can embrace a language that expresses that story, we will feel a great release. We will discover a remarkable power to act and to do so in such a way that we will feel true to ourselves.

For example, in the context of immigration, Saul (2008, p. 316–7) argues:

> our assumption that the newcomer will quickly come into the circle and join our family. Immigration is an engagement leading to marriage. The psychological assumption is one of dignity based on the inevitability of a future family relationship. This is the old Aboriginal idea.

John Braithwaite, in his address at Dalhousie, argued that the lived experience of democracy is alienation, that elites run things, that we don't have a say in any legitimate way. If Saul (2008) is right, at least in the Canadian context, it is because elites do not understand the Canadian ethic of fairness and inclusion and that this involves embracing the inherent tension of social life, that of the individual and the group (ibid., p. 318).

> The Aboriginal idea of a circle is based upon the idea of tension. [Canadians] need to redesign our [institutions] to do the same. When I say it needs to be

> about thinking, not training, I could equally say it needs to be about engagement and aggressive debate, not about smooth expertise and passive service.

To develop a normative restorative justice framework that works for Canada we must change that focus from training people to deliver different models of restorative justice, to developing community-led praxis that engages citizens in the values of a just society, a fair country.

Canadians are born of a 'circle that welcomes and adapts' (ibid., p. 322); yet, are Canadians ready to embrace a Metis identity? Rauls argues that Canadians have a history of slipping back into colonial insecurities, to the detriment of advancing Canadian interests. That the Canadian struggle is not between the citizen and the state, as it is in Europe and the United States: 'Rather, we are dependent on the personal engagement of the citizen, both as an individual and as a bulwark of the state (ibid., p. 318)'. If this is the case, the first step in embracing a normative theory of restorative justice is to claim this national ethic of fairness and inclusion and overcome our colonial insecurities. Through the indigenous roots of the circle, Canadians have an opportunity to embrace the heart of the tension between the individual to the group. Such a process could re-define citizenship, and justice, based on fairness, inclusion, and responsible citizenship in Canada.

Zehr (2000) has characterized restorative justice as a journey to belonging. For all Canadians to belong, a common story of belonging must emerge within those 'small places close to home' – be it the community of the neighborhood, the school, the factory, farm or office. It is these communities that must hold the story of rights and restoration in their hands, and their hearts. The emergent values of restorative justice – forgiveness and reconciliation – can only be given as gifts, one Canadian to another. The launch of Reconciliation Canada in 2012 is a bold visionary step in this direction, an invitation by Chief Dr. Robert Joseph, of the Gwawaenuk Nation, to embrace a common humanity and future:

> Let us find a way to belong to this time and place together. Our future and the well-being of all our children, rests with the kind of relationship we build today.

References

Ahmed, E., Harris, N., Braithwaite, J. and Braithwaite, V. (2001) *Shame Management Through Reintegration*. Cambridge: Cambridge University Press.

Archibald, B. (2008). Let My People Go: Human Capital Investment and Community Capacity Building via Meta/Regulation in a Deliberative Democracy – A modest contribution for Criminal Law and Restorative Justice. HeinOnline – 16 *Cardozo Journal of International and Comparative Law*.

Archibald, B. and Llewellyn, J. (2006). The Challenges of Institutionalizing Comprehensive Restorative Justice: Theory and Practice in Nova Scotia, *Dalhousie Law Journal*, 29, 297.

Braithwaite, J. (1996). Restorative Justice and a Better Future, *The Dalhousie Review*, 76(1), 9–32. (Reprinted in E. McLaughlin, R. Fergusson, G. Hughes and L. Westmorland (eds), *Restorative Justice: Critical Issues*. London: Sage, 2003).

Braithwaite, J. (2002a). *Restorative justice and responsive regulation*. New York: Oxford University Press.

Braithwaite, J. (2002b). Setting standards for restorative justice. *British Journal of Criminology*, 42(3), 563–77.

Braithwaite, J. (2006). Accountability and responsibility through restorative justice. In: M.D. Dowdle (ed.) *Public accountability, designs, dilemmas and experiences*. Cambridge, UK: Cambridge University Press,(pp. 33–51.

Braithwaite, V. (2009) Dismissive and Resistant Defiance, paper presented at Legitimacy and Compliance in Criminal Justice: An International Symposium, University of Leeds, Leeds, 25–6 June.

Braithwaite, V. (2009) Introducing Responsive Regulation, paper presented at the Child Protection as Regulation: Clarifying Principles Conference, Australian National University, Canberra, 5–6 November.

Charbonneau, S. (2005). The Canadian Youth Criminal Justice Act 2003: A step forward for advocates of restorative justice. In: E. Elliot and R.M. Gordon (eds) *New directions in restorative justice: Issues, practice, evaluation*. Cullompton,: Willan Publishing, pp. 75–86.

Chatterjee, J. and Elliott, L (2003). Restorative policing in Canada: the Royal Canadian Mounted Police, community justice forums, and the youth criminal justice act', *Police Practice and Research*, 4(4), 1

Christie, N. (1977). Conflict as property. *British Journal of Criminology* 17(1), 1–14.

Clairemont, D. (2005). *The Nova Scotia Restorative Justice Initiative: Final Evaluation Report*, Pilot Research, Bedford, Nova Scotia.

Cormier, R (2002) *Restorative Justice: Directions and Principles – Developments in Canada*. Ottawa: Department of the Solicitor General Canada.

Crnovich, M. (1995). *Report on sentencing circles in Nunavik*. In Pautuutit Women's Association, Inuit Women and Justice: Progress Report No. 1.

Cunneen, C. and Hoyle, C. (2010). *Debating restorative justice*. Oxford: Hart Publishing.

Dandurand, Y. and Griffith, C.T. (2006). *Handbook of Restorative Justice Programmes*. New York: United Nations Publication.

Daubney, D. (2010, November). *The role the 1987–88 Justice Committee of the House of Commons played in encouraging the use of restorative justice in Canada*. Paper presented at Restorative Justice Week 2010, Canada.

Dickson-Gilmore, J. and La Prairie, C. (2005). Will the Circle be Unbroken: Aboriginal Communities, Restorative Justice and the Challenges of Conflict and Change. Toronto: University of Toronto Press.

Doosje, B., Branscombe, N.R., Spears, R. and Manstead, A.S.R. 1998. Guilty by association: When one's group has a negative history. *Journal of Personality and Social Psychology*, 75, 872–86.

Ellemers, N., Doosje, B. and Spears, R. 2004. Sources of respect: The effects of being liked by ingroups and outgroups. *European Journal of Social Psychology*, 34, 155–72.

Griffiths, C.T. and Hamilton, R. 1996. Sanctioning and healing: Restorative justice in Canadian Aboriginal communities. In B. Galaway and J. Hudson (eds), *Restorative justice: International perspectives.* Monsey, NY: Criminal Justice Press, pp. 175–92.

Hornsey, M. 2008. Social Identity Theory and Self-categorization Theory: A Historical Review *Social and Personality Psychology Compass* 2(1): 204–22; 10.

House of Commons. 1998. *Taking responsibility: Report of standing committee on justice and Solicitor General on its review of sentencing, conditional release and related aspects of corrections.* Canada: Standing Committee on Justice and Solicitor General.

House of Commons Justice Committee. 2010. *Cutting crime: The case for justice reinvestment.* (HC 94–1). London: The Stationery Office Limited.

Hutchison, K. 2006. *Walking After Midnight.* Vancouver: Raincoast Books.

Jenkins, T. 2012. *Forgiveness as a Healing Agent in Cases of Traumatic Violence.* MA Thesis held at Simon Fraser University.

Kelly, R. 2006. *From scoundrel to scholar…The Russ Kelly Story.* Self Published.

Kelly, R. 2010, November. *The Elmira case…and beyond!* Paper presented at Restorative Justice Week, Canada.

Lewin, K. 1951. *Field theory in social science; selected theoretical papers.* D. Cartwright (ed.). New York: Harper & Row.

Llewellyn, J.J. 2011. A relational vision of justice. Revisioning Justice. Restorative Justice Week. Correctional Services of Canada.

Marshall, T.F. 1996. The evolution of restorative justice in Britian. *European Journal of Criminal Policy and Research*, 4(4), 21–43.

McDonald, J., Thorsborne, M., Moore, D., Hyndman, M. and O'Connell, T. 1995. *Real justice training manual: Coordinating family group conferences.* Pipersville, PA: Piper's Press.

Moore, S.A. and Mitchell, R.C. eds. Power, Pedagogy and Praxis: Social Justice in the Globalized Classroom. Rotterdam: Sense Publications.

Moore, S.A. and Mitchell, R.C. 2011. Rights-Based Restorative Justice in Canada: From Silence to Citizenship. In: M. Freeman (ed.), *Current Legal Issues.* Oxford: Oxford University Press, x; pp. 202–18.

Morrison, B.E. 2007. *Restoring safe school communities: A whole school response to bullying, violence and alienation.* Sydney: Federation Press.

Morrison, B.E. 2010. From Social Control to Social Engagement: Finding the time and place to talk. Contemporary Issues in Criminal Justice Policy. American Society of Criminology Annual Meeting.

Morrison, B.E. and Pawlychka, C. 2012. Juvenile Justice and Restorative Justice: Reflections on Developments in British Columbia. In J. Winterdyk and R. Smandych (eds), *Youth at Risk and Youth Justice: A Canadian Overview*. Toronto: Oxford University Press.

Nova Scotia Human Rights Commission 2012. Restorative Boards of Inquiry: Fostering Dignity and Respectful, Responsible Relationships.

Pinker, S. 2011. *The Better Angles of our Nature*. New York: Penguin Books.

Pranis, K., Stuart, B., and Wedge, M. (2003). *Peacemaking Circles: From Crime to Community*. Living Justice Press.

Rudin, J. 2008. Aboriginal Over-representation and R. v. Gladue: Where We Were, Where We Are and Where We Might Be Going. *Supreme Court Law Review*, 40 (2d).

Rudin, J. 2010. Eyes Wide Shut: The Alberta Court of Appeal's Decision in *R. v. Arcand* and Aboriginal Offenders. *Alberta Law Review*, 48(4).

Saul, J.R. 2008. *A fair country*. Toronto: Penguin.

Schabas, W.A. 1998. Canada and the Adoption of the Universal Declaration of Human Rights. *McGill Law Journal, 43*, 403.

Sharpe, S. 1998. *Restorative Justice: A Vision for Healing and Change,* Mediation and Restorative Justice Centre, Edmonton, AB.

Sherman, L.W. 1993. Defiance, deterrence, and irrelevance: a theory of the criminal sanction. *Journal of research in Crime and Delinquency*, 30 (4), 445–73.

Sherman 2003. Reason for emotion: Reinventing justice with theories, innovation, and research. *Criminology*, 41, pp. 1–38.

Sherman, L.W. and Strang, H. 2007. *Restorative justice: The evidence.* London: The Smith Institute.

Stuart, B. 1996. *Circle Sentencing in Yukon Territory, Canada: A Partnership of the Communityand the Criminal Justice System* International Journal of Comparative and Applied Criminal Justice. 20(1 and 2): 291–309.

Tajfel, H. and Turner, J.C. 1979. An intergrative theory of intergroup conflict. In W.G. Austin and S. Worchel (eds), *The Social Psychology of Intergroup Relations* (pp. 33–47). Monterey, CA: Brooks/Cole.Tomporowski et al. (2010)

Turpel-Lafond, Judge M.E. 1999. Changing Punishment at the Turn of the Century. Finding Common Ground, Sentending within a Restorative Justice Paradigm. Procedural Implications of R. v. Gladue 1999 2. Paper presented at the CIAJ in Sasktoon, Saskatchewan, Canada, Sept. 26–9. *Criminal Law Quarterly*.

Turner, J.C. 2005. Explaining the nature of power: A three-process theory. *European Journal of Social Psychology*, 35, 1–22.

Turner, J.C., Hogg, M.A., Oakes, P.J., Reicher, S.D., and Wetherell, M.S. 1987. *Rediscovering the Social Group: A self-categorization Theory*. New York: Blackwell.

Tustin, L. and Lutes, R.E. 2010. *A guide to the Youth Criminal Justice Act.* Toronto, ON: Butterworths.

Tyler, T.R. 2006. Restorative justice and procedural justice. *Journal of Social Issues*, 62, 305–23.

United Nations. 2006. *Handbook on restorative justice programs: Criminal justice handbook series*. United Nations Office on Drugs and Crime.

Van Ness, D. 2003. Proposed basic principles on the use of restorative justice: Recognising the aims and limits of restorative justice In: A. von Hirsch, et al. (eds), *Restorative justice and criminal justice: Competing or reconcilable paradigms?* Oxford: Hart Publishing, pp. 157–76.

VanNess, D. and Johnstone, G. 2007. *Handbook of restorative justice*. Cullompton: Willan Publishing.

Virk, M. 2008. Reena Virk: A Father's story.

Walgrave, L. 2008. Restorative justice, self-interest and responsible citizenship. Culumpton: Willan Publishing.

Wenzel, M., Woodyatt, L. and Hedrick, K. (2012). No genuine self-forgiveness without accepting responsibility: Value reaffirmation as a key to maintaining positive self-regard. *European Journal of Social Psychology*, 42(5), pp. 617–27.

Wohl, M.J.A. and Branscombe, N.R. 2005. Forgiveness and collective guilt assignment to historical perpetrator groups depend on level of social category inclusiveness. *Journal of Personality and Social Psychology*, 88, 288–303.

Wachtel, T. 1997. *Real Justice: How We Can Revolutionize Our Response to Wrongdoing*. Pipersville, PA: The Piper's Press, .

Zehr, H. 1990. *Changing lenses: A new focus for crime and justice*. Scottsdale, PA: Herald Press.

Zehr, H. 2002. *The little book of restorative justice*. Intercourse, PA: Good Books.

Chapter 11
Conflict Resolution: Theory, Practice and Challenges that Lie Ahead

Maria Hadjipavlou

Background

The interdisciplinary field of conflict resolution both theoretically and in an applied fashion has developed out of the need to challenge the traditional theories and methods in solving problems whether at the international, local, institutional or the interpersonal levels. My chapter focuses on the use of different conflict resolution tools specifically in ethnonational and international conflicts and its conversation with feminist theory. What are the underlying assumptions about international conflict from a conflict resolution and feminist perspective? Why such an approach gives considerable emphasis on the subjective elements of conflict (misperceptions, miscommunication, unintended escalation, enemy imaging, the dichotomy of 'us' and 'them', etc), and thus the centrality of improving communication, emphasizing basic human needs theory as an explanation for 'deep-rooted conflict'. Why societal attitudinal changes toward the Other as well as relationship building are important factors in restoring traumatized communities which are in a conflict-habituated system? How are issues of power asymmetries and security being addressed from a conflict resolution and feminist perspectives? There is a lot of similarity in the application and tools used by both Restorative Justice and Conflict resolution. Both support unofficial processes where the grievances of both sides are addressed and mutual recognition of harm done to the other. The need for apology and reconciliation processes as well as truth commissions have been used as alternative tools as well as the interactive Problem-Solving Workshop in putting the foundations for a peace culture and sociopolitical change. I would suggest that a conversation among disciplines, theoreticians and practitioners is of paramount importance in rebuilding traumatized communities and restoring dignity and trust.

I was among the fortunate ones to have participated at the International symposium on Restorative Justice and Human Rights held on the island of Skopelos in June 2012. The Symposium and the participants' presentations took place in different locations around the island (a very unconventional academic conference, indeed!). This method was intentional and deeply appreciated by all participants. Both the natural environment, the sea, the secluded spiritual sites, the reconstruction of ancient Greek dwellings, the 19th century mansion and the intellectual energy have enriched my thinking on numerous questions that were raised during these encounters. One of the questions raised was : 'does Restorative Justice (RJ) need a theory'? This led me pose the same question with regard to Conflict Resolution (CR). Thus, in my chapter, I will try to highlight the common values, and practices which CR and RJ share and how each can learn from the other. I will also support each other in the bigger overarching shared goal which is to make our world a better, fairer and safer place and our relationships healthier and more trusting. Hopefully, my contribution will help develop furthering thinking and questioning for the development of a firmer philosophical foundation for RJ.

Like RJ, the interdisciplinary field of CR both theoretically and applied has developed out of the need to challenge the traditional theories and methods in solving problems whether at the international, local, institutional or the interpersonal levels. In this chapter I will argue that CR which Burton called a philosophy (Burton 1972) still lacks a coherent and widely accepted theory which can explain the causes of war and ethno national conflicts. All we have to work with are different theories/assumptions stemming from international relations politics, political and from social psychology or psycho-dynamic theories. In this chapter I will attempt the following: I will first tackle briefly the concept 'conflict' and then outline the major theories which try to help us explain the phenomena of war and conflicts; second, I will mention the major CR tools with specific reference to the Interactive Problem-Solving Workshop (IPSW) which I have used in my practice and how this connects to RJ as an approach; third, I will address the learnings from the IPSW and its limitations. I will conclude with some challenges that lie ahead in the field of CR and RJ and finally propose the need for a multi-theory interdisciplinary model.

Major CR Theories

It has been often said that conflict is an inevitable and inseparable part of our life. Conflicts occur at all levels: personal, interpersonal, community (for instance class issues, ethnic issues, race issues, gender issues, religious issues); at the international level (interstate differences, international crises, cold wars, armed conflicts and so on). Social conflicts, that is conflicts between or among groups have always existed (as in Homer's Iliad and the Peloponnesian wars; since ancient times many thought of wars as 'God's will', a justification that still abounds in our days!) A multi-level analysis can help us make comparisons among the different levels, but more importantly it allows us to have different points of entry for interventions and this is where CR and RJ do intervene. Of course, conflict can also be desirable. As sociologists inform us without conflict (clashes of ideas and social class struggles and big challenges of status quo) we would not have had social, cultural or political change (Coser 1956, Dahrendorf 1959). Here, however, I will be speaking about destructive armed conflicts or crimes which lead to killings, violations of human rights, breakdown of trust and safety, displacement of people, missing persons, rape of women and girls and economic and cultural catastrophes.

The study of conflict at all levels became significant after the Second World War and special attention was given to prevention and resolution of conflicts. The theory then prevailing, Realism of International Relations. had proven inadequate to resolve conflicts and was defensive of 'power over', such as coercion (Hadjipavlou-Trigeorgis, 1987).It was challenged by the new types of conflicts which arose especially after the end of the so-called 'cold war' era which are mostly intra-state and inter-societal generating ethnic and racial violence. Major questions raised in the 1950s, 1960s and continue to busy our minds, such as 'what makes people use violence and want to kill? The philosophical ambition of this book and chapter also allows me to carry on further with my open-ended questions such as, How can we prevent violence?'Social scientists from various disciplines also wondered 'what makes people become so 'monstrous'?' What causes wars and conflicts? What are the sources of aggression in national populations? What can be done to predict and prevent armed conflicts? What causes changes in popular attitudes? How do we construct the enemy remember Rwanda in the 1990s, the Tutsis became cockroaches and had to be crushed. What is the role of the state in such conditions? What kinds of conflicts exist? What is the role of academics and intellectuals? How can an applicable theory of conflict and restoration develop? Is there one?

The other focus of these scholars was also to establish a new profession that would be available to advise policy makers, judges and law makers. The pioneers of the conflict resolution movement who contributed to the establishment of research Centres (from Oslo, Norway, to University of Michigan, Miami University, University of Chicago, London University, and many others) for the study of war, security policy and peace, were Quincy Wright, Fred Cottrell, Robert Heffner, William Barth, John Burton, Herbert Kelman, Daniel Katz, Kenneth Boulding, Anatol Rapporort, Harold Lasswell, Theodore Lentz, Elise Boulding. They all lay the foundations for programmes for conflict and peace research as a scientific discipline. New academic Journals were established such as the *Journal of Conflict Resolution,* the *Journal of Social Issues,* the *Bulletin of Research Exchange on Prevention of War, the Journal of Peace Research* founded by Kenneth Boulding, the *Negotiation Journal* founded by Jeremy Rubin and Roger Fisher. Johan Galtung (1969) was the first to distinguish between *direct* and *structural* violence. The former includes every day violence when an individual or group suffers physical or emotional pain as a result of direct action (like a gun shot or verbal abuse). Structural violence is caused by institutions (church, army the state, the family) and structures of society (hierarchies, class system, race system) which result in inequality or oppression among individuals or social groups (minorities, women, migrants, homosexuals). This typology was also spoken on by feminists and was developed further to speak of many other forms of violence starting from the personal to the international (Cockburn 2004, Hadjipavlou 2010)

So since the late 1960s many new academic programs emerged on 'Conflict and Peace Studies', or on 'Conflict Analysis and Resolution' (Burton 1990, Boulding 1990, Gultung 1975, Kelman 1979, etc.). We still, however, do not have one commonly agreed upon and generally accepted theory to explain why destructive conflicts and wars arise.

But do we need one? The old question of 'are human beings inherently 'good' or inherently 'bad' still continues? Some attribute destructive conflict to the constitution of human nature, that is because of 'bad people with bad instincts', and frustrations leading to aggression and hatred (Waltz 1959); others attribute it to particular circumstances and situations, 'bad societies with bad political structures' such as patriarchy, and unfair constitutional type of governance and bad economy(Dahrendorf 1959); and others attribute it to the bad international system which is flawed and lacks a central authority to reconcile disputes and enforce codes of contacts among nations (Heraclides 2002). The constructivists tell us that one is not born a 'killer' or torturer' but is made due to the situations (Fatourou, 1995). People learn to make war (as we also learn to make peace), consider all the institutions that the state uses to prepare citizens for war or socialize them to the idea of war and enemy making.

A similarity that CR and RJ share is that they are not fixed concepts but are historically and culturally situated discourses; both have used the academy as a substantial site of growth and development so as to create multidisciplinary bodies of scholarship and to emphasize the relationship between theory, research and practice. This approach was also reflected in the Skopelos Symposium and the mixed background of its delegates added to this interdisciplinarity. As discussed in chapter 1 by Gavrielides and Artinipoulou, RJ and CR are constantly developing. Moreover, both disciplines have used non-traditional methodologies such as action research, participatory research method, qualitative and focus group discussions, dialogue, negotiation, biographical method, the narrative, etc. Both fields have also paid attention to individual and group experiences; both sought to empower grass roots and civil society; both have advocated non-violence and the values of difference as means for addressing competing interests and needs; both situate a problem in its historical and sociopolitical context which a feminist analysis also considers paramount; both fields of inquiry have challenged and diverged from the traditional realist school of thought about 'power-based theory' and redefined both the concept of power and its application. Moreover, conflict resolvers, as did the feminists, have redefined and expanded the concepts of 'national security' to include 'human security' which encompasses psychological, economic and social security and reject the culture of militarization and hegemonic masculinity as sources of 'safety' in patriarchal contexts.

Needs-Based Theory

Normative political theory viewed conflict as a contest to be won, either by the one or the other side, thus in a zero sum way. By contrast needs-based theorists viewed conflict as a shared problem to be solved in a cooperative manner and encourage win-win solutions, a view that restorative justice practitioners also hold. John Burton, a former diplomat turned academic, developed the 'Basic Human Needs Theory' of conflict resolution. His assumption is based on the fact that when these basic human needs (BHNs) which include identity, security, recognition, justice, dignity and participation, are frustrated and remain unfulfilled then crisis and violent conflict break out. These he called 'ontological needs' and are non-negotiable and universal. Thus in any conflict resolution process these BHNs have to be addressed and taken into account and be fulfilled, otherwise the settlement will remain fragile and renewed crisis will emerge (consider the cases of Cyprus, Lebanon, Bosnia, Iraq, Syria). Burton also made a distinction between needs, values and interests. While he defines needs as ontological and non-negotiable, he views values as offering some limited opportunities for negotiation; interests on the other hand are tangible issues which can be negotiated such as territory, resources and economic benefits. Burton also used different terms to refer to the above distinctions,'*conflict*' is about needs, whereas '*dispute*' is over negotiated values (such as gender equality, prohibition of smoking, no guns, no war games, etc). He also distinguished the terms *conflict resolution* (which is about resolving deep seemingly intractable issues such as identity), from *conflict management* and *conflict settlement* which address 'tangible ' factors of conflict such as natural resources or territory. In my view they are all interconnected because we cannot solve identity which is connected to a particular territory without looking at dissemination of resources and power issues which I believe feminist scholars did make this connection.

Nevertheless, Burton also spoke about transformation of relationships by the solution of those issues and behaviours which led to the creation of the conflict or crime originally; this is exactly what RJ also does. Relationship mending and healing has also been one of goals and values of RJ approach (Gavrielides 2012). Both John Burton and Herbert Kelman used the BHNs approach in their 'third party interactive problem solving workshops' about which I will mention below (Kelman 1997). Kelman has been applying this approach to his work in the Middle East and specifically to the Israeli–Palestinian conflict (Kelman 1979). Ron Fisher and others also developed this approach further (Fisher 1997). It was coined 'track II' approach to distinguish it from 'Track I' which is the official diplomatic or judiciary process. Ron Fisher, Kelman and I have used the same approach and the tool of IPSW in our work in different conflict societies, including Cyprus (Hadjipavlou 2012a, 2012b).

Interest-Based Negotiations Theory

Roger Fisher of Harvard Law School was the father of the 'Getting to Yes' approach to conflict resolution in which he introduced the term 'principled-negotiations' which aims to resolve conflict by differing judgement to a moral principle (Mills, 2006). Such an approach advocates the need for interest based negotiations in contrast to those based on 'positions'. Fisher suggests that an interest would include issues like security, esteem, pleasures, s sense of belonging, recognition, control over one's life (similar to Burton's BHNs) whereas positions refer to how one would achieve those interests. Fisher encourages the need for empathy and asks the question 'why does one hold one position, and another holds a different one?' The aim through 'principled negotiation' is to make concessions and search for mutually profitable solutions. Thus the parties move beyond position-based bargaining to underlying interests (Fisher and Uri 1981).

Paul Lederach (1997) and other scholars developed the *Transformation theory* which views conflict as an opportunity (Chinese character of conflict both as 'crisis' and as 'opportunity') and propagates that building sustainable peace requires far more than elite agreements. Input and involvement must also come from middle and grass toots levels of society and must be incorporated in the peace agreements. Likewise, empowerment theory advocates for the active participation of citizens in peacebuilding campaigns. *Empowerment theory* is closely connected with social justice theory whose main objective is the liberation of the oppressed through dialogue at the grassroots level and social action against impediments that serve to perpetuate conflict (see Freire, 1970). All these theories are in full support of the assertion that input be largely solicited from below. Needless to say that RJ aims similarly.

Kelman (1997) and Ron Fisher (1997) viewing conflict from a social psychological perspective claim that cultural perceptions and ethnic stereotypes need to be factored in any response to ethnic conflict. Specifically, Fisher (1997) argues that the *mindsets*, or *cultural lenses*, with which the disputing parties, (and the potential interveners), view the world are crucial factors for understanding and responding to ethnic disputes. To further the case for grassroots level analyses, research clearly demonstrates that the ways in which the stakeholders frame the issues and the conflict itself explain collaborative success or failure.

To this day, as I mentioned earlier, we do not have a commonly agreed upon theory to explain why destructive conflict and wars arise. Social psychology developed some theories, one of them being the 'Realistic Group Conflict Theory' with an optimistic view. M. Sherif and his group (1966) investigating intergroup conflict found that real intergroup conflict over objective and scarce resources (territories, limited resources or dominance) precedes the phenomena of prejudice and hatred of the Other. Hatred is caused by competition and sociopolitical factors. Take these away, they claim, and we eradicate prejudice and hatred. He used the famous 'Robber Cave' experiment to prove his theory. These scholars proposed the concept of 'superordinate goal' as a means to reduce intergroup hostility which means people will cooperate not because they 'love' each other but because they see shared interests and a win-win possibility. In other words, real conflicts over scarce resources, territories, or dominance result in perception of threat which in turn causes attribution to negative characteristics to the threatening group in order to explain the experienced threat (Bar-Tal 2007b).Thus satisfactory political, economic, social and cultural cooperation, the experience of shared values, experiences of friendship, security and mutual support can enhance conflict reduction and changes in partisan perceptions, negative stereotyping and mutual fears.

The other social psychological theory is the 'Social Identity' theory (pessimistic view) which was developed by Tajfel and his colleagues, (1982). The view is that a central part of our identity is made up of group affiliation (such as our ethnic group, our nation, our state, etc.) and we tend to view 'our group' as better than the Other (thus we construct the 'us' and 'them' dichotomy which then lead to issues of inclusion and exclusion). We have the tendency to downgrade the other because of the human motivation to have feelings of personal worth and positive self-esteem. Individuals constantly classify others into social categories and evaluate them on this basis. Group members ascribe to members of other groups homogeneous traits, intentions and other characteristics (stereotypes). Is it a human need to favour ones' own group at the expense of the out-group? Do we thus despair? Or should we invest time and effort to counteract prejudice and hatred as being causes of destructive conflict? New findings, however, showed that stereotypic content is not universal, but it is culturally and individually bound. That is different groups usually hold different stereotypic contents about the same group, and within the same group, individual group members may hold different stereotypic contents about a particular out-group (Bar-Tal 1998).

Another model as developed by Bar-Tal (1990), the *ethnocentric* model, proposes that the human tendency to perceive the other group by virtue of its mere otherness as different and devalued becomes the underlying basis for negative stereotyping. This tendency prevails when the out-group differs and arouses despise or fear (as in relations between whites and blacks, Turks and Greeks, Jews and Arabs) To address this 'pessimistic view' Allport and others developed the '*Contact*_Theory' (Allport 1954) which informs us that lack of knowledge and information about the other is the father of evil. Creating conditions for groups in conflict to meet and get to know each other as human beings, engage in dialogue and open to new information helps break down negative stereotyping and prejudices. RJ makes use of this theory to get the parties to acknowledge the hurt and harm caused to the other (Gavrielides 2012). However, for this model to work certain conditions are needed such as institutional support; acquaintance potential; cooperative atmosphere; and equal status. Problem-solving workshops, intercommunal dialogue and third party facilitated conflict resolution workshops all are tools in reducing intergroup ignorance, potential conflicts and tensions and enhance mutual understanding and empathy building.

Thus a number of theories and assumptions can inform CR and RJ in the effort to use alternative ways to violence or the formal justice system to address group or individual grievances, fundamental issues and historical traumas and felt injustices.

I will now deal with a specific method CR uses to bring members from adversary groups together to engage in dialogue and I believe this workshop tool of IPS is relevant to the RJ goals and practice and can be used accordingly.

Interactive Problem-Solving Workshop (IPSW)

There is no doubt that most conflict is over real incompatibilities in resources, values, or power, but it is assumed that all conflicts are a mix of objective and subjective factors, and that both of these sets must be addressed for resolution to occur. It is further assumed that subjective factors play a more influential role as conflict escalates to higher levels of intensity, thus increasing the relevance of methods that address subjective elements can contain the tensions(Fisher and Keashly 1991, Fisher 2009). Therefore, IPSWs which I describe in details below focus on a range of perceptual and relationship factors such as misperceptions, misattributions, self-serving biases, unwitting commitments, mistrust, miscommunication, adversarial interactions, self-fulfilling prophecies, and unmet human needs for security, identity, and distributive justice, all of which can be important factors in causing and escalating the conflict.

It is also assumed that authentic and constructive face-to-face interaction is necessary to confront and overcome the many distorted and invalid cognitive elements and to change the adversarial orientations and patterns of interaction that characterize destructive conflict (Fisher 2009). Kelman (1992), one of the pioneers of IPSW, tells us that:

> Workshops are designed to promote a special kind of interaction or discourse that can contribute to the desired political outcome. … the setting, ground rules, and procedures of problem-solving workshops encourage (and permit) interaction marked by the following elements: an emphasis on addressing each other (rather than one's constituencies, or third parties, or the record) and on listening to each other; analytical discussion; adherence to a 'no-fault principle; and a problem-solving mode of interaction. This kind of interaction allows the parties to explore each other's concerns, penetrate each other's perspectives, and take cognizance of each other's constraints. As a result they are able to offer each other the needed reassurances to engage in negotiation and to come up with solutions responsive to both sides' needs and fears (p. 85).

In relation to this kind of interaction induced by IPSWs, it is further assumed that the facilitative and diagnostic role of an impartial and skilled third party is essential to elicit and maintain problem-solving motivation, to support accurate and respectful interaction, to create a mutual analysis that transcends biased narratives, and to assist in the creation of directions and options that will help to de-escalate and resolve the conflict (Fisher, 1972, 2009). Essentially, the role of the third party is to facilitate productive confrontation between the participants, whereby they focus directly on the issues in the conflict as they see them, and then work together to develop strategies to move out of their impasse.

Using the social psychological perspective the focus is on how individuals are connected to social systems, and in this respect, it is assumed that individual changes in perceptions and attitudes that occur as a result of participation in an

IPSW must be transferred to the social system in question for any effects on the conflict to be realized. Individual participants can influence public opinion and policy making in their respective collectivities in many ways, through the roles they enact (for instance advisor, journalist, academic) and through their carrying of information to public constituencies (writings, speeches) and to various decision makers (negotiators, policy makers, leaders). Thus, the process of transfer, by which individual changes come to influence the social system, is a central concern of the IPSW methodology (Fisher 2004, 2009).

The assumptions and general rationale of the IPSW provide a framework in which to articulate the detailed rationale for effecting individual, interactive and systemic changes that are claimed by the methodology. Thus, concepts and processes from a number of levels (individual, group and intergroup) can be used to provide a detailed rationale for the IPSW (Fisher 1990, 2009).

Thus the underlying assumptions the IPSW is based upon when addressing international or intercommunal conflicts, include the following:

a. International conflict is nor viewed only as a conflict between states, (gets away from the nation state centric and realist approach) but it is also a conflict between societies, thus we should pay attention to the importance of sociopsychological and cultural factors in the analysis of conflict along with legal, military, economic and geostrategic ones.
b. Third party efforts need to be directed toward a solution between collectivities rather than simply a settlement between governments.
c. Transformation of the relationship between the parties presupposes that the solution must come from the interactions of the parties themselves who will jointly address their needs.
d. It is assumed that conflict resolution requires direct, bilateral interaction between the key parties, as well as multilateral efforts involving related actors.
e. This interaction in the workshop setting must have a growing character in which the parties can observe directly their differing perceptions and reactions in which they can jointly shape new insights and ideas for the solution.
f. The satisfaction of basic human needs as articulated through identity groups is the ultimate criterion of a satisfactory resolution.
g. It is through interaction around needs and related fears that the parties can identify actions of mutual assurance that are essential to deescalate existential conflicts involving identity and security.
h. Parties must come to understand the constraints which escalate or maintain the conflict and the broader range of influence process that are needed to transform the relationship and the conflict.
i. Finally the assumption that change is possible and parties need to recognize the opportune moments.

j. The IPSW is facilitated by a third party usually of social scientists from various disciplines who are knowledgeable of the issues involved. Surely, some of these assumptions are useful to RJ.

The role of the third party in the ipsw process
The third party is neither a mediator nor a judge but a facilitator who:

a. Provides the framework and appropriate atmosphere for the parties to talk/listen to each other under a set of norms that provide communication and new learnings.
b. Serves as a repository of trust for both sides and encourages the development of a 'working trust' by acknowledging common interests despite differences.
c. Guides the participants through the agenda and the various phases of the workshop.
d. Makes theoretical interventions about group dynamics.
e. Makes content observations about points being made.
f. Makes process observations that suggest how interactions in the workshop may reflect intergroup relations between the sides.
g. It is knowledgeable about the conflict but does not take positions or adjudicate differences but encourages an analytical process which means gaining entry into the other's perspective, trying to understand the situation from where the other comes from and, in the process, integrates it into their own perspective.
h. From time to time summarizes what each side has said so as to move the process ahead.
i. Provides a loose agenda which is often rearranged depending on the questions and priorities raised by the parties.
j. Provides ground rules.

Ground Rules
Why are ground rules important and how they help the process? They provide:

a. Confidentiality which is a very important element so as to allow participants feel free and safe to express themselves.
b. Ask of participants to be respectful and not interrupt the other.
c. Manage anger and strong feelings.
d. Whatever is said in the room stays in the room unless all the participants agree to issue a statement at the end of the workshop and release any outcome or decision taken by the parties.
e. The participants are not there to debate and act as negotiators for their own side but as individuals to listen and learn. They hold no commitment to their leaders and should feel free of official constraints.

The Structure of the IPSW
There is the pre-workshop phase whose purposes include:

a. Selection of the participants. Kelman will always select participants who are influential in their respective communities and spend a great deal of time on this. The idea being the products of the workshop (new ideas, new insights about the other's constraints, fears, etc) be easily transferred to the macro level of each community. Thus most participants come from the unofficial elite level.
b. The convenor of the workshop meets with each individual separate to explain what the workshop process is about, and answers any questions the participant might have, the idea being to create familiarity with the process and build trust with the third party.
c. The participants usually come from a broad ideological spectrum, representing the main trends in their society, they are not all 'peace lovers'.
d. The convenor asks for full commitment to stay on for the duration of the workshop which normally lasts three days.

Workshop phases
Below I present the different steps the IPSW is structured:

Session One: The third party meets separately with all the members of the one party to the conflict and then with the other. Each side is asked to describe to them the situation and the main political issues on the ground. It is an opportunity for the third party and the participants from each side to get to know each other and also exhibit intra-differences; not all come with the same views and perspectives though they are from the same community (intra-party ideological differences, position differences and gender differences emerge). This might last for three hours or more.

Session Two: In this session the two groups meet together with the third party.
a. They are asked to introduce themselves to the other.
b. The Third party introduces the ground rules and the norms of the workshop
c. Each side presents to the other the political situation on the ground, their view of the conflict and the positions of their side. The other can ask clarification questions. (this is usually a 'hot' emotional session because each one wants to project their victimhood and their own justice or injustices suffered because of the Other and occurrence of violations of human rights). It is an emotionally-loaded session and the third party tries to contain aggressive behaviour.

Session Three: The analytic phases begins
a. Each side is asked to present their fundamental fears, concerns and basic needs that any agreement should include and address.

b. Once the needs and concerns are heard and understood by each side there follows a discussion on what would be acceptable by both sides. This means brainstorming on new ideas and new insights which they jointly develop. (this is a creative session but sometimes elements of regression, going back to the 'correct history version' of their side might emerge. (The process is not linear).

Session Four: Once joint acceptable options for possible solutions are worked out by both sides then

a. They start the discussion on the political difficulties, psychological constraints and resistances that such a possible proposed options for a solution would encounter in their respective communities in preparing the societies for a solution (mutual acknowledgement and empathy starts developing here as well as a deeper understanding of macro level and societal constraints that would need to overcome).

Session Five: The discussion now moves to

a. How to overcome these constraints and difficulties and educate the public back home to accept the other's ontological needs and rights.
b. How to help each other in the transfer and implementation of these new ideas and joint agreement (cooperation and understanding each other's societal complexity and difficulties). This is the stage where joint project designs might emerge.
c. Session Six:
d. Next steps after they leave the workshop and the re-entry experience; they each make individual and group commitments to continue the work outside the workshop context.
e. Evaluation of the experience. Usually we see the development of personal connections and friendships across conflict lines which continue back home after the workshop experience is over. A new community of peace builders is gradually being formed and the challenge is how to sustain it?

Benefits of the workshop for the participants
The participants:

a. Learn new skills on analytical thinking and conflict analysis
b. Learn perspective taking
c. Gain new insights and knowledge about the Other's situation and how their own side's official statements affects the Other –and vice versa
d. Develop new friendships from the other side and learn that there are people in the 'enemy camp' with whom they can speak to and cooperate
e. Acknowledge change in their perceptions and attitudes and ideas thus allowing the participants to move away from official rigid positions and develop a different analysis which takes into account both multiple histories and mutual fears and levels of mistrust.

f. Learn the value of compromise and respect for the Other's Basic Human Needs
g. Learn that the IPSW has both educational and political aims
h. The political is how to feed back to one's community the new learning and changes encountered and communicate to the officials the new ideas and options which have been jointly produced in the workshop setting and thus broaden the understanding of positions on each side and what needs and interests lie underneath. It is educational in the sense of personal and group change in attitudes, perceptions and behaviours and learning about the Other from direct experience.
i. It is believed that the new ideas will contribute to making the official negotiation agenda flexible and inclusive of micro level's concerns and fears.

Benefits for the Third Party and the field of CR

a. Commitment to the role of scholar practitioner and that a social scientist has a role to play in international conflict situations
b. Applying in practice theories on the social psychology of international conflict
c. Produce new theoretical knowledge on international conflict resolution through their academic publications, thus IPSW can serve as an action research tool.
d. Show the need for diplomats and officials in negotiations to consult with both third party conflict resolution practitioners/academics and legitimate the contribution of IPSW as an unofficial process to citizens' unofficial diplomacy and conflict resolution.
e. Connection of academia with the societal and policy making levels

The Power Asymmetry Issue

One of the issues that has often been raised in IPSW is the asymmetric relationship the parties in conflict have. The more powerful one in terms of military and economic power usually is perceived as not motivated to want a solution or interested in alternative methods and tools to reach a solution. However, the field of conflict resolution generally posits a broader definition of conflict, seeing it as the ability to bring about desired outcomes (Coleman, 1997). Morton Deutsch, (1973) tells us that it is useful to see power as a relational construct linking the individual actor to the environment, rather than simply as a resource or capability possessed by one or more parties. The view of power as relational has been advocated by feminist scholars who see that the effective use of power depends on the party's motivation, skill and judgement to use their resources to influence others in jointly working together. Feminists make a distinction between 'power over' which is coercive and domination and 'power with' which is enabling the other to act together and cooperate, this being close to CR and RJ processes

(Hadjipavlou 2006). In addition, the dynamic of power is embedded in social relationships in that the use of power needs to be endorsed and legitimated by those who are the targets of influence in order for it to be effective (Folger, Poole, and Stutman, 2009, Fisher 2009).Feminists also critically analyze the patriarchal system, its structures and institutions which are male dominated and marginalize women as agents thus making women vulnerable victims due not only to gender but race, ethnicity and sexual orientation both in domestic violence and other forms of violences (Artinopoulou 2012)

Thus feminist definitions and distinctions of power asymmetries have important implications for the IPSW and RJ methods and their capacity to deal with power dynamics in conflict and issues of human rights violations. The acknowledgement of power imbalances limiting the potential effectiveness of IPSWs occurred fairly early on in the development of the method (Fisher, 1972) and remains an issue which both the third party facilitators and the all the parties involved have to reckon with.

According to Fisher 2009 the IPSW, in contrast to many other types of forum, offers a degree of procedural justice to both parties, but this quality is particularly appealing and useful to the weaker party in asymmetric conflicts as it provides a rare space to present their narrative and to confront the more powerful party. In its design and execution, the IPSW offers all of the essential characteristics of procedural justice identified by Tyler (2000) and other scholars in the field, such as: participation or voice, neutrality and trustworthiness of the third party, and treatment with dignity and respect.

At the same time, most studies of procedural justice in the field of conflict resolution deal with interactions and methods that involve making decisions about the outcome of the conflict, such as plea bargaining, or arbitration. The IPSW does not seek the final outcomes of a conflict, although it may produce principles or creative options that move in that direction. This is a difference from RJ which usually seeks a solution or closure in the relationship mending process. Thus the capacity of the IPSW to provide a forum of equality to parties of unequal power and to operationalize the components of procedural justice should be noted.

In terms of distributive justice, the IPSW also provides a forum for constructive discussion on the inequitable apportioning of resources which is often a primary source of many ethnopolitical conflicts. Burton and other conflict theorists actually include distributive justice in the list of basic human needs, so that a Needs analysis engendered by the IPSW method automatically deals with such issues.

Social Justice Issue

CR has had to also deal with an interesting concept of justice in social relations and in situations of social/political conflict. Justice is a sense of fairness and rightness in social relations and outcomes, and is commonly broken down into two major types: 1) Procedural Justice which is a judgement of how decisions are made and parties in conflict are treated in terms of opportunities to participate and be heard, the perceived neutrality of and trust in the motives of authorities or third parties, and being accorded respect and dignity in the process (Taylor, 2000), and 2) Distributive Justice which is determined by an evaluation of the fairness of outcomes in terms of the distribution of limited resources or incurred costs to the parties (Deutsch 2006, Fisher 2009). Of course, the two forms of justice are linked in reality in that perceptions of fair process tend to lead to perceptions of just outcomes. Research has informed our understanding of conflict and our practice of conflict resolution along with work on a variety of related topics including the sense of injustice, moral exclusion, retributive and restorative justice, oppression and cultural imperialism (Deutsch 2006, Gavrielides 2012). Tyler (2000) informs us that:

> ...research findings about social justice can truly make a contribution to our understanding of how to resolve conflicts and promote stable and lasting peaceful relationships among individuals and groups. ...
>
> One clear possible avenue for the peaceful resolution of conflicts is through an understanding of the psychology of social justice. People's views about what is just or fair are a social facilitator through which the interaction among people and groups is enabled (p. 117).

There is no doubt that feelings of injustices and inequities are crucial elements in protracted and deep-rooted ethnonational conflicts (Hadjipavlou 2006b). Marginalized groups or ethnic minorities often bring forth their grievances of exclusion, humiliation and inequitable access to resources as well as not being given a voice to articulate their just cause and their needs. Often the apparatus of the state which is controlled by the dominant group or a coalition is used to maintain the system of injustice through the application of coercive practices (Fisher 2009, Hadjipavlou-Trigeorgis 1998). In such situations the IPSWs can provide such a forum for the articulation of such injustices. Rouhana (2000), however, thinks that the IPSW has not devoted adequate time to the issue of justice as they do to the cognitive and relationship building issues. And he comments on this issue as follows:

In many approaches there seems to be an underlying assumption that the problem between two ethno national groups is in the way people solve problems (a cognitive problem) or in the way people interact (a relationship problem). Thus, if we can only address the cognitive obstacles and find a formula to solve the conflict or if we can improve mutual perceptions between the protagonists and lead to better relationships between them, the ethnonational conflict can be solved. This is often assumed regardless of what is happening on the ground in terms of realistic conflict over tangible resources, power relations and the related motivations of each side, societal dynamics, international dynamics, the nature of the conflict itself, and the role of ideologies (p. 325).

Rouhana has in mind here the Israeli –Palestinian conflict. And the question arises whether IPSW as was developed in the Western world is promoting real social change toward greater equality and justice? Proponents of the method believe that IPSW is a mechanism for real social change in that it focuses on deep and underlying causes of the problem, relationship mending, healing of ethnic wounds and creation of new ideas to move forward (Hadjipavlou-Trigeorgis 1998).

In general CR as does RJ are founded on the idea that the sources of violence, and the identity and nature of its promoters and perpetrators, must be understood if they are to be combated. Supporters of IPSW and RJ know too well that in many situations the odds are stacked against it, and that it will take great skill and steadfastness and patience to overcome them. They accept that conflict is an essential part of social change and that conflictants will have different interests and perceptions, but insist that conflicts be pursued in a way that recognizes the humanity of those with whom we find ourselves in conflict. The basic approach of the IPSW is to provide equality of status and voice to participants from the two sides of the conflict and to operate with third party impartiality regardless of power differences. Participants are usually selected from the same levels of social status and often matched in terms of education, profession, political orientation and connection to the leadership of their respective societies. Equal numbers are invited from each side regardless of population ratios, and equal opportunities for input into the discussions are assured. The operating norms or ground rules of IPSWs typically safeguard equality and fairness of representation. Fisher supports this view and the ground rule calls for the equality of the two parties within the workshop setting. Asymmetries in power, moral position, or reputation clearly play an important role in the conflict and are usually brought up during the workshop discussions.

I come from Cyprus which has been ethnically divided for nearly four decades due to a coup d'etat and the Turkish invasion in 1974. A conflict culture prevails to this day in both Cypriot communities, the Greek Cypriots and the Turkish Cypriots. Each sees itself the victim of the other. Mutual stereotyping, historical grievances and violations of human rights abound on both sides. Each side excludes the story of the other. The official adversarial discourses often unintentionally promote separation than the professed reunification of the island through intercommunal peace talks which both sides engage in with United Nations good services. There have been, however, groups of citizens, non-governmental organizations and individuals who have been challenging the monolithic and one-sided narratives and propose a more complex analysis and inclusion of the other's grievances and needs (Hadjipavlou 2003, 2006). Numerous CR workshops and dialogue groups across the divide have taken place both on the island and abroad. The use of IPSW has been applied and groups have produced new ideas and creative options for reunification and coexistence. In these workshop settings despite the power asymmetries on the ground both Turkish Cypriot and Greek Cypriot participants are equals in the workshop setting in the sense that each party has the same right to serious consideration of its needs, fears, grievances and concerns. Within the rules of the workshop, Greek Cypriot participants cannot dismiss Turkish Cypriot concerns on the grounds that the Turkish Cypriot minority considers itself the weaker party versus the majority Greek Cypriot community. Neither can the Turkish Cypriot participants dismiss the Greek Cypriot security concerns on the grounds that Turkey is the invader and occupier. This micro level processes and community-led initiatives can complement the peace work at the official level and legitimate citizens' contribution to the bigger reconciliation goal. The challenge remains as to how the macro level utilizes these citizens' new ideas (Hadjipavlou 2012b).

Limitations of IPSW and Normative Implications for RJ

As we have noted there are a number of assumptions that govern the application of IPSW. One of them which also relates to JR approach is the willingness of the parties to interact with the other on the basis of equality and more important exhibit trust in the process and the third party facilitation role. Kelman (1990) points out that for the stronger party this means that they have to accept that past patterns of domination are illegitimate, and for the weaker party that they have reached the stage of confrontation in the conflict and both had a role in the violence. This is not easy and it takes courage and determination to get out of the box!

Another assumption concerns the transfer of the change and new ideas that occur during the workshop interactions. In other words, how the changes in individual participants' perceptions, attitudes and orientations are translated into changes in policy making or public opinion? The method is not a substitute for negotiations Kelman (1972) insists that IPSWs can play a complementary role at all stages of negotiations. This could also mean that RJ is not a panacea by itself but it is a strong alternative to other institutional /structural methods. This too presupposes commitment on the part of participants to link the micro level change to the macro level for both policy goals and influencing the dynamics of the conflict. In the case of Cyprus I noted that for this to happen the unofficial process used by citizens needed to be legitimated by the macro level as a useful tool in informing their work with new ideas that were produced in a non-binding context that could benefit both sides in different ways. Many of the ideas produced in the framework of IPSWs were often viewed as a threat to the entrenched positions of officials on both sides and the participants were criticized for not promoting their community's 'national interests' as defined by the male-dominated elites, which is usually in the context of an 'us' and 'them' dichotomy (Hadjipavlou 2006, 2012b). In the same way that RJ can be viewed by skeptics in the judiciary that it is a 'soft' way of dealing with offenders. However, its strength, like that of CR lies within communities and unofficial settings rather than formal structures thus generating change from below.

When the political culture resists new ideas then an alternative approach maybe is to take very small steps, understand where the resistance stems from and try to develop civil society presence and respect for diversity of views, needs and opinions. Other chapters of this book have discussed the issue of power and how it impacts on the implementation of justice processes including RJ at both the national and international level.

Sometimes the climate of the conflict is charged with negative emotions and restrictive norms on expressing new and conciliatory ideas which are produced at the micro level of the IPSWs, such as changing societal beliefs about the adversary or transforming the relationship between the two parties. Could this be due to lack of clarity about goals, or the absence of theoretical connections between objectives of the problem-solving workshop and the desired effects on the conflict, and the evaluation of impact in terms of demonstrable achievements? In protracted and intractable problems (such as the Cyprus and the Israel/Palestinian conflicts) the challenge to achieve positive changes and impacts on the dynamics of the conflict both within and across communities is indeed daunting.

Nevertheless both the IPSW and RJ approach can establish a situation and a climate which enables the authentic exchange of information and ideas between the participants in a mutually empowering manner. (See for instance the argument developed in Chapter 15 by Gavrielides).

The IPSW operates under the norms and principles of procedural justice, thus providing a rare and valuable forum, particularly for the weaker party, in which acknowledgement and respect are provided and expected. Both RJ and IPSW draw on the Needs theory, the acknowledgement for healing of trauma and historical wounds as well in the transformation of relations between the parties. When both parties become more receptive to a conciliatory and cooperative orientation and are willing to engage in a mutual search for a better understanding of the conflict or offense then the effectiveness of all methods of conflict resolution, including IPSWs, and RJ will be greatly enhanced.

Concluding Thoughts, a Multi-theory Model?

As I have stressed in this chapter, conflicts are complex and complicated and can occur in multiple levels and be of different kinds. I claim that we need a multi-level analysis to inform us about the roots, the consequences and the impact of the conflict on communities, their social relationships and their needs, fears, expectations and values. To do so we need to have at our disposal a number of tools, concepts and theories which will inform a multi-theoretical model which I believe it is more appropriate in our endeavour to understand the deep underlying issues involved in the working of conflicts and crises and of course their management and resolution. Both subjective and objective factors and the dialectic between the two contribute to the creation of conflicts, stresses and destabilization of our daily social worlds.

As it is stressed in the RJ approach and processes used in response to crime and conflict, we need to be adaptable to different groups of people's environments, political, social and cultural systems and basic human needs of safety, recognition, dignity, fairness, respect and well-beingness.

The symposium at Skopelos brought together academics, scholars, practitioners and activists incorporating different disciplinary lenses and the diversity of questions raised enriched the discussion and created a unique synergy which one cannot find in the conventional academic forums. This to me is a testament that the input of different theories and even clashes of ideas provided a new collaborative thinking and sharing in the same goals to bring about a new style of learning and new levels of intellectual curiosity, elements that both the IPSWs and RJ approaches promote on both a theoretical, philosophical and applied fashion. For me the Skopelos experience created a network of minds and bonding of individuals committed to social change and acceptance of differences but above all openness to continue the journey of learning and being curious. The choice of different locations around the island further reinforced the connection between our natural world and our mental, intellectual and relationship building landscapes. A multi-level theory would encompass knowledge and tools from various disciplines thus breaking down the 'expert' notion of disciplinary boundaries and would open up for all of us a new imaginary to engage in. This might be a shared challenge to jointly start imagining.

References

Allport, G.W. 1954. *The Nature of Prejudice*. Reading, MA: Addison Wesley.

Artinopoulou, V. 2012. *Epanorthotiki Dikaiosini (Restorative Justice)* Athens: Nomiki Bibliothiki Group.

Bar-Tal, D. 1990. *Israel-Palestinian Conflict: A Cognitive Analysis*. Oxford: Oxford University Press.

Bar-Tal, D. 1998. Societal Beliefs in Times of Intractable Conflicts: The Israeli Case. *International Journal of Intercultural Relations*, 14, pp. 7–29.

Bar-Tal, D. 2001 Why does Fear Override Hope in Societies Engulfed in Intractable Conflict as it does in the Israeli Society? *Political Psychology*, 22, pp. 601–27.

Boulding, K.E. 1990. *Three Faces of Power*. Thousand Oaks: Sage.

Burton, J.W. 1972. *World Society*. Cambridge: Cambridge University Press.

Burton, J.W. 1990. *Conflict: Human Needs Theory*. New York: St. Martin's Press.

Cockburn, C. 2004. *The Line, Women, Partition and the Gender Order in Cyprus*. London: Zed Books.

Coleman, P.T. 1997. Redefining Ripeness: A Social Psychological Perspective. *Peace and Conflict: Journal of Peace Psychology*, 3, pp. 81–9.

Coser, L. 1956. *The Functions of Social Conflict.* London: Routledge and Kegan Paul.

Dahrendorf, R. 1959. *Class and Class Conflict in Industrial Society.* London: Routledge and Kegan Paul.

Deutsch, M. 1973. *The Resolution of Conflict: Constructive and Destructive Processes*. New Haven, CT: Yale University Press.

Deutsch, M. 2006. Justice and Conflict in *The Handbook of Conflict Resolution: Theory and Practice* edited by M. Deutsch, P.T. Coleman and E.C. Marcus. San Francisco, CA: Jossey-Bass, pp. 46–68.

Fisher, R.J. 1972. Third Party Consultation: A Method for the Study and Resolution of Conflict. *Journal of Conflict Resolution,* 16(1), pp. 67–94.

Fisher, R.J. 1990. *The Social Psychology of Intergroup and International Conflict Resolution*. New York: Springer-Verlag.

Fisher, R.J. 1997. *Interactive Conflict Resolution.* Syracuse NY: Syracuse University Press.

Fisher, R.J. 2004. The Problem-Solving Workshop as a Method of Research. *International Negotiation*, 9, pp. 385–95.

Fisher, R.J. 2009. Issues of Power Asymmetry and Justice in Problem-Solving Workshops. Paper presented at the *32nd Annual Scientific Meeting of the International Society of Political Psychology.* Dublin, Ireland, 14–17 July.

Fisher, R.J. and Keashly, L. 1991. The Potential Complementarity of Mediation and Consultation within a Contingency Model of Third Party Intervention. *Journal of Peace Research*, 28(1), pp. 29–42.

Fisher, R. and Ury, W. 1981. *Getting to Yes: Negotiating an Agreement without Giving In*, London, Sydney, Auckland: Bergvlei SA, Business Books Limited.

Folger, J.P., Poole, M.S. and Stutman, R.K. 2009. *Working Through Conflict* (fifth edition). New York: Longman.

Galtung, J. 1969. Violence, Peace and Peace Research. *Journal of Peace Research*, 6.

Galtung, J. 1975. *Peace: Research, Education, Action.* Copenhagen: C.Eljers.

Gavrielides, T. (ed.) 2012. *Rights and Restoration within Youth Justice*. de Sitter Publications.Hadjipavlou, M. 2003. Inter-ethnic Stereotypes, Neighborliness, and Separation Paradoxes and Challenges in Cyprus. *Journal of Mediterranean Studies*, 13(2), pp. 281–318.

Hadjipavlou, M. 2006. No Permission to Cross: Cypriot Women's Dialogue Across the Divide. *Gender Place and Culture: A Journal of Feminist Geography.* 13(4), pp. 329–51.

Hadjipavlou, M. 2010. *Women and Change in Cyprus. Feminisms, Gender in Conflict*. London: I.B.Tauris.

Hadjipavlou, M. 2012a. An Approach to Empathy Building and Reconciliation: The case of Turkish, Greek and Cypriot Youth in *Rights and Restoration within Youth Justice* edited by T. Gavrielides. Whitby, ON: de Sitter Publications, pp. 367–97.

Hadjipavlou, M. 2012b The Third Alternative Space: Bicommunal Work in Divided Cyprus. *Palestine–Israel Journal of Politics, Economics and Culture Studies,* special issue on Civil Society 18, 2 & 3, pp. 156–85.

Hadjipavlou-Trigeorgis, M. 1987. *Identity Conflict in Divide Societies: The Case of Cyprus*. Unpublished PhD thesis. Boston University, USA.

Hadjipavlou-Trigeorgis, M. 1998. Different Relationships to the Land: Personal Narratives, Political Implications, and Future Possibilities. In: *Cyprus and its people, Nation, Identity, and Experience in an Unimagined Community. 1955–1997,* edited by V. Calotychos. Boulder, CO: Westview Press. pp. 251–77.

Heraclides, A. 1997. Ethnicity, Secessionist Conflict and the International Society: Toward a Normative Paradigm Shift. *Nations and Nationalism*, 3, 4. pp. 156–83.

Kelman, H.C. 1979. An Interactional Approach to Conflict Resolution and its Application to Israeli-Palestinian relations. *International Interactions*, 6, pp. 99–122.

Kelman, H.C. 1992. Informal Mediation by the Scholar/Practitioner in *Mediation in International Relations: Multiple Approaches to Conflict Management* edited by J. Bercovitch and Rubin J. New York: St. Martin's Press, pp. 64–96.

Kelman, H.C. 1997. Social Psychological Dimensions of International Conflict. In: *Peacemaking in International Conflict* edited by I.W. Zartman and J.L.Rasmussen. Washington, DC: United States Institute for Peace.

Lederach, J. 1997. *Building Peace: Sustainable Reconciliation in Divided Societies*. Washington, DC: US Institute of Peace Press.

Sherif, M. 1966. *In Common Predicament: Social Psychology, Intergroup Conflict and Cooperation*. Boston: Houghton Mifflin.

Tyler, T. 2000. Social Justice: Outcome and procedure. *International Journal of Psychology*, 35, pp. 117–25.

Tajfel, H. 1982. *Social Identity and Intergroup Relations*. Cambridge: Cambridge University Press.

Waltz, K. 1959. *Man the State and War. A Theoretical Analysis*. New York: Columbia University Press.

PART III
Back to Basics for Restorative Justice

Chapter 12

Returning Conflict and Justice to Aboriginal Peoples: Restorative Justice Reconsidered

Judah Oudshoorn

Introduction

Written from a Settler perspective, this chapter explores the role of restorative justice practitioners in addressing root causes of crime. Is it expedient to only start restorative justice when a crime happens? What would it mean for restorative justice practitioners to live justice more meaningfully – to support Aboriginal peoples in moving towards self-determination and governance? Using a conflict model of law theory and relevant ideas about legal pluralism, this chapter follows the troubling contours of colonialism in Canada, to point towards a more enduring, peaceful and just relationship between Settler and Aboriginal peoples. This chapter will contribute to a more well-rounded restorative justice ethos by addressing the following questions. If crime is rooted in social causes, how do we better confront both? Or, more specifically, for the purposes of this chapter: if justice has been stolen, how do we (Settlers) return it to Aboriginal peoples?

Terms

Aboriginal

The term Aboriginal is not a perfect descriptor and I am conscious of the problematic nature of imposing labels on first peoples (Proulx, 2003). However, I will follow the lead of many Aboriginal academics in using it for this chapter, as it can inclusively represent a diversity of people under its umbrella (Restoule, 2008). By Aboriginal I mean indigenous, the Metis and Inuit people that live in the country now known as Canada. These are the original inhabitants. Capitalizing Aboriginal indicates that, although this group is not homogenous, each Aboriginal person is deserving of nation-like status, similar to calling a person Canadian. Reasons for this will become self-evident below.

Locating Self as a Settler

I was born in London, Canada to a mother with Scottish heritage and a father who emigrated from the Netherlands as a child. A few years ago I would not have described myself as a settler, as I wrongly assumed that Canada's colonial days were a thing of the past. I grew up with a few Aboriginal friends. In high school I played on the rugby team. My position was called hooker, a front row position in the middle of the scrum. Barely weighing 120lbs when soaking wet I was afforded the protection of two large Aboriginal friends who played on either side of me. We went into rugby battle together. At the end of the day they would bus back to the nearby Reserve – small, often inadequate tracts of land given by the British Crown to Aboriginal peoples during colonial times – while I went to my comfortable, suburban home. I was clueless of the suffering of their people, let alone the sweeping nature of colonialism. I owe much to them, on the field and off.

Waking up to this reality, albeit slowly, I am coming to understand the plight of Aboriginal people and my ignorant complicity in it; colonialism is not a thing of the past. Why is this important? For two reasons. First, a caveat, I am still learning. Will I continue to make choices that support processes of decolonization, or is the status quo an easy way out? Second, what I have to say is more for other non-Aboriginal Canadians, colonizers like me, settlers in someone else's land.

Moving Restorative Justice Beyond Individual Crime

It is not surprising that restorative justice has found applicability beyond criminal justice. Although its initial advent in the 1970s was in this sphere (cf. Gavrielides, 2011), many now apply it to conflict and violence in other settings. Some of this has to do with the normative nature of restorative justice. It articulates a way we *ought* to address harm. Not limited to a particular practice, or simply an alternative methodology for punishing people, Howard Zehr (1990) in *Changing Lenses* suggests it is a paradigm in its developmental stages (p. 180). Paradigms identify issues or problems, while also predicting solutions. As Zehr (1990) says, 'They provide the lens through which we understand phenomena. They determine how we solve problems' (ibid., pp. 86–7). To respond to the problem of harm, he composed a set of guiding questions for restorative justice:

1. Who has been hurt?
2. What are their needs?
3. Whose obligations are these?
4. Who has a stake in the situation?
5. What is the appropriate process to involve stakeholders in an effort to put things right? (Zehr 2002, p. 38)

Where the harm is a crime, restorative justice practitioners have found these questions useful. Likewise there is resonance in other social settings. Educators are using them, as are some people working in child protection. Still others have discovered applicability in the home. Indeed, as a parent, I often use the guiding questions for teaching my children about the impacts of their choices, taking responsibility, as well as understanding what they need when they are hurt. However, as much as these questions enable harm to be addressed more holistically, there are some obvious limits. What if my children are acting up because I have not given them the attention they need, or because they are tired or hungry? What if a child hurts their sibling because a peer is bullying them at school? The point is this, behaviours are influenced by social contexts. One shortcoming of the above five questions is that root causes are ignored (Price Lofton, 2004).

Restorative justice responses to crime often do this. For example, as a restorative justice practitioner, I ask offenders: 'What does it mean to take responsibility for your crime, given the fact that no one is ever likely to be accountable for harm done to you?' I've asked it of adults who perpetrate domestic violence, but grew up witnessing it as children. I've asked it of people who had experienced sexual abuse as children and gone on to perpetrate it later in life. I've asked it of people caught stealing to support a drug habit, who are using to cope with a history of abuse. The list goes on. Does this mean that each of these people is not to be accountable for their own actions? No. Rather, the purpose of identifying this is to say that when a crime is divorced from its context, it is more likely to be repeated in the future.

Even though restorative justice is paradigmatically different from criminal justice, the starting point is often the same. Neither intervention is mobilized until after a crime takes place. However, beginning at the same point as criminal law does can lead to similar problematic outcomes for restorative justice. Criminologist Nils Christie says we place an overwhelming significance on specific crimes, to the exclusion of the particular circumstances that give rise to it. He says, 'the crime is the decisive factor' that puts 'the whole machinery of the state in motion' (Christie, 1981, pp. 44–5). Yet crime does not happen in a vacuum. By conducting justice as such, we are at risk of what Johnstone and Ward (2010) call 'the individualization of blame', whereby criminal law deflects culpability onto the individual perpetrator rather than the societal conditions that influence those actions (ibid., pp. 16–17). As one offender said to me: 'prisons are like putting a band-aid on cancer'. Without getting at root causes, is restorative justice simply dressing a wound while ignoring a disease?

This critique is not new to restorative justice, yet it is significant (Braithwaite, 2002; Price Lofton, 2004). Indeed, it also matters to victims of crime. One of the most common things I hear from victims is that they want to ensure that what happened to them, never happens to anyone else. This is a twofold process. One, individual offenders do need to take responsibility for their crimes. Two, society needs to be accountable for conditions that foster those crimes. Without both, the past is often repeated. As such, Howard Zehr now asks, alongside his guiding questions of restorative justice, What are the root causes of the harm?

A second shortcoming of using crime as the launching point for restorative justice is that harm is not always criminal. As such, some harm will avoid intervention. As Zehr (2002) says, crime is nothing more and nothing less than a law broken (p. 21). The following example illustrates this point. Rule of law in Canada is supposed to mean that everyone is presumed equal before law. Whether a person is prime minister or homeless, neither is allowed to steal bread. Society deems this action illegal. It is criminal. Yet, comparing the lifestyle of the two, why is it allowable for a prime minister to live in wealth, while the homeless person panhandles for survival? Why is opulence, in the face of debilitating poverty, not a crime? Is this not equally, if not more, harmful than stealing for sustenance? Certainly, if the homeless person breaks into the residence of the prime minister to steal a loaf of bread he will be criminally liable. The answer is simple, one is socially acceptable, the other not. One is a crime, while the other is legal. If crime were primarily about harm, the reverse might be true.

Embedded within this discussion is the issue of justice beyond the criminal. As law professor John Braithwaite (2002) suggests, restorative justice runs the risk of ignoring, if not making worse, social injustice (p. 151). He says of Aboriginal imprisonment in his home country of Australia: 'Thus far we have failed badly in Australia to use restorative justice to reduce Aboriginal imprisonment rates. This has been the biggest disappointment to date in the way restorative justice has developed in Australia' (ibid., p. 155). Although he rejects the hypothesis that restorative justice is unimportant to struggles for social justice, he claims that whether or not it contributes positively depends on (a) 'the centrality of freedom as nondomination as a restorative justice value' and (b) 'if restorative justice succeeds in giving voice to dominated Indigenous people' (ibid., p. 157). To advance these two possibilities, restorative justice practitioners can learn from critical theorists. The question is, when the machinery of criminal justice is mobilized whose interests are being served? Is it the rich or poor, prime minister or the homeless, those perpetuating injustice or those struggling for justice? Crime is defined as it is because of the complexity of social relations that it emerges from. This chapter adopts the idea that criminal law reflects the values and interests of the elite over those on the margins of society.

A Framework for Understanding Crime as a Social Phenomenon

Conflict Model of Law

This understanding of social relations regarding crime is known as a conflict model of law. It is contra a consensus one, as articulated by sociologists such as Emile Durkheim and Talcott Parsons in the early and middle parts of the twentieth century. These social scientists described the formation of law as a collective activity; that is, law emerges from a society's common consciousness or shared values (McGarrell and Castellano, 1991). The key point being that law favours the common good. A conflict model, sometimes called moral Marxism, challenges these ideas. Although Marx did not dedicate an entire volume to the study of law, many of his protégés have articulated law as a tool of the elite, using his description of unequal social relations in order to explain this. The central premise is that law is one of the primary instruments used by those who have political and economic power to control and dominate those who do not (Litowitz, 2000; McGarrell and Castellano, 1991; Tifft and Sullivan, 1980).

The Indian Act, enacted in 1876 in Canada, could be characterized as one such example. It was implemented when the nation of Canada was just over ten years old. Although early agreements, like Two Row Wampum, between the British Crown and Aboriginal people described (if not dictated) the relationship between these groups as nations peacefully supporting yet running parallel to each other, Canada imposed the Indian Act on Aboriginal peoples. Rather than sharing land and resources while maintaining independent governance structures, Canada legislated small tracts of land to Aboriginal peoples called Indian Reserves. These places had little to do with traditional lands and disconnected Aboriginals from each other as well as from their primary means of subsistence (Gordon, 2010). Todd Gordon (2010), in his book *Imperialist Canada*, argues that this was a way for the government elite to keep Aboriginals away from coveted resources, while isolating them from organizing and rising up in opposition (p. 72). Today, it is these same laws that oppress Aboriginal peoples in Canada. Not only does this example highlight how law maintains the interests of the elite, it also hints at a deeper reality. Aboriginal people are similarly marginalized to the homeless person described above, but differently in the sense that they are a colonized people. The relationship is not nation to nation, as the Two Row Wampum agreement commands, instead it is one of colonial imperialism.

Conflict of Laws and the Legal Pluralism

Since Aboriginal peoples never relinquished their rights to self-determination and governance then the Indian Act, among other legislation, is in direct competition with Aboriginal laws. There is, in fact, a conflict of laws here. Aboriginal legal scholar Taiaiake Alfred (2009) says 'that Settlers will need to grow beyond their cultural arrogance and learn to be pluralist in their worldviews … this means committing … to make fundamental shifts in relations of power between peoples. We must move from colonial-imperialist relations to pluralist multinational associations of autonomous peoples and territories that respect the basic imperatives of indigenous cultures as well as preserve the stability and benefits of cooperative confederal relations between indigenous nations and other governments' (pp. 266–7). Many settlers have wrongly assumed the absence of Aboriginal legal reality, or chosen to ignore it. This cultural arrogance, as Alfred terms it, denies the value of Aboriginal traditions.

A better understanding of legal pluralism might help settlers return what has been stolen. Legal pluralism acknowledges that all social groups adopt some form of legal structure or ways of managing behaviour. They require some ordering and ways to restore equilibrium when things are off balance. This exists across cultures. Legal scholars often describe this as legal pluralism (Griffiths, 1986; McNamara, 2000; Proulx, 2003). Rather than understanding law as one single entity, or code, it is more practical to recognize multiple legal orders in a society. Social groups like family, schools, faith communities and so on, function within a set of implicit and/or explicit rules or guidelines. Legal scholar John Griffiths (1986) claims that legal pluralism is 'an attribute of all social fields' and that it is a universal component of social organization (p. 38). Some critics of legal pluralist perspectives argue that it is at this point that the term legal pluralism becomes meaningless, as it is impossible to compare the law of a social group with that of a state (von Benda-Beckham, 2002). The critique is that the definition of law goes on *ad infinitum*. However, one proponent in favour of legal pluralism, Franz von Benda-Beckham (2002), argues that any theory on it needs grounding in empirical reality, when it is soon discovered that law is 'a dimension of social organization ... the summary indication of ... normative conceptions for which validity for a certain category of people or territory is asserted' (p. 48).

The growing movement of restorative justice points in this direction. By identifying restorative justice as normative, we are able to see how it is occupying space that was previously described as legalistic, or similar to the functioning of a formal legal system. The administrator at a school might deal with a fight on school property by determining who is the instigator, assigning guilt and subsequently suspending the offending party from attending school. Rather than mimicking a punitive justice system, some schools are now adopting restorative justice approaches. There is still opportunity for the separation of unsafe individuals, but more and more students are meeting to discuss needs and outcomes. The social ordering of the school is a kind of legalism.

In case the reader thinks that the above example is rather spurious, similar to the critique above that the law of a school social group is not comparative to the law of a country, Luke McNamara (2000), a professor studying law and sentencing circles, says this kind of law is equally significant. Discussing Aboriginal law he says it, 'is a matter of empirical reality for First Nation peoples in Canada, irrespective of whether the relevant state legal system can be said to be pluralist in the juristic sense' (p. 10). Griffiths (1986) takes this further, 'An important part of the ideological heritage of the bourgouis revolutions and liberal hegemony of the last few centuries is a complex of ideas concerning the nature of law and its place in social life. According to what I shall call the ideology of legal centralism, law is and should be the law of the state, uniform for all persons, exclusive of all other law, and administered by a single set of state institutions. To the extent that other, lesser normative orderings, such as the church, the family, the voluntary association and the economic organization exist, they ought to be and in fact are hierarchically subordinate to the law and institutions of the state' (pp. 2–3). Thus, again, the law of the state comes to be dominant over other sets of laws. It becomes a monolithic entity, subsuming other plural, legal realities.

The above is not an argument *per se* against some version of the rule of law and the inherent benefits of equality, but it is a reminder that rule of law is defined and wielded by the political elite. Another Aboriginal legal scholar, John Borrows, describes the purpose of rule of law. Citing Aristotle, he outlines how rule of law creates greater opportunity for justice and goodness among the members of a state than the personal rule of man (Borrows, 2002). However, Borrows (2002) argues that Canada contravenes rule of law by arbitrarily ignoring Aboriginal consent and law in the formation of such legislation as the Indian Act: 'The Supreme Court [of Canada] has not effectively articulated how, and by what legal right, assertions of Crown sovereignty grant underlying title to the Crown or displace Aboriginal governance' (p. 117). Without some acknowledgement of legal pluralism, Aboriginal laws, both in substance and process, can be (and are) ignored (McNamara, 2000).

Once a legal plurality is recognized, a conflict of laws approaches and allows new questions: do Canadian courts have jurisdiction to define what crime is for Aboriginal peoples? And, perhaps more importantly, does the Canadian judiciary have the power to define processes of justice for Aboriginal peoples? These are fundamentally important for those practising restorative justice in Canada. Indeed, the advancement of rule of law in societies with many cultures naturally calls for recognition of this diversity (Council of Europe, 2011). Before beginning to offer some preliminary answers to these, a few more comments on the history of Canada's criminal acts towards Aboriginal peoples is necessary. A fuller picture of the context will help restorative justice practitioners think more clearly about Howard Zehr's question about root causes.

What are the Root Causes? Colonialism in Canada

> Violations of solemn promises in the treaties, inhumane conditions in residential schools, the uprooting of whole communities, the denial of rights and respect to patriotic Aboriginal veterans of two world wars, and the great injustices and small indignities inflicted by administration of the Indian Act — all take on mythic power to symbolize present experiences of unrelenting injustice (Royal Commission on Aboriginal Peoples, 1996, p. 30)

My own gateway into understanding Aboriginal issues in Canada happened in two ways. One, I was invited to participate in a healing circle, a gathering of Aboriginal people with some church groups, ones that had been responsible for the crimes of residential schools (explained in part below) towards their children and families. I was profoundly moved by the generosity of the Aboriginal people. It is hard to describe their kindness towards church members who, although they were not direct offenders, still represented the institutions responsible for perpetrating this atrocity. I thought that I would simply observe on coming into the circle. I left thinking of myself for the first time as a settler, a colonizer. Not because anyone shook a finger at me, told or judged me; rather, I began to recognize the history I had learned in school was skewed, only taught from one side, the dominant one. I had learned that my heritage was one of exploration, not conquest; that my history was about new ways of life, not death, dominance and displacement of Aboriginal peoples. This awakening also led me to study restorative justice and subsequently to practise it in Canadian penitentiaries. It was in prisons that I began to meet more Aboriginal people, many more. Actually, they are significantly overrepresented in Canadian prisons. It is this issue that I will use as a window into viewing colonialism.

In 1996, as a measure to correct this overrepresentation of Aboriginals in Canadian federal prisons, the Criminal Code was changed to include section 718.2(e), 'all available sanctions other than imprisonment that are reasonable in the circumstances should be considered for all offenders, *with particular attention to the circumstances of Aboriginal offenders*' (emphasis added). Significantly, in the eight years following this decision the opposite happened, although inmate populations deflated by 13 per cent overall, yet the number of Aboriginals behind bars ballooned up 22 per cent (Correctional Investigator Canada, 2006). In fact, by the year 2006, Aboriginals represented almost 20 per cent of people incarcerated while constituting less than 3 per cent of the total populace (ibid.). What does this tell us? Are Aboriginal peoples more likely than others to behave as criminals? Or is there some deeper explanation?

From the late 1800s to the early 1990s – essentially most of Canadian history – the federal government, along with the active participation of numerous Christian churches, removed over 150,000 Aboriginal children from homes, communities and cultures into residential schools (Truth and Reconciliation Commission of Canada, 2012). Disguised as an exercise in nation building, the process was actually racist and traumatizing. The purpose was assimilation, the vision articulated by its founders, that 'the "savage" was to be made civilized' (Report of the Royal Commission on Aboriginal Peoples, 1996, p. 312). Not allowed to speak their own languages or live within the safety and security of their own families, many Aboriginal people grew up deeply wounded and wholly disconnected from loved ones. The legacy is a tragedy. Generations are traumatized.

Today, even in the year 2013, the Canadian government carries this cycle of violence forward. Residential schools may be abolished, shunned as vestiges of a racist past, however, with each Aboriginal person removed from home, community and culture into a Canadian prison a question appears: what is the nature of the relationship between Aboriginals and non-Aboriginals? Is this residential schools all over again? Has it ever stopped? Fundamentally, it seems to be a further amputation of a people from the limbs of family, home, health, history, culture, identity and so forth. It might, *might*, be justifiable if 3 per cent of the inmate population were Aboriginal, not 20 per cent.

There is much debate about what is causing this overrepresentation. Some say it is a culture conflict, an Aboriginal world view of justice that does not fit with a Eurocentric one. Others claim it is poverty and substance abuse that cause a lot of criminal behaviour in Aboriginal communities. It is the argument of this chapter that these two first points are only partially correct. Really, at the foundation of poverty, substance use and cultural conflict is the fact that Canada has treated Aboriginal people in a criminal, colonial way for the entire history, including the present day, of white Europeans being on Aboriginal soil. Indeed, historian John S. Milloy (1999) even calls his pivotal work on the history of residential schools in Canada *A National Crime*. As such, Aboriginal people are entering into a Canadian criminal justice system as unequals because of colonialism. And, tweaks to the law like section 718.2(e) fail to remedy this because law is accountable to a judiciary that simply perpetuates colonial approaches to relating to Aboriginal people.

In 1982 the Charter of Rights and Freedoms was made into law in Canada. In fact, it was entrenched in the Constitution. This human rights document gave the opportunity for judicial review of Canadian legal cases and provided a framework for an independent judiciary to apply rule of law more fairly. What has been the impact on Aboriginal communities? Although the Charter gives more power to the judiciary to remedy unjust laws, the impact has been almost non-existent.

In his paper titled *The Charter of Whiteness: Twenty-five Years of Maintaining Racial Injustice in the Canadian Criminal Justice System*, lawyer David M. Tanovich (2008) argues that the Charter has had little impact on Aboriginal overrepresentation in prisons because judges are often hostile towards (read, against) Charter challenges based on race and lawyers are not eager to bring them forward. In Tanovich's words: 'These instances of judicial reluctance and hostility certainly tend to confirm the theory that the composition of the judiciary and inherent conservatism of judicial review are some of the biggest hurdles in using litigation as a political tool of change. There is no question that increasing the diversity of the bench is one of the most pressing issues facing the justice system and that it will have a big impact on increasing the cultural competence of the judiciary' (ibid., p. 672).

It is significant that the race of the judge himself (they are mostly male) has an impact on outcomes. Tanovich (2008) suggests that law is typically applied by white, middle-class judges. In his penultimate work, legal scholar William J. Stuntz (2011) claims that the collapse of American criminal justice – or the rise of a racist system – is largely a result of a centralized approach to justice where judges have no stake in the communities where they are imposing sentencing outcomes. Applying this to the Canadian context, judges are white, middle to upper class with no real, shared connection with Aboriginal communities. The result is that the judiciary is blind to white privilege. Donna Coker suggests, 'The … problem for confronting white complacency (or encouragement) of race disparities in the criminal justice is the invisibility (to whites) of white privilege. Whites seldom think of themselves through the lens of race; whiteness is invisible to most whites. Rather, whites see themselves and other whites as individuals.

Because they cannot see the privilege that protects them from police maltreatment and suspicion, they have difficulty believing that such treatment is not in some way invited or provoked when it happens to others' (as quoted in Tanovich, 2008).

Indeed, where law is outsider imposition, it takes on an apparition-like quality, elusive to those on the margins. In *The Law is a White Dog: How Legal Rituals Make and Unmake Persons*, legal scholar Colin Dayan (2011) describes this: 'Persons judged outside the law's protection and marked as enemies of the community resort to an alternative understanding of law. Degraded and socially excluded, they interpret legal precepts and proscriptions for themselves and reconceive the rules: not the opposite of law but its haunting' (p. 252). The opposite of animate is a delusion. What are judges animating, if Canadian justice appears a delusion to Aboriginal nations?

Thus, the overrepresentation of Aboriginal peoples in Canadian prisons exemplifies the colonial nature of the relationship. With judges who are white, law that is an apparition and often impotent, the remedial nature of section 718.2(e) is a band-aid on a cancer. A logical solution would be to return justice to Aboriginal peoples, while supporting their capacity to do so.

Returning Justice to Aboriginal Peoples

> 'We make the case, in this and subsequent volumes, not only for more just treatment of Aboriginal people now and in the future but also for restorative justice, by which we mean the obligation to relinquish control of that which has been unjustly appropriated: the authority of Aboriginal nations to govern their own affairs; control of lands and resources essential to the livelihood of families and communities; and jurisdiction over education, child welfare and community services. We also argue for measures to achieve corrective justice, eliminating the disparities in economic base and individual and collective well-being that have resulted from unjust treatment in the past.' (Royal Commission on Aboriginal Peoples, 1996, p. 28)

The general concern of this chapter is that if practitioners are facilitating restorative justice programs with Aboriginal peoples, or in Aboriginal communities, without proper attention to colonialism, they might be participating in a similar type of oppression to the criminal justice system. *A restorative justice process ought to be about returning justice to Aboriginal peoples.*

Who Has Standing to 'Do' Justice?

Although the language of 'doing' justice is problematic, particularly from the perspective of many Aboriginal people, the question is purposeful. As I contemplate this from my position as a white male of European descent, also coming face-to-face with these circumstances as a restorative justice mediator in Canada's federal prisons, I cannot help but wonder whether the Canadian justice system *deserves* to punish Aboriginal people? Or, for the purposes of this chapter, do restorative justice practitioners of settler descent, deserve to facilitate justice processes for/with Aboriginal people?

Some in the United States of America have started to ask similar questions, although more from an African American perspective. Bryan Stevenson, an anti-death penalty advocate, argues that without knowledge of their history a people is bound to repeat the ills of the past (www.TED.com, 2012). He wonders why African Americans are being given the death penalty at dramatically higher rates than white Americans, on the very land where people of colour were lynched in the decades of segregation (ibid.). Comparing this to Nazi Germany, he states that German scholars have deemed it unconscionable to imagine the death penalty being legal in their country (ibid.). How could a country that systematically imprisoned, tortured and executed millions of Jews reinstitute a similar scheme? It would be outrageous. To implement one would be a denial of history and responsibility for mass atrocities and genocide. Put another way, what would the national reaction be if today the largest proportion of inmates in German prisons were Jewish? There would be an outcry, not only locally but also globally. Really, it is inconceivable. Nonetheless, in Canada the harmful legacy of residential schools has now translated into disproportionate imprisonment for Aboriginal people. Yesterday's residential student is today's inmate. Who will take responsibility for this?

Given the colonial reality of Canada's history, do settlers have any business deciding justice between an Aboriginal victim and an Aboriginal offender? Of course, with many Aboriginal people now living in urban settings, the reality is that it is not likely for both a victim and an offender to be of Aboriginal descent. This increases the complexity (conflict of laws) of the situation, but does not rule out consideration of the appropriateness of settler power, and authority to do justice, in this context.

One place restorative justice has been involved in this kind of situation is *vis-à-vis* sentencing circles. Because much has been written about this topic (cf. Green, 1998; Pranis, Stuart and Wedge, 2003; Pranis, 2005; Proulx, 2003; Ross, 1996), I will not describe the particulars of one. Rather, the case alluded to in the introduction is described below with an explanation of how its outcome adds to the discussion.

Case Study

Context

In 2008, a drunken Aboriginal father abandoned his inadequately dressed children to die in a snowstorm. The conditions for this to happen grew out of 100 years of the sober – intentionally planned – tyranny of a Canadian nation with its disregard of Aboriginal peoples."

Questions for Consideration

The question is not which is worse, the choices of one person or one nation (both are harmful), or who deserves to be accountable, but rather, why does Canada believe it can punish this Aboriginal man and still call it justice? Given the harms to his people through colonial mechanisms like fraudulent treaties, how can what was stolen – the process of justice – be returned to Aboriginal communities?

Story

The morning of 28 January 2008 ended in tragedy for Kaydance and Santana, aged 3 and 15 months respectively. In the days prior, their father, Christopher Pauchay was taking care of the children on his own after a fight with his common-law spouse. In spite of this responsibility he engaged in heavy drinking on the night of 27 January. At some point in the early hours of January 28, thinking that something was wrong with one of his daughters, Christopher Pauchay stumbled outside, incoherently inebriated, into subzero temperatures with the younger one in his arms, to find help. The older girl followed close behind, but both were somehow separated from their father and lost. Sadly, Kaydance and Santana succumbed to hypothermia and froze to death wearing only T-shirts and diapers.

Admitting his wrongdoing, Pauchay pleaded guilty to criminal negligence causing death. Since Pauchay was Aboriginal, the judge in the case, Barry Morgan, honoured his request for a sentencing circle. Bringing together family members, including Tracey Jimmy (his common-law spouse and the mother of the children), Aboriginal elders, community members, the judge, the crown prosecutor, the defence lawyer and Pauchay, the circle met to make sentencing recommendations. The circle suggested a conditional sentence, whereby Pauchay could be reunited with Tracey and a third daughter who had been removed from the family by Children's Aid, receive drug and alcohol counselling and work with the elders for the rest of his life so as to be on a healing journey (*R. vs. Pauchay 2009*). The Yellow Quill First Nation people, although traumatically impacted by the offence, were very supportive of Pauchay and keenly interested in his rehabilitation, which they termed healing.

However, in making his sentencing decision the judge *overruled* the circle. He claimed to factor in Pauchay's Aboriginal heritage as is required by law. In Judge Morgan's words: 'In this case, I am mindful of the background from which Mr. Pauchay comes, and I have considered to what extent he has, to use a phrase from *Cappo*, "been disadvantaged in any way that could be related to the offence which he committed". Although there is no doubt that Mr. Pauchay has been exposed to substance abuse both in his home and in his community, and that poverty has always been a part of his life, that does not end the inquiry. Alcohol was the precipitating factor here, but it cannot act in mitigation in these circumstances, given his lengthy record, and considering his past failure to address his alcohol issues despite numerous opportunities to do so' (R. vs. Pauchay, 2009).

Taking the recommendation of the crown prosecutor he claimed that it would not be possible to give a conditional sentence given the gravity of the offence. In his words: 'I have determined that a proper balancing of the principles of sentencing requires a term of incarceration in a federal penitentiary for a term of three years. In mitigation, whereas I acknowledge that Mr. Pauchay no doubt feels remorse and grief for the devastating consequences of his actions, and that he has entered an early guilty plea, the fact remains that two defenceless young victims lost their lives as a direct consequence of his reckless behaviour. He has a lengthy criminal record, and he has done little, over the years, to deal with the alcohol abuse that is so much a part of his offending behaviour. The principle of denunciation, and the need to foster respect for the judicial system, mandates a significant response. Although I appreciate the input of the community of Yellow Quill, as expressed through the process of the Sentencing Circle, I cannot agree with the recommendations of that circle. Nor do I have the jurisdiction, even were I so inclined, to construct a sentence that would place Mr. Pauchay under community control in the manner suggested; the maximum duration of a probation order is three years. It will be up to Mr. Pauchay to decide, upon his release from prison, whether he wants to access the community support that is available to him at Yellow Quill First Nation' (ibid.). Morgan's decision affirmed denunciation and deterrence as the most important factors for this decision.

What is also affirmed in the Case Study is Canada's dominant, colonizing role over Aboriginal peoples. The sentencing circle is a version of restorative justice and, in some ways, what happened here was an attempt to give power back to Aboriginal peoples. The Gladue legislation, acknowledges overrepresentation of Aboriginal peoples in Canadian prisons. Sentencing circles seek to place justice in the hands of those most affected by a crime. Indeed, Pranis, Stuart and Wedge (2003) argue that circles give voice to those on the margins. Yet, the overarching power of the judge and the Canadian legal system ended up overruling the justice of the community. Do the community members not understand the gravity of the offence? Does the mother of the deceased children not understand the harm that has been done? Similar questions could be asked of the judge: how has deterrence and denunciation been working for Aboriginal peoples in regards to justice? Obviously it has not, as the Aboriginal prison population continues to grow.

Sentencing circles would be more aptly titled if they were called Recommendation Circles instead. Essentially, that is what they are. A judge is ultimately responsible for a sentencing decision and the recommendations of a circle are only one option at his or her disposal, and they are not the strongest one. Without justification in the Criminal Code, a judge must rely on case law to determine whether or not recommendationsfit firstly with the law as code and secondly with case law. It is hard to imagine, then, that sentencing circles are much more than a way of appeasing communities – in this case, Aboriginal ones – that have been ravaged by crime and the ensuing parade of people into prison. Some might call this hegemony, oppressors finding a way for the oppressed to acquiesce to their suffering and domination (Litowitz, 2000).

There is some debate in the literature about this. Some argue that sentencing circles are in fact a move in the right direction (for example Zellerer, Chapter 13 in this volume). McNamara (2000) argues that, although sentencing circles operate under some constraint, they are putting judicial decision-making in the hands of Aboriginal peoples: 'the Canadian criminal justice system has been motivated, at least in part, by a genuine recognition of the legitimacy, relevance and value of Aboriginal law and justice processes, cultural values and perspectives (including the authority of Aboriginal Elders)' (McNamara, 2000, p. 29). Kay Pranis, cited in Braithwaite (2002), claims that human beings are storytelling creatures. Her hope is that sentencing circles prove a positive way forward in addressing social injustices, as there is opportunity for people to truly hear each other. Others like John Borrows (2002) believe that without further acknowledgement of the validity of Aboriginal laws, not much will change. He says that in spite of case law and history to prove otherwise, many believe Aboriginal law and processes to be inferior (Borrows 2002). Craig Proulx (2003), a Metis scholar specializing in Aboriginal justice issues among others, makes a case that sentencing circles are part of the slow process of 'building capacity for eventual self-government in justice' (ibid., p. 32). Crown Attorney Rupert Ross and Aboriginal Judge Murray Sinclair – who have both had significant roles in sentencing circles in Canada – argue that sentencing circles can be more aligned with Aboriginal communities and less with the system; that is, where communities are more involved in initiating and supporting the process, and where processes are focused on Aboriginal healing, there is a greater likelihood for success (Green, 1998). This seems to indicate there is a cautious role for restorative justice in Aboriginal communities.

However, at the heart of the debate, is the question of authority. Aboriginal people want settlers to know that there are alternative epistemologies and ways of doing justice (Proulx, 2003; Alfred, 2009). If sentencing circles are limited by law, or a judge's unwillingness to apply sentencing differently, I have to wonder why power – judicial discretion and authority – is not vested in a person of Aboriginal descent who speaks for Aboriginal people.

Aristotle in *Nicomachean Ethics* describes a judge as 'a sort of animate justice' responsible for restoring equality (p. 115) (see also Artinopoulou and Gavrielides, Chapter 2 in this volume). This highlights what is vested in judicial power: a way of bringing justice to life. It is descriptive of section 718.2(e) of the Canadian Criminal Code, which allows for a judge to look beyond the code. It draws judicial notice to the humanity, the life, of the offender. In the landmark case of *R. vs. Gladue* (1999) the Supreme Court of Canada decided that lower courts had erred in the application of 718.2(e) (described above), by ignoring the Aboriginal heritage of a particular offender in sentencing. Significantly this ruling stated: 'The provision is not simply a codification of existing jurisprudence. It is remedial in nature and is designed to ameliorate the serious problem of overrepresentation of Aboriginal people in prisons, and to encourage sentencing judges to have recourse to a restorative approach to sentencing. There is a judicial duty to give the provision's remedial purpose real force' (R. vs. Gladue, 1999). Thus, discretion is important because it recognizes that justice cannot be one size fits all in its approach. It is about bringing justice to life. The way forward might be in thinking about 'living' justice rather than simply 'doing' it. Living justice might be about appropriately sharing power and returning it to those it has been misappropriated from.

Who Has the Standing to 'Live' Justice?

Once settlers like myself recognize that we do not necessarily have the standing to 'do' justice to Aboriginal peoples, what then is the role of the restorative justice practitioner? There are two possibilities. One, from an individual case perspective, when it is still conceivable that a practitioner might be invited to facilitate a restorative justice process involving Aboriginal people. Two, in light of settler treaty obligations there is much work to be done to consider the social crimes perpetrated by settlers. Both of these are more about 'living' justice than 'doing' it. Proulx (2003) says the following about Aboriginal justice: 'Justice and law for many Aboriginal people in the past were not separated from everyday life. They were integral parts of daily life. This understanding is still held by many Aboriginal people, and today they are trying to revive this understanding and re-inculcate it within the lives of Aboriginal people who have lost or were never taught it. One way this is being taught is that justice and law, on the most basic level are about relationships' (p. 39). There are ways for restorative justice practitioners to live a more just relationship with Aboriginal peoples from a case and a community perspective.

Living justice: from a case perspective (starting from an individual crime)

(I) SHARING POWER WITH THE PEOPLE: HOW CAN ONE BE A COORDINATOR NOT MEDIATOR?

The restorative justice practice of Family Group Decision Making (FGDM) is one possible template for forging a shared power relationship between a practitioner and an Aboriginal community. FGDM is an inherently democratic process since it seeks to put power in the hands of people most directly affected by a crime; in practice, FGDM, is mostly used in child protection cases (Merkel-Holguin, 2004, p. 155). Recognizing the inherent difficulty and potentially traumatic impact of removing children from families, FGDM seeks to do child protection in a way that honours the decision-making abilities of families, even ones where child safety has been put at risk. A restorative justice practitioner is not a mediator or even a facilitator in this situation. Rather, they are a coordinator, responsible for bringing together all people significantly connected to a child, family, kin and other supporters. In fact, during the restorative justice process, the coordinator is not present as part of the dialogue. Only family, kin and supporters are responsible for discussing and developing a plan of care for the child. When the family does not have capacity to understand an issue, professional support and expertise is offered.

This model is significant for its locus of power, as well as its ability to impact social and power relations. In fact, researchers are finding that it is changing the relationship between the state and families, as well as between the community and state (ibid., p. 167). In this sense, families are given the ability to self-govern and respond to their own needs, with some support from the state. Most studies find high levels of satisfaction among family members. Joan Pennel (2006), a lead researcher in this area, says that instead of being a state imposition FGDM are noted for 'democratic decision processes of consensus … yield[ing] plans that families from diverse cultures are willing to put their best effort into carrying out' (p. 276). The work of the restorative justice coordinator, then, is in strengthening informal networks of support for the child and the social capital of all involved (ibid.).

So, what would it look like for restorative justice practitioners to apply some of this approach in Aboriginal communities? Could this be another step in moving Aboriginal justice towards being self-governing? This takes restorative justice beyond case processing towards community building. In the words of restorative justice researcher Elizabeth Elliott (2011): 'When restorative justice practices are motivated by a community-building focus rather than a case-processing criminal-justice mandate, opportunities for encountering and addressing inequalities and social justice issues become clear' (p. 191).

(II) EXPANDING THE CIRCLE: WHO ELSE NEEDS TO BE INCLUDED?

The coordinator in FGDM is responsible for finding out who to invite to a meeting. If justice is about relationship, I wonder who else needs to be invited into a restorative justice circle in Aboriginal communities. I learned about the plight (and strength) of Aboriginal peoples in Canada through an invitation to attend a healing circle. At the time I saw myself as an outsider coming to observe, through participation I recognized the role, the responsibility, that I needed to take as a settler. With the permission of the primary participants in a restorative justice process, it might be helpful to think about circles as inclusive, community building processes. Are there students who could take part? What about political leaders? Justice as relationship advocates that change happens when we hear each other's stories (Braithwaite, 2002). Could expanding the circle of an individual restorative justice case, improve the likelihood that it also addresses root causes?

Living justice: from a community perspective (starting from a social crime)

(I) COUCHING ABORIGINAL ISSUES IN SETTLER PROBLEMS: HOW CAN SETTLERS TAKE RESPONSIBILITY?

The Violence Against Women (VAW) movement has done an excellent job helping society understand violence as something that is gender-based. Yet in continuing to refer to it as VAW, we sometimes cloud the reality that males, whether against women, children, or other men, perpetrate the majority of violence. By focusing (necessary) attention on the victims, the root of the issue – male violence – can at times remain unexamined. My concern is similar when it comes to Aboriginal issues. Yes, we need to identify issues affecting Aboriginal peoples in Canada as the 1996 Royal Commission on Aboriginal Peoples has done. However, what about an examination of the other side? An Aboriginal Commission on Settler People. As restorative justice practitioners, it is important for us to advocate for victim needs, while also continuing to put the spotlight on those needing to take responsibility.

(ii) The needs of Aboriginal peoples: how can settlers listen and follow their lead?

What are Aboriginal people asking for? Although, as mentioned at the outset, this is not a homogenous group of people, there are significant treaty obligations that settler people are not following through on. From a human rights perspective, the United Nations has consistently damned Canada for its abhorrent treatment of Aboriginal peoples (cf. United Nations Committee on the Elimination of Racial Discrimination). Yet many in the Aboriginal community have consistently offered a meaningful way forward. A recent example of this is a pamphlet put together by Aboriginal leaders Taiaiake Alfred and Tobold Rollo (2012) titled *Resetting and Restoring the Relationship between Indigenous Peoples and Canada*. I quote five of their ideas verbatim:

> 1. Declaration of Responsibility.
>
> To restore this relationship, the Government of Canada must acknowledge the systematic nature of Canada's colonial past and present. Recent governments have issued apologies for specific colonial programs, such as the Residential School System, but have yet to acknowledge responsibility for the full range of colonial institutions, including legislation currently enforced under the Indian Act.
>
> 2. Legislated Recognition of Political Authority.
>
> The Government of Canada must enact legislation that recognizes the inherent rights of Indigenous Nations to designate political authority according to their own laws, governing principles, and customs. The law will provide guidance and give expression to the already existing recognition of the right of self-determination found in Section 35 of the Canadian Constitution and the nation-to-nation relationship established by previous treaties and agreements. In addition, it will allow systems of political authority and accountability to take root in Indigenous communities that will correct the democratically defective and dysfunctional Indian Act system.
>
> 3. Legislated Devolution of Governance.
>
> The Government of Canada must devolve control over social, cultural, economic, housing, health, and educational services to Indigenous governments,

> in accordance with Section 35 of the Constitution of Canada. The current 'duty to consult' must be replaced with federally structured shared-jurisdiction over lands consider for urban and economic development. Indigenous jurisdiction will provide a stop-gap measure against the erosion of environmental protections under external pressures.
>
> 4. Legislation of Crown Fiduciary Duty.
>
> The Government of Canada must provide funding, training, and resources sufficient to assist Indigenous nations while they re-establish their capacities and autonomy as Indigenous Nations. As these capacities are realized, the cost to Canada will diminish sharply until it is no longer needed.
>
> 5. Unrestricted Modern Treaty Process.
>
> The Government of Canada must remove formal and informal restrictions placed on treaty negotiations with Indigenous governments over rights to land and culture. A refusal to negotiate in good faith amounts to a bare assertion of colonial sovereignty, which stands as an affront to international law and to the Constitution of Canada itself. (p. 2)

If we want to take the next step in acknowledgement and repair of harm, we will need further systemic change. The relationship between Aboriginal peoples and settlers needs to be rewritten. Taiaiake Alfred (2009) says we need to go beyond reconciliation. He argues that reconciliation will simply perpetuate the status quo. What is called for is resurgence, based on restitution and compensation to support Aboriginal peoples in re-establishing what was never surrendered: self-determination and governance (Alfred, 2009). What was stolen must be given back: 'When we say to the Settlers, "Give it back," are we talking about them giving up the country and moving away? No. Irredentism has never been the vision of our peoples. When we say "Give it back," we're talking about Settlers demonstrating respect for what we share – the land and its resources – and making things right by offering us the dignity and freedom we are due and returning our power and land enough to be self-sufficient' (Alfred, 2009: 153).

(III) SETTLERS AS ALLIES – HOW CAN WE WALK ALONGSIDE ABORIGINAL PEOPLES?

Following (i) and (ii) – from Aboriginal issues towards settler problems, from colonial imposition to following the lead of Aboriginal peoples – the logical next step is for settlers to function as allies, supporting Aboriginal peoples in accomplishing the five points above. As I put the finishing touches to this chapter, Chief Theresa Spence of Attiwapiskat, a small Aboriginal Reserve in Canada, is over thirty days into a hunger strike. Her community is ravaged by poverty and traumatized by the colonial nature of the relationship with Canada. She is currently living in a tent fifteen minutes walk from the Parliament of

Canada and is demanding a meeting with the prime minister and governor general, or Queen's representative. The role of settler allies is to support her, to call attention to her struggle, to challenge our political leaders to listen, to make changes. This, along with a growing grassroots movement of Aboriginal peoples called #idlenomore, challenges all settlers to learn, to be re-educated about our history and present and to walk alongside Aboriginal peoples to make our future one where right relationships, based on the Two Row Wampum, are established.

Conclusion: Directions for Restorative Justice

Articulating a clearer restorative justice ethos ought to involve a strengthened relationship with human rights. Therefore much of this chapter is about advocating self-determination, equality and fairness for Aboriginal peoples. Each of these is a value of human rights (see Gavrielides, 2012). This is as much about entrenching Aboriginal rights in law – like section 35 in the Constitution of Canada – as it is about creating safe and respectful social processes for implementation. Most philosophies of restorative justice suggest putting power in the hands of people most affected by harms (Zehr, 2002). Yet, as this chapter suggests, when starting points are legal definitions of crime or outcomes are limited by the state (as in the Pauchay case), we might simply be perpetuating the opposite: colonialism, inequality and injustice. Restorative justice processes are moving in the direction of living justice when the following are asked:

- What are the root causes of a particular crime?
- Who is to be accountable for these causes (like the state)?
- What is the best process for righting these social harms?
- And, more specifically, from the Case Study in this chapter:
- How can the state focus on the root cause, while supporting the capacity of stakeholders to meet the justice needs of those affected by a crime?
- What in law needs to change (for example, principles of sentencing), in order for judges to return the power of self-determination and justice to Aboriginal peoples?

In these ways restorative justice, as a practice, can better intervene in crime, recognizing its emergence in social harms. Living restorative justice is about meaningful interventions that address the justice needs of those most affected by harms. But, it does not stop there. Living restorative justice is about protecting individual human rights while also acknowledging the power of groups to determine their own meanings of justice.

References

Alfred, T. 2009. *Wasase: Indigenous Pathways of Action and Freedom*. North York: University of Toronto Press.

Alfred, T. and Rollo T. 2012. *Resetting and Restoring the Relationship Between Indigenous Peoples and Canada*. Pamphlet.

Aristotle translated by Irwin, T. 1999. *Nicomachean Ethics*. (second edition). Indianapolis: Hackett Publishing.

Borrows, J. 2002. *Recovering Canada: The Resurgence of Indigenous Law*. Toronto: University of Toronto Press.

Borrows, J. 2010. *Canada's Indigenous Constitution*. Toronto: University of Toronto Press.

Braithwaite, J. 2002. *Restorative Justice and Responsive Regulation*. New York: Oxford University Press.

Christie, N. 1981. *Limits to Pain: The Role of Punishment in Penal Policy*. Eugene: Wipf and Stock Publishers.

Correctional Investigator Canada. 2006. *Backgrounder: Aboriginal Inmates* [online]. Available at: http://www.oci-bec.gc.ca/rpt/annrpt/annrpt20052006info-eng.aspx [accessed: 8 May 2012].

Council of Europe. 2011. *Meeting the Challenge of Inter-faith and Inter-Cultural Tensions at a Local Level* [online]. Available at: https://wcd.coe.int/ViewDoc.jsp?id=1767329&Site=DC [accessed: 19 January 2013].

Dayan, C. 2011. *The Law is a White Dog: How Legal Rituals Make and Unmake Persons*. Princeton: Princeton University Press.

Elliott, E.M. 2011. *Security With Care: Restorative Justice and Healthy Societies*. Black Point: Fernwood Publishing.

Gavrielides, T. 2011. Restorative Practices: From the Early Societies to the 1970s. *Internet Journal of Criminology* [online]. pp. 1–20. Available at http://www.internetjournalofcriminology.com/ijcarticles.html [accessed: 5 July 2012].

Gavrielides, T. 2012. *Rights and Restoration in Youth Justice*. Whitby, ON: de Sitter Publications.

Gordon, T. 2010. *Imperialist Canada*. Winnipeg: Arbeiter Ring Publishing.

Green, R. 1998. *Justice in Aboriginal Communities: Sentencing Alternatives*. Saskatoon: Purich Publishing.

Griffiths, J. 1986. What is Legal Pluralism? *Journal of Legal Pluralism*. 24, pp. 1–55.

Johnstone, G. and Ward, T. 2010. *Law and Crime: Key Approaches to Criminology*. London: Sage Publications.

Litowitz, D. 2000. Gramsci, Hegemony, and the Law. *Brigham Young University Law Review*, 2000(2), pp. 515–51.

McGarrell, E.F. and Castellano T.C. 1991. An Integrative Conflict Model of the Criminal Law Formation Process. *Journal of Research in Crime and Delinquency*, 28(2), pp. 174–96.

McNamara, L. 2000. The Locus of Decision-Making Authority in Circle Sentencing: The Significance of Criteria and Guidelines. *Windsor Yearbook of Access to Justice*, 18, pp. 60–114.

Merkel-Holguin, L. 2004. Sharing Power with the People: Family Group Conferencing as a Democratic Experiment. *Journal of Sociology & Social Welfare*, 31, pp. 155–73.

Milloy, J.S. 1999. *A National Crime: the Canadian Government and the Residential School System 1879 to 1986*. Winnipeg: The University of Manitoba Press.

Pennell, J. 2006. Restorative Practices and Child Welfare: Toward an Inclusive Civil Society. *Journal of Social Issues*, 62(2), pp. 259–79.

Pranis, K. 2005. *The Little Book of Circle Processes: A New/Old Approach to Peacemaking*. Intercourse: Good Books.

Pranis, K., Stuart B. and Wedge M. 2003. *Peacemaking Circles: From Crime to Community*. St. Paul: Living Justice Press.

Price Lofton, B. 2004. Does Restorative Justice Challenge Systemic Injustices?, in *Critical Issues in Restorative Justice*, edited by H. Zehr and B. Toews. Monsey: Criminal Justice Press.

Proulx, C. 2003. *Reclaiming Aboriginal Justice, Identity, and Community*. Saskatoon: Purich Publishing.

Report of the Royal Commission on Aboriginal Peoples. 1996. Canada.

Restoule, J.P. 2008. The Values Carry On: Aboriginal Identity Formation of the Urban-Raised Generation. *Canadian Journal of Native Education*, 31(2), pp. 15–33.

Ross, R. 1996. *Returning to the Teachings: Exploring Aboriginal Justice*. Toronto: Penguin Canada.

R. vs. Gladue. 1999. ABCA 61 (CanLII) [online]. Available at: http://canlii.ca/t/22kpp [accessed: 8 May 2012].

R. vs. Pauchay. 1999. SKPC 35 (CanLII) [online]. Available at: http://canlii.ca/t/22pqh [accessed: 8 May 2012].

Stevenson, B. 2012. *We Need to Talk About an Injustice* [online]. Available at: http://www.ted.com/talks/bryan_stevenson_we_need_to_talk_about_an_injustice.html [accessed: 15 March 2012].

Stuntz, W.J. 2011. *The Collapse of American Criminal Justice*. USA: Harvard University Press.

Tanovich, D.M. 2008. The Charter of Whiteness: Twenty-Five Years of Maintaining Racial Injustice in the Canadian Criminal Justice System. *Supreme Court Law Review*. 2008(2d), pp. 655–86.

Tifft, L. and Sullivan, D. 1980. *The Struggle to be Human: Crime, Criminology and Anarchism*. UK: Cienfuegos Press.

Truth and Reconciliation Commission Canada. 2012. *Residential Schools* [online]. Available at: http://www.trc.ca/websites/trcinstitution/index.php?p=4 [accessed: 8 May 2012].

von Benda-Beckham, F. 2002. Who's Afraid of Legal Pluralism? *Journal of Legal Pluralism*, 2002(47), pp. 37–83.

Zehr, H. 1990. *Changing Lenses: A New Focus for Crime and Justice* (third edition). Scottdale: Herald Press.

Zehr, H. 2002. *The Little Book of Restorative Justice*. Intercourse: Good Books.

Chapter 13
Realizing the Potential of Restorative Justice

Evelyn Zellerer

Introduction

Restorative justice is a rapidly growing global movement with a variety of programmes in countries all over the world. After more than 30 years of practical experience and an explosion of literature on the topic, this is a good time to revisit and reflect on the vision of restorative justice. This book's ambition to reconstruct restorative justice philosophy provides a good framework and opportunity to pose questions. This chapter centres on two broad inquiries: What is the potential of restorative justice? What could guide us in realizing its potential? We need more 'clarity about where the restorative justice "train" should be headed and, in some cases, to nudge the train back onto the track' (Zehr, 2002, p. 5).

We continue to grapple with terminology, definitions and parameters. It was not until the 1990s that 'restorative justice' became the most accepted and all-encompassing term for what we were envisioning and doing. Restorative justice has been conceptualized in different ways, as summarized by Van Ness (2006, p. 13, emphasis in original; see Johnstone and Van Ness 2007):

> 'Restorative justice' is sometimes used narrowly to refer to programmes that bring affected parties together to agree on how to respond to crime (this might be called the *encounter* conception of restorative justice). It is used more broadly by others to refer to a theory of reparation and prevention that would influence all criminal justice (the *reparative* conception). Finally, it is used most broadly to refer to a belief that the preferred response to all conflict – indeed to all of life – is peacebuilding through dialogue and agreement of the parties (the *transformative* conception).

Restorative justice is an umbrella term, with a variety of practices and programmes that fall under it. One misidentification is that restorative justice is a particular practice, for example conferencing. Practices and programmes are different expressions of how the vision of restorative justice can manifest. One of the gifts of restorative justice is that it is dynamic and invites us to continually engage with individuals, groups, organizations and communities to co-create ways that best meet everyone's needs and resolves the issues at hand in a generative way.

I concur with Zehr (1990, 2002) that restorative justice is a change of lenses. It provides an alternative holistic framework for understanding and responding to conflict and harm. Ultimately, it is an 'approach to life, interpersonal relationships and a way of prioritizing what is important in the process of learning how to coexist' (Gavrielides, 2007, p. 139).

I use the term in a broad transformative sense because the vision of restorative justice is transformation. Transformation is multifaceted, applying to how we perceive and respond to conflict and crime; how individuals, communities and governments engage; the possibilities of outcomes; and current structures like the justice system itself.

To fully appreciate its vision and realize its transformative potential, we need to view restorative justice from a broader perspective. In this chapter, I posit that there are two overarching ways of being that operate in the world. One I call the separatist paradigm and the other the wholeness dimension. While restorative justice was born from the wholeness dimension, it is mainly practised within the separatist paradigm. This poses some challenges which I highlight.

Restorative justice is poised to make a significant contribution to the broader paradigm shift occurring in the world. There is also the possibility that it will be co-opted or subsumed by current systems, thereby making improvements but not substantive changes or realizing its full potential. I suggest that shared values offer guidance to ensure that we are operating within and contributing to the restorative vision and human rights, as well as to the emerging wholeness dimension. Peacemaking circles are then described as an exemplar.

Paradigms and the Current Shift

The first known modern usage of the Greek word 'paradigm' was in the fifteenth century. It was primarily used in reference to language. Since the 1960s, the term has been applied to the sciences and then to other disciplines and broadly means 'a philosophical or theoretical framework of any kind' (Merriam-Webster Dictionary).

Kuhn (1970) is famous for explaining how paradigms operate within science and over time. A paradigm directs us to both problems and solutions, telling us what is to be observed, the kind of questions to ask, and how research is to be conducted and results interpreted.

A paradigm has within it a set of values, assumptions, theories, generalizations and practices. It dictates how we perceive, evaluate and ultimately experience reality. What we consider 'normal' exists for a period of time until we go through a paradigm shift, whereby our understanding of reality changes. Kuhn (1970, p. 92) explains that a growing sense that 'existing institutions have ceased adequately to meet the problems posed by an environment they have in part created' can lead to a crisis and then a revolution. For example, Einstein challenged two hundred years of Newtonian understanding of force and motion with his work on relativity; new physics was created.

I posit that similarly, restorative justice challenges the 'normal' reality in relation to crime and justice (Zehr, 1990, 1995; Barnett, 1977; Christie, 1977). While we can talk about paradigms of justice, the criminal justice and restorative justice approaches themselves belong within two different broader frameworks. We can call one the separatist paradigm and the other the wholeness dimension.

The separatist paradigm is the philosophy of separation, disconnection, objectivity, dichotomous thinking and justified violence. It is an ordered, linear, hierarchical approach to the world. This is a Hobbesian, Newtonian and Darwinian world view. For example, Thomas Hobbes argues in his book Leviathan (1651) that man's state of nature is one of violence and war, whereby life is 'solitary, poor, nasty, brutish and short'. We therefore require 'the terror of some power', to be ruled by an absolute sovereign.

Within this separatist paradigm, the modern criminal justice system was conceived and thrives. A judge presides over an adversarial battle between the state and the defence lawyer representing the accused. It is a game of win or lose. Those deemed guilty must get their just desserts through punishment. Justice, within this paradigm, is retributive, punitive and proportionate.

Prisons are used to separate and punish the guilty, 'bad people' (see Foucault, 1977). Within prisons, segregation cells were built for the bad of the bad. And the death penalty allows the state to kill the worst of the worse. It is a never-ending spiral downward into how we identify, separate, punish and take out the people who break laws; we just have to get tough enough. It has led us to backlogged courts, mandatory minimums, three strikes and you're out laws and overflowing prisons.

This is the reality of polarities and dichotomous thinking, which creates right and wrong, good and bad, black and white, us and them. Individuals and institutions operating within this paradigm believe that only one truth exists, with a capital T, within an objective reality. This forces people to pit themselves against each other to prove the supremacy and rightness of their truth. Judgments and sanctions are designed to be declaratory (declaring what is right and wrong) and punitive (punishing those who are judged wrong). Who decides what is right and wrong? Those with the structural power to do so on our, the people's, behalf decide (judges and government officials). As Christie (1977) points out, the state stole conflict from individuals and communities.

Within the separatist paradigm, there is a consistency in what decisions are made and justified. There is a distortion of power and a manufacturing of power imbalances. Note that other chapters in this book elaborate on the role of power and how it interferes with the delivery of justice, including restorative justice. Within the separatist paradigm, the force of one person or group against another is seen as the way to produce desired results. We wage war against the enemy, dropping bombs to create peace; hit children to teach them a lesson; practise eugenics and genocide to create a superior race; put animals through excruciating experiments to advance knowledge; confine whales in aquariums for amusement; clear cut rainforests to provide resources. George Bush (USA), Stephen Harper

(Canada), Omar al-Bashir (Sudan) and Pieter Botha (South Africa) are just some of the leaders who operated within this paradigm.

What has this paradigm created and how is it working for us? Take a look around! At every level we are disconnected and destroying each other and the planet. It is not sustainable. The evidence for the failures of criminal justice is massive and clear. Punishment and locking people up in prison does not reduce crime; recidivism rates in North America, for example, are high at about 70 per cent. I have always loved singer Holly Near's revealing question: 'why do we kill people who are killing people to show that killing people is wrong?'

The separatist paradigm, and the criminal justice system within it, are breaking down and are in a state of crisis. Many refer to the criminal justice system as archaic. We have known of this impending breakdown and the need for alternatives for some time. In an early article Barnett (1977) promotes an examination of the underlying assumptions and errors of the present system and calls for a new paradigm: 'In the criminal justice system we are witnessing the death throes of an old and cumbersome paradigm, one that has dominated Western thought for more than 900 years.'

What Else is Possible?

There is another way of being we can choose, which is becoming more prominent with the global shift in consciousness now occurring. I call this the wholeness dimension. I use the more conventional word paradigm to describe the separatist way of being. You can imagine paradigm as a box within which reality is defined and, by its very nature, is limiting. To convey more accurately the essence of the emergent way of being, I introduce a new phrase using the word dimension rather than paradigm, as it is a very different reality. As our awareness expands, paradigmatic boxes become transparent and we are able to perceive different realities and limitless possibilities. The separatist paradigm does not disappear, we now see it clearly for what it is and can consciously choose if and how we engage with it.

Interconnection, interdependence, cooperation and collaboration are integral aspects of the wholeness dimension. It is illustrated by the new sciences, especially quantum physics. Science is proving that everything is energy and is intricately interconnected to everything else; that the observer is not separate from the observed but an intrinsic part, as both influencer and influenced, of what is observed.

We are the creators and generators of our reality. It is not 'I'll believe it when I see it', it is 'I'll see it when I believe it'. Instead of being bound by linear, hierarchical and positivist thinking, it is a multidimensional universe with awareness of and from multiple perception points. There is room for multiple truths and different perceptions of the same experience.

This is a reality beyond polarities. There is no us and them. It is only us. What we do to others, we do to ourselves. There is no superior race and there are no disposable people. We share one home, mother earth.

How do we bring about change from this dimension? Rather than through the force of power over, change occurs through our innate power of being and the synergy that occurs when people operating from their true potency come together. We use non-violence, caring, invitation and collaboration. There is a great misconception that this is soft or ineffectual. Great power arises from this dimension, it just looks different. It is exemplified by leaders such as Martin Luther King, Gandhi, Nelson Mandela, the Dalai Lama and many more. Grassroots initiatives that operate from this dimension are also potent and some have toppled governments.

Various social movements are 'advocates of humbling power' (Braithwaite, 2012, p. 1). In terms of restorative justice, Pranis (2007, pp. 71–2) explains: 'One of the paradoxes of restorative justice is that it is a vision of radical change, but it asks us to make those changes in a gentle way. Restorative justice asks us to create change without attempting to decide for others, because to control them violates the values of restorative justice. This vision is contrary to our usual sense of making social change … we create change while proceeding with compassion towards those with whom we disagree.'

The wholeness dimension is not some kind of utopia. The wholeness dimension invites us to be simply who we truly are, authentic and conscious. When we show up in the world that way, change occurs (as in Heer, 2011). As Gandhi (1913, p. 241) said, 'We but mirror the world ... If we could change ourselves, the tendencies in the world would also change. As a man changes his own nature, so does the attitude of the world change towards him … A wonderful thing it is and the source of our happiness. We need not wait to see what others do.' This became popularized with the paraphrase: 'be the change you wish to see in the world'.

Consciousness includes everything and is a state of non-judgment. Our journey into full conscious awareness is not a direct ascent. 'Consciousness is not a steady state for most of us, not an uninterrupted ascent of growth. We awaken, fall back, awaken more fully, go through periods of intense insight, plead for a little status quo to rest' (Baldwin, 1998, p. 13).

It is not entirely accurate to depict the separatist paradigm as old and wholeness dimension as new. We have chosen the former for thousands of years so yes it is historically old. It has served its purpose and as a species we are evolving beyond its limitations. It is now crumbling. Its reign started coming to an end in the 1960s, with the rise of the civil rights, women's liberation, environmental and peace movements. This paradigm continues to be challenged by people rising up, such as through the Arab Spring, Occupy and Idle No More movements. It is like we are waking up and unplugging from the separatist matrix.

The wholeness dimension has actually always existed. It is expressed in ancient teachings such as the Medicine Wheel from Aboriginal peoples (see Bopp et al., 1985) and ubuntu from southern Africa (see Schoeman, Chapter 14 in this volume). Early non-state societies were kin-based, supported collective responsibility and practised restitution and restoration, which could be characterized as restorative justice (Gavrielides, 2012a). Braithwaite (2002a, p. 5) contends that restorative justice was the dominant model 'throughout most of human history for perhaps all the world's peoples'. Starting in the Middle Ages, with the emergence of centralized rulers and the state, restorative approaches were replaced by a state controlled criminal justice system. The restorative approach 'was not voluntarily abandoned by the people; it was deliberately and forcibly co-opted by the crown and then discarded' (Weitekamp, 1999, p. 89). Gavrielides (2012a, p. 23) believes that while restorative justice 'remained dormant and relatively inactive, it was never forgotten by the communities'.

The possibility of both has been alive for all of human existence. The separatist paradigm, however, has been the dominant choice. The wholeness dimension is now re-emerging fully through a new consciousness that is being born on our planet. This is not about going back to the good old days. It is not helpful to romanticize the past or kin-based societies. Slavery, blood revenge and power imbalances existed. 'Most premodern societies sustained side-by-side restorative traditions and retributive traditions that were in many ways more brutal than modern retributivism' (Braithwaite, 2002a, p. 5). It is about learning from the ancient teachings, honouring the contributions of indigenous peoples who have much to offer given their traditional alignment with the wholeness dimension, and also awakening into a fuller consciousness.

Various prophesies have spoken of such an awakening. For example, Morales (2012), President of Bolivia, explained at the UN General Assembly that according to the Mayan calendar, 21 December 2012 marked:

> the end of the Macha and the beginning of the Pacha, it is the end of selfishness and the beginning of brotherhood, it is the end of individualism and the beginning of collectivism ... The scientists know very well that this marks the end of an anthropocentric life and the beginning of a bio-centric life. It is the end of hatred and the beginning of love, the end of lies and beginning of truth. It is the end of sadness and the beginning of joy; it is the end of division and the beginning of unity. This is a theme to be developed … to constantly look for economic and social equality among all human persons. This is the time to bring dignity to all inhabitants.

I posit that the philosophy and practice of restorative justice originates from the wholeness dimension. And it is from this source that the vision of restorative justice can be fully realized. Yet the majority of our work and practice occurs within the separatist paradigm. We need to be aware of which paradigm we are operating from and in, and make conscious choices that are most generative to what we would like to ultimately create.

Contributions of Restorative Justice

One thing I appreciate about restorative justice is that it has always been profoundly pragmatic. It did not start as a theory, it started as practice. Restorative practices have developed ahead of our language to describe them.

The first modern restorative process is attributed to the Elmira case in 1974 in Kitchener, Canada (Peachey, 2003; Nyp, 2004). After two young men pled guilty to a vandalizing spree involving 22 properties, probation officer Mark Yantzi and Mennonite Central Committee worker Dave Worth initiated this seemingly impossible, pie in the sky idea of the offenders meeting their victims. Judge McConnell surprised them by ordering a remand so this could occur. The two youths met with 21 of the 22 victims and successfully worked out restitution. There was no precedent or roadmap for what they did. It inspired the development of what became victim offender reconciliation programs (VORP).

Pioneers like these followed their awareness that something had to change and had the courage to try something radically different. For example, Barry Stuart was the Chief Judge of the Yukon Territorial Court when he chose to work together with community and justice officials to explore ways to make a difference in the obvious failings of the adversarial-based sentencing process. He knew something more than tinkering was required. He stepped off the bench, removed his robes and invited the community and justice officials to sit in a circle to explore how to better serve the interests of the community. He blended principles of contemporary consensus processes and traditional circles to create a safe space for the essential and difficult discussions to unfold among all participants affected by sentencing decisions. Initially called sentencing circles, this process directly engaged offenders, victims and representatives from all sectors of the community, justice and relevant agencies (education, health and economic development) in dialogue to develop a comprehensive sentencing plan for each case (personal communication, Stuart, 1996).

Stuart ended up setting legal precedent in Canada (R. v. Moses, 1992). He later coined the term peacemaking circles to capture what was being created in practice (Pranis, Stuart and Wedge 2003).

There are many stories from around the world of individuals and communities creating new approaches to resolving issues in creative and generative ways. While we have come a long way in developing both theory and practice, and are more sophisticated in both arenas, we are still essentially pioneers.

We must be careful not to limit or stop the further development and unfolding of the restorative vision. Imposing one generic model or coming to conclusions on what restorative justice has to look like constrains its transformative potential and hampers its organic development. It is about aligning with restorative values and principles and collaboratively developing an appropriate process to fit each situation and cultural context, and to meet the needs of all parties involved. If we simply impose a generic model or programme we become similar to the current justice system in that we force the situation and parties into a predetermined judicial process.

It is important to be aware of our alignment with the heart of restorative justice. Like many others, I am concerned about how some restorative processes are focusing on expediency and reaching agreements without engaging with deeper transformational opportunities. There is a danger that the time and attention given for values and relationships 'are seen as somehow getting in the way of achieving "win-win" agreements … thinking centres on material concerns such as compensation and restitution and on achieving agreements about "how much" is appropriate.' (Ross, 2006, p. xvi). Ross calls this a 'stuff-centred' focus that does not align with the restorative vision where harm is 'only peripherally about "stuff". Instead, the harm is understood in the relational realm … It's almost as if we cannot escape our technology-obsessed world where product rules over process, quantity over quality, speed over thoroughness, contract over caring' (ibid., xvii–xviii).

Conversations about guidelines, standards and the regulation of restorative justice are worthwhile (see Johnstone, 2012). We do need clarity and guidance. There are, unfortunately, some terrible, even harmful, practices that do not coincide with the values or principles yet call themselves restorative justice. We need to prevent unequivocal poor practice and to ensure human rights are upheld. However, I too am wary of 'a Western accreditation agency telling an Indigenous elder that a centuries-old restorative practice does not comply with the accreditation standards' (Braithwaite, 2000, p. 1). Or that lay practitioners would need government permission to hold a circle to resolve an issue. I think restorative justice is all about empowering people and communities more and more to resolve their own conflicts. As Braithwaite (2002b, p. 564) says, 'if restorative justice is about shifting power to the people, surely reimposing the state to set standards for restorative justice shifts the power back to the state?'

If restorative justice becomes standardized, prescribed and state regulated, we will miss the opportunity for realizing its full potential. We will become subsumed by current systems rather than creating true alternatives. Practitioners need the freedom to be innovative, creative and responsive to each situation and cultural context. 'If governments are truly committed to promoting restorative justice, then they need to work closer with the communities that create the various models through which this abstract umbrella notion of restorative justice is delivered … Try to mould and standardize restorative justice and all you will achieve is its McDonaldisation. Its diversity … creativity and innovation will all die out' (Gavrielides, 2012b).

One possibility could be to 'craft open-textured restorative justice standards that allow a lot of space for cultural difference and innovation while giving us a language for denouncing uncontroversially bad practice' (Braithwaite, 2000, p. 1). New Zealand, for example, went through a two-year process in considering standards. The Restorative Justice Network concluded that the optimal approach was to develop values-based guidelines (Boyack, Bowen and Marshall, 2004).

The Ministry of Justice (2004), in collaboration with practitioners, published *Restorative Justice in New Zealand: Best Practice* to provide guidance for delivering restorative justice using principles and values.

Pranis (2007, p. 71) reminds us:

> One of the great strengths of the restorative justice movement is that it is not dependent upon a centralized source of legitimacy or support … A clearly articulated vision and values to guide action replace prescribed actions and extensive control mechanisms. Values-guided practice can respond to unique circumstances or unexpected developments in ways that technique-driven practice cannot. If there is agreement on vision and values, there can be an enormous amount of local autonomy for practitioners with local efforts contributing to the larger shared vision. A powerful way to bring change is to think globally and act locally with autonomy. The shared values synergize countless discrete activities happening at the local level into a whole that is greater than the sum of its parts. By avoiding the need for centralized control enormous amounts of energy are freed to be invested in the actual work.

Restorative justice could be a contribution to a paradigm shift. This requires us to think outside the box. As Kuhn (1970) explains, a paradigm shift is arduous. The separatist paradigm has a lot invested in making sure it is perpetuated. It is rare for those entrenched in this reality, especially authorities, just to give up their perspective, structural power and control voluntarily. The separatist paradigm seems like common sense and there is often a refusal to perceive beyond accepted modes of thinking. Those entrenched only see the world through that lens. Institutions are committed to it and structures are protected by controlling reform. The co-optation and subversion of alternatives is a well-known, documented phenomenon. We have already seen how easy it is for restorative justice to be diluted or co-opted by the criminal justice system. Unless we approach restorative justice with conscious awareness and choice, we may get lost in the separatist paradigm and end up not making real, substantive changes.

Rupert Ross (2006, p. xvi), a crown attorney who has been exploring criminal, restorative and Aboriginal justice for years, found that 'Restorative justice processes require such a fundamentally different way of thinking that even the best-motivated people seem to be having problems escaping the preconceptions and commandments of our western way of seeing.' While it would be easy to be cynical, he acknowledges: 'Perhaps it will just take a while for the differences to be understood and for western-educated people to begin to feel comfortable working in the un-bounded relational realm' (p. xviii).

We need to continue to ask questions about the development of restorative justice and its relationship to the current legal system. There are many discussions and debates about the distinction between restorative and retributive justice. Braithwaite (2002a, p. 16) says:

> The most fraught issue in the values debate is whether values such as retribution, just desserts, and fair punishment should be accommodated in a restorative justice framework. Many of the most distinguished restorative justice thinkers think they should. My own inclination is to think they should not .... restorative justice should be explicitly about a values shift from the retributive/punitive to the restorative.

I concur. As Zehr (1995, p. 207) points out: 'Unless underlying traditional assumptions and values are transformed to alternative assumptions and values, alternative processes will rarely end up as real alternatives.'

An incredible contribution that restorative justice could make is to create an entirely different reality around conflict, crime and justice. As Braithwaite and Strang (2000, p. 208) point out, 'There is no problem so serious that restorative processes and values might not be morally superior to formally retributive processes and values.' They mention apartheid, mass murder, genocide and nuclear safety as examples.

Van Ness and Strong (2010) offer models for how restorative justice might be configured and ways to assess whether what we are doing is partly or more fully restorative (see also McCold and Wachtel 2002). They propose five possible models: (1) an augmentation model, whereby restorative programmes augment and are offered as alternatives to criminal justice processes. This is how the majority of restorative practices operate now; (2) a dual track model, where criminal and restorative justice systems operate side by side yet independently, with occasional cooperation; (3) a safety net, whereby the dominant, preferred system is restorative, with the criminal justice system used as a back-up when a restorative approach cannot or does not work to bring about resolution; (4) a hybrid model where parts of the system are restorative and other parts operate as criminal justice; and (5) a unitary model, which is a fully restorative system as the only approach, created either by converting the criminal justice system or by replacing it.

As next steps in our evolution, I would like us to create restorative justice as the first response to conflict and harm and make it the new norm. We need to build bridges from the separatist paradigm to the wholeness dimension. Old systems, like criminal justice, can be consciously used to help us during development phases. While some people can take quantum leaps, it can be scary to let go of what is familiar and deemed true or necessary. Sometimes it is helpful to have some familiarity and reassurance. We could conceive of the criminal justice system like scaffolding, supporting us while we build new approaches. As we progress, the scaffolding is no longer needed and can fall away. As Richard Buckminster Fuller observed, 'You never change things by fighting the existing reality. To change something, build a new model that makes the existing model obsolete.'

It is a journey and there will be iterative results along the way. We need to be mindful of our role of consciously creating true alternatives so we don't inadvertently get lost. It would be unfortunate if restorative justice was absorbed by the separatist paradigm rendering it unable to fulfil its potential as an effective catalyst for change. There is the possibility of restorative justice becoming one of the cogs in the criminal justice wheel. Instead, restorative justice could be the light leading the way towards a society beyond crime and punishment. From the wholeness dimension, such constructs as crime, victim, offender and punishment no longer make sense. I think the bigger promise of restorative justice is contributing to a new reality surrounding crime and justice and to the broader paradigm shift into wholeness. We have only just begun to realize our full humanity and capacities.

It is now time for the restorative justice movement to choose. It can become defined and confined by the current justice system and broader separatist paradigm, whereby its full potential remains unrealized. Restorative justice would make many improvements, but not fundamental, substantive changes.

Another choice is for restorative justice to become more firmly and fully committed to its roots in the emerging wholeness dimension and part of the new consciousness we are creating on our planet. It would require us to keep asking questions and make conscious choices each step of the way from our ever expanding awareness of possibilities. It would mean getting more comfortable being in the 'un-bounded relational realm' as Ross (2006) called it.

How can we know when we are moving in the direction of, or operating from, the wholeness dimension, rather than being influenced or absorbed by the separatist paradigm?

Principles are certainly important and helpful, and there is extensive literature referring to restorative principles. The United Nations (2002), for example, produced a document on the basic principles for restorative programmes in criminal matters. Zehr and Mika (1998) provide a summary of fundamental principles of restorative justice that includes three main ones, with further details given within each: (a) crime is fundamentally a violation of people and interpersonal relationships; (b) violations create obligations and liabilities; and (c) restorative justice seeks to heal and put right the wrongs.

Numerous authors intermix principles and values, creating some confusion. Is there a difference between them? I see them as different yet close cousins. Values are our inner compass or guidance system, which inherently influence our lives whether we are conscious of them or not. Principles are external precepts we identify as contextually important and use to guide and evaluate behaviour and processes. They act as an external application of values. Zehr (2002, p. 35) says 'principles of restorative justice are useful only if they are rooted in a number of underlying values … to apply restorative justice principles in a way that is true to their spirit and intent, we must be explicit about these values'.

I concur with Pranis (2007, p. 59):

> As the weaving of practice and philosophy has developed and the variety of practice has grown, it has become increasingly evident that the movement needs unifying concepts that are flexible enough to encompass new practice

possibilities, but clear enough to preclude that which is not restorative. Restorative values are emerging as a unifying concept that grounds theory and guides practice.

Shared Values

Values are qualities seen as intrinsically valuable, worthwhile and desirable. They are captured by a single word or short phrase and are revealed in our attitudes and behaviour. Rokeach (1972, p. 159) postulates: 'Once a value is internalized it becomes consciously or unconsciously, a standard or criterion for guiding action, for developing and maintaining attitudes towards relevant objects and situations.' Values are 'our compass' (Pranis, Stuart and Wedge, 2003, p. 33).

I think it is helpful to recognize three kinds of values: individual, cultural/ societal and universal. What is most important is the process of going within and discovering what our values are and seeing whether we are acting in accordance with them. A facilitator, parent, teacher, religious leader or president can proclaim what our values ought to be. Yet the process of self-examination – including individual, group, societal and global – creates awareness, moral development, empowerment and choice. Zehr (2002, pp. 35–36) believes that 'perhaps one of restorative justice's greatest attributes is the way it encourages us to explore our values together'.

While individuals and cultures have a diversity of values, patterns are also present. For example, Valerie Braithwaite (1998; Braithwaite and Blamey, 1998) found different prioritization of values among individuals but also identified patterns and consistency. After measuring values of Australians over a 25-year period, she concluded that the values patterns were relatively stable over time and across populations. The variation among individuals is explained by two major value orientations or systems, one she calls harmony and the other security. Both the security and harmony values are embraced by the vast majority of that population, they just differed in how they prioritized them. How values were prioritized, in turn, was found to influence responses to policies. Interestingly, and not surprisingly, people who are security oriented are most likely to support tougher laws and penalties.

I posit that the choice and prioritization of values is related to the extent to which individuals and cultures are operating from the separatist paradigm. Recall that people immersed in the separatist paradigm are in a state of disconnect. They are disconnected from each other as well as from their own inherent state of being (wholeness). As such, people will feel a need for values like safety and security. Whereas individuals who are less immersed within the separatist paradigm and closer to the wholeness dimension (our natural state of being), will more likely connect with values like harmony and love.

Can values change? Could we move towards embracing values conducive to restorative justice and more aligned with the wholeness dimension? Based on my knowledge and experience, I say yes. The Dalai Lama explains that the process of learning and incorporating a virtue requires 'constant practice and familiarization so that it becomes spontaneous. What we find is that the more we develop concern for others' well-being, the easier it becomes to act in others' interests. As we become habituated to the effort required, so the struggle to sustain it lessens. Eventually, it will become second nature.' (1999, pp. 124–5)

Further insight into values and their evolution is offered by Beck and Cowan (1996) who advanced the theory of human and cultural development called spiral dynamics. Humans construct ever new, more complex conceptual models of the world. These models are organized around what they call memes or core value systems, applicable to both individuals and cultures. Different subcultures, societies and entire nations are at different levels of emergence. Beck (nd) outlines eight stages of value systems, where each is a prelude to the next. He states:

> Cultures, as well as countries, are formed by the emergence of value systems (social stages) in the response to life conditions. Such complex adaptive intelligences form the glue that bonds a group together, defines who they are as a people, and reflects the place on the planet they inhabit … While they are all legitimate expressions of the human experience, they are not 'equal' in their capacities to deal with complex problems in society.

One of Beck's twelve postulates is to 'reframe globalization issues around value system codes'. He explains: 'By understanding these deeper value system currents or complexity strata, it becomes possible to develop more realistic big picture views and craft practical, appropriate solutions to real problems.'

Values are thus expressive and pragmatic, as well as evolving. What about shared universal values, do they exist? I think they do and many throughout history think so too.

A quick perusal of the literature shows philosophical, religious and governmental leaders within both eastern and western nations identifying universal values. Philosophers such as Socrates, Plato and Aristotle devoted attention to identifying human values that were most significant for a good life (see Artinopoulou and Gavrielides, Chapter 2 in this volume). Every major religion champions universal values, such as forgiveness. While there is not a consensus among scholars, many researchers have also concluded that universal values exist. For example, social psychologist Schwartz (1992, 1994), who studied thousands of people in over 40 countries, identified and categorized universal values. Based on their review, Kinnier, Kernes and Dautheribes (2000, p. 11) created a short list of universal values, concluding that 'values that consistently appear throughout history and across many of the major religions and secular organizations cannot be dismissed'.

The 1948 Universal Declaration of Human Rights is an articulation of our shared values on a global scale. This is the first comprehensive agreement among nations of the rights and freedoms of all human beings. The rights described in the 30 articles include personal, social, civil, political and economic rights. These fundamental rights reflect our shared values – such as dignity, equality, freedom – and are meaningful and applicable to every human being, everywhere and at all times. The document preamble begins with: 'recognition of the inherent dignity and of the equal and inalienable rights of all members of the human family is the foundation of freedom, justice and peace in the world.'

I echo Prosser's (2012, emphasis in original) conclusion that the UN Charter, Universal Declaration of Human Rights and subsequent treaties, covenants and declarations demand a universal approach to human rights and contribute to 'the even broader framework of *universalistic* human values'.

I posit that the Declaration and much of our current work with human rights aligns with the emergence of the wholeness dimension. Mary Robinson (1998), former President of Ireland and the first High Commissioner for Human Rights, called the Declaration 'an extraordinary vision for an interdependent and interconnected world'.

Just as restorative justice could get co-opted and subsumed by the separatist paradigm, as described earlier, Harvey (2012, p. 69) similarly cautions that human rights as a movement, discipline and discourse 'is at risk of losing its way'. Its emancipatory potential 'is being steadily buried under the conventional worlds of law and politics. Disturbing forms of legalism put at risk the critical practice of rights (and restorative justice)'. We need to stay mindful that human rights and restorative justice do not end up inadvertently being absorbed by the legalist culture and institutions of the separatist paradigm, so that legitimization overshadows transformation.

One key to preventing such absorption and staying true to our vision is 'alternative processes that are consciously and explicitly built upon alternative values' (Zehr 1995, p. 207). Human rights could contribute to restorative justice and vice versa. For example, Braithwaite (2002a, p. 13) suggests:

> fundamental human rights should set legal limits on what restorative processes are allowed to do. But I also suspect that UN human rights instruments can give quite good guidance on the values restorative justice processes ought to observe. Integrating the rights-constraining and values-guiding requirements for restorative justice … might make for decent and practical global social movement politics for the movement for restorative justice.

What are the values of restorative justice? I like Pranis's (2007, p. 60) explanation of restorative values as 'those things that feel deeply important to the essence of the restorative impulse and are carried in the spirit of what we do and how we do it.'

Restorative values have been articulated in different ways, yet as Pranis (2007) reveals, there is consistency. Overall, we have an emerging general consensus on what the values are. Core values identified in the literature include respect, dignity, inclusion, responsibility, humility, mutual care, reparation and non-domination.

As mentioned earlier, it is difficult to distinguish values from principles in the literature. Various authors have articulated guiding principles of restorative justice that relate to, or are the same as, values. Pranis (2007, p. 60) clarifies that restorative values can be divided into process values and individual values: 'Some values, such as respect, appear in both groups. Some, such as honesty, relate primarily to the individual participants while others, such as inclusion, are relevant to the process. The process values encourage or enable the participants to exhibit the individual values. Both are critical for the transformative outcomes sought in restorative interactions'.

Values can be 'the benchmarks of our accountability', to ourselves, to each other and for restorative processes (Elliott, 2011, p. 109). In terms of guiding restorative justice more specifically, according to Braithwaite (2002b), we can place values into three groups. Some values provide procedural safeguards, what he describes as constraining values (for example, empowerment, accountability, appealability and respect for fundamental human rights). Others are maximizing values that should be promoted but participants can ignore, like restoration of property loss. The third type is emergent values, such as remorse, forgiveness and mercy, which are not to be actively encouraged or prescribed, but simply allowed to emerge.

Some people may say values are too vague. 'Yet standards must be broad if we are to avert legalistic regulation of restorative justice, which is at odds with the philosophy of restorative justice. What we need is deliberative regulation where we are clear about the values we expect restorative justice to realize' (Braithwaite, 2002a, p. 15).

Universal shared values, as discussed in this section, are a powerful, effective means to guide our actions. As Kay Pranis suggests (2007), we need to continually keep asking the question: does this move us in the direction of our shared values?

What can this look like in practice? How can we realize human rights and the transformative potential of restorative justice? Peacemaking circles are a potent exemplar.

Peacemaking Circles

Peacemaking circles are a values-based, structured yet flexible approach for engaging with others (see Pranis, Stuart and Wedge, 2003; Pranis, 2005; Boyes-Watson, 2008). It would be simplest to place peacemaking circles (hereafter Circles) as one particular practice under the umbrella of restorative justice. When used for conflict and crime situations, Circles certainly align with and fit within restorative justice. Yet Circles are used for a multitude of purposes and have their own history and philosophy. I see them as parallel to and synergistic with restorative justice.

Circles are ancient (see Baldwin, 1998). They are a universal form and belong to all of us. Our ancestors have gathered in circles for thousands of years. Cultures all over the world have continued to gather in circles. First Nations and indigenous peoples in particular have kept the teachings and practices alive through the generations.

Circles today draw upon ancient and contemporary wisdom and are used for a wide range of purposes such as talking, learning, decision-making, healing, conflict, sentencing, strategic planning and development. Circles are used in families, schools, communities, workplaces and justice systems. Boyes-Watson and Pranis (2010, p. 29) offer one definition: 'The circle is a structured process for organizing effective group communication, relationship building, decision-making, and conflict resolution'.

Circles are holistic and balanced in terms of both individuals and process. Circles acknowledge and invite the mental, emotional, physical and spiritual aspects of individuals and human experience. Participants physically sit in a circle with no barriers between them. The process begins with getting acquainted, developing relationships and creating the foundation for how we are going to talk, before dealing with the issues at hand.

There is an assumption and actualization of equality. Everyone in the Circle is a participant, seen as having inherent dignity and something of value to offer. Each participant is invited to speak in their own voice and to share whatever is relevant to them, their own truth. Emotions are welcome and given the space to be fully expressed.

We are all gifting and receiving, teachers and learners. We are each unique yet part of the whole and we benefit from the collective wisdom that emerges out of the Circle. It is not about eliminating differences; it is about respecting them and tapping into what they contribute. Circles offer a space to uncover and amplify the greatness of the individual and of the group.

Circles are a sophisticated way to balance individualism and collectivism. We engage with and meet the needs of individuals and the group at the same time, and no compromise is required. We acknowledge individuality and diversity, and that each person, situation and context is unique. At the same time, we know we live in an interconnected and interdependent universe. Conflict and harm are experienced by individuals and affect the collective. Therefore, we attend to individual and social harms, among other things, and focus on the relationship between the persons who chose to harm and persons who experienced harm as well as the larger web of relationships.

Peacemaking circles operate from the wholeness dimension. They are paradoxical, creating gateways for change: 'They're both structured and open, ordered and spontaneous, framed and free, limited and unlimited ... It's as if the structured, ordered, framed, and limited parameters of the Circle provide the springboard for participants to come together in ways that are open, spontaneous, freeing, and unlimited in possibilities. The latter experience is what each Circle discovers on its own.' (Pranis, Stuart and Wedge, 2003, p. 7).

One unique aspect of Circles is the *talking piece*. This is an object that gets passed around the Circle and only the person holding it has the floor to speak, if they choose. The other participants receive them by giving their attention and listening. It is a powerful equalizer, creating a space for uninterrupted sharing, deep listening, silent reflections and 'heart speak'. It literally changes the dynamics of the conversation and creates dialogue. The talking piece is one of the gifts from the teachings of Aboriginal peoples. It appears that talking pieces have been used in various cultures. I was intrigued to learn from my colleague at the Greek symposium, Dr. Artinopoulou, that a talking stick was used in ancient Greece.

One of the most important aspects of Circle processes is that we consciously create a space based on shared values. 'The values we bring to a situation determine how we respond. Before dealing with any conflict, therefore, we need to clarify our values.' (Pranis, Stuart and Wedge, 2003, p. 33).

Barry Stuart developed an exercise in the 1970s where a scenario of a family conflict is provided and individuals identify how they hoped they would have responded. Participants then come up with a consensus of shared values. Those of us training and facilitating peacemaking circles have been replicating this exercise in numerous settings with diverse groups around the world and observing consistent results. What we find is that every group is coming up with virtually the same list of values. Pranis, Stuart and Wedge (2003, p. 33) point out that 'the type of value is always the same: positive, constructive, healing values – values supportive of the best in ourselves and others.'

Pranis (2007, 2001) shares a story of how staff in a correctional facility said they have different values than young offenders. Pranis did peacemaking circle training with these youth and they indeed came up with basically the same list of core values as the staff! She also noticed that the values identified by participants in Circles are the same ones restorative proponents articulate in the literature. She asks:

> Why is it significant that members of my audiences and restorative justice writers produce similar lists of values? Because the similarity means that restorative justice processes do not impose a foreign set of values on participants but, instead, create environments in which participants are able to operate according to the values they themselves affirm … when people do not act according to those values, it is often because they do not feel safe doing so. And this is why there is a need for restorative justice – not to force an alien approach on parties in dispute, but to create a safe environment in which they can apply what they themselves acknowledge to be the best approach. (Pranis, 2007, p. 63)

People of varying ages, genders, cultures, religions, socioeconomic status and upbringing are coming up with virtually the same list of values. And these are basically the same values that underlie the Universal Declaration of Human Rights. Therefore, the 'core values that support good relationships with others seem to be universal' (Pranis, 2007, p. 64).

Even though we see a consistency in the values that are identified, the process of individuals and groups discovering their own values is an incredible contribution to awareness, empowerment and choice. Each group needs to learn and experience how to engage with one another and work through issues. As shared values are uncovered, individuals and groups can agree to have them as their foundation and compass, guiding them through difficult conversation, pain and conflict in a generative way.

For example, I worked with one department that had a long history of various issues and conflict. Things had escalated to a union grievance. I met with each individual separately and invited them to a Circle. Everyone voluntarily showed up. We went through the values exercise and they were surprised, given their behaviour, what they uncovered as their shared values. We began to explore their relationships and interactions using a talking piece. This was the first truly equalized, respectful conversation they had experienced as an entire department. A conflict was resolved when one party spontaneously apologized and shook hands with the other party.

It is common for groups to behave different from or counter to their shared values without even realizing it. Underlying this disparate behaviour is a sense of personal vulnerability, people don't feel safe. Individuals operating within the separatist paradigm feel disconnected, so they tend to try to protect themselves and their behaviour is reactive rather than responsive. Circles provide a safe space to practice being who we authentically are and to act in accordance with shared values, experiencing wholeness. We get to physically, mentally, emotionally and spiritually experience what this feels and looks like through a co-creative process. We build our muscle so that it gets easier to be our authentic selves and act in alignment with our shared values outside the Circle, thus contributing to the broader creation of a new conscious reality.

This uncovering and commitment to act in alignment with our shared values also acts as a bridge to human rights. When people discover their values, which are in effect human rights (like respect, dignity and equality), and choose to act according to those values, then human rights are realized. Circles are designed to assist us in realizing our common humanity and, therefore, provide an avenue to actualize human rights in the world.

Values-based processes like Circles are bridges between the separatist paradigm and the wholeness dimension. Through the Circle process, each participant has the opportunity to recognize their authentic state of being and remember our shared humanity. Individuals are changed by this experience which can, through their new awareness and behaviour, create ripples into the larger community and society.

A Non-conclusion: An Invitation

Like the Greek symposium out of which this paper emerged, this has been a journey of asking questions, grappling with answers, receiving inspiration, taking risks and sharing ideas with colleagues (Zellerer, 2012). I hope you, the reader, have enjoyed the journey through this paper and feel inspired to explore your own awareness more fully.

This was a good opportunity to step back, revisit and reflect on the potential of restorative justice. What is restorative justice and what are we hoping to create? How can restorative justice contribute to the current global shift in consciousness? What can guide us?

I invite us to think of ourselves as pioneers. We are at a new frontier and we have choices. Restorative justice philosophy invites us to create true alternatives to how we perceive and respond to conflict and crime. Restorative justice is fundamentally about transformation. The challenge is that we are doing transformative work in what I call the separatist paradigm, where the criminal justice system thrives.

We have to be careful not to get lost inadvertently in that reality. Let's not impose a generic model or come to conclusions about what restorative justice has to look like. A standardized, state regulated process could take the life force out of restorative justice, when what we need to do is stay attuned to the greater potential of restorative justice. Its potential flows from what I call the wholeness dimension.

The key is to be aware of which paradigm we are working within and contributing to. If restorative work is done consciously, even within the separatist paradigm, we can create viable alternatives to current structures. This would create bridges between the separatist paradigm and wholeness dimension. It requires us to continually ask questions, be responsive and adaptive to each situation and make choices based on our awareness as it expands into ever new possibilities.

Universal values offer effective guidance. Using values-based practices to uncover and consciously choose to act in accordance with our shared values invites us to be authentic and ensures that we are being restorative and actualizing human rights. Peacemaking circles were described as an exemplar of what this can look like in practice.

Restorative justice could become a compelling beacon of transformation. As we develop alternatives and people are transformed by their experiences, the old structures and paradigm will be able to fall away. Restorative justice has the potential to be an integral part of a global paradigm shift, if we so choose. Just as some groups are working to create a new economic reality and others a different educational reality, restorative proponents could create a new justice reality. Ultimately, I think restorative justice envisions a world beyond the constructs of crime, victim, offender and punishment.

I echo Rumi: 'Out beyond ideas of wrongdoing and rightdoing, there is a field. I'll meet you there.'

Acknowledgements

I thank Vasso Artinopoulou and Theo Gavrielides for their generosity and vision in organizing an exceptional international symposium and in editing this book. I am grateful for Joanne Pulis for her reflections, awareness and meticulousness in working with me on this paper.

References

Baldwin, C. 1998. *Calling the Circle: The First and Future Culture*. New York: Bantam Books.

Ball, J., Caldwell, W. and Pranis, K. 2010. *Doing Democracy with Circles*. St. Paul, MN: Living Justice Press.

Barnett, R. 1977. Restitution: A new paradigm of criminal justice. *Ethics: An International Journal of Social, Political, and Legal Philosophy*, 87(4), pp. 279–301.

Beck, D.E. [nd]. *Stages of Social Development*. Center for Human Emergence. Available at: http://www.humanemergence.org/essays.html.

Beck, D.E. and Cowan, C. 1996. *Spiral Dynamics: Mastering values, leadership, and change*. Malden, MA: Blackwell Publishing.

Bopp, J., Bopp, M., Brown, L. and Lane, P. 1985. *The Sacred Tree*. Lethbridge, Alberta: Four Worlds Development Press.

Boyack, J., Bowen, H. and Marshall, C. 2004. How does restorative justice ensure good practice? in *Critical Issues in Restorative Justice*, edited by H. Zehr and B. Toews. Monsey, NJ: Criminal Justice Press.

Boyes-Watson, C. 2008. *Peacemaking Circles and Urban Youth*. St. Paul, MN: Living Justice Press.

Boyes-Watson, C. and Pranis, K. 2010. *Heart of Hope*. Center for Restorative Justice, Suffolk University.

Braithwaite, J. 2000. Standards for Restorative Justice. Paper presented at the *Ancillary Meetings of the Tenth United Nations Congress on the Prevention of Crime and Treatment of Offenders*. Vienna, Austria, 10–17 April.

Braithwaite, J. 2002a. *Restorative Justice and Responsive Regulation*. New York: Oxford University Press.

Braithwaite, J. 2002b. Setting standards for restorative justice. *British Journal of Criminology*, 42, pp. 563–77.

Braithwaite, J. 2012. Rights and restoration, in *Rights and Restoration within Youth Justice*, edited by T. Gavrielides. Whitby, ON: de Sitter Publications, pp. 1–4.

Braithwaite, J. and Strang, H. 2000. Connecting philosophy and practice, in *Restorative Justice: Philosophy to Practice*, edited by H. Strang and J. Braithwaite. Aldershot: Ashgate, pp. 203–20.

Braithwaite, V. 1998. The value balance model of political evaluations. *British Journal of Psychology*, 89, pp. 223–47.

Braithwaite, V. and Blamey, R. 1998. Consensus, stability and meaning in abstract social values. *Australian Journal of Political Science*, 33, pp. 363–80.

Christie, N. 1977. Conflicts as property. *British Journal of Criminology*, 17(1), pp. 1–15.

Dalai Lama. 1999. *Ancient Wisdom, Modern World: Ethics for the New Millennium*. London: Little Brown.

Elliott, E. 2011. *Security with Care*. Halifax and Winnipeg: Fernwood Publishing.

Foucault, M. 1977. *Discipline and Punish: The Birth of the Prison*. New York: Pantheon Books.

Gandhi, M. 1913. General Knowledge About Health, in *The Collected Works of M.K.Gandhi*. Vol 13. New Delhi, India.

Gavrielides, T. 2007. *Restorative Justice Theory and Practice: Addressing the Discrepancy*. Helsinki: HEUNI.

Gavrielides, T. 2012a. Bridging restorative justice and human rights for youth justice, in *Rights and Restoration within Youth Justice*, edited by T. Gavrielides. Whitby, ON: de Sitter Publications, pp. 15–43.

Gavrielides, T. 2012b. The McDonaldisation of a community-born and community-led ethos: My reflections on the restorative justice week past, in *Blog, IARS*, Available at: http://www.iars.org.uk/content/mcdonaldisation-rj.

Harvey, C. 2012. Reconstructing and restoring human rights, in *Rights and Restoration within Youth Justice*, edited by T. Gavrielides. Whitby, ON: de Sitter Publications, pp. 67–89.

Heer, D. 2011. *Being You, Changing the World*. Big Country Publishing.

Hobbes, T. 1651. *Leviathan*

Johnstone, G. 2012. The standardization of restorative justice, in *Rights and Restoration within Youth Justice*, edited by T. Gavrielides. Whitby, ON: de Sitter Publications, pp. 91–115.

Johnstone, G. and Van Ness, D. 2007. The meaning of restorative justice, in *Handbook of Restorative Justice*, edited by G. Johnstone and D. Van Ness. Devon and Portland: Willan Publishing, pp. 5–23.

Kinnier, R., Kernes, J. and Dautheribes, T. 2000. A short list of universal moral values. *Counseling and Values*, 45, pp. 4–16.

Kuhn, T.S. 1970. *The Structure of Scientific Revolutions*. (second edition). Chicago: University of Chicago Press.

McCold, P. and Wachtel, T. 2002. Restorative justice theory validation, in *Restorative Justice: Theoretical Foundations*, edited by E. Weitekamp and H. Kerner. Devon and Portland: Willan Publishing, pp. 110–42.

Ministry of Justice. 2004. *Restorative Justice in New Zealand: Best Practice*. Wellington, New Zealand.

Morales, E. 2012. Address, *General debate of the 67th Session of the General Assembly of the United Nations*, New York, 26 September 2012.

Nyp, G. 2004. *Pioneers of Peace*. Kitchener, ON: Community Justice Initiatives.

Peachey, D. 2003. The Kitchener experiment, in *A Restorative Justice Reader*, edited by G. Johnstone. Cullompton: Willan Publishing, pp. 178–86.

Pranis, K. 2001. *Lessons from incarcerated youth: Values and Relationships*. Minnesota, MN: Department of Corrections.

Pranis, K. 2005. *The Little Book of Circle Processes*. Intercourse, PA: Good Books.

Pranis, K. 2007. Restorative values, in *Handbook of Restorative Justice*, edited by G. Johnstone and D. Van Ness. Cullompton: Willan Publishing, pp. 59–74.

Pranis, K., Stuart, B. and Wedge, W. 2003. *Peacemaking Circles: From Crime to Community*. St. Paul, MN: Living Justice Press.

Prosser, M.H. 2012. Universal human rights as universal values, in *Values at the Theoretical Crossroads of Culture*, edited by S.J. Kulch and M.H. Prosser. Shanghai: Shanghai Foreign Language Education Press.

R. v. Moses [1992] 71 C.C.C. (3d) 347 Yukon Territorial Court.

Robinson, M. 1998. Address. *The Fiftieth Anniversary of the Universal Declaration of Human Rights: From words to deeds*. New York: United Nations.

Rokeach, M. 1972. *Beliefs, attitudes and values: A theory of organization and change*. San Francisco: Jossey-Bass.

Ross, R. 2006. *Returning to the Teachings: Exploring Aboriginal Justice*. Toronto: Penguin.

Schwartz, S.H. 1992. Universals in the content and structure of values: theory and empirical tests in 20 countries, in *Advances in Experimental Social Psychology*, edited by M. Zanna. New York: Academic Press. 25, pp. 1–65.

Schwartz, S.H. 1994. Are there universal aspects in the content and structure of values? *Journal of Social Issues*, 50, pp. 19–45.

Stuart, B. 1996. Circle sentencing in Yukon Territory, Canada: a partnership of the community and the criminal justice system. *International Journal of Comparative and Applied Criminal Justice,* 20(1 and 2), pp. 291–309.

United Nations Economic and Social Council. 2002. *Basic Principles on the Use of Restorative Justice Programmes in Criminal Matters*. No. 2002/12. 24 July.

Van Ness, D. 2006. *RJ City: Phase I Final Report*. Washington, DC: Prison Fellowship International.

Van Ness, D. and Strong, K.H. 2010. *Restorative Justice* (fourth edition). New Providence, NJ: Anderson Publishing.

Weitekamp, E. 1999. The history of restorative justice, in *Restorative Juvenile Justice: Repairing the harm of youth justice*, edited by L. Walgrave and G. Bazemore. Monsey: Criminal Justice Press.

Zehr, H. 1990. *Changing Lenses*. Scottsdale, PA: Herald Press.

Zehr, H. 1995. Justice paradigm shift? Values and visions in the reform process. *Mediation Quarterly*, 12(3), pp. 207–16.

Zehr, H. 2002. *The Little Book of Restorative Justice*. Intercourse, PA: Good Books.

Zehr, H. and Mika, H. 1998. Fundamental concepts of restorative justice. *Contemporary Justice Review*, 1(1), pp. 47–55.

Zellerer, E. 2012. How is as important as what: international symposium on restorative justice and human rights Part II, in *Evelyn's Blog, Peace of the Circle*. Available at: http://www.peaceofthecircle.com/evelyns-blog/

Chapter 14
The African Concept of Ubuntu and Restorative Justice

Marelize Schoeman

Abstract

Africans have always presented a world view which diametrically opposes traditional Western philosophy. In traditional Africa the concepts *ubuntu, community, indigenous justice* and *restoration* are interlinked and aimed at the restoration of victims and the reintegration of offenders back into the community. The restoration of relationships and social harmony undermined by the conflict are also of importance.

Modern restorative justice and indigenous justice practices share many similarities. The same values and principles that underpin the African philosophy of ubuntu are also embodied in restorative justice. This intersection of restorative justice and ubuntu philosophy is of broader relevance as it demonstrates how global and African philosophies have the potential to contribute to restoration and conflict resolution in diverse societies.

This chapter explores the interconnectedness of restorative justice values and the ubuntu world view as a medium to bridge the divide between traditional culture and modern day life in Africa, as well as the Western world in general. A plethora of writings investigating restorative justice from a Westernized perspective has been published but few studies exploring the normative roots of restorative justice as an enduring practice in African and other traditional cultures exist. The first section of the chapter focuses on the ubuntu philosophy and the influence it has on traditional justice practices in Africa. This is followed by an exposition of ubuntuism in a restorative justice context in which the relevance of similarities between ubuntu and restorative justice are explored. Lastly, the chapter examines the interconnectedness of ubuntu and restorative justice and asks what the relevance of these similarities are in the normative development of restorative justice as well as in the administration of justice in modern day society and the Western world in general.

Introduction

In traditional Africa the concepts ubuntu, community, indigenous justice and restoration are interlinked. The African ethic and humanistic philosophy of ubuntu encompasses issues of human dignity and respect within the understanding that an individual's humanity is interconnected with the dignity and humanity of others (Mabovula, 2011). Hence, concepts of community, peace and justice do not stand apart from the African way of life, but is emergent in the African peoples' world. Ubuntu is thus more than a moral philosophy, it encompasses African life on an ontological level in that it relates to the essence of being, identity and living. As such, it also underpins the conception of justice. The restoration of harm done is central to ubuntu justice and it is believed that it is the interconnectedness of human beings that brings about restoration and healing in the resolution of conflicts, inclusive of criminal actions. It therefore adds a new dimension to the debate on justice as an integrated part of being a person and, in this context, guides us to question what effect this has on the administration of justice.

The Western colonization of Africa in the nineteenth and twentieth centuries had a profound effect on the political and sociocultural ethos of African people and brought about a breakdown in traditional social structures related to governance, justice and laws, creating uncertainty and mistrust between post-colonial African countries. Even though ubuntu principles are still entrenched in modern day Africa, globalization and the accompanying westernization resulted in acculturation associated with the erosion of traditional values, subsequently creating a state of anomie (Biakolo, 1998). Against this background it is asked whether, within a culturally diverse Africa, ubuntuism remains an acknowledged way of life and whether traditional practices can be justified in a westernized Africa.

In this chapter it is proposed that there is a significant correlation between traditional justice practices as found in the ubuntu philosophy and restorative justice theory and practice. During the last three decades restorative justice has emerged worldwide as an alternative approach to dealing with offending behaviour. This is also the case in Africa where various countries, such as South Africa and Nigeria, are currently utilizing restorative justice in a criminal justice setting and civil society alike as a method of adjudication and alternative conflict resolution. These developments encourages us to examine the normative roots of restorative justice in general, begging us to question the role traditional cultures played in shaping modern day restorative justice practices.

A plethora of writings exploring restorative justice from a westernized perspective has been published. In contrast, few studies exploring the normative roots of restorative justice as an enduring practice in African and other traditional cultures exist. Ignoring these cultural roots can be compared with 'An unknowable, a Ding an sich, a sound of one hand clapping' (Bateson, 1979, p. 78). The purpose of this chapter is to explore traditional indigenous justice practices indicative of the ubuntu philosophy as well as the traditional African understanding of the concepts of crime and criminality. It focuses on the humanistic character of the ubuntu world view and how the interdependence between individuals and the community affects the African concept of justice. The chapter ends by examining the interconnectedness of ubuntu and restorative justice asking what the relevance of these similarities are in the normative development of restorative justice as well as in the administration of justice in modern day society and the Western world in general.

Ubuntuism

According to Nafukho (2006) the ubuntuism concept is based on the African philosophy and way of life known as ubuntu. The ubuntu concept is present in most African cultures and represents an ontological awareness of what it means to be African (Ovens, 2009). In South Africa, the word ubuntu has its roots in the Nguni family of languages (Ndebele, Swati/Swazi, Xhosa and Zulu). It is referred to as *omundu/muntu* by Eastern African Bantu speaking people, *botho* by Tswana speaking people in Botswana and in the case of the Swahili language *mtu* (Nafukho, 2006). Even though the multitude of ethnic groups in Africa uses different terminologies to describe the ubuntu way of life, in essence this philosophy underpins a recognized African way of being. As such, the term ubuntu will be used in this chapter to represent this philosophy. In the same way African is used to depict the salient moral beliefs and presuppositions indicative of the Sub-Saharan African people.

Ubuntu in essence is a traditional moral theory that encompasses the normative set of social rules and principles that guide the conduct of people in African societies (Metz, 2011). It is a communal and humanistic morality which focuses on the welfare and interests of each member in a society. This is entrenched in the notion of common good where the aspirations and needs intrinsic to human fulfilment are sought out. Gyekye (2011) warns that the common good is not the sum of various individual goods, but embraces the communal needs that are basic to the enjoyment and fulfilment of all the members of the community. Institutions in the community, such as legal, political and economic systems are thus set up to enhance social order and peace. Even though these systems might originate from a governing structure, it is important that their foundations are in the community in order to serve the community. The common good is thus a notion that is associated with the concept of community and is espoused by the communitarian African society. Questions that should be asked in this regard are firstly, what are the roots of this form of morality? And secondly, if the emphasis is predominantly placed on the well-being of the community what place does the individual have in such a society?

In answering the first question, no clarity exists about the roots of ubuntu morality, hence conflicting arguments exist about whether its roots are religious or humanitarian in nature (Gyekye, 2011). Philosophers postulating that ubuntu has a religious foundation proposed that religion provides the necessary justification for moral values and beliefs associated with the ubuntu philosophy. They also clarified moral concepts, such as good, bad, right and wrong as religious dogma (Gyekye, 2011). The predominant criticism of this point of view is that antisocial behaviour is a wrongdoing against individuals in society and not the breaking of divine or religious creeds. Furthermore, stating that religion is the basis of people's morality is to infer that without it people will not be able to act in a moral and responsible way (Gbadegesin, 1998). African spirituality is as diverse as the multitude of ethnic affiliations found on the African continent. This begs the question, if ubuntu is grounded in religious dogma then which of the religious affiliations is it associated with? In light of the fact that the ubuntu philosophy is a shared philosophy throughout Africa it can thus be deduced that even though spirituality is central to Africa's people it is not the root of the ubuntu philosophy. While religion inspires morality, ubuntu ethics is more pragmatic and focused on the realities of everyday life. Ubuntu transcends an individualistic world view, recognising the epistemological roots of knowledge as given by ancestors to benefit communities and in recognition of the intrinsic potential of each human being (Cornell, 2008). Prinsloo (1998) highlights that as such, it is the way in which human dignity gains prominence in relation to both morality and rationality. It can therefore be argued that ubuntu is a humanistic ethic and morality with human welfare as the focal point.

The advocates of this humanistic viewpoint postulate that ubuntu morality is rooted in considerations for human welfare and interest, and not in divine pronouncements (Gyekye, 2011). Attributes aimed at enhancing social well-being in society, such as honesty, compassion and generosity that bring about peace, justice and respect are viewed as the foundation of this morality. What is good is therefore defined as deeds, habits, and behaviour patterns that are considered by society as of value because of their contribution towards human welfare. In other words, actions that promote human welfare and interest are perceived as good, while those that detract from human welfare are bad in the world where individuals function. Within Africa, humanity is not just an anthropological concept, it is a moral term and reflects the association between all people with shared aims and interests (Gyekye, 2011). This relationship goes beyond ethical and racial divides and recognizes humanness as the single criteria that constitutes all human beings into one universal family of humankind which adheres to the morality of a shared humanity. The Akan maxim 'man's brother is man' alludes to this idea of universal brotherhood and unity (Gyekye, 2011).

The humanistic character of the African ubuntu world view is conceptualized through the proverbs '*umuntu ngumuntu ngabantu*' meaning 'a person is a person through other persons' (Nafukho, 2006, p. 409). Other maxims associated with ubuntu, such as 'it is through others that one attains selfhood' and the Venda saying '*Muthu u bebelwa munwe*', translated as 'a person is born for the other', emphasize the importance of the community in self-definition (Nussbaum, 2003). It is this rootedness of the self-in-community that captures the interdependence between self and community. Within this relationship ubuntu represents rules of conduct and/or social ethics central to the collective consciousness of the people of Africa (Nafukho, 2006). This perception of the interconnectedness between the individual and community is also reflected in Aristotle's Politics (328 BC) where he postulates that 'Man is by nature a social animal; an individual who is unsocial naturally and not accidentally is either beneath our notice or more than human. Society is something in nature that precedes the individual. Anyone who either cannot lead the common life or is so self-sufficient as not to need to, and therefore does not partake of society, is either a beast or a god.' (Zion, 1998)

The ubuntu philosophy subscribes to values of true humanness, care, sensitivity to the needs of others, respect, empathy and congruence (Biakolo, 1998). It encompasses issues of human dignity and respect with the understanding that a reciprocal relationship exists between the humanity of an individual and the dignity and humanity of others (Mabovula, 2011). Hence, ubuntu encapsulates the capacity in African culture to express compassion, reciprocity, dignity, harmony and humanity in the interests of building and maintaining community.

This brings us to the question of whether an individual has a place in such a communal society? Ubuntu is often criticized because of its focus on a philosophy that values shared humanity and community, thus being perceived as not acknowledging the value of individualism and individual freedom (Metz, 2011). This perception is not accurate as the individual is recognized as being part of the larger community and as such the contribution an individual's behaviour makes to the well-being of the group is recognized. The difference in comparison to a westernized paradigm is that the individual's actions are not driven by utilitarian but by humanitarian motives. For instance, even though the concept of justice may cut across all cultures, the idea of placing an individual at the centre of justice is problematic in communitarian cultures as the adjudication of justice does not reside in the individual but in the community (Mangena, 2012). African individuality can therefore not be separated from the identity of the individual as part of the larger group. In ubuntu societies every member is expected to contribute to society by virtue of their individual talents and attributes and thereby visibly participating in society and not disappearing in the whole. Moral personhood is therefore of importance.

Similar to the concept of brotherhood, personhood is also a moral term and something that has to be attained. For example, the statement 'he is a person' is a normative judgment implying that 'he has good character' and is a generous, humble, respectful and peaceful person. Similarly, a person whose behaviour is unethical will be judged as being someone that is not a human and thus has no character (Gyekye, 2011). In a number of Sub-Saharan African languages there is no word for ethics or morality, which are replaced with the concept of character. It is interesting to note that the English word ethics is derived from the Greek word ethike, which also means character. In an African context, character is acquired in direct proportion to one's participation in communal life from birth onwards. In this regard socialization plays an important role in the development of an ubuntu morality. The Igbo and Yoruba (Nigeria) proverb 'It takes a whole village to raise a child', acknowledges that a child's upbringing is a communal effort and the responsibility of the larger extended family and wider community. Other maxims in Africa voicing a similar sentiment are the Sukuma (Tanzania) proverb 'One knee does not bring up a child', and the Swahili (East and Central Africa) proverb 'One hand does not nurse a child'. As such, the African ubuntu ontology encompasses the essence of being African. It transcends individualistic identity offering a holistic perception of an African view of the world.

The concept of personhood furthermore infers that an individual can be a human being without being a person because the individual does not act for the common good. That said, it does not imply that if someone is considered 'not a person', that such an individual will lose his or her rights as a human being, or that the community will cease to act with ubuntu towards that individual. In contradiction, an individual who acts immorally is not rejected and isolated from society but rather is drawn in closer in order to assist the individual to become a person and live with ubuntu. In this instance restorative justice practices, similar to those in African traditional justice, are used to restore the imbalance caused by the harm done and thereby attain restoration for the victim and the community, as well as the wrongdoer. Hence, retribution and a punitive paradigm are foreign to the African concept of justice.

Ubuntu thus acts as a fundamental ontological and epistemological world view in Africa. It reflects shared knowledge that has been passed from one generation to the next. For instance, elders who are considered to be the foundation of wisdom will educate the children, often through storytelling, on how to behave and how to live well with others (Mangena, 2012). These teachings also act as a moral compass to measure against whether behaviour could be deemed as moral or immoral. The value of the knowledge lies within the teachings, which are geared towards seeking consensus and mutual understanding and the maintenance of harmony. According to Archbishop Desmond Tutu (1999), a person with ubuntu is open and available to others, affirming of others, and does not feel threatened by the fact that others are able and good. This opinion is based on a self-assurance that comes from the knowledge that he or she belongs in a greater whole. In such a society, it is recognized that one is diminished when others are humiliated or tortured and oppressed.

That said, the question remains whether ubuntuism is an acknowledged way of life within a culturally diverse Africa and broader international community. Globally ubuntuism is not a foreign concept and can be linked to the philosophy of collectivism that, similarly to ubuntu, emphasizes the interdependence of human beings. It is also reflected in the moral philosophy of Alexander Pope (Barnes, 1990) and Marcus Aurelius's work *Meditation,* where the interconnectedness of human beings and the universe in general is recognized (Gavrielides, 2005). In all instances the purpose of this interconnectedness is to aspire to the common good.

The ubuntu philosophy also greatly influenced Jung's views on the collective subconscious and the role it plays in the development of ethnicity. In his paradoxical exploration of the relationship between individualism versus the collective consciousness, he came to the realization that consciousness emerges gradually from encounters with the other (Blackmun-Eskow, 2009). Jung (Brooke, 2008a, p. 38) expounded on this idea stating that 'If a man is capable of leading a responsible life himself, then he is also conscious of his duties to the community', thus highlighting the reciprocal relationship between the community and the individual. Brooke (2008a), further exploring the relationship between individuation and the collective conscious within the paradigm of Jungian psychology, used the concept ubuntu to bring an ethical dimension to the individualism versus collective consciousness debate. She postulates that ubuntu is a term that defines what it is to be a person, where being a person is both a given and a task of self-realization. Ubuntu, thus becomes the personification of all the virtues we admire in others, namely personal responsibility, ethical self-knowledge, strength and courage, humility, forgiveness, human understanding, a knowledge of history, and a sense of the sacred (Brooke, 2008b). In answering the question of whether ubuntuism is an acknowledged way of life it can be concluded that the ubuntu philosophy transcends national and cultural differences and fundamentally acknowledges our shared humanity on a global level.

Ubuntuism in a Westernized Africa

Senghor (1993) argues that Africans have always presented a world view which diametrically opposes a traditional Western philosophy. He perceives the Western world to be an individualistic culture, in comparison to the collective identity of the African cultures, with a somewhat selfish concern for oneself and the small group of people close to oneself. In individualistic cultures, emphasis is placed on independence, achievement, freedom, high levels of competition and pleasure. Collectivist cultures, such as found in African society, emphasize interdependence, harmony, family security, social hierarchy, cooperation and low levels of competition (Triandis, 1989). In comparison to western cultures, collectivism is still one of the foremost cultural differences that is evident in Africa in this day and age, even though large sections of the society have westernized to some extent.

This brings us to the question of whether ubuntu's existence can be justified in a westernized Africa. This question is complex and cannot be answered before we explore why Africa has lost its traditional cultural roots (Schoeman, 2012). Colonization had a profound effect on the political and sociocultural ethos of African people. Even though there have been some positive effects of colonialism on Africa, such as opening the continent up to international trade, in general the effects have been far more destructive than beneficial. This is especially evident in the countries of the Sub-Saharan region. Most African states or countries grew directly out of the Western colonization of African societies. This in itself contributed to a breakdown in traditional social structures related to governance, justice and laws, creating uncertainty and mistrust between post-colonial African counties (Okafo, 2006). Furthermore, colonialism in Africa resulted in an imposition of foreign rule over the indigenous traditional political setting and dominance of African people in all spheres of their social, political, cultural, economic and religious development (Arowolo, 2010). Globalization continues to exacerbate both relative deprivation and crises of identity, resulting in the disintegration of traditional communities and value systems. Merton (Messner, 2010) postulates that such a breakdown of social bonds between the individual and a community, and the fragmentation of social identity as well as the rejection of self-regulatory values, can result in a state of anomie.

Defining anomie, Merton (Zhao and Cao, 2010, p. 1,212) states, 'In a word, the degree of anomie in a social system is indicated by the extent to which there is a lack of consensus on norms judged to be legitimate, with its attendant uncertainty and insecurity in social relations.' Anomie is thus associated with the normlessness or chaos that takes place when social structures break down due to rapid changes in a society (Tibbetts and Hemmens, 2010). In Africa, this was primarily caused by the paradigm shift from an African to a Western ideology, a shift that ontologically opposed the African way of life. Research recognizes that colonization produces increased levels of anomie with regard to economic and social development (Biakolo, 1998). This occurs when highly developed societies, via globalization, encounter people living in traditional social structures. This is more relevant in countries with a strong cultural identity and where a sense of group cohesion exists. A case in point is African communities where there is a direct correlation between the identity of the individual and the identity of the group on an ontological, metaphysical and epistemological level. In this regard Kuhn (Gavrielides, 2005) claims that such a shift in reality causes a paradigm crisis resulting in an inability to comprehend new data and resolve problems.

The basic presumption is that the percentage of anomic individuals gives an indication of the degree of anomie in society. In other words, the more individuals share traits of anomic dispositions, the higher the degree of anomie is in a society (Huschka and Mau, 2006). This interface between globalization and culture is known to trigger cultural conflict. In Africa this state of anomie is evident in the violent methods of conflict resolution, racial and ethnic intolerance and high crime rate evident in society today. In African society anomie is furthermore intensified by the apparent lack of fit between traditional collectivistic social structures and the consumerism-driven cultural norms and individualistic westernized structures found in post-colonial Africa (Kasingo, 2010). Mimiko (in Arowolo, 2010) argues that westernization in Africa resulted in the erosion of the social fabric, and the growth of a culture of violence. According to him, traditional African systems of conflict resolution were destroyed and nothing was put in their place. Arowolo (2010) concurs, stating that the state of cultural emptiness caused by globalization is the foundation of cultural extinction and a drought of African values evident in modern day Africa.

This brings to mind the question of whether Africa would have been better off had colonization never taken place. There are contradictory opinions in this regard, but Atteslander (2007) warns against forgetting the positive aspect of anomie, namely that without a certain degree of anomie social change is impossible. Hence, it is important to develop a better understanding of the structures and functioning of anomie in Africa in order to govern social change effectively while avoiding social conflicts. In this regard Cornell (2008, p. 7) acknowledges the role the ubuntu philosophy can play to build, enhance and repair the moral and social fabric in anomic communities and African society in general.

Ubuntu remains a recognized philosophy in Africa and is still entrenched in sociocultural practices and legislation. According to Metz (2011) ubuntu is not only applicable to the normative theoretical understanding of morality in Africa, but also creates a precise and clear account of the importance of individual liberty in present day societies, creating a promising foundation for human rights in Africa. This requires the refashioning of the interpretation of ubuntu to characterize current day realities and how it is construed in the light of our understanding of what morality is. In essence, ubuntu boils down to figuring out what institutes performing morally right actions. As such, this debate has remained current and relevant throughout modern times. Furthermore, this is as much a global debate as it is an African one.

Justice in Africa

Eurocentric pro-colonialist opinion postulates that European colonialists brought criminal justice, law and order to Africa (Dalgleish, 2005). This assumption has been proven incorrect by historical information which found a number of parallels between the criminal justice system in pre-colonial Africa and the one found in Britain's criminal justice system of the same period (ibid.). Traditional justice is encapsulated in the ubuntu philosophy and has always been humanistic and restorative in nature.

Traditionally, ubuntu philosophy was used to maintain law and order in African society. Native African traditions, customs and laws served as the foundations for control and justice on the continent. This changed with the colonization of Sub-Saharan Africa. In terms of the justice system African colonialization brought about the introduction of Western-based criminal justice systems resulting in the disintegration of Africa's rich indigenous justice traditions. The African traditional form of societies and restorative traditions were replaced by a Western individualistic and retributively oriented justice system (Omale, 2006). According to Elechi (2004) African peoples' disillusionment with a westernized justice system derives mostly from their perception of the system's concept and practice which they found alien and antithetical to the African concept and practice of justice. For instance, the formal punitive processes in the English judicial system contradict the spirit of traditional African justice that emphasizes righting wrongs and reconciliation (Okafo, 2006). Notwithstanding this, although there is no uniform justice system, the justice system used in modern day Africa is predominantly based on Western judicial ideologies. In order to understand the cause of this disillusionment it is necessary to take a step back to explore the traditional African understanding of the concept of crime and criminality.

In traditional African communities crime was seen as a conflict between people and not a violation of State Laws. The terms offenders and victims are modern legal terms and in traditional communities they were referred to as the wrongdoers and the parties wronged (Kinyanjui, 2009). The epistemology underpinning traditional justice in Africa is entrenched in experiential knowledge that was passed down from one generation to another (Nasseem, 2002). Within an African context it should be noted that this knowledge is also based on the shared social dimension not of *I* know, but *we* know (Ovens, 2009). Indicative of the ubuntu philosophy, traditional justice also focus on practices that is grounded in such a cultural epistemology. Maintaining positive relations within the society is therefore recognized as a collective responsibility and a dispute between fellow members of a society is perceived not merely as a matter of curiosity with regard to the affairs of one's neighbour but a conflict belonging to the entire community (Murithi, 2006). Similarly, if an individual is wronged he or she may depend on the group to remedy the wrong and, because of the strong sense of group identity, the community takes ownership of the individual's ill-treatment. This perception of crime as social harm is also reflected in the justice system where African justice and law are instrumental in the generation of societal cohesion, rather than being agents for advancing individual or factional group interests as seen in a westernized legal system (Okafo, 2006).

From the above discussion it is clear that on an ontological level African judicial practices are rooted in the ubuntu philosophy. Nussbaum (Elechi, Morris and Schauer, 2010) noted that traditional African culture and principles of justice are also founded on the supposition of companionship, reciprocity, dignity, harmony and humanity in the interests of building and maintaining a community characterized by justice and mutual caring. The primary goal of African indigenous justice systems is the restoration of victims, the community and also the offenders. A criminal offence is seen to have caused a breach in individual and communal relationships and the purpose of the judicial process in this context is to heal the breach, to restore good relationships and to redress the balance. The sense of community is reflected in the treatment of offenders. Offenders are not ostracized but encouraged to understand and accept responsibility for their actions, thereby promoting reconciliation between victim, perpetrator and community. Even though sanctions, such as fines or a short exile during imprisonment, may be part of the adjudication of justice, the fundamental purpose of the judicial process remains to heal (Tutu, 2004). Hence, victims, offenders and the entire community are involved and participate in the definition of harm and search for a resolution acceptable to all stakeholders (Elechi, 2004). This approach to adjudication provides offenders with support, guidance and healing.

African justice is thus contradictory to a retributive Western justice system in that it is conciliatory in nature and seeks to restore peace and harmony between community members. Harm caused by criminal behaviour can therefore not be considered fully resolved, until the peace, the relationships and the social harmony damaged by the crime, have been restored. The values of ubuntu are thus both personal, in that individual growth is achieved through interaction with others, and normative, in that it fosters pro-social attitudes and restoration (Giddy, 2012).

In this regard, traditional African justice and restorative justice are analogous in philosophy and practice. This will be discussed in more detail later on in this chapter.

Even though a post-colonial westernized legal system is still evident in the majority of modern day Sub-Saharan African countries aspects of ubuntu and traditional justice are also recognized. This is evident in the African Charter on Human and Peoples' Rights which promotes human rights that are relevant to Africa. The emphasis of the Charter is on the protection of national communal rights, rather than individual rights. The intention of the African Charter is to recreate the bonds of the pre-colonial era among individuals and between individuals and the state (Mutua, 1995). The Constitution of the Republic of South Africa Act 108 of 1996 and the South African Traditional Courts Bill 2008 are further examples of legislation that aims to affirm ubuntuism and strives to reintroduce customary law and practices in adjudication.

It can therefore be concluded that ubuntu creates a philosophical foundation that is of relevance in African justice. It creates an ontological world view and epistemology geared towards seeking consensus, justice and the maintenance of harmony. It humanizes the judicial process and recognizes crime as interpersonal harm and conflict, which can only be resolved through reconciliation and healing for the common good.

Ubuntuism in a Restorative Justice Context

Braithwaite (2002) has argued that we have yet to discover a culture which does not have some deep-seated restorative traditions. It is therefore widely acknowledged that modern restorative justice theory and practice have been enriched through learning from indigenous justice practices (Tshehla, 2004). Johnstone (2004) argues that in order to obtain a comprehensive understanding of restorative justice it is necessary to explore its roots in traditional and contemporary indigenous communities. In this regard, Africa's restorative tradition is deeply rooted in the ubuntu philosophy and as such a significant correlation exists between restorative justice practices and those in African traditional justice. Clear similarities can be identified between the philosophy, values and practices of restorative justice and ubuntu.

Philosophical Similarities

Both restorative justice and ubuntu promote a normative system that recognizes the interconnectedness between individual and community and strives towards achieving a more communitarian approach in adjudication and conflict resolution. As such, the African indigenous justice system is community based and human centred and employs restorative and transformative principles in conflict resolution. Restorative justice is negotiative and democratic, hence it empowers the community to use mediation during conflict resolution (Elechi, 2004). Restorative and ubuntu justice is an interactive process that provides opportunities for dialogue between the victim, offender and other affected parties in the community. It encourages community participation and ownership of the process. In this instance dialogue represents close-knit relationships in which all members of society are acknowledged and respected (Ovens and Prinsloo, 2010). Traditionally African societies relied on dialogue to make sense of life. Dialogue is used to negotiate and conceptualize what can be understood as being a 'common moral position' meant to safeguard the interests of the community as a whole (Mangena, 2012). According to Bangura (2005) ubuntu inspires people to expose themselves to others and to embrace the differences in their humanness in order to inform and enrich their own lives. This refers to the willingness to learn from others as a means to build knowledge and wisdom (Nafukho, 2006). Ubuntu, like restorative justice, incorporates dialogue by intertwining relationships and closeness (ibid.). Hence, the dialogue is more than a linguistic exchange, it acknowledges the human rights and dignity of all individuals in society (Ovens and Prinsloo, 2010). However, the ability to use dialogue to achieve peaceful reconciliation seems to be no longer respected in many contemporary African societies, as is evident from the violent protests and wars seen in Africa.

Similarities in the Value System Supporting Restorative Justice and Ubuntu

Dignity and respect are viewed as central values in ubuntu and restorative justice. In African culture, dignity is very important and is also linked to the philosophy of ubuntu (Skelton, 2007). The goal of African justice is the restoration of victims and the reintegration of the offender back into the community. African indigenous justice is a victim-centred process; hence the starting point for African justice is the affirmation of victims' needs for information, validation, social support and vindication (Elechi, 2004). Both justice systems acknowledge the offender's needs for support, guidance and healing. As mentioned before, offenders are not shunned but guided to understand the impact of their wrongdoing and accept responsibility for their actions. The purpose of this is to promote healing through reconciliation between victim, perpetrator and community.

Similarities also exist in the process and individual values of ubuntu and restorative justice. In restorative justice the process values address the quality of the restorative process while individual values focus on promoting the nurturing of individuals (Pranis, 2007). Process values guide the practices and processes responsible for restoration and conflict resolution, ensuring that the adjudication process takes place in an environment that supports values such as respect, honesty, humility, mutual care, accountability and trust (Dyck, 2004). In traditional justice traditional leaders and community elders played an important role in conflict resolution. The victim and offender were represented by elders from their clan with both parties given the opportunity to state their case. Once both cases were heard, the elders deliberated on the best resolution to the conflict. The concept of guilt used in contemporary criminal law is inconsequential since the aim of the decision was to cater for the needs of the victim as well as to promote reconciliation within the community (Kinyanjui, 2009). These traditional processes are similar in nature and objective to those found in restorative justice mediation.

Individual values in restorative justice strive to encourage humanitarian behaviour towards others. In this regard it aims at enabling individuals to actualize their inner potential and to act with respect, honesty, accountability, compassion and patience (Pranis, 2007). It also supports reconciliation and healing for both the victim and perpetrator. Sullivan and Tiff (2004) emphasize that at its core restorative justice is not selective but seeks to meet the needs of all who find themselves in a situation of harm. From this perspective restorative values are not foreign to African society but are affirmed in the ubuntu philosophy.

Similarities in the Practices Associated With Restorative Justice and Ubuntu

Both restorative and African traditional justice aim to promote reconciliation and to restore peace and harmony in the community. This emanates from the understanding that an individual's humanity is interconnected with the dignity and humanity of others, as discussed previously. Traditional African culture has an infinite capacity for the pursuit of consensus and reconciliation similar to that found in restorative justice. In Africa consensus building is used to regulate and manage relationships between members of the community (Murithi, 2006). Hence, African-style democracy operates in the form of lengthy discussions where each speaker is generally provided with an equal chance to speak up until an agreement and/or group cohesion is reached. The format of the discussion, referred to as *legothlas*, is similar to the process followed in restorative circles and mediation sessions. The final agreement in the African dispute-building process was signified by *omulembe/amani,* peace; *obulala*, togetherness; *umoja*, oneness; and the concept of *simunye*, translated as we are one and unity is strength (Nafukho, 2006). The consensus tenet of ubuntu requires an authentic respect for the human rights of cultures within and outside Africa.

Both restorative justice and traditional ubuntu justice practices are focused on righting the harm done to individuals as well as the broader community and not on abiding to established legalistic judicial processes and laws. It is therefore a creative process that follows a more flexible approach to find the best solution for the specific problem raised in a dispute. Restorative justice and ubuntu justice thus deal with antisocial behaviour in a fundamentally different way to most conventional justice systems. Crime, according to Zehr (1990), is viewed as a violation of people and interpersonal relationships and not a dispute between an individual and the State. This is similar to the view held in the ubuntu philosophy as discussed earlier. Gavrielides (2005) postulates that restorative justice replaces conventional criminal justice processes with a new *telos*, moving away from retributive justice's focus on the violation of the law to focusing on the violation of people and relationships. On a fundamental level a restorative paradigm offers an opportunity for the victim and offender to explore the real effect of the harm done and to find a solution that fits the unique circumstances associated with the conflict. Consequently, the outcomes in both traditional ubuntu justice and restorative justice processes, unlike judicial law, are not based on prior pronouncements of law by other courts. In other words they are not subject to the rule of *stare decisis*, or the law of precedent, it is therefore not necessary in restorative justice processes to consider the outcome of previous cases (Skelton, 2007).

In summary, the primary purpose of both restorative and ubuntu justice practices is to restore. In consequence, if we, on a theoretical level, acknowledge the similarities between these two justice systems it raises the question of their relevance to modern day society?

Finding Solutions Within a Pluralistic Society

In the previous discussion we acknowledged that the ubuntu and restorative justice paradigm is philosophically congruous as both make use of the interconnectedness of human beings to bring about restoration and healing in the resolution of conflicts, inclusive of criminal actions. Anderson (2003) is of the opinion that while restorative justice functions as a response to crime, ubuntu is much more since it not only focuses on restoring an imbalance created by criminal conduct but also acts as a normative world view proactively aiding in conflict resolution, reconciliation and establishing peace within communities. In this regard some restorative justice practitioners are moving towards a similar perspective with regards to restorative justice postulating that restorative justice theory has the same potential as it also has a transformative dimension. Johnstone (2012) proposes that an alternative way of constructing restorative justice is as a loosely linked assortment of beliefs, practices, values and ways of life, which can be broken down into a set of teachings on how we should conduct ourselves in the world, see and relate to others and deal with problems we might encounter. Furthermore, he emphasizes the power of restorative justice processes and their ability to achieve restorative goals, such as reparation of harm, reconciliation of conflicted parties and in general bringing about public safety. Even though it is outside the scope of this discussion the author is of the opinion that the potential value of restorative justice as a proactive crime prevention and restoration mechanism, not just for reactive adjudication, is overlooked and is an area worth exploring in more depth.

In some African countries, such as South Africa, restorative justice within the formal criminal justice system predominantly functions within child justice and domestic violence disputes. It is rarely used on an informal level as a mechanism for alternative community-based interventions. Government support for restorative justice initiatives is mostly limited to their application in the criminal justice system, while community-based interventions are driven by non-governmental and church-based organizations in civil society. Restorative justice services in general are funding driven and rarely sustainable (Merrifield, 2010). In the most instances funding for restorative justice initiatives in the criminal justice sector comes from government sources. This top-down approach is not ideal as it marginalizes services because they are driven from a political power base. Ubuntu's power as an ontological philosophy has steadily diminished in Africa even though it is recognized in legislative frameworks such as the African Charter. This, as discussed earlier, can be largely ascribed to colonization and, more recently, the globalization taking place in Africa. With the interest in finding an alternative to the current retributive justice system in Africa, restorative justice and subsequently traditional justice practices associated with ubuntu are becoming more prominent. One of the reasons for this, specifically in South Africa, is that in the search for reconciliation and reconstruction, after the legacy of apartheid restorative justice was used to bring about reconciliation. As such, South Africa is an example of an African country poised to develop modern restorative justice processes within and alongside the existing criminal justice system. As is the case in many African countries, the danger exists that this may be derailed by the struggle to deal with the culture of violence, as is evident in the serious violent crime seen in modern day South Africa. It can therefore be argued that the challenge in Africa is not to introduce a new restorative justice paradigm but rather to reintroduce restorative justice practices as found in traditional ubuntu justice.

In Africa society is not solely made up of traditional communities but is characterized by ethnic diversity as well as overlapping affinity groups that are broader than mere race and ethnicity. Cultural values and practices are also influenced by urbanization, level of education and acceptance of postmodern notions. African culture has been in a transitional phase, shifting from traditional to modern, for many years. According to Ovens and Prinsloo (2010) this has influenced individuals' identification with their own ethnicity, which is a product of adaptation to the influences of Western culture. In order to reignite ubuntuism and introduce the concept of restorative justice in modern Africa it is therefore necessary to redefine the traditional concepts that were historically defined through cultural and regional boundaries, such as community. Furthermore, as mentioned earlier, it is also necessary to reconceptualize and contextualize ubuntu within modern day Africa and explore the role restorative justice can play in finding a universally acceptable philosophy for adjudication and crime prevention within a pluralistic African society.

In the search for a universally acceptable philosophy in Africa care should be taken not to fall into the trap of unanimism. Unanimism is an unwarranted assumption that all the inhabitants of this vast and varied continent can be supposed to resemble each other in any salient characteristic of thought or culture (Ovens and Prinsloo, 2010). In this regard Van der Merwe (Ovens and Prinsloo, 2010) poses the question of whether Africans do adhere to ubuntu, or at least endeavour to do so? He believes that South Africa is an example of such an ethos of solidarity where a commitment to peaceful coexistence is emerging amongst ordinary South Africans in spite of their differences. This ethos is grounded in the spirit of ubuntu and is evident in the relatively non violent transition of South African society from a totalitarian state to a multi-party democracy. Cornell (2008, p. 7) proposes that in striving to achieve solidarity the saying '*a botho bag ago a nne botho seshabeng'*, which literally means 'let your welfare be the welfare of the nation', is of relevance as it points us to how ubuntu calls us to be an aspirational community in which an individual's well-being or welfare is developed and enhanced by seeking the well-being of the larger community. However, attempting to integrate traditional values with modern practices remains a complex issue when, to a large extent, the law still follows a predominantly Western tradition. Despite the complexity of this challenge, De Liefde (2003) argues that the call for inclusive responsibility on a broad, social level is gaining momentum resulting in people committing to principles of ubuntuism inclusive of social responsibility and restorative justice. It is within this discourse that the numerous similarities between the tenets of restorative justice and ubuntu as discussed in this chapter are of relevance.

Conclusion

In this chapter the author explored the role that ubuntuism as an African philosophy plays as a moral theory in traditional and modern day Africa. It was concluded that there are resounding similarities between restorative justice and the traditional justice practices found in ubuntu philosophy. Colonization in Africa contributed to the disintegration of traditional communities and value systems resulting in acculturation and the westernization of society in general. Consequently, South Africa has become a society that is not only made up of traditional communities but is also characterized by ethnic diversity and a modernized culture.

In seeking an answer to address the fundamental cultural differences between African and Western culture, the paper does not propose that African society should revert back to traditional systems of adjudication, or even way of life, but rather that the differences between Western and African philosophies be recognized and sensitivity developed to the different epistemological and ontological points of departure. In this regard, the tenets of restorative justice are not foreign to African society but reflective of the system of beliefs found in the ubuntu philosophy. It is therefore proposed that both ubuntu and restorative philosophies are relevant in modern day Africa.

The intersection of restorative justice and ubuntu philosophies is also of broader relevance. The author briefly touched on the potential transformative dimension associated with both ubuntu and restorative justice practices. This is of value since it demonstrates how Western and African philosophies have the potential to contribute to inclusive social transformation and restoration on a global level. It would therefore be of value to conduct a more in-depth examination thereof. That said, this review is in no way proposed as a complete discussion of the interconnectedness between the African ubuntu and restorative justice philosophies but rather strives to generate a critical discourse on the role and place of indigenous philosophies in the reconstructing of restorative justice philosophy.

References

Anderson, A.M. 2003. Restorative Justice, the African Philosophy of Ubuntu and the diversion of Criminal Prosecution, *17th International Conference of the International Society for the Reform of Criminal Law*. The Hague, Netherlands, 24–28 August 2003.

Arowolo, D. 2010. The effects of western civilisation and culture on Africa. *Afro Asian Journal of Social Sciences* 1(1), Quarter IV. Available at: http://www.onlineresearchjournals.com/ aajoss/art/53.pdf [accessed: 21 November 2012].

Atteslander, P. 2007. The Impact of Globalization on Methodology. Measuring Anomie and Social Transformation. *International Review of Sociology*, 17(3), pp. 511–24.

Bangura, A.K. 2005. Ubuntugogy: An African educational paradigm that transcends pedagogy, andragogy, ergonagy and heutagogy. *Journal of Third World Studies*, 22(2), pp. 13–53.

Barnes, J. 1990. Partial Wholes. *Social Philosophy and Policy*, 8 (1), pp. 1–23.

Bateson, G. 1979. *Mind and Nature*. London: Fontana.

Biakolo, E. 1998. Categories of Cross cultural cognitions and African condition, in *Philosophy from Africa. A text readings*, edited by Coetzee, P.H. and Roux, A.P.J. Halfway House: International Thomson Publishing, pp. 1–14.

Blackmun-Eskow, S. 2009. *Jung in Africa: Africa in Jung*. Available at: http://fielding.academia.edu/SarahBlackmunEskow/Papers/934711/Jung_in_Africa_Africa_in_Jung [accessed: 12 June 2012].

Braithwaite, J. 2002. *The Fall and Rise of Restorative Justice*. Available at: www.oup.org [accessed 22 November 2012].

Brooke, R. 2008a. Cultural reflections on Jung's concept of individuation. *Psychological Perspectives*, 51, pp. 36–53.

Brooke, R. 2008b. Ubuntu and the Individuation Process: Toward a Multicultural Analytical Psychology. *Psychological Perspectives*, 51, pp. 36–53.

Cornell, D. 2004. A call for a More Nuanced Constitutional Jurisprudence: Ubuntu, Dignity, and Reconciliation. *Suid-Afrikaanse Publiekreg/ South African Public Law*, 19(1), pp. 666–75.

Cornell, D. 2008. uBuntu, Pluralism and the Responsibility of Legal Academics to the New South Africa, paper presented at thc *Inaugural lecture by Professor Drucilla Cornell Department of Private Law*. Faculty of Law, 10 September. Available at: http://www.uct.ac.za/downloads/uct.ac.za/news/lectures/inaugurals/Drucilla_Cornell.pdf [accessed: 6 November 2012].

Dalgleish, D. 2005. Pre-Colonial Criminal Justice In West Africa: Eurocentric Thought Versus Africentric Evidence. *African Journal of Criminology and Justice Studies*, 1(1), pp. 55–69.

De Liefde, W.H.J. 2003. *Lekgotla. The art of leadership through dialogue*. Houghton: Jacana.

Dyck, D. 2004. Are We – Practitioners, Advocates – Practicing What We Preach?, in *Critical issues in Restorative Justice*, edited by Zehr, H. and Troews, B. New York: Criminal Justice Press.

Elechi, O.O. 2004. Human Rights and the African Indigenous Justice System, *18th International Conference of the International Society for the Reform of Criminal Law*. Montreal, Quebec, Canada, 8–12 August 2004. Available at: www.restorativejustice.org/articlesdb/articles/5450Cached [accessed: 14 August 2012].

Elechi, O.O., Morris, S.V.C. and Schauer, E.J. 2010. Restoring Justice (Ubuntu): An African Perspective. *International Criminal Justice Review*, 20(1), pp. 73–85.

Gavrielides, T. 2005. Some Meta-Theoretical Questions for Restorative Justice. *Ratio Juris*, 18(1), pp. 84–106.

Gbadegesin, S. 1998. Eniyan: the Yoruba concept of a person, in *Philosophy from Africa. A text readings*, edited by Coetzee, P.H. and Roux, A.P.J. Halfway House: International Thomson Publishing, pp. 1–14.

Giddy, P. 2012. Philosophy for Children in Africa: developing a framework. *South African Journal of Education*, 32, pp. 15–25.

Gyekye, K, 2011. African Ethics, *The Stanford Encyclopedia of Philosophy*, Fall Edition. Available at: http://plato.stanford.edu/archives/fall2011/entries/african-ethics/ [accessed: 22 November 2012].

Huschka, D. and Mau, S. 2006. Social Anomie and Racial Segregation in South Africa. *Social Indicators Research*. 76, pp. 467–498.

Johnstone, G. 2004. How and in what terms should restorative justice be conceived? in *Critical Issues in Restorative Justice*, edited by Zehr, H. and Toews, B. New York: Criminal Justice Press.

Johnstone, G. 2012. The teachings of restorative justice, *1st International Symposium on the Philosophy of Restorative Justice and Human Rights*. Skopelos Island, Greece, 2–7 June 2012.

Kasingo, A. 2010. Impact of Globalization on Traditional African Religion and Cultural Conflict. *Journal of Alternative Perspectives in the Social Sciences*. 2(1), pp. 309–22.

Kinyanjui, S. 2009. Restorative Justice in Traditional Pre-Colonial Criminal Justice Systems in Kenya. *Tribal Law Journal*. 10, pp. 1–16.

Mabovula, N.N. 2011. The erosion of African communal values: a reappraisal of the African Ubuntu philosophy. *Inkanyiso*, 3(1), pp. 38–47.

Mangena, F. 2012. Towards a hunhu/ubuntu dialogical moral theory. *Phronimon*, 13(2), pp. 1–17.

Merrifield, M. 2010. *Khulisa Crime Prevention Initiative*. Personal Interview. 20 July.

Messner, S.F. and Merton, Robert K. Social Structure and Anomie, in *Encyclopedia of Criminological Theory*, edited by Cullen, F.T. and Wilcox, P. Thousand Oaks, CA: Sage.

Metz, T. 2011. Ubuntu as a moral theory and human rights in South Africa. *African Human Rights Law Journal*, 11(2), pp. 532–59.

Murithi, T. 2006. Practical Peacemaking Wisdom from Africa: Reflections on Ubuntu. *The Journal of Pan African Studies*, 1(4), June, pp. 25–34.

Mutua M.W. 1995. The Banjul Charter and the African Fingerprint: An Evaluation of the Language of Rights and Duties. *Virginia Journal of International Law*, 35(2), pp. 339–40.

Nafukho, F. M. 2006. Ubuntu world view: a traditional African view of adult learning in the workplace. *Advances in Developing Human Resources*, 8(3), pp. 408–15.

Nasseem, S.B. 2002. African heritage and contemporary life, in *Philosophy from Africa* (second edition) (eds) Coetzee, P.H. and Roux, A.P.J. Oxford: Oxford University Press.

Nussbaum, B. 2003. Ubuntu: Reflections of a South African on Our Common Humanity. *Reflections*, 4(4), pp. 21–6.

Okafo, N. 2006. Relevance of African Traditional Jurisprudence on Control, Justice, and Law: A Critique of the Igbo Experience. *African Journal of Criminology and Justice Studies*, AJCJS, 2(1), pp. 37–62.

Omale, D.J.O. 2006. Justice in History: An Examination of 'African Restorative Traditions' and the Emerging 'Restorative Justice' Paradigm. *African Journal Of Criminology and Justice Studies*, 2(2), pp. 33–63.

Ovens, M. 2009. *The significance of 'Africanness' on the development of contemporary criminological propositions*. Available at: www.unisa.ac.za/contents/.../col.../ SignificansAfricanness.doc [accessed: 5 November 2012].

Ovens, M. and Prinsloo, J. 2010. The Significance of 'Africanness' for the Development of Contemporary Criminological Propositions: A Multidisciplinary Approach. *Phronimon*, 11(2), pp. 19–33.

Pranis, K. 2007. Restorative values, in Johnstone, G. and van Ness, D.W. (eds). *Handbook of Restorative Justice*. Oregon:Willan Publishings.

Prinsloo, E.D. 1998. Ubuntu culture and participatory management, in *Philosophy from Africa. A text readings*, edited by Coetzee, PH. and Roux, A.P.J. Halfway House: International Thomson Publishing.

Schoeman, M. 2012. A philosophical view of social transformation through restorative justice teachings – a case study of traditional leaders in Ixopo, South Africa. *Phronimon* 13(2), pp. 19–38.

Senghor, L. 1993. Negritude: A Humanism of the Twentieth Century, in *Colonial Discourse and Post-colonial Theory: A Reader*. Williams, P. and Chrisman, L. (eds), New York: Harvester Wheatsheaf.

Skelton, A. 2007. Tapping indigenous knowledge: traditional conflict resolution, restorative justice and the denunciation of crime in South Africa. *Acta Juridica*, pp. 228–46.

Sullivan, D. and Tiff, L. 2004. What are the implications of Restorative Justice for society and our lives, in *Critical issues in Restorative Justice*, edited by Zehr, H. and Troews, B. New York: Criminal Justice Press.

Tibbetts, K.G. and Hemmens, C. 2010. *Criminological theory: A text/reader*. California: Sage Publications.

Triandis, H.C. 1989. The Self and Social Behaviour in Differing Cultural Contexts. *Psychological Review*, 96(3), pp. 506–20.

Tshehla, B. 2004. The restorative justice bug bites the South African criminal justice system. *South African Journal of Criminal Justice*. 1, pp. 1–16.

Tshehla, B. 2005. Traditional leaders' role in justice and crime prevention. *SA Crime Quarterly*, 11, March, pp. 15–20.

Tutu, D. 1999. *No Future without Forgiveness*. New York: Doubleday.

Tutu, D. 2004. The Truth and Reconciliation Process – Restorative Justice. *Lecture, Longford Lecture Series*, Canada, 16 February 2004. Available at: http://www.longfordtrust.org/lecture_details.php?id=11 [accessed: 24 August 2012].Zehr, Howard. 1990. *Changing Lenses: A New Focus for Crime and Justice*. Scottsdale: Herald.

Zhao, R. and Cao, L. 2010. Social Change and Anomie: A Cross-National Study Social Change and Anomie: A Cross-National Study. *Social Forces*, 88(3), pp. 1,209–29.

Zion, J. 1998. The Dynamics of Navajo Peacemaking. *Journal of Contemporary Criminal Justice*, 14(1), pp. 58–74.

Chapter 15
Restorative Pain: A New Vision of Punishment

Theo Gavrielides

My 'Painful Statement'

Since I first started writing about restorative justice I have struggled with the concept of punishment and whether, or how, it reconciles with restorative practices. In the eyes of any layperson, punishment is something unpleasant; it is seen as a necessary consequence resulting from wrongdoing. This understanding, however, opens a Pandora's Box of questions. Who is to say that the punished action is wrong and who is to decide the type and level of punishment? And what is punishment, given that we all punish whether in our capacity as parents, partners, friends, justice agents or even victims?

On the other hand, the majority of proponents of restorative justice claim that it is an alternative to punishment, as it moves away from state-inflicted retributive responses and the exclusion of affected parties in the decision-making process of justice. There have also been some views that restorative justice is an alternative punishment. Both of these positions will be explored in detail in this chapter.

I want to start by putting down my own position on the relationship between restorative justice and punishment. For now, I am going to use brash and simple words in the hope that this position is made clear. Then, I will plunge into the realms of philosophy and Greek tragedy to justify my normative thinking.

Since the beginning of recorded history the ideas on how to respond to wrongdoing have been limited, unimaginative and rather elementary. This is probably because they are based simply on common sense. If somebody harms another then we can try to stop them from doing it again, teach them a lesson, keep them away from the people and the environment that they harmed or take the time to teach them to help themselves.

The criminal justice system aspires to all of the above. It then justifies its practices through a number of schools of thought, primarily Liberalism and Utilitarianism, particularly the strands of retribution (just desserts) and rehabilitation. Specifically in relation to punishment theories, Braithwaite and Strang (2000) write: 'Since Kant, Hegel and Bentham made their seminal contributions, the philosophy of punishment has been one of the dullest, least inspired fields within both philosophy and criminology, even though it has attracted contributions from many of law and philosophy's brightest and best' (p. 203).

Therefore, I must ask, if these are the common sense responses to doing harm, then what is the proposition from restorative justice? Put another way, is restorative justice simply a variation of what has already been stated, or does it propose something different? How commonsensical is restorative justice?

For instance, a number of restorativists, whose writings I will explore in detail later, reject the functionality of retribution (eye for an eye), and claim that helping the wrongdoers to help themselves is constructive. In their view, restorative justice aims to do just that. Again, I have to ask, is restorative justice therefore a repackaging of rehabilitation and a branch of liberal philosophy? If this is the case, then why so many attacks against the premises of the current criminal justice system?

Here is my position. I claim that restorative justice is neither punishment nor an alternative to punishment. The restorative justice experience offers something new. It is restorative punishment. And I am borrowing the word punishment with extreme caution, as its modern interpretation is so ingrained in our hearts and minds that it does not allow us to see beyond what is stated. But I decided to persist with this term despite criticism when presenting it at public lectures.[1] There is a reason for this persistence, which I will also explain later.

My notion of restorative punishment sits outside the current paradigm of viewing, understanding and thus dealing with wrongdoing and harm. To view my notion, we need to do what Zehr (1990) says and 'change lenses'. In fact, this paper counts on the reader being able to change lenses as various terms are used, including punishment, crime, wrong, harm, victim, pain, restitution, offender and so on.

I believe that restorative justice theorists and practitioners have struggled with finding a place for restorative practices because we have not been able to articulate their philosophical foundations, which would then allow the construction of a paradigm through which we can understand and justify their propositions.

For two decades (1970s–1990s) after restorative justice was brought back into the literature and criminal justice practice, its proponents presented it as a polar opposite to current criminal justice system. Bianchi (1973), Cantor (1976), Christie (1977), Barnett (1977), Eglash (1977) and Zehr (1990) spoke of a different paradigm of justice, which sees crime as a violation not of the law but of human relationships. Despite being premature, these claims made absolute sense as they brought restorative justice from the shadows to the centre of academic discussions. What followed were volumes of writings on restorative justice and an explosion of claims about what restorative justice can achieve for the offender, crime rates, recidivism, victims and the community.

I am not suggesting we return to the old times of Abolitionism. These debates have served their purposes and it is only through listening to the needs of our times that we can make philosophy and normative theory useful for practice (Braithwaite

1 See for instance, my Liz Elliot memorial lecture 2012, *Restorative Punishment*, http://www.iars.org.uk/content/RJpunishment (accessed December 2012).

and Strang, 2000). And I am stressing normative theory as opposed to grounded or empirical theory.

We must accept that we are still faced with a normative gap and a philosophical challenge for restorative justice (Braithwaite and Strang, 2000; Haines, 1998; Gavrielides 2012a). The late Liz Elliot (2011) said: 'Restorative justice must be more than a programme within the current system – it must be a new paradigm for responding to harm and conflict with its own philosophical and theoretical framework' (back cover). The Hon. Sir Anthony Mason warned that the contribution of restorative justice will remain limited until a more ambitious philosophical framework is pursued for its practices. 'We cannot expect too much from a system of one-off conferencing … we should be looking to anchor the concept as an element in a more extensive culture shift (Mason, 2000, p. 2)'. Haines reminds us of our responsibilities as theorists since 'the failure to theoretically and practically operationalise the concept of restorative justice is an abrogation of responsibility on the part of those involved in promoting its concept and a serious weakness of the literature' (Haines, 1998).

I am conscious that I have not yet suggested anything that is radically new. As early as 1999, Bazemore and Walgrave argued that restorative justice is a 'third way'. However, they agreed that restorative justice denies both the retributive and rehabilitative elements of justice. So, here is my contribution.

I claim that restorative justice embraces both the retributive and rehabilitative elements and adds an additional burden on the parties involved and their community. That is the *restorative pain*, which serves as the trigger of *restorative catharsis*, a natural by-product of successful restorative processes (for example Gavrielides 2012b; 2012c). To use Braithwaite's language, this catharsis should not be seen as a must but as a gift of restorative justice (Braithwaite, 2002). I add that this gift is painful, retributive and dangerous but rehabilitative and constructive.

My understanding of punishment is broader than Garland's (1990), who sees it as a social institution that extends beyond a mere repertoire of penal sanctions. Garland (1990) claims that punishment has a whole range of possible referents and it is likely to exhibit internal conflicts and ambiguities. His framework may allow some to conceptualize restorative justice within a broader construct of punishment as a social institution. But, as already stated, my restorative punishment lives in a different paradigm that resulted from a mere evolution and is a consequence of time, societal change and historical change. However, to explain this paradigm, I must step out of the realm of social institutions and constructs. I identify my restorative catharsis in the works of Greek tragedy and philosophy.

I thus become conscious that my restorative punishment will need moral justification. Duff explains that what makes a theory morally problematic is that it 'involves doing things to people that (when not described as punishment – or in our case as restorative measures) seem morally wrong' (Duff and Garland, 1997, p. 2). In the case of restorative punishment, the infliction of pain, as I will argue it, causes moral implications that need to be justified. But how? Surely not via the schools of thought used by the criminal justice system? If a different paradigm is to be used to view restorative punishment, then a philosophy for restorative justice must be identified.

Given the above, this chapter is divided into three main sections. The first is a descriptive account of how punishment is currently perceived. The second section then aims to develop the concept of restorative punishment. To this end, I attempt to deconstruct the concept of punishment and push the reader to take a leap into the unknown paradigm of restorative justice. I will refer to some case studies combined with normative thinking drawn from Greek tragedy, Classical Greek philosophy – particularly the teachings of Aristotle – as well as the writings of contemporary thinkers such Nietzsche. The third section takes a bold step in constructing a philosophical justification for my proposed notion of restorative punishment. I will do so by building on existing thinking, principally from the school of Collectivists. While writing this paper, I remember Aristotle's warning: 'Nothing is more likely to bring a system of justice into disrepute more quickly than inconsistency in punishment.'

Punishment as it Stands

To deconstruct any notion, first we have to identify it within a generally acceptable conceptual framework. The concept of punishment has been the centre of countless debates, theories and critical writings since early societies. It has appeared in religious statements (as in an eye for an eye), ancient laws and community rules (Gavrielides and Winderdyk, 2011).

Let us view punishment through the lenses of the current criminal justice paradigm. Punishment is defined as the infliction of pain for a wrong actually, or perceived to have been, committed. The various definitions in the literature tend to be informed by the philosophical school to which they subscribe, the two dominant being the retributive and the utilitarian theories. These various understandings of punishment are classified as follows:

- Punishment and guilt (as in imposing it because of one's guilty behaviour).
- Punishment as pain (as in its manifestation through the experience of unpleasantness).
- Punishment and blame (as in imposing it to express disapprobation).
- Punishment and authority (as in its imposition by a person in authority).

Under the retributive understanding of punishment, the receiver is seen as someone deserving to suffer. Although there are various variations of this retributive understanding, their common belief is that it should inflict the suffering that offenders deserve. In particular, there are three key lines of arguments that are accepted by all retributive theories of punishment:

> Just Desserts, or the Proportionality Principle: in simple terms, this means that the punishment must be equivalent to the level of wrongdoing. Just Desserts has been criticized for its simplicity as it does not really provide a justification for punishment. It simply acts as a restraint on it.
>
> Punishment is good in itself: this position argues that punishing criminals is itself just. This has also been criticized, as there is no real explanation as to why it is good to inflict pain on criminals. Some theorists tried to justify it by explaining that it can lead to repentance, self-reform, reparation and reconciliation or to restore the fair balance of benefits and burdens, which were redistributed by crime. But the actual practice of imprisonment as the main vehicle for inflicting this pain has proved unsuccessful in living up to all these promises.
>
> Punishment only for the guilty: this argument simply says that only those who are blameworthy deserve punishment and that this is the sole justification of punishment. Therefore, punishment is only justified in cases of deliberate wrongdoing. The criticism that this argument has received centres on the fact that it doesn't actually justify punishment. Rather, it acts as a constraint on the circumstances in which punishment may be administered. It does not even try to justify the link between crime and punishment.

Under the utilitarian understanding of punishment, the picture is clearer. In simple terms, utilitarianism posits that the morally right action is that which produces the greatest amount of utility. Utility has been defined in the following ways:

> As happiness or pleasure, which is the sole intrinsic good. Pain is the sole inherent evil.
>
> As happiness combined with other intrinsic goods such as knowledge, love and beauty. Consequently, the ultimate goal is the pursuit of these virtues. The criticism that this approach has received is that we do not tend to pursue these values for their own sake but for hedonistic and egoistic purposes.
>
> As preference or desire satisfaction, meaning that it is broad enough to include fulfilling what one desires. In this way, there should be no conflict between hedonistic and preference utilitarianism.
>
> As the extent to which the rightness of an act is compliant with the rules that maximize it. Therefore, utility is used as a guide for the rules we should follow as distinct from the particular actions we should perform.
>
> As dominion, which is a republican concept of liberty where people are free from non-interference by others by virtue of the protection of the law and related

> social institutions and whereby people enjoy equality before the law (Braithwaite and Pettit, 1990; von Hirsch and Ashworth, 1992).
>
> Nowadays, the concept of punishment primarily exists within the sphere of criminal law and justice and it is manifested through the practice of imprisonment. In certain societies, punishment was, and on many occasions still is, manifested through the infliction of physical pain or even the taking of life.

Punishment is also understood in the form of rehabilitation. Von Hirsch explains: 'Rehabilitation is the idea of curing an offender of his or her criminal tendencies. It consists, more precisely, of changing an offender's personality, outlook, habits, or opportunities so as to make him or her less inclined to commit crimes (1998, p. 1).' This definition may ring some alarm bells for certain restorativists. Von Hirsch continues: 'Often, rehabilitation is said to involve helping the offender, but a benefit to the offender is not necessarily presupposed: those who benefit are other persons, ourselves, who become less likely to be victimied by the offender (ibid., p. 1).'

Today's dominant understanding of punishment as retribution and rehabilitation resulting from wrongdoing is the outcome of historical events and the demands of modern society. In Europe, what is really believed to have caused this change was the increasing power of kingships as trans-local and trans-tribal institutions. This is mainly because they united the tribes and large areas, changing in this way the structure of societies from communitarian/tribal to hierarchical/feudal. Sharpe (1980), Rossner (1989) and Gavrielides (2007) explain that in Europe contemporary punishment was constructed after the Norman conquest when crime was seen as a violation of the King's law. The understanding of what is crime and harm was key in defining society's response.

Also important were the interests that were being compromised as well as who had the power to respond to them. Here power is understood through the current lenses of criminal justice. Therefore, power is not the ability to observe oneself. It is not the pursuit of self-improvement and ultimate utility either. Power is understood as the financial, political, social and biological circumstances that allow a unit (whether an individual, a state, a group or an agent) to proceed with action for their own or others' ends.

In the pursuit of increasing the success of the criminal justice system as constructed within the aforementioned understanding, crime control was formalized in communities. Cohen (1985) describes how justice and social control were reconstructed from being informal local and regional control systems to becoming a centralized machinery of processing justice. Foucault (1970; 1991) described this system as 'alien' bringing 'an abrupt change' (ibid, 1991) as tavern closing times and curfews became common and regulation of the dinner hours of labourers was encouraged.

The formalization and professionalization process of the criminal justice system was also a key consequence of trade development and economics (Marx, 1954).

Michalowski (1985) claimed that formal law emerged as a means of controlling property and relations, and that the concept of individual property and the history of law were inseparable from then on. As Bentham (1996) put it, property and law are born together and die together.

Barnett (1977) also reminds us of the role of religious institutions and the significance of the ecclesiastic law of that time. This claim is also supported by Tallack (1900) who noted that the greedy ecclesiastical powers of the time aimed to exact a double vengeance upon the offenders by taking their property and by applying corporal punishment or imprisonment. Braithwaite's (1998) critique is along the same lines:

> Long before the Inquisition, church leaders were among those who sought to secure their power through retributive affliction on the bodies of their flock … It was the church that established prosecution as a central authority to assert its will and church heresy. The barbarism of the Inquisition was justified, because crime was committed not against a victim, but against the moral order of the church.

In consequence, as the rights of the state gradually overshadowed those of the victim, the concept of punishment took on a more punitive meaning. What also emerged from this development was the division of law between public and private. Crime was mostly dealt with as an act against the state and the public interest, while offences against individuals' rights were pursued separately as torts. The terms offender and victim started to be used.

During this period, political philosophers Jeremy Bentham (1748–1832) and John Austin (1790–1859) argued that the law is a phenomenon of large societies with a sovereign. This can be a determinate person or group who have supreme and absolute *de facto* power. The laws in these societies, including our Western countries, are a subset of the sovereign's commands. These are general orders that apply to classes of actions and people and are backed up by threat of force or sanction. This imperatival positivist theory identifies the existence of legal systems with patterns of command and obedience that can be ascertained without considering whether the sovereign has a moral right to rule or whether his commands are meritorious.

Deconstructing Pain and Reconstructing Punishment for Restorative Justice

By now, we should have gathered some elementary understanding of contemporary punishment and the historical circumstances (sociological, financial, political) that led to its construction. Turning our attention to the relationship between punishment and restorative justice, we notice that the extant literature has been generous. For instance, Daly (2000) takes restorative justice to be punishment, because it leads to obligations for the offender. She backs up her position with the results of a qualitative analysis on young offenders who had experienced family group conferencing (Daly, 1999). On the other hand, McCold (1999) rejects the idea of including coercive judicial sanctions in the restorative process. Marshall (1996) claims that coercive processes are not unavoidable and that they must be considered. However, this should be done through the criminal justice system. He argued that this is where restorative justice should end and where the traditional system should take over (Marshall, 1996). On the other hand, Braithwaite believes that if a restorative process fails, it should be tried again and again; in his own words: 'restorative justice rewards the patient' (Braithwaite, 1999b). However, he envisages 'not a future where punishment is abolished, but a future where punishment is marginalized' (Braithwaite, 1999a). Finally, Walgrave believes that restorative practices include coercive actions as well as voluntary processes, and that the coercive intervention should also be reasonable, restorative and respectful (Walgrave, 2001).

For the sake of brevity, I will divide the many views on the relationship between restorative justice and punishment into two broad categories. The first denies that restorative justice measures can, in any way, be punitive (Wright, 1996). The second argues that restorative justice is not alternative to punishment, but alternative punishment (Duff, 1992). The argument of the first group is that the primary purpose of restorative measures is to be constructive. Therefore, they are not inflicted 'for their own sake' but for a higher purpose (Walgrave, 1999, p. 146). The second group, however, argues that, 'this purported distinction is misleading because it relies for its effect on the confusion of two distinct elements in the concept of intention. One element relates to the motives for doing something; the other refers to the fact that the act in question is being performed deliberately or wilfully (Dignan, 2003, p. 179).'

This paper argues that restorative justice is neither punishment nor alternative to punishment. It puts forward the concept of restorative punishment that sits outside of the literature's aforementioned two lines of argument. To understand restorative punishment the current concept must be deconstructed.

A brief account of the many historical sources can help indicate that punishment, in today's sense, was the exception rather than the norm. For example, the *Code of Hammurabi* (c.2380 BC), which is one of the first samples of written law, espoused the practice of individual compensation. On several occasions, this served as a substitute for the death penalty. Furthermore, in the Ninth Book of the *Iliad*, Homer referred to the case of Ajax, who criticized Achilles for not accepting Agamemnon's offer of reparation. In his criticism, Ajax pointed out to Achilles that even a brother's death may be compensated by the payment of money. It is worth noting that the word guilt may derive from the Anglo-Saxon word *geldam*, which means payment.

The bulk of the available historical sources on punishment suggest that the concept was used for both property and personal crimes. Moreover, according to Diamond's (1935) research on the sanctions imposed for homicide, monetary restitution was an accepted form of penalty throughout the Western world.

Barnett (1977) also claimed, 'of 100 scattered tribal communities, as to which the information is of undoubted reliability, 73% called for a pecuniary sanction versus 17% that called for a certain number of persons to be handed over to the family of the victim as a sanction'. In addition, Shafer noted that among Indian Hindus and Semitic nations the death fine and restitution were used, and continued to prevail for centuries: 'he who atones is forgiven'.

As argued, the current understanding of punishment is the outcome of historical events, the development of societal norms, institutions and structures as well as economics and politics. Current practice is still placed within this understanding and hence to be able to view my proposition of restorative punishment, the reader is asked to switch lenses by viewing an alternative paradigm.

Let us take a step back to ask what is a paradigm, and why we need to speak in terms of paradigms. 'A paradigm is an achievement in a particular discipline which defines the legitimate problems and methods of research within that discipline (Barnett, 1981, p. 245).' Paradigms shape our understanding of the notions that come under a specific discipline. As Zehr puts it, 'They provide the lenses through which we understand phenomena' (1990, p. 86). Moreover, they form our common sense and guide us in our understanding of what is possible and what is impossible. All in all, to the common eye, things falling outside the paradigm seem absurd and abnormal. Common sense reasoning is again brought into the discussion.

Paradigms are particular ways of constructing and organizing reality (ibid., p. 87). They shape how we define problems and what we recognize as appropriate solutions. For instance, once parliaments or law enforcement authorities decide to criminalize a certain action, our reality is defined accordingly. The current punishment paradigm is such a construct. As such, notions and definitions that fall under the criminal justice umbrella are the result of the understanding that is available under the punitive matrix. As with all paradigms, this one also creates its own reality.

Nevertheless, constructs can and do change. One of the most influential books about paradigm changes is the *Structure of Scientific Revolutions* by Thomas Kuhn (1970). According to Budd and Hill (2007), 'Very few works have had the impact that Structure has had.' Indeed, from 1999 to 2007, the book was cited 9,268 times (Web of Science).[2] Kuhn (1970) says:

> The term paradigm is used in two different senses. On the one hand, it stands for the entire constellation of beliefs, values, techniques, and so on shared by the members of a given community. On the other, it denotes one sort of element in that constellation, the concrete puzzle-solutions which, employed as models or examples, can replace explicit rules as a basis for the solution of the remaining puzzles of normal science (p. 175).

2 www.thomsonreuters.com/web-of-science.

Kuhn claims that paradigms can replace each other, causing a revolution in the way we view and understand the world. *Paradigm revolutions* constitute one of the primary sources that lead to changes in scientific outlook. What causes such a change is a *paradigm crisis*. At the beginning, the paradigm seems to fit most phenomena. Over time, however, dysfunctions begin to develop as more and more phenomena stop fitting the paradigm. In Barnett's terms: 'As the paradigm develops and matures, it reveals occasional inabilities to solve new problems and explain new data (Barnett, 1981: 245).'

An example of a *paradigm crisis* that led to a *paradigm change* is the Ptolemaic Paradigm, which used to shape Western understanding of the *cosmos* until the seventeenth century. Under this paradigm it was common sense that *cosmos* was a series of concentric crystalline spheres with the Earth at the centre. However, after time and new discoveries more and more phenomena stopped fitting the paradigm, which started to face a crisis. As a result, Isaac Newton's new theory constituted the *coup de grâce* of the old paradigm, which was replaced by a better, more accurate one.

Similarly, Barnett (1977) suggested that we stop attempting to make the facts fit the old punitive paradigm of justice and make the effort to view criminal justice through a more accurate matrix; that he names *restitution*. The history of our justice paradigm, he said, shows some of the symptoms of *paradigm change*.

It is through this evolved paradigm that we now need to view the concept of pain and how it is manifested, experienced and used in restorative practice. I will start by sharing my own experience from sitting in a restorative circle with 22 male prisoners from Ferndale prison[3] in British Columbia.

My Story From Ferndale Prison

It was a rainy November evening when Brenda Morrison and I visited Ferndale prison. The circle took place in the chaplaincy and the majority of participants were serving a life sentence (meaning that they had been convicted of manslaughter). The circle took place not with the intention of mitigating their life sentence, but as part of a routine healing process that the institute had adopted and supported for years.[4] The participants shared their story in the usual way. I told them about mine. One participant said: 'My pain, which I want to share with you all, is not that I am going to be in this place for yet another Christmas and probably for the rest of my life. I know what I did. My pain is that my ill mother is also being punished by not being with me on her last Christmas.' He then told us about his mum's frail state, how much he loves her and how important it was for her to spend her

3 Further on Ferndale institution http://www.csc-scc.gc.ca/text/facilit/institutprofiles/ferndale-eng.shtml (accessed December 2012).

4 It is worth noting, that this initiative was championed by the late Prof. Liz Elliott http://www.sfu.ca/crj/about/liz-elliot.html (accessed December 2012).

last Christmas with her only son whom she had forgiven. This story acted as a catalyst for the remaining stories as the circle participants expressed their own pain and stories. It then hit me. I could no longer see pain as a state-inflicted form of punishment. For most of the participants, their state-inflicted sentence was something they had already accepted.

The restorative process of the circle allowed the identification, expression and sharing of a far more constructive type of pain. This pain was neither shameful nor stigmatizing, as Braithwaite (1989) or the Stigmatizing Theory would see it. It was very personal and could not be generalized. It was the outcome of the individual circumstances surrounding each participant, whether it related to their loved ones, their life or something they felt they had lost having observed themselves in pain. This pain found its way into our discussion, as the prisoners felt safe in a space and company that encouraged them to use it as a tool for communication and bonding.

Therefore, I must conclude, that restorative justice does entail pain, but of a different kind, not pain that is triggered by state and top-down punishment, as we understand it through the current paradigm. Restorative justice triggers pain that is personal and specific to each participant and is the consequence of his or her own actions, behaviour, self-observation and self-reflection. This pain is a gift and is not always present. It cannot be imposed but it can be nurtured.

We have argued that the retributive understanding of punishment identifies the existence of two basic elements. The first is the communicative and the second the retributive. Duff explains that punishment under the current paradigm aims to communicate with the receiver, imposing 'the suffering which she deserves for her crime' (Duff, 1992, pp. 53–4). Punishment is thus justified as an intrinsically appropriate response to crime.

The restorative understanding of punishment is a fundamentally different one. If we accept the retributive position that punishment consists of two elements, the expressive and the retributive, restorative measures would certainly deny the second element. Retribution is completely taken out of the restorative picture. However, the expressive element is desirable, as it promotes restorative goals. Feinberg (1965) claims that punishment, no matter the type, should serve an expressive function. Nonetheless, as Duff points out (1992; 1996; 2001) being merely expressive would not be enough for restorative justice 'because it should be a two-way communication, not a one-way directive aimed at a passive wrongdoer' (1992, p. 53). All parties need to be heard in the process and contribute to the restorative outcome.

Von Hirsch and Ashworth (1998) and Duff (1999) agree that punishment is conceptualized as a form of censure and that the vehicle through which blame is expressed is the visitation of deprivation (harsh treatment). While Duff argues that deprivation can itself be explained in reprobative terms providing a kind of secular penance, Von Hirsch believes that it has to do with helping to keep predatory behaviour within tolerable limits. Yet, he acknowledges that:

> One might still wish to devise another way of issuing authoritative judgements of blame, for such predatory behaviour as occurs. But those judgements, in the interest of keeping state-inflicted suffering to a minimum, would no longer be linked to purposive infliction of suffering' (von Hirsch and Ashworth, 1998, p. 70).

Restorative punishment is such a device, as it is able to issue a new authoritative judgement of blame, without using the deprivation (harsh treatment) element. However, restorative punishment is not interested in 'keeping state-inflicted suffering to a minimum'. This is because it is not imposed by the state; it is a voluntary agreement reached by the parties with the help of the state (through its representatives, the facilitators). Von Hirsch was also right in one more thing, that the new device 'would no longer be linked to purposive infliction of suffering' (ibid., p. 70).

Going back to the notion of pain as a restorative gift, Walgrave (1999) claims that the difference between punishment and what he calls 'painful restorative obligation' can be identified in the intention of the punisher.

> It is the punisher who considers a certain action to be wrong and who wants the wrongdoer to suffer for it. However, defining every unpleasant obligation as a punishment, in fact, places the distinction between punishment and non-punishment on the experience and the interpretation of the person who is subjected to the treatment. (Walgrave, 2001, p. 22)

Therefore, he refuses to call restorative sanctions punishments, since those who agree on them have no intention of making the offender suffer. In a similar vein, Wright claims that punishment practices are the intentional or 'deliberate imposition of pain' on offenders, which would include incarceration and fines. He distinguished the intentions of legal authorities, arguing, 'Whereas punishment is an intended deprivation, non-punishment is intended to be constructive' (Wright 1991, p. 15). However, as Daly pointed out, this distinction 'overlooks decades of critique of the rehabilitative ideal, with its associated treatment-oriented intervention' (Daly 2000, p. 39). Wright 'equates punishment with being punitive and non-punishment with being non-punitive' and that this argument 'exemplifies how elites may delude themselves into thinking that what they intend to do is in fact experienced that way by those at the receiving end' (ibid.).

I argue that restorative punishment is triggered by constructive pain that is private and self-inflicted. It aims to restore and to be cleansing. Deterrence (general or specific) might be welcomed as a side effect, but is not among the primary goals of restorative measures, nor is retribution for what was done.

Thus, we notice a difference of aims in the restorative vs. punitive punishment comparison. As a restorative measure, punishment aims to cleanse, restore, create, construct, repair and reintegrate. Restorative measures can entail education *per se* as they can teach communication, negotiation, compromise and related skills.

A Philosophical Justification for Restorative Punishment

Wright once asked me[5] why one needs to know the philosophical foundations of a practice, whose central aim is to repair harm and promote good. Three reasons come to mind as to why restorative punishment and pain are morally problematic. The first relates to the process of awakening restorative pain, as described above. To identify and communicate this pain during the restorative process there first needs to be a breakdown of fears and the encouragement of sharing and storytelling. Figley's Empowerment Model (1998) helps us identify the stages of the restorative and healing process: (a) building commitment to therapeutic objectives, (b) framing the problem, (c) reframing the problem, (d) developing a healing theory, and (e) closure and preparedness. Figley's model of intervention emphasizes a communication process aimed at developing a healing theory. This process gives opportunities for storytelling, a reinterpretation of symptoms, a clarification of insights and correction of distortions, and answers to questions central to healing.

This is a hard and difficult venture that, if not carefully balanced, may result in several problems. For instance, if restorative pain is not organically developed through mutual feelings of trust among participants it may end up being coerced, similarly to state-inflicted punishment. The literature on coerced restorative practices and their consequences is rich. Moreover, if the specific needs and circumstances of the involved parties are not carefully assessed, the restorative pain may end up repunishing them. Schiff (1999) explains that some young offenders who had experienced mediation had characterized it as a kind of double punishment.

The second concerns language, which is the key tool used to identify, extract and externalize restorative punishment. The dangers associated with any language-/dialogue-based approaches are well documented. For instance, Wind noted: 'While language can offer hope in the healing process, it may also profoundly exacerbate the trauma (Wind, Sullivan and Levins, 2008, p. 251)'. For language to be healing, it needs to be reordered and reimagined away from the world of retriggering and into a world where siblings, parents and others engage in conversations of acceptance of the abuse and its ongoing consequences.

The third relates to the pain itself. Although this is constructive, cleansing and honest, it is still tough. Hume's discussion on the paradox of tragedy comes to mind. 'It seems an unaccountable pleasure, which the spectators of a well-wrote tragedy receive from sorrow, terror, anxiety and other passion, which are in themselves disagreeable and uneasy' (*Of Tragedy – Four Dissertations*). With this statement, Hume helps us to understand why pain as received through the restorative process in the form of sorrow, anxicty, fear, pity and various other passions, is still welcomed by all parties involved. Remember the example of Ferndale.

5 Martin Wright, e-mail on Fri 28/09/2001 00:16.

One also has to ask why humans are drawn to stories of brokenness and pain. Nietzsche's 1872 seminal work *The Birth of Tragedy* is relevant. In reading Nietzsche, Price calls this paradox the 'tragic pleasure' (1998, p. 385). First seen in the Greek tragedies of *Oedipus* and *Antigone* (300 BC) the desire to dissect and clarify our response to this unsettling material has historically centred on the oxymoronic idea of constructing through pain. The communicative elements of Greek tragedy are found later in the works of Shakespeare (for instance *Hamlet* and *King Lear*) and even in modern films.

Aristotle calls this pain catharsis (see *Poetics*). It aims to awaken feelings of fear and pity. Hence, any good Greek tragedy should be able to thrill the viewers with 'horror and melted them to pity at what takes place' (Aristotle, *Poetics*). This is necessary and welcomed as the upsetting process is purgative and engenders a sense of catharsis at the removal of debilitating emotions otherwise built up and trapped inside. Price (1998) explains that the specific pleasure found in tragic drama is in the period of reflection immediately following the experience during which this process of cleansing occurs. Aristotle concludes that this type of pain reminds us that life is fundamentally painful and in need of justification, of redemption from suffering. Nietzsche agrees and adds that the release of these pent-up emotions is not only therapeutic and redemptive for viewers, but also so strong that it actually draws them to the tragic drama for this experience of restoration (Deleuze, 1983).

But it seems that we have already entered the debate on the justification of restorative pain. Again, I am going to use Greek tragedy as my starting point. Aristotle defines tragedy as:

> The imitation of an action that is serious and also as having magnitude complete in itself; in language with pleasurable accessories, each kind brought in separately in parts of the work; in a dramatic, not in a narrative form; with incidents arousing pity and fear, wherewith to accomplish its catharsis of such emotions. (Aristotle, 1965, p. 348)

Putting it in the context of Greek tragedy, restorative pain is not pleasurable in the sense that spectators of a tragic drama do not enjoy the death of Hamlet, the suffering of Oedipus or the execution of Desdemona in the same way that they enjoy a good meal (Price, 1998). Nietzsche argues that this does not mean that the experience of this pain cannot be gratifying on a far more fundamental level. For Nietzsche the initial pain must be examined for it is not entirely unpleasant and on some deeper level actually provides a sense of euphoria.

> Affirmation of life even in its strangest and sternest problems, the will to life rejoicing in its own inexhaustibility through the sacrifice of its highest types – that is what I call Dionysian … Not so as to get rid of pity and terror … but, beyond pity and terror, to realise in oneself the eternal joy of becoming – that joy which also encompasses destruction. (Nietzsche, 1878, p. 5)

Price argues that what we learn when experiencing pain as described above and through the eyes of Greek tragedy is a way to acknowledge misfortune within the boundaries of our human nature (Price, 1998). Humans aware of this necessity of overcoming, submit to their basest desires and seek out the tragic in the hope of inflicting pain upon themselves, destroying the self and finally being reunited in the 'mysterious primordial unity' (Nietzsche, 1872, p. 37).

German philosopher Schopenhauer also spoke of this constructive pain. He encourages his readers to submit themselves to the tragic predicament and in it find rest (Soll, 1988). But Nietzsche (1872) takes a step further as he finds at the heart of the tragic paradox of our restorative pain a great sense of hope, 'the joyous hope that the spell of individuation may be broken in augury of a restored oneness' (p. 74).

Jim's Story

I first met Jim in March 2012 and then again in November that year, when I visited Vancouver to give some lectures on restorative justice. Although not an academic, Jim came to all the lectures and introduced himself as someone who has been in hell. During his childhood, Jim was repeatedly abused sexually, physically, emotionally and psychologically. He then lived on the streets for years succumbing to the predations of paedophiles and to addiction. He joined several gangs and did multiple stints in prison. Eventually, Jim became a physical wreck facing cardiac arrest at twenty-two. He now has a loving partner and spends his time principally as a youth worker giving speeches in schools and youth institutions. He shares his story openly and honestly and has written a book where he reflects on his experiences, both the good and the bad (Mandelin, 2012). I had the chance to speak to Jim on several occasions. We had dinner together and exchanged a few chats both face-to-face and online. I could not understand what makes a man transform in such a way. Jim said:

> My journey, our journey seems to be a journey of plowing through some very dense, thick brush. This makes the journey so dark at times and so weary for the travellers. I have been on a road of seeking justice, been through the criminal justice system but yet feel I have not been a part of any real and healing justice myself. I have healed in spite of my bully's not coming to the circle. Actually I should say, I am still healing but I am much better as the years have gone by. I have managed to heal by sitting in restorative circles, sometimes small and sometimes big. I have healed from the process that these circles provided me, I began feeling the pain inflicted on me in my childhood with others who have experienced the same as they have sat with me in the circle. This became my community of healers. This support helped me to accept the truth about my abuse and this feeling work has led to trusting my own intuition about what is right. Deep down inside of me someplace, it has given me new eyes. There

> are few filters left for me from which to dilute the truth with, so pain of the brightness of this truth, a knowing pain, is the result, a pain that makes me stronger not weaker. The pain actually never is all gone because as I heal I see my 'brothers' and 'sisters' pain and I feel the same pain. It is in this circle that we all fit, we all feel and we all heal.

Through Jim's words I found the connection between restorative justice, restorative punishment, pain and the catharsis that needs to be experienced in order to heal and move forward whether as victims or offenders – labels that I could not use for Jim. Catharsis is not a moment but a process. In Jim's case, this process is his life. He pursues it via dialogue and self-reflection and restorative justice is one way to achieve this.

Therefore, I must conclude that catharsis is the outcome of our restorative punishment and the justification for the pain that is associated with it. Remembering his medical training, Aristotle asserted that catharsis is a 'form of homeopathic treatment – curing emotion by means of an emotion like kind but not identical' (Woodfin and Groves, 2006, p. 157). Catharsis derived from the Greek word *κάθαρσις* meaning to cleanse.

In referring to his Dialectic Method (in *Phenomenology of Mind*, 1910), Hegel explains that catharsis works as a thesis that moves to its opposite, the antithesis by principle of negativity. It is via this negative that a new state, called synthesis (Mueller, 1958; Abdulla, 1985), is arrived at through the clash of the two opposite forces. This new state of synthesis, while sharing traits of both thesis and antithesis, produces a discovery of the two opposite forces, or a 'reconciliation of the two' (Abdulla, 1985). Hegel believes that all things are related and nothing can stand in isolation. He claims that everything in one way or another influences and is being influenced by the forces around it. He moves on to explain that the dialectical procedure that results in catharsis could be transferred into restorative justice and our restorative pain revealing conflict ideas or beliefs not as disjunctions but as conjoined. Such is the synthesis, a category of becoming.

Therefore, catharsis as pursued by the restorative dialogue is an important transformative discovery. Like the spectators to a Greek tragedy, the parties in a restorative process will go through tragic, dramatic experiences and pass catharsis (if achieved as a gift), only then to realize that catharsis is not the final state in itself but rather a reaching to the state of synthesis, recognition, understanding or discovery. Remember Jim's life story. This is the experience of wonder that we find beautiful despite its tragic nature. It is a glimpse of the moment of sublimation. Aristotle reminds us that these are the moments that affirm the beauty of life, the connection between individuals and then between the individual and their community.

Here we have to pause to attempt to make a missing connection. One between cathartic action as experienced in the context of Greek tragedy and our everyday lives. How does catharsis justify restorative punishment and hence pain once harm has been committed? Why is catharsis so important as to justify such action and pain and from where does it draw its significance?

To answer these questions we need to view crime through Zehr's eyes as a 'wound in human relationships' and an action that 'creates an obligation to restore and repair' (Zehr, 1990). 'Crime is fundamentally a violation of people and interpersonal relationships' (Zehr and Mika, 1998, p. 17), a conflict not between the individual and the state, but between individuals.

By restricting criminal procedure and law to the narrow legal definition of what is relevant and what is not, the victim and the offender cannot explore the real effects of the case and the degree of their culpability. Wright claimed, 'The boundary between crime and other harmful actions is an artificial and constantly changing one … Crimes are actions by which people cause certain types of harm, prohibited by law, and for which, if a person is convicted of them in court, a sanction may be imposed (Wright, 1996).'

This new understanding of crime transcends the burden of the criminal process, introducing a new target: the restoration of the relationship between victims and offenders and offenders and their communities. As Zehr put it, the restorative justice understanding of crime 'creates an obligation to make things right'. A question that follows from this, and which is important in understanding the significance of catharsis as a justification of pain, is what created this relationship that restorative justice aims to restore?

Restorative justice assumes the existence of, what I called, a 'social liaison' that bonds individuals in a relationship of respect for others' rights and freedoms (Gavrielides, 2005). Restorative justice assumes that this liaison has always been with us because it is innate in our nature as human beings. We cannot see it, but we can feel it in moments of danger or of extreme happiness. Individuals are not really strangers and that is why victim and offender are not enemies.

I remember walking over London Bridge in the evening of 7 July 2005 when the multiple bombings took place. There was no public transport so all Londoners had to walk home, the streets were full and the bridge packed with sad faces. We all looked at each other that day feeling that strong sense of connection and a sense of despair and care. I had never met those people and yet I was drawn to them. I wanted to tell them that we would get through this. I wanted to know that they were safe and that they shared my own feelings of loss and sadness. That day I felt the social liaison that connects me with my city and its people.

Sullivan, Tifft and Cordella described this relationship in a slightly different way: 'The restorative justice ethic is based in a spiritual sense that sees us all connected to each other at a fundamental level and, as such, requires of us a more heightened and pervasive sense of justice' (1998: 16). Morris and Young also argued (2000): 'Restorative justice endorses a collective ethos and collective responsibility. Thus, it emphasizes the existence of shared values, which can be used to address the offending and its consequences and to reintegrate victims and offenders at the local level … In essence, the social values underlying restorative justice rely on connections; connections between offenders, victims and communities (pp. 14, 15).'

The pre-existence of this social liaison that restorative justice aims to restore gives context and grounding for catharsis through constructive pain. To understand this better we resort to the teachings of Collectivists. In Barnes' words, Collectivists' 'oddities and accidents may be individual and independent, their movements and machinations largely self-determined, but in their essence they are necessarily bound to others; for all are adjuncts and elements of a larger whole' (1991, p. 1).

Alexander Pope, at the end of the first Epistle of the *Essay on Man* said: 'each of us, like any other natural object, is a part of the universe; it is folly to deny the fact – and folly to wish it changed ... for our good is determined and our moral comportment should be governed by our partial statues in the universal All' (Mack, 1950). On the other hand, each of us is not only a part, but also a system or a whole. We are what Barnes (1988) calls 'partial whole'. We are parts of a greater whole, and again wholes with parts of our own.

Marcus Aurelius' work *Meditations* (Rutherford, 1989) is said to be the closest ancient parallel to Pope's views (Barnes, 1991, pp. 1–23). He insisted that we are a part (*μέρος*) of Nature (*φύσις*), or of the universe (*κόσμος*), or of Fate (*ειμαρμένη*). He said that we stand to the universe as our hands and feet stand to our bodies and that, as with organic parts, we have mutually interdependent functions and activities, working together (*συνεργούσιν*) to a common end, a common good. In other words, 'we are interdependent parts of an organised whole, and our mutual dependencies determine our nature and our function' (Barnes 1991: 7).

What restorative justice takes from these philosophies is their central feature of interdependency, determination and self-assurance through the realization of the existence of others. This reality creates the social liaison which connects individuals, and which might be broken if a crime occurs.

Barnes said: 'Systems, or integral wholes, are wholes which have (at least) one special sort of partition. This is characterized by the fact that its members are united by a special relation (or set of relations); they form a family. Families are defined in terms of binary relations (Barnes, 1991, p. 13).' The broken social liaison, or what Barnes called the 'special relation', between individuals and individuals and their community is the focus of restoration.

In restorative justice victim and offender are treated as free individuals, responsible for their actions and decisions. They are not strangers, but related because of the 'social liaison' that connects them. It does not matter whether they have met before or not. What is important is that they live in the same environment; whether it be social or legal.

As free individuals, both have rights that need to be respected and protected. They also have obligations (Braithwaite, 2002) among which are restoring the balance in the community that the harm had disturbed. Therefore, what restorative justice calls them to do is to restore the broken liaison that used to bond them. To this end, the experience of pain is welcomed and justified.

This pain cannot be transferred. It is private and personal and has to be experienced by the parties involved. They are considered the most appropriate for this experience, but need to be guided and supervised by an impartial third party chosen by the community, such as a mediator. But restorative justice assumes that the parties are mentally competent and hence morally culpable actors, who are willing to take responsibility for their actions, not only to the parties directly injured, but perhaps also to a wider community. (Daly, 2000, pp. 35).

In this matrix, victim and offender are seen as two sides of the same coin. The offender is not dealt with as a parasite of society, but as one of us. Offenders distort the social liaison, but this does not make them our enemy.[6] On the contrary, their actions are seen as an opportunity to prevent greater evils, 'to confront crime with a grace that transforms human lives to paths of love and giving' (Braithwaite, 1999b). Again, in the context of Greek tragedy and catharsis, their suffering during the restorative process is encouraged and should be welcomed as a gift. It is an opportunity to experience life through tragic sharing and pain.

Restorative justice makes one more assumption, that individuals are dependent on their communities; that their lives gain meaning from the aggregation and their happiness is linked to the existence of the aggregation that witnesses it. That is why the restoration of their relationship is important enough to justify pain and enjoy catharsis. But how realistic is this assumption in today's society?

It appears that when translating this into action, restorative justice assumes a kind of relationship between people, which is difficult to accept or even comprehend in modern Western societies. Sullivan, Tift and Cordella (1998) argued that restorative justice promotes a social ethic 'that differs radically from that prevalent in our current political economy' (p. 16). Accordingly, many restorativists suggest that we try to understand this relationship, not by comparing it with how we live today in our societies (where the social liaison is less visible), but with what communities such as the Navajo Nation experience. Yazzie (1994) explains how their spiritual approach to life and human relationships leads them to define the Navajo sense of justice as peace making.

But again, isn't this a bit far-fetched? How can we expect our modern societies to transform themselves into indigenous models of community living? McCold and Watchtel (1998) argues that the only way we can comprehend what community really means under the restorative paradigm is to interpret it in the broadest way possible. Restorative justice requires that we rethink what constitutes community and that we begin to accept the fact that community is far more than a place. However, this does not mean that we have to change the structure of our communities; only the normative idea we have planted in our

6 In *Meditations* Marcus Aurelius noted, 'For in a way all things are interwoven with one another, and all things are for this reason friendly to one another. One thing is continuous with another because of the tonic motion and the conspiration and the unity of substance' Aurelius, Marcus (167 ACE) *The Meditations*. trans. G. Long, VI, xxxviii.

minds. In *Community is not a Place*, McCold and Wachtel (1998) proposed a reconceptualization of community that is more consistent with restorative justice.

Now, bearing in mind the assumption of the pre-existence of a social liaison, the central characteristic of a restorative community is that it provides the environment for growing human relations. Its size does not really matter.

The existence of community is a prerequisite for the liaison that relates individuals and hence justifies restorative pain. The community strives to instil a sense in individuals to respect and protect the liaison. It attempts this by keeping a liaison between itself and the individual; not a liaison of control and power, but of care. The imposition of state-inflicted punishment is therefore irrelevant. The self-infliction of restorative pain through community care is paramount. A central belief in the restorative thought is that 'it is wiser to strengthen our relationship with offenders rather than weaken it' by segregating and ostracizing them (Johnstone, 2001, p. 13). That is why 'it makes sense to show them that we care about them' (ibid.). Accordingly, 'offenders are provided opportunities and encouragement to understand the harm they have caused to victims and the community, and develop plans for taking appropriate responsibility. Voluntary participation is maximised; coercion and exclusion are minimised' (Zehr and Mika, 1998, p. 51). The pursuit of catharsis and the experience of restorative pain must be accepted. As Elliott put it, *Security with Care* (2012). The liaison between communities of care and individuals can educate and indeed promote a feeling of responsibility, especially to those who violate their connection with other individuals and with their communities.

Finally, it is important to add that the community 'wants reassurance that what happened was wrong, that something is being done about it, and that steps are being taken to discourage its recurrence' (Zehr, 1990, p. 195). Indeed, restorative justice embraces the idea of individual freedom and liberty. Consequently, the community aims to protect humans' relations by giving them the voice and choice to amend and restore their broken liaisons. The community can supervise them, but should not control them. However, as Johnstone (2001) notes, 'the community must be prepared to become involved in the resolution of conflict' (p. 14). In fact, in the mind of a restorativist, government cannot effectively address crime without the moral authority and informal social control provided by community.

Concluding Reflections

Building a philosophical justification for a notion is a process. This paper is part of such a journey and has used previous thinking hopefully to add to the much-needed normative thinking for restorative justice. It was not the intention of this paper to make an argument for or against restorative justice. If comparators with the criminal justice system were used, it was for the purpose of helping the reader put the arguments in the context of current reality. This is exactly why I chose to persist with the term punishment, as I noted in my introduction. Although I fear its connotations with imprisonment and state-inflicted forms of pain are difficult to overcome, I am hopeful that by now the reader is ready to put their limits to the test. That is, if they are able to say the word and observe that they do not relate it to state-inflicted pain then my first goal has been achieved.

My second goal was to allow this self-observation to progress into becoming an ability to view this word through different lenses. These lenses should explain how this new punishment relates to the pain described by Jim and others I referred to. This is also the foundation for understanding my restorative catharsis and, by extension, the ultimate goal of restorative justice; a notion that aims to bring balance to the social liaison that connects us all.

One of the goals of normative writing is to allow the expansion of our thinking and, through this, the development of practices that we understand and implement better. It should also help us identify a conceptual framework for our chosen definitions and arguments. I consciously avoided the use of grounded theories and empirical findings. These would have distracted me from my aforementioned two goals. There are also volumes of this type of writing on restorative justice and we have already accepted that there is a gap in its philosophical development.

Like any cathartic moment, the opportunity to reflect through these words should leave the reader changed or being changed. This is a process of sublimation, of self-overcoming and of challenging concepts and norms that define our common sense and reality. It is in this sublimation of self-overcoming that I believe lies the biggest contribution of this chapter. It is in this process of questioning and redefining that, as one of the joint Editors of this volume, I see the book's biggest challenge and value.

References

Abdulla, A. 1985. *Catharsis in Literature*. Bloomington: Indiana University Press.

Aristotle 1965. *Poetics* in J.D Kaplan, *The Pocket Aristotle*, New York: Washington Square Press, pp. 340–79.

Aurelius, M. 167 ACE. *The Meditations*, trans. G. Long.

Barnes, J. 1988. 'Bits and Pieces' in *Matter and Metaphysics*, edited by M. Mignucci, Naples: Bibliopolis, pp. 223–94.

Barnes, J. 1991. 'Partial Wholes' in *Ethics, Politics, and Human Nature*, edited by J. Paul. Cambridge: Basil Blackwell, pp. 1–23.

Barnett, R. 1977. 'Restitution: A New Paradigm of Criminal Justice' 87(4) *Ethics: An International Journal of Social, Political, and Legal Philosophy*, pp. 279–301.

Barnett, R. 1981. 'Restitution' in *Perspectives on Crime Victims*, edited by J. Hudson, London: The C.V Mosby Company.

Bazemore, G. and Walgave, L. 1999. *Restorative Juvenile Justice*. Monsey: Criminal Justice Press.

Bentham, J. 1996. *An Introduction to the Principles of Morals and Legislation*, edited by J.H Burns and H.L.A Hart. Oxford: Oxford University Press.

Bianchi, H. 1973. 'Tsedeka Justice', *Review for Philosophy and Theology*, pp. 306–17.

Braithwaite, J. 1989. *Crime, Shame and Reintegration*. Cambridge: Cambridge University Press.

Braithwaite, J. 1998. 'Restorative Justice', in *Handbook of Crime and Punishment* edited by M. Tonry, Oxford: Oxford University Press.

Braithwaite, J. 1999a. 'A Future where Punishment is Marginalised: Realistic or Utopian?' 46 *UCLA Law Review*, pp. 1,727–50.

Braithwaite, J. 1999b. 'Restorative Justice: Assessing Optimistic and Pessimistic Accounts', *25 Crime and Justice, 1.*

Braithwaite, J. 2002. *Restorative Justice and Responsive Regulation*. New York: OUP.

Braithwaite, J. and Pettit, P. 1990. *Not Just Desserts: A Republican Theory of Criminal Justice*. Oxford: Clarendon Press.

Braithwaite, J. and Strang, H. 2000. *Restorative Justice: Philosophy to Practice*. Aldershot: Ashgate.

Budd, J. and Hill, H. 2007. '*The Cognitive and Social Lives of Paradigms in Information Science*', paper presented at University of Missouri, DC.

Cantor, G. 1976. 'An End to Crime and Punishment', *39(4) The Shingle (Philadelphia Bar Association)*, pp. 99–114.

Christie, N. 1977. 'Conflicts as Property' *17(1) British Journal of Criminology*, pp. 1–15.

Cohen, S. 1985. *Visions of Social Control: Crime, Punishment and Classification*. Cambridge: Cambridge University Press.

Daly, K. 1999. 'Does Punishment have a place in Restorative Justice?' in *The Australia and New Zealand Society of Criminology Annual Conference*.

Daly, K. 2000. 'Revisiting the Relationship between Retributive and Restorative Justice' in *Restorative Justice: Philosophy to Practice*, edited by J. Braithwaite and H. Strang. Aldershot: Ashgate, pp. 33–54.

Diamond, S. 1935. *Primitive Law*, London: Longmans, Green & Co.

Deleuze, G. 1983. *Nietzsche and Philosophy*, New York: Columbia University Press.

Dignan, J. 2003. 'Towards a systemic model of Restorative Justice' in *Restorative Justice and Criminal Justice: Competing or Reconcilable Paradigms?*, edited by A. Von Hirsch et al. Oxford: Hart Publishing.

Duff, A. 1992. 'Alternatives to Punishment or Alternative Punishments?' in *Retributivism and its Critics*, edited by W. Cragg, Stuttgart: Franz Steiner, pp. 44–68.

Duff, A. 1996. 'Penal Communications: Recent Work in the Philosophy of Punishment' in *Crime and Justice: A Review of Research*, edited by M. Tonry, Chicago: University of Chicago, pp. 1–97.

Duff, A. 1999. 'Response to Von Hirsch' in *Punishment and Political Theory*, edited by M. Matravers, Oxford: Oregon, pp. 83–5.

Duff, A. 2001. *Punishment, Communication, and Community*. Oxford: Oxford University Press.

Duff, A. and Garland, D. 1997. *A Reader on Punishment*. Oxford: Oxford University Press.

Elliott, E. 2011. *Security with Care*. Halifax: Fernwood Publishing.

Eglash, A. 1977. 'Beyond Restitution: Creative Restitution' in *Restitution in Criminal Justice*, edited by B. Galaway. Lexington, MA: DC Heath and Company.

Feinberg, J. 1965. 'The Expressive Function of Punishment', *49 The Monist*, pp. 397–408.

Figley, C.R. 1998. *Burnout in families: The systemic costs of caring*. New York: CRC Press.

Foucault, M. 1970. *The Order of Things: An Archaeology of the Human Sciences*. London: Tavistock.

Foucault, M. 1991. *Discipline and Punish: The Birth of the Prison*. London: Penguin.

Garland, D. 1990. 'Punishment as Atonement', *46 UCLA Law Review*, pp. 1,801–58.

Gavrielides, T. 2005. 'Some Meta-theoretical Questions for Restorative Justice', *18:1 Ratio Juris*, pp. 84–106.

Gavrielides, T. 2007. *Restorative Justice Theory and Practice: Addressing the Discrepancy*. Helsinki: HEUNI.

Gavrielides, T. 2012a. *Rights and Restoration within Youth Justice*, Whitby: ON de Sitter Publications.

Gavrielides, T. 2012b. 'Clergy Child Sexual Abuse and the Restorative Justice Dialogue', *Journal of Church and State*.

Gavrielides, T. 2012c. 'Contextualising Restorative Justice for Hate Crime'. 27(18) *Journal of Interpersonal Violence*, pp. 3,624–43.

Gavrielides, T. and J. Winterdyk 2011. 'The fall and rise of restorative justice: a historical account of its notion, practices and possible lessons learned', *Vol 2 and 3 Pakistan Journal of Criminology*, pp. 107–25.

Haines, K. 1998. 'Some Principled Objections to a Restorative Justice Approach to Working with Juvenile Offenders' in *Restorative Justice for Juveniles: Potentialities, Risks and Problems for Research*, edited by L. Walgrave, Leuven: Leuven University Press.

Hall, S. 2012. *Theorizing Crime and Deviance,* London: Sage.

Hegel, G. 1910. *The Phenomenology of Mind*, New York: Macmillan.

Johnstone, G. 2001. *Restorative Justice: Ideas, Values, Debates*. Cullompton: Willan Publishing.

Kuhn, T. 1970. *The Structure of Scientific Revolutions*, Chicago: University of Chicago Press.

Mack, M. 1950. *The Poems of Alexander Pope III.* London: Methuen.

Mack, M. 1985. *Alexander Pope*. New Haven: Yale University Press.
Mandelin, J. 2012. *A Life Worth Dying For*, Victoria: Friesen Press.
Marshall, T. 1996. 'The Evolution of Restorative Justice in Britain' *4:4 European Journal on Criminal Policy and Research*, pp. 21–43.
Marx, K. 1954. *Capital*, London: Lawrence and Wishart.
Mason, A. 2000. 'Restorative Justice: Courts and Civil Society' in *Restorative Justice Philosophy to Practice* edited by J. Braithwaite and H. Strang, Dartmouth: Ashgate Publishing.
McCold, P. 1999. 'Toward a Holistic Vision of Restorative Juvenile Justice: A Reply to Walgrave' in *The 4th International Conference on Restorative Justice for Juveniles*. Leuven, Belgium
McCold, P. and Wachtel, B. 1998. 'Community is not a Place: A New Look at Community Justice Initiatives' *1:1 Contemporary Justice Review*, pp. 71–85.
Moberly, W. 1968. *The Ethics of Punishment*. London: Faber and Faber.
Michalowski, R. 1985. *Order, Law and Crime*, New York: Random House.
Morris, A. and Young, W. 2000. 'Reforming Criminal Justice: The Potential of Restorative Justice' in *Restorative Justice: Philosophy to Practice*, edited by J. Braithwaite and H. Strang. Aldershot: Ashgate.
Mueller, G. 1958. 'The Hegel legend of thesis, antithesis and synthesis', *19 Journal of History of Ideas*, 411–14.
Nietzsche, F. 1872. *The Birth of Tragedy*, Ed. W. Kaufmann, New York: The Modern Library.
Nietzsche, F. 1878. *Twilight of the Idols*, New York: Viking Press.
Price A. 1998. 'Nietzsche and the Paradox of Tragedy', *38:4 The British Journal of Aesthetics*, p. 385.
Rossner, D. 1989. 'Wiedergutmachen statt Ubelvergelten', in *Tater-Opfer-Ausgleich: Vom zwischenmenschlichen Weg zur Wiederstellung des Rechtsfriedens* edited by E. Marks and D. Rossner, Bonn: Unveränderte Auflage.
Rutherford, R. 1989. *The Meditations of Marcus Aurelius: A Study*. Oxford: Clarendon Press.
Schiff, M. 1999. 'The Impact of Restorative Interventions on Juvenile Offenders' in *Restorative Juvenile Justice: Repairing the Harm of Youth Crime*, edited by G. Bazemore and L. Walgrave, Monsey: Criminal Justice Press.
Sharpe, J. 1980. 'Enforcing the Law in the Seventeenth Century English Village', in *Crime and the Law* edited by V. Gatrell, London: Europa.
Soll, I. 1988. 'Pessimism and the Tragic View of Life' in *Reading Nietzsche,* edited by E. Solomon and K. Higgins, New York: Oxford University Press, p. 107.
Sullivan, D., Tifft, L. and Cordella, P. 1998. 'The Phenomenon of Restorative Justice: Some introductory Remarks', *1 Contemporary Justice Review,* pp. 7–20.
Tallack, W. 1900. *Reparation to the Injured and the Rights of Victims of Crime Compensation*, London: Wertheimer

von Hirsch, A. 1999. 'Punishment, Penance and the State', in *Punishment and Political Theory*, edited by M. Matravers. Oxford: Hart Publishing, pp. 69–82.
von Hirsch, A. and Ashworth, A.J. 1992. 'Not Not Just Desserts: A Response to Braithwaite and Pettit'. *12 Oxford Journal of Legal Studies,* pp. 83–98.
von Hirsch, A. and Ashworth, A.J. 1998. *Principled Sentencing*. Oxford: Hart Publishing.
Walgrave, L. 1999. 'Community service as a cornestone of a systemic restorative response to juvenile crime' in *Restorative Juvenile Justice: Repairing the Harm of youth Crime*, edited by G. Bazemore and L. Walgrave. Monsey: Criminal Justice Press, pp. 129–55.
Walgrave, L. 2001. 'On Restoration and Punishment: Favourable Similarities and Fortunate Differences' in *Restorative Justice for Juveniles: Conferencing, Mediation, and Circles* edited by G. Maxwell, Oxford: Hart.
Wind, L., Sullivan, J. and Levins, D.J. 2008. 'Survivors' Perspectives on the Impact of Clergy Sexual Abuse on Families of Origin', *17(3–4) Journal of Child Sexual Abuse*. pp. 238–54.
Woodfin, R. and Groves, J. 2006. *Introduction: Aristotle*, Cambridge: Icon Books.
Wright, M. 1991. *Justice for Victims and Offenders*. Philadelphia: Open University Press.
Wright, M. 1996. *Justice for Victims and Offenders: A Restorative Response to Crime*. Winchester: Waterside Press.
Yazzie, R. 1994. 'Life comes from it: Navajo Justice Concepts', *24 New Mexico Law Review*, pp. 175–90.
Zehr, H. 1990. *Changing Lenses: A New Focus for Crime and Justice*. Scottsdale: Herald Press.
Zehr, H. and Mika, H. 1998. 'Fundamental Concepts of Restorative Justice', 1 *Contemporary Justice Review*, pp. 47–55.

Chapter 16
Epilogue: Reconstructing Restorative Justice Philosophy

Theo Gavrielides and Vasso Artinopoulou

A Summary of Discourses

Blackburn (1999, p. 5) said, 'Our ideas and concepts can be compared with the lenses through which we see the world. In philosophy the lens is itself the topic of study.' Our authors treated philosophy as a way of life; elements and structures through which to view the world, the implementation of values in justice systems, and the imagination of a restorative world were some of the issues examined in their chapters.

The discourses in this volume reflect the structures with which justice systems are built. The journey from practice to theory and back and the continuity of practice are also key points in the structure of the chapters; they were not merely an attempt to theorize practice or practice theory. It was a dialectic relationship between practice and theory, which facilitated a broad focus on worldwide social structures and justice systems. The discourse of the chapters lies in the lens through which we view social structures, justice systems, human rights institutions, communities and individuals.

So, this is a discourse on the chapters' discourses, like the final varnishing of the painting. Some colours in the painting are bold, some are pale, but each viewer has his or her own perception. However, we can distinguish a few of the painting's components and formulate a varnish which complements the whole.

The first part of this final chapter serves as a gathering, highlighting and organization of the themes and issues which have arisen in the preceding chapters. We appreciate that each reader will have their own perspective on what they have read and we do not attempt to analyze critically the key discourses which have arisen from the chapters. This will be done in the second part. The main issues addressed in the volume, were:

1. Restorative justice philosophy is neither a solid perspective nor a global theory. Restorative justice philosophy helps how and what to think, how and what to say, how to act. With a glance at the past, we live the present, looking to the future. In other words 'fixing the past, into the focus of the present and to some extent with the future' (Mackay, Chapter 6).

According to Mackay, restorative justice aims to restore and repair the harm done to individuals and/or communities. Individual personalities, institutions, groups, identities, values and principles, ideologies, representations and feelings are all involved in the transformative and interactive process of restoring and healing the harm.

It is clear that most of our authors (particularly Johnstone, Oudshoorn and Schoeman) have intended to widen the restorative justice lens to other matters, including guidance on how we should live our everyday lives, giving justifications and teachings of restorative justice. Restorative justice becomes an archetype of thinking and living. In other words, focusing only on restorative justice practices (such as mediation, conferences, cycles) is like seeing the trees but failing to see the wood.

> 2. Restorative justice philosophy has both transformative and relational effects at all levels of social reality (individuals, communities, groups, societies, nations, supranational structures).

The concept of transformation through restoration and healing is a key point in the Zellerer, Schoeman, Hadjipavlou and Yiallourides/Anastasiadou chapters. Transformation as a dynamic and interactive process of (social) change is reflected in justice systems, crime components, communities and values from a restorative justice perspective. Relational repair is the *sine qua non* precondition of achieving transformation.

According to Sharpe's chapter, relationality in justice, in communities, in crime components, in the individuals while healing the harm or trauma and in the relational approach to rights, reflects the radical transformation of subjectivity from modern to postmodern conditions.

According to Gavrielides (Chapter 15), restorative punishment and catharsis procedures are to be found in relationships and the social liaison that binds us all. They are all components of the restorative justice philosophy discourse, an updated or 'new born' discourse in the continuum of restorative justice knowledge (or due to the Foucaultian genealogy of discourses as pointed out by Maglione in Chapter 4).

Through restorative justice's relational effects, justice in social relations achieve and operate the mechanisms for social change:

> 3. What we live today is the deadlock of injustice, reflected not only in traditional justice systems, but also in the current crisis environment. Colonialism, authority, power structures, and dominant discourses in social institutions, reflect the social crisis we live with nowadays in Europe and US. (Hadjipavlou, Chapter 11).

A sharp fall in human rights implementation is reflected in national and supranational institutions; human rights have grown up from the first generation to the fourth one. Cornescu (2009) argues that there are four stages in the historical evolution of human rights: positivation, generalization, internationalization and specialization. Currently, we are at the specialization stage, meaning specialization of human rights in criminal justice systems, in communities, in middle level social institutions (such as schools) and in social and minority groups. Restorative justice aligns with that specialization focus in the levels of social reality, from international to interpersonal conflicts. Both restorative justice lenses and human rights lenses are focussed in our eyes.

According to Mackay and Yiallourides, peacemaking theory of law and restorative justice are the two faces of Janos. Institutions, social practices and communities have to recognize the different kinds of rights.

Focused on implementation of human rights and restorative justice in everyday life, most authors suggest we move our restorative justice vision from justice systems to everyday living justice (for instance see Oudshoorn, Chapter 12).

> 4. Restorativists are all those who share that holistic restorative justice vision and compose the restorative justice movement. Shared values and principles, such as equity and fairness, social justice and equality, human rights protection structures and humanitarian practices, are the common places – τόποι – where human rights and restorative justice meet (Artinopoulou and Gavrielides, Chapter 2)

Aristotle's theory on justice and restorative justice as a form of social justice took centre stage once more in the history of theories and ideas. Moreover, according to Schoeman (Chapter 14), pro-restorative perspectives and reimaginations of justice and fairness are brought to the forefront as demands reflect the restorative vision of world. Nevertheless, the discourses are often developed through conflict theories of law (Chapters 7, 8 and 12); surprisingly enough they align with the justice values, equity and fairness, Ubuntu philosophy and practice (Chapter 14), Aboriginal cycles (Chapter 12 and 13) and Aristotle's theory on justice (Chapter 2).

So, how do we reach *topoi* in current complex societies? The restorative justice movement lives its own formulation process. It is an open-ended question whether a global restorative justice movement is to be structured; Maglione asks what arevthe demands and who are the leaders. As political and social theories testify, social movements are in the process of social formulation, depending on the wider context if they succeed in putting their demands on the agenda of decision-making centres and spreading their ideology in communities, gaining supporters.

> 5. We need a multidisciplinary background to attain interdisciplinary approaches. Interestingly enough, and despite the multiple backgrounds of the authors, there were many coincidences in the chapter discourses that interlinked the chapters and led to a conceptualized framework of current restorative justice (Chapter 2).

Interdisciplinarity is a process of synthesis. As Editors, we learnt that a way from multi- to inter-disciplinarity exists, either as a narrow path or as a large avenue. We, all the contributors to this volume, were lucky to feel liberated enough to enjoy our journey to Ithaca (Chapter 1). Reconstruction processes are a form of interdisciplinary synthesis. However, we concentrated mostly on the process and not the final outcome, as we are detached from generalizations and holistic schemes. Finally, this discourse on the chapters' discourses contains values, practices and vision. Equity, peace, fairness, rights, relational repair and justice are the key points, the τόποι, where the humanitarian philosophical ways of thinking are crossed. Only the priority level changes, not the content itself.

A Different Zeitgeist

This book attempted to treat restorative justice as a form of pursuing, reaching and maintaining justice. The need to place justice and the system that delivers it within cultural, historical and societal contexts was taken as a given. Through the writing for this volume and the extant literature, we observed that there is a shift in the tectonic plates of justice; a different Zeitgeist. This observation is not attached to a particular country, continent or legal system. It relates to how you and I view, pursue, achieve and indeed want to experience justice at the inter-personal, inter-community and inter-state levels. Where the literature is thin, we listen to the stranger passing by, who is witnessing this change. This makes both our questioning and this book timely.

It is a common mistake when thinking about restorative justice to compare it with something that isn't. This comparator is an easy aid particularly since most often we resort to comparing it with what we are used to. In paradigm language, this is called our common sense.

However, in our current reality, where justice systems are forced to reconsider not only their own sub-systems[1] but also the entire framework within which they operate, our common sense is questioned. The paradigm stops fitting the facts. The chapters in this volume pointed out a number of reasons for this questioning: increasing inequalities, the uneven distribution of wealth, the power and interest battles within and outside the restorative justice movement, the increasingly stronger community voice, the world economic crisis, stronger social movements, the globalization of civic society, as well as the role of academia and research.

Aristotle and his followers explain that justice is hardly a subjective notion. It is made of ingredients that are pure and easy to identify in nature. It is the theories that have been developed to explain these ingredients that are human constructs and hence subjective. For example, for the advocates of divine command theory justice is the authoritative command of God. On the other hand, the Pythagoreans

---

1 For instance in the case of criminal justice systems their sub-systems are the police machinery, the prosecution, the courts, prison and the probation service.

defined justice as reciprocity, in that A shall have done to him what he has done to B or, as the Old Testament put it, 'An eye for an eye, and a tooth for a tooth' (Lex Talionis). Others, such as Plato, have argued that justice is in the interest of the strong (a name for whatever the powerful or cunning ruler has managed to impose on the people).[2] For Nietzsche, justice is part of the slave morality of the weak many, rooted in their resentment of the strong few, and intended to keep the noble man down.[3] Thomas Hobbes sees justice as a collection of enforceable, authoritative rules created by the public and hence injustice is whatever those rules forbid, regardless of their relation to morality.[4] Thinkers belonging to the social contract tradition would argue that justice is derived from the mutual agreement of everyone concerned or from what they would agree to under hypothetical conditions. These examples are only meant to be illustrative of the variations of interpretations of the norm of justice, which we have accepted to be objective.

Why would the notion of restorative justice be any different? The objectivity of restorative justice is reflected in the 'natural objects' that comprise it. John Stuart Mill said that mankind is always predisposed to believe that any subjective feeling is a revelation of some objective reality. In the case of restorative justice our task was to determine whether the reality, to which this feeling of justice corresponds, is one that needs any such special revelation. For the purpose of this inquiry, 'it is practically important to consider whether the feeling itself, of justice and injustice, is sui generis, like our sensations of colour and taste, or a derivative feeling, formed by a combination of others'.[5]

In other words, if we were to test objectively the image of restorative justice as it is portrayed in modern society, how satisfactory would the outcome be? But what is restorative justice, and how is it reconstructed in contemporary terms? The truth is that we tend to think of restorative justice as a notion that has, or should have, a physical or conceptual existence within the real word. Some have attempted to explain its physical existence by defining it through process-based descriptions and by giving real life examples that may include practices such as mediation, conferencing, circles etc. Others have asserted that restorative justice may be more than a practice encompassing a set of principles or teachings. Therefore, they provide value-based understandings and theories that may, or may not, be susceptible to testing and empirical verification.

Here, we take a bold but firm step by stating that the past struggles of restorative justice are due to the limited vision of its proponents. We posit that restorative justice is indeed more than a series of practices or a set of values. As

2 See Plato's *Republic*, esp. Thrasymachus.

3 Nietzsche said: 'Justice (fairness) originates among those who are approximately equally powerful', Nietzsche F, Human, *All Too Human*, Cambridge: CUP, 1986.

4 See, Hobbes Thomas, *The Elements of Law, Natural and Politics*, 1889, ed. F. Tönnies, including 'Short Tract on First Principles', 1889 (written 1630–36).

5 Mill S John, *Utilitarianism, On Liberty, Considerations on Representative Government*, London: Everyman, 1993, pp. 43–4.

we reconstruct its philosophy, we assert that restorative justice is a comprehensive set of justifications of structures, or lack of structures, for the pursuit of justice.

When making this statement, we bear two things in mind. First, that we respect what has already been developed, accepting and building on both the process-based and value-based understandings of restorative justice. As it will be argued in detail, both sets of knowledge are used in our two models of reconstructing restorative justice philosophy. Second, we are mindful not to propose anything that can exist instead of something. We are not abolitionists. All authors, including the Editors of this book, are realists with a genuine interest in unravelling the hidden dimensions of restorative justice. Again, as it will become clear, our proposition accepts the implementation of restorative justice within an integrated model of justice.

We also assert that restorative justice is not a uniform notion. Despite its objective existence, it is an evolving norm as its constituent objects are to be found in living nature. These objects are continuously moving – τα πάντα ρεί και ουδέν μένει. Therefore, restorative justice will always be accused by empirical researchers of lacking clarity. Restorative justice is a shortcut term constructed with the mentality of our busy and managerial lives. Therefore, attempts that continue to define restorative justice in the narrow sense will remain vain and out of touch with its evolving and ever changing nature. Scientists will look at water and define it as H_2O.But in the pursuit of truth, and a higher sense of knowledge, we may see water as an untamed form of nature that can take almost unlimited shapes, forms and roles. We also get to realize that it is not always good. Where it gives life it can also take it away. The definition H_2O suddenly becomes shallow and mundane.

We have used the various objects making the restorative justice justification in a collective fashion, missing what the notion is actually about. However, to identify the common attributes in this variety of objects that constitute restorative justice, it is vital that we survey their concrete nature. The chapters in this book help us do just that. We must accept, nevertheless, that a medium such as a book has its limitations and this is reflected in the number of issues exposed and the objects discussed. More symposia are needed to continue this journey.

Arguably, each legal system is based on the perceived notion of justice by the society which then entrusts its application and enforcement to legal practitioners, such as judges and lawyers. This statement leads us to assume two things; first, that there are different legal systems and second that there are different types of justice depending on national and local understandings. Although this might be true, what is undeniable is that justice has a normative concept, a universal truth.

This book is not about revealing this universal truth. It is about surveying the colours of restorative justice in the concrete and finding that final varnish we believe complements and brings out these colours in the best way.

In the preceding chapters, justice is spoken of in two ways: the lawful and the fair. The law is a human construct that is devoted to the advantage of all, or to the advantage of the best, or to the advantage of those in power, or to the advantage of those representing it. The law commands us to act according to the mean. A well-written law follows the mean well and a poorly written law does not. On the other hand, fairness is a principle sometimes materialized through the law and the given justice system. The two are not mutually exclusive. As Aristotle put it: 'Justice in this sense, that of obedience to law, is thus co-extensive with virtue, but the terms are not identical in meaning' (Ethics). Therefore, although justice is an objective concept, it is divided into the human construct of the law and value-based fairness.

This led us to conclude that, for any analysis of restorative justice, its objective norm will be moulded into the form that we experience in a legalized justice system and that it will be delivered through bottom-up and unstructured mechanisms of fairness. Again, our interest is not in advocating for or against these two forms. Our aim is to understand them.

The preceding chapters also helped us to understand that, although we can be more demanding in terms of the representation of justice (the law), we have to remain reasonable in our expectations of the agents attempting to represent justice (the value). We would be obtuse to expect any judge or lawyer to represent the normative concept of justice (fairness). Their job description stops where justice (the law) is done. The question is, what sort of justice do we want to pursue? Put another way, what will satisfy your sense of justice post the experience of harm and conflict?

This book is not about helping you to decide whether restorative justice can lead to a better sense of justice. That is a task for its campaigners (or indeed its adversaries). Here, as modern philosophers, we try to understand restorative justice and its justification in the world of theory and practice in the hope that others, who either accuse or praise its empirical manifestation, can have a more informed discussion.

It is in human nature to hope for something better. Take the Utilitarians, for instance, who base their entire school of thought on the pursuit of utility (the ultimate good and happiness). Therefore, it should come as no surprise as to why most of our authors want to see restorative justice as a tool that can help us experience a better sense of justice. But criticism was also present, as well as some genuine attempts to construct self-assessment methodologies for our claims.

The authors were also critical of the means for delivering justice. In short, there is the informal delivery system, encompassing our day-to-day treatment and interaction with others. This is where justice is delivered informally by each one of us in our daily activities and within our communities. The second system of justice, the formal one, encompasses the justice system that has been constructed to deliver justice through the law and its institutions.

The chapters also reminded us that the individual is essentially a member of society or, as Aristotle put it, a 'social animal', whose identity is determined, but not limited, to its membership of different social groups.[6] We cannot understand

6 However, as various libertarians would argue, although our membership of different groups (ethnic, religious, national) is influential, our identity cannot be reduced

our existence if we don't place it within the existence of others. Our world and realities are defined by our surroundings and, for those rare thinkers whose views do not conform to what is common sense, things become complex as we tend to ostracize or label them as abnormal. Therefore, a common thread running through almost all the contributions is the significance of interconnectedness and the pre-existence of a social liaison that binds us all in a social relationship.

More importantly, all contributions in this book – particularly the chapters by Zellerer, Gavrielides and Sharpe – serve as a wake-up call from the deep sleep our current justice paradigm has put us all under. The tinted lenses through which we view justice will continue to obstruct our attempts to understand and implement restorative justice. It is only after we challenge this common sense that we will be able to divert to the various modes of action and arrangement of human affairs that are classed by universal or widely spread opinion as just. This approach will help us return to the basics of restorative justice, breaking free from the Macdonaldised version of justice.[7] Our objective here is to reconstruct the notion of restorative justice using objective tools and principles.

Restorative Justice Philosophy Reconstructed

To reconstruct restorative justice philosophy as a comprehensive set of justifications for the pursuit of justice, we first need to identify a common starting point. To pursue justice we must accept that there is an injustice, an imbalance in the *status quo*. We call this imbalance *conflict*. This can be between individuals, communities, states or even ourselves. The opposite is what Schiff, Yiallourides and Anastasiadou name in this volume as *peace*.

We have also accepted that there are two forms of justice: the lawful and the fair. Both are desirable and can co-exist. However, whereas the lawful requires a structure and a system of regulation, the fair is value-based and can be attained through loose and bottom-up methods. There is enough empirical evidence to show that restorative justice exists in both forms; the structured and unstructured – the lawful and the fair. There is no better or worse form. There is also no reason for comparing it with what isn't. Our reconstructed vision of restorative justice philosophy has a dual dimension: structured and unstructured restorative justice. So let us focus on understanding it as it is.

---

to membership of a single group. Each one of us is defined by a unique combination of characteristics that make up our personality.

7 See 'The McDonaldisation of a community born and community led ethos' by Gavrielides http://www.rj4all.info/content/mcdonaldisationrestorative justice (accessed February 2013)

Structured Restorative Justice

To understand the formal delivery system of justice, we only need to follow a law's journey from its conception to its delivery. To deliver justice (the law) formally, first there needs to be an injustice done to society, in this case we named it *conflict*. This needs to be identified and publicly condemned. It also needs to be backed up by a pattern of unjust behaviour. Through this, the need for regulation arises. This requires a mixture of skills and professions, including politicians, the media, academia, market research, economics, campaigners and so on. Once a law has been produced to regulate this pattern of injustice and conflict, then a further series of actors come into play to represent and deliver justice, including lawyers, courts, judges, administrators, prosecutors, prison and probation staff. Once this law is delivered, then a further chain of maintenance is observed encompassing educational institutions, the media, campaigners, politicians and so on. All these agents and institutions are engaged to contribute to the formal system of delivery and representation of justice.

Structured restorative justice is placed within this machinery and organized sub-systems of pursuing, delivering and maintaining justice after a conflict has occurred. But these institutions are not equal and the agents delivering or representing justice share various positions of power depending on their roles and place in society. This creates the power imbalances that a number of chapters in this book talked about. These power structures and imbalances are additional to those that may lead to conflict in the first place. These types of imbalances are to be found within the very machinery that is set up to address conflict and its underlying causes.

To counterbalance this distortion we have introduced legal standards. Contributors to this volume called them rights, or human rights, and placed them within both international and individual spheres. In this case, rights and human rights were understood as justiciable standards implemented by the very system that they aim to correct. They are, of course, based on our common humanity and are informed by the living experiences of those they aim to protect. But they do not have any significance until they take the form, or have the protection, of the law. Thus they must be introduced into the machinery of the structured systems and sub-systems that have been set up to address injustice and conflict.

Chart 1 illustrates how this structured way of delivering justice and restorative justice works. Within this model, conflict creates crime, offenders and victims. All three are placed within a funnel. Emptying the funnel will bring peace. Exit from the funnel can be achieved through a legalized and structured justice system that is served by structured institutions. The power imbalance that this structure creates is meant to be contained by the outside layer of the funnel which is made of human rights as they are materialized through the law. Structured restorative justice is one way of emptying the funnel and is part of many other structured forms of delivering and maintaining justice and bringing peace.

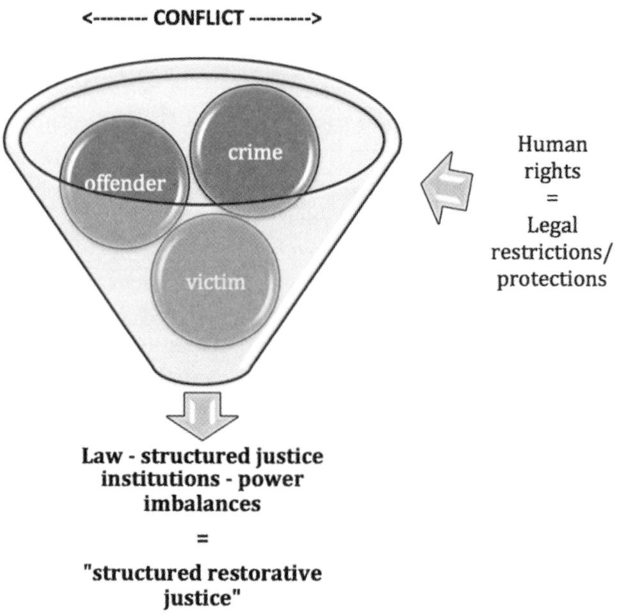

Figure 1 Structured Restorative Justice

Unstructured Restorative Justice

To understand the informal delivery of justice, we need to put conflict, our common starting point, within the context of doing harm. Conflict in the form of harm causes a broken liaison between individuals, communities, the individual and the community, the individual and the state or even between states. It also creates harmed parties independently of whether these are labelled as victims or offenders. In this model it does not matter who did what to whom. What matters is that the conflict has caused harm and a broken liaison in the pre-existent relationship of the harmed parties.

Going back to our funnel, this time it is filled with different ingredients (harm, broken social liaison and harmed parties). Again, to achieve peace we must empty the funnel. Only this time the intervention of the law will not be enough. The community must intervene and various emotions must be employed. This intervention can take various shapes and forms. Restorative justice practice may offer one such a form. Unlike in the previous funnel, loose and bottom-up mechanisms that aim to restore harm and mend broken social liaisons are used. These are not dependent on formalized sub-systems. They use localized and informal projects to bring peace.

A common feature of both funnels is the power structures that are created through the mechanisms of emptying them. These powers are not observed within

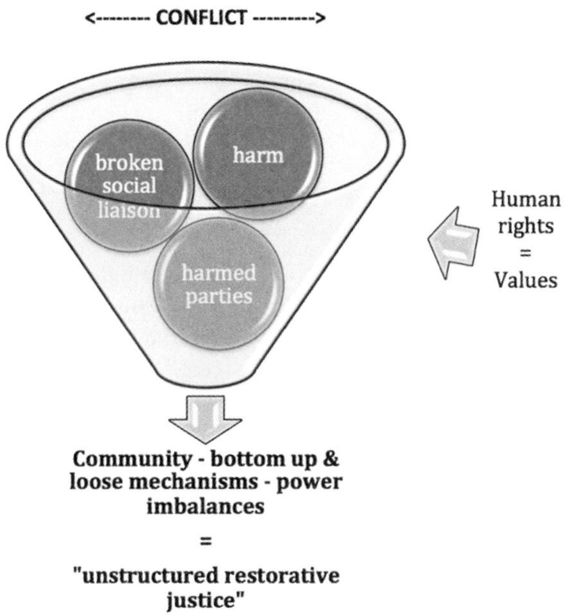

Figure 2 Unstructured Restorative Justice

and between institutions, they are created among those community representatives delivering justice. They can also be created between the harmed parties themselves as their labels and roles are removed.

Another shared denominator between the two funnels and forms of delivering justice is the role of human rights as a restraining standard. In this case, human rights are not enforced as legal restrictions but as a value-based code of behaviour and practice. Whether they are justiciable or not is irrelevant to the community-led and bottom-up structures that are called on to empty the funnel of harm, broken social liaisons and harmed parties. What these justice projects need, including unstructured restorative justice, is the manifestation of value-based guidelines. These are the set of values that we often confuse with restorative justice. This is also where the overlap between restorative justice and human rights is found, or as Artinopoulou and Gavrielides note in Chapter 2, this is the *topoi* where the two disciplines meet.

Where Do We Go From Here?

We agreed from the outset that any philosophy must be grounded in practice and be able to contribute to a better future for what it aims to understand and justify. Our reconstructed restorative justice philosophy put the value-based and process-based understandings of restorative justice within a normative framework of justifying structured and unstructured mechanisms of delivering justice. What does this mean then for researchers, practitioners and policymakers taking an interest in restorative justice today?

The End of Definitions

There are already enough excellent papers in the literature on the definition and meaning of restorative justice (see Braithwaite and Strang, 2000; Johnstone and Van Ness, 2003; Zehr, 2003; Roche, 2001; Gavrielides, 2007, 2008; Johnstone, 2011). Therefore, our discussion purposely steered away from getting involved in yet more similar definitional arguments. Moreover, as already pointed out, trying to define water too narrowly will prevent philosophers from seeing its other properties.

In making this statement we accept the concerns that have already been expressed in the literature. There are too many to capture here, but to mention a few, a narrow understanding is necessary for the evaluation of the restorative justice practice, the setting of training and accreditation standards, the mapping and researching of its existence. Roche writes: 'In the same way that counterfeit goods may tarnish the good reputation of a manufacturers' brand label, programmes that are called restorative when they are not can tarnish the concept' (2001, p. 343). In another article Roche (2006) goes on to criticize the narrow approach that has been adopted for restorative justice claiming that it has led us to think of it only in criminal justice terms. He then lists a number of areas, including social welfare and education, corporate regulation and community governance, that can come under the umbrella of restorative justice.

We agree with Johnstone (2011) that 'there is not likely to be (indeed perhaps should not be) a single accepted conception of restorative justice. Instead, we must acknowledge the differing and indeed competing ideas about its nature' (p. 14). He makes this point again in his chapter in this volume giving the example of conferencing.

We also assert that there is no longer a need to be defensive. If a practice claims to be punitive but in fact isn't, does it need to be corrected? Why does restorative justice have to explain itself? Here we have provided a far more worthwhile justification and explanation. Our reconstructed restorative justice should also explain why Johnstone's statement matters. In other words, why and how can you define a collection of justifications of structured and unstructured ways of delivering justice? Further efforts need to be made in the theoretical understanding and development of our reconstruction as well as empirical testing of the various shapes and forms that restorative justice takes at both ends of the funnels.

The End of Abolitionism

There is general consensus in the literature that writings in the 1970s and 1980s on restorative justice presented its concept as in complete opposition to the dominant way of delivering justice, in the hope that enough attention was given to the ideas that were put forward. As we moved away from the era of experimentation and entered the times of implementation and maturity, we realize that ideas of abolishing and replacing are out of date and naïve.

There is one more reason why these discussions do not sit well with a value-based system such as restorative justice. Oudshoorn writes in this Chapter 12 about the negative impact of Colonialism and the replacement of respected Aboriginal traditions with something alien. While this statement has its merits we must be careful not to turn restorative justice into a colonial power itself. For instance, if a Western tradition is not organically prepared for restorative justice, then it should not be introduced as a more informed option deriving from a higher authority. Remember the funnel. Whether in the structured or unstructured systems of delivering justice, restorative justice forms only one of the options available for emptying the funnels. Both systems of justice put restorative justice next to other forms of justice.

A common mistake is confusing the paradigm language with abolishing what is. We have made a strong point in this book that unless we change our lenses we will not be able to view our reconstruction. This statement uses paradigm language in the sense that what is being questioned is: 'what is common sense?' But this does not mean that we are proposing abolishing what is. We are simply saying that there are other means of delivering justice beyond what we are used to seeing. So let's view them for what they are without the need to remove what is. The abolitionism debate should be over.

Ending the Bottom-Up or Top-Down Divide

There can be no doubt that restorative justice is back on the agenda. Governments are becoming interested in its propositions and are trying to find ways of using it more extensively and consistently. Here is not the place to explain the reasons for this increasing interest. The literature has captured some of these factors (Gavrielides 2012a; 2012b). It has also highlighted some dangers and pitfalls that are associated with this expansion. Gavrielides (2013) and Umbreit (2001) call these dangers the Macdonaldisation of restorative justice. By using this term they want to describe the process of taking away the community heart of restorative justice and replacing it with fast food mentality of business-focused goals and readily available quick fixes.

While these fears might be justifiable, our reconstruction helps us understand that whether through a structured/top-down system or one that is bottom-up and loose, restorative justice can still deliver. Whether we end up regulating restorative justice practice through legislation or we leave it in the hands of localized and unregulated projects it will still deliver. However, we must remember that if the structured system is applied, then restorative justice will be emptying the funnel from crime, victims and offenders. If we wish to achieve peace by empting the funnel from harm, the broken social liaison and harmed parties, then a top-down approach, such as legislation, will not be enough. A value-based system of community trust and care must be employed. But this does not mean that one is better than the other or that the two cannot coexist. However, we do disagree that one is dependent on the other. For example, we do not need legislation in order for value-based, unstructured restorative justice to be implemented. The examples of the old bear evidence to this claim. Likewise, the cold letter of the law does not need warm hearts and value-based localized systems to deliver structured restorative justice. This can still be applied by criminal justice agents such as the police, prosecution, probation and prison staff. There are enough empirical studies bearing evidence to this claim. Enough time has been spent defending our preferred practices. After all, much of the success of restorative justice is to be found in its plurality, diversity and living nature as a continuously evolving system of justice.

Understanding Campaigning

Much energy has been spent and a number of high profile articles have been published focusing on the advantages (or indeed disadvantages) of restorative justice. Advantages tend to include higher victim satisfaction rates, reducing reoffending, cutting costs and increasing efficiency. Indeed these are the areas that government and most funders are interested in. Therefore, we would be naïve to dismiss the significance of these questions. Answering them may also help us understand the limitations or potential of the restorative justice practice. What our answers should not try to do is prove or disprove that restorative justice, whether in its structured or unstructured form, can provide a better sense of justice. It is what it is and our energy should be spent in developing its principles and practices and not in campaigning for its superiority. This is yet one more reason why campaigners and advocates of restorative justice should let its researchers and theoreticians remain objective and open to questioning. Much controversy and battles between interests have been formed within the restorative justice movement because of this reason. This should not exclude practitioners and policymakers who remain suspicious and isolated.

Getting Our Values Language Right

As argued, restorative justice is more than a set of values. What these values are has been the focus of a number of papers, including some chapters in this volume. What we have shown here is that these values are what makes the outside layer of our funnel. This layer aims to bring balance to the power battles that are to be found in the exit strategies of both of our funnels. They are not *restorative*

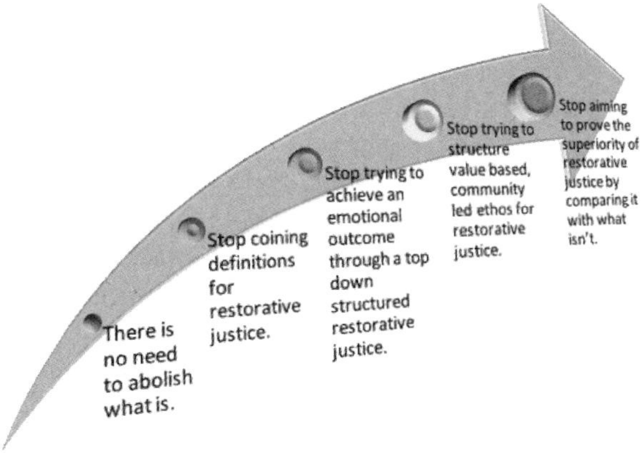

Figure 3 Moving forward: Five rules for restorative justice

justice, but a *part* of it. The relationship between restorative justice and human rights must also be put right. We agree with Braithwaite that human rights act as the restraining values in restorative practice (2000). We make a distinction, however, between human rights as legal standards that exist within a structured system of justice and those that are value-based and are to be applied within a loose methodology. The shared *topoi* where restorative justice and human rights meet was revealed and hence their respective movements can now find a common ground for further collaboration and support.

As we move forward with new research, empirical testing and theoretical development for restorative justice, we propose that we apply the following rules:

Rule 1: There is no need to abolish what is.

Variation: Focus on understanding where structured and unstructured restorative justice can help empty the funnel.

Rule 2: Stop coining definitions for restorative justice.

Variation: Focus on understanding and developing its values (protective layer) and practices (funnel exit).

Rule 3: Stop trying to achieve an emotional outcome through a top-down structured restorative justice.

Variation: Crime, victims and offenders are legal constructs of a structured system of justice and should be treated as such.

Rule 4: Stop trying to structure value-based, community-led ethos for restorative justice.

Variation: Harm, the broken social liaison and harmed parties should be served through relational approaches that are motivated by values and the community.

Rule 5: Stop aiming to prove the superiority of restorative justice by comparing it with what isn't.

Variation: Evaluation and empirical studies should focus on the question 'what happened' and not 'what works'.

References

Blackburn, S. 1999. *Think: A Compelling Introduction To Philosophy.* Oxford: Oxford University Press.

Braithwaite, J. and Strang, H. 2000. *Restorative Justice: Philosophy to Practice.* Aldershot: Ashgate.

Cornescu, A. 2009. *The generations of human rights, Days of Law: the Conference Proceedings*. Brno: Masaryk University.

Gavrielides, T. 2005. Some Meta-theoretical Questions for Restorative Justice. *Ratio Juris*, 18(1), pp. 84–106.

Gavrielides, T. 2007. *Restorative Justice Theory and Practice: Addressing the Discrepancy*. Helsinki: HEUNI.

Gavrielides, T. 2012a. *Rights and Restoration within Youth Justice*. Whitby: ON de Sitter Publications.

Roche, D. 2006. Dimensions of restorative justice. *Journal of Social Issues*, 62(2), pp. 217–38.

Index